For Reference

Not to be taken from this room

Health Care Policy and Politics

A to Z

Health Care Policy and Politics

A to Z

Julie Rovner

CQ PRESS

A DIVISION OF CONGRESSIONAL QUARTERLY INC.
WASHINGTON, D.C.

CQ Press

A Division of Congressional Quarterly Inc.

1414 22nd St. N.W.

Washington, D.C. 20037

(202) 822-1475; (800) 638-1710

http://books.cq.com

Health Care Policy and Politics was designed and typeset by Kachergis Book Design, Pittsboro, North Carolina.

Printed in the United States of America

03   02   01   00   99   5   4   3   2   1

LIBRARY OF CONGRESS CATALOGING-IN-PUBLICATION DATA

Rovner, Julie.

Health care policy and politics A to Z / Julie Rovner.

     p.   cm.

    Includes index.

    ISBN 1-56802-437-1

    1. Medical policy—United States. 2. Medical care—Political aspects—United States. 3. Public health—Political aspects—United States. I. Title.

    RA395.A3R685   1999

    362.1'0973—dc21   99-40972

Contents

Preface

A couple of years ago, I was attending a function at C-SPAN, the cable public affairs network, where I ran into one of its top executives. "Are you STILL covering health care?" he inquired with some incredulity. "Aren't you bored with it yet?" In fact, I was not bored with covering health policy, which has been my professional focus since 1986, and still am not bored today. I remember exactly what I told him, and it remains true—health policy doesn't get boring because the issues keep changing. Who could have predicted in 1986 that little more than a decade later Congress would be debating things like a ban on the cloning of humans or discrimination based on genetic makeup?

Unlike many of the issues debated in Washington, health care affects all Americans, and it affects them in literally life-or-death ways. But health policy, like health care in general, is dauntingly complicated, rife with jargon and long-running conflicts that have raged for years. Even those who want to learn more about Medicare reform, to name just one example, are often put off by conversations that seem to take place in another language or by experts who presume everyone knows as much as they do about the history of the program and the various fights that have taken place over the years. Yet politicians are frequently able to trade on the public's lack of knowledge about important programs, leading to unchecked demagoguery.

This volume is intended to permit lay people to join the continuing conversation about health policy issues. Its goal is to provide background information on the broad array of health issues on the national agenda. It presumes at least a high-school-civics' understanding of how the federal government works but assumes no expertise in health care. Its intended audience includes high school and college students writing term papers, professional government-watchers new to health policy, and even those who merely want to be better able to follow the debates in the media.

Although many books and glossaries define health care terms, this one focuses on the conflict, background, and history of health policy issues. This kind of information is more difficult to come by than definitions; making such critical context available should enable many more citizens to join the national conversation over the direction of health care policy.

This work is also very "Congress centric" because, for better or worse, the U.S. Congress is where much of the nation's health policy is made. While those who rail against "big government" campaign to prevent the federal government from getting more involved in the nation's health care system, the federal government continues to provide, by nearly any measure, the lion's share of funding for health care. Medicare alone is the nation's largest single health insurance program, and in 1997 the federal government paid $367 billion of the nation's total $1.1 trillion health care bill. Congress, as the holder of the federal purse strings, cannot help but want to dictate the policies that accompany those dollars.

Yet although health care, according to pollsters, is usually among voters' top concerns, it has in the past commanded surprisingly little respect among policymakers, compared with such "big ticket" issues as taxes, trade, and national security. The situation, however, is likely to change in the future. One reason is the inexorable aging of the massive baby boom generation. That fact will bring health care issues front and center, since older people consume more health care dollars than younger people. The financial future of Medicare, the subject of an ongoing battle, is just one of a long list of issues related to the aging "boomers" with which Congress will be forced to grapple. New technology is also driving current and future health policy. Scientists' ability to do new and marvelous things often prompts significant ethical questions, as well as the need to set new spending priorities. Finally, the rapidly changing private health care marketplace is not going unnoticed by lawmakers, if only because dislocations are drawing complaints from constituents and driving the number of uninsured Americans ever higher.

It should be emphasized that health policy is an ever changing issue. This volume offers a snapshot view of the issue's many aspects at the end of the century. As the health policy debate—its content and coverage, as well as the commentary and analysis that it inevitably provokes—continues to evolve, so will this guide. Any mistakes or omissions are mine alone, and comments will be gratefully accepted for future editions.

A Note on Sources

The majority of information in this volume comes directly from my own reporting: seven years covering health and welfare for the *Congressional Quarterly Weekly Report*, a year and a half covering health for Medical News Network, four years for National Journal's *CongressDaily*, and a year for National Public Radio.

In compiling this volume I made liberal use of my own previously published material, particularly that from CQ *Weekly Report*s and *Almanac*s. Other helpful information was drawn from reports prepared or funded by the Commonwealth Fund, Henry J. Kaiser Family Foundation, Robert Wood Johnson Foundation, Alliance for Health Reform, and the Urban Institute.

Among the most valuable primary sources I used were the *Green Book*, published annually by the House Ways and Means Committee, which provides background and statistics on Medicare and other programs the committee oversees; the *Medicaid Source Book*, prepared by the Congressional Research Service for the House Energy and Commerce Committee; and Paul Starr's seminal *Social Transformation of American Medicine.*

I am also indebted to the public affairs staffs of several organizations, particularly the Department of Health and Human Services, the Health Care Financing Administration, the American Medical Association, and the American Association of Health Plans, which provided too many background papers and materials to be noted here.

Acknowledgments

Learning an area as complex and diverse as health policy requires many teachers, and I am privileged to have been taught by some of the best. I want especially to thank the following people, many of them current or former Capitol Hill staff aides, for their patient explanations and unfailing availability on deadline, often provided at the expense of sleep following days or even weeks of around-the-clock drafting or negotiation sessions.

Medicare experts include the following current or former Hill staff: David Abernethy, Brian Biles, Mike Hash, Chip Kahn, Tricia Neuman, Karen Pollitz, Bill Vaughan, and Marina Weiss. Off the Hill, Diane Archer, Marty Corry, Geri Dallek, Karen Davis, Judy Feder, Ed Howard, Marilyn Moon, Ron Pollack, John Rother, Patricia Smith, and Gail Wilensky provided invaluable background.

I learned Medicaid at the knee of three of the most formidable experts in the field: Sara Rosenbaum, Diane Rowland, and Andy Schneider. Also adding to my understanding were Howard Cohen and Karen Nelson of the House Commerce Committee.

David Schulke and Chris Jennings of the Senate Aging Committee taught me the intricacies of prescription drug prices and other issues concerning the Food and Drug Administration. Tobacco experts Matt Myers and Cliff Douglas were invaluable in helping me understand that complicated issue. Chai Feldblum and Pat Wright helped me through the debates over the Americans with Disabilities Act. Of the many people who guided me through the abortion debates on Capitol Hill, Rachel Gorlin, Jo Blum, and Douglas Johnson stand out as those I could not have done without.

Although I am grateful to all of my sources, two of

them, Tim Westmoreland, formerly of the House Energy and Commerce Committee and now at Georgetown University Law Center, and David Nexon of the Senate Health, Education, Labor and Pensions Committee, most influenced my thinking and understanding on a wide range of health issues, from AIDS to insurance coverage to public health programs.

At CQ Press, I want to thank Dave Tarr for suggesting the idea for the book and for sponsoring the development of the manuscript. Christopher Karlsten contributed his editing expertise and gently shepherded the manuscript through the production process. Freelance editor Joanne Ainsworth edited many of the articles.

Finally, I also want to thank all of my various editors at my "real" jobs: Lou Peck, Keith White, and Charlie Mitchell at National Journal's *CongressDaily;* Anne Gudenkauf and Joe Neel at National Public Radio; and Martha Kerr and Sarah Masters at Reuters Health Information Services, who were so cooperative in putting up with me while I was working on this project in my "spare" time.

A

AAPCC (Medicare)

See ADJUSTED AVERAGE PER CAPITA COST.

Abortion

Abortion is perhaps the most polarizing social issue in American politics, not just in the arena of health policy making. After more than three decades of strife, the United States appears no closer to a compromise position than it was in the late 1960s, when the issue took center stage on the national agenda.

Politically, although support for abortion is generally associated with the Democratic party, and opposition with Republicans, abortion is not as strictly partisan an issue as many think. Although the Democratic party platform has since 1976 supported leaving the landmark *ROE V. WADE* Supreme Court ruling intact, as many as a third of Democrats in Congress vote against abortion in many if not most circumstances. Indeed, it was a prominent prolife Democrat, Pennsylvania governor William Casey, who signed into law the statute many thought the Court would use to overturn *Roe* in 1992. Similarly, though the GOP platform has embraced a "right to life for the unborn," also since 1976, a significant portion of Republicans (around 25 percent) support abortion rights some or most of the time.

Both sides of the abortion debate have sought to win public support with colorful appeals. Here, an antiabortion protester dressed as "Death" speaks to a crowd gathered in Washington, D.C., to mark the Supreme Court's Roe v. Wade *decision. Source: Vidal Medina, Reuters*

Abortion may be the most polarizing issue in American politics. Although activists at the extremes of the debate have long dominated policy discussions, public opinion polls have shown the majority of Americans believe that abortion should be legal, but also limited to certain situations. Source: R. Michael Jenkins, Congressional Quarterly

One of the reasons it is difficult to generalize about abortion politics is that lawmakers differ on various abortion-related issues. Many lawmakers who generally support a woman's right to choose abortion do not support the use of public funds to pay for it. Similarly, many legislators who oppose abortion in most instances support it in cases of rape or incest.

Although purists on both sides berate those policymakers who waver on the issue, those very policymakers reflect the significant ambivalence most Americans have about abortion—an ambivalence that has persisted over the decades the abortion wars have been fought in the legislatures, the courts, and the streets in front of clinics. In general, Americans want abortion to be available but discouraged. They want it used only in rare or tragic cases (such as rape, incest, or severe birth defects), but don't want to see abortion recriminalized. In a 1998 *New York Times* poll, half of those surveyed said they thought abortion "is the same thing as murdering a child," but 61 percent said it should be permitted in the first three months of pregnancy. At the same time, though only 15 percent of respondents said abortions should be available during the second three months of pregnancy, 60 percent said the Court's landmark *Roe v. Wade* decision—which banned states from outlawing abortion during those second three months—was a good thing.

It is this ambivalence that has set the parameters of the public debate over abortion in the seventies, eighties, and nineties. Although the public debate does not reflect it, those who think abortion should be legal all the time or illegal in every circumstance make up a small minority of the population. The only way to prevail in an abortion debate is to capture enough of the "muddled middle" to make a majority. That explains why Republicans in the early 1980s failed in their efforts to pass a constitutional amendment to ban abortion, and why Democrats in the early 1990s could not muster the votes for their FREEDOM OF CHOICE ACT, which not only would have codified the tenets of *Roe* but also would have struck down many restrictions the post-*Roe* Court found acceptable.

Instead of seeking the middle ground, each side has concentrated on the issues on which it thinks it can muster a majority. For abortion rights forces, those include rape and incest, fetal tissue research, and early forms of abortion, like the abortion pill RU486. For abortion opponents, the issues on which the public is most on their side include involving parents in the abortion decision and establishing guidelines for abortion procedures later in pregnancy. Pushing a ban on what they call PARTIAL-BIRTH ABORTIONS helped antiabortion forces in Congress persuade large majorities of legislators and the public to support an antiabortion cause from 1995 on, coming within three votes of overriding President Bill Clinton's veto in the Senate.

Statistics

The term *abortion* applies to any premature expulsion of a fetus from a woman's womb. *Spontaneous abortion* is the medical term for a miscarriage and occurs naturally for a variety of reasons related to the health of the woman or the fetus. The term *abortion* refers to what is medically known as *induced abortion,* sometimes called *elective abortion,* one brought about deliberately by a medical procedure.

Abortion has been declining in recent years. In 1996, according to the Alan Guttmacher Institute (AGI), which has been collecting abortion statistics since 1973, the abortion rate (number of abortions per one thousand women), the abortion ratio (percentage of pregnancies that end up in abortion), and the number of abortions performed were at their lowest in twenty years.

There were 1.37 million abortions in 1996, according to AGI, down 11 percent from the 1.53 million abortions in 1992 and the 1.6 million in 1990. At the same time, the abortion rate dropped to twenty-three per one thousand women, the lowest since 1975. That rate, however, is still higher than those in other Western developed nations. In 1995 Sweden had an abortion rate of eighteen per one thousand women, Canada had a rate of sixteen, and England and Wales, fifteen. Also down in 1996 was the ratio of pregnancies ending in abortion. It was 26 percent, down from 28 percent in 1990.

Analysts say abortions are declining for several reasons. One is changing demographics. The huge baby boom generation is getting older, and older women generally have lower pregnancy rates. At the same time, teenage pregnancy rates are falling, partly because of better use of contraception.

Another reason some say abortions are going down is that there are significantly fewer providers. The AGI survey found 338 fewer facilities providing abortions in 1996 than in 1992, a decrease of 14 percent. That decrease was nearly twice the drop between 1988 and 1992 (8 percent) and more than three times the drop between 1985 and 1988 (4 percent). Among those most likely to have discontinued providing abortions are physicians' offices and hospitals, particularly those in rural areas. In 1996

Reported Abortions, Abortion Rate, and Abortion Ratio, United States, 1973–1996

Year	Abortions (in thousands)	Abortion rate	Abortion ratio
1973	744.6	16.3	19.3
1974	898.6	19.3	22.0
1975	1,034.2	21.7	24.9
1976	1,179.3	24.2	26.5
1977	1,316.7	26.4	28.6
1978	1,409.6	27.7	29.2
1979	1,497.7	28.8	29.6
1980	1,553.9	29.3	30.0
1981	1,577.3	29.3	30.1
1982	1,573.9	28.8	30.0
1983	(1,575.0)	(28.5)	(30.4)
1984	1,577.2	28.1	29.7
1985	1,588.6	28.0	29.7
1986	(1,574.0)	(27.4)	(29.4)
1987	1,559.1	26.9	28.8
1988	1,590.8	27.3	28.6
1989	(1,566.9)	(26.8)	(27.5)
1990	(1,608.6)	(27.4)	(28.0)
1991	1,556.5	26.3	27.4
1992	1,528.9	25.9	27.5
1993	(1,500.0)	(25.4)	(27.4)
1994	(1,431.0)	(24.1)	(26.7)
1995	1,363.7	22.9	26.0
1996	1,365.7	22.9	26.1

Source: Alan Guttmacher Institute, December 1998.

Note: The abortion *rate* is the number of abortions per one thousand women ages fifteen to forty-four; the abortion *ratio* is the number of abortions per one hundred pregnancies ending in abortions or live births. Figures in parentheses are estimates based on interpolations of abortion numbers.

abortions were unavailable in 86 percent of all U.S. counties and in one-third of U.S. cities (89 of 320 metropolitan areas). In twenty-one states 90 percent of counties had no abortion provider. Seventy percent of all abortions in 1996 took place in clinics specializing in the procedure.

In addition, states have imposed more restrictions on the procedure in the wake of Supreme Court decisions allowing them. A 1999 survey of state laws by the NATIONAL ABORTION AND REPRODUCTIVE RIGHTS ACTION LEAGUE found that women had less access to abortion that year than they had had in 1973, the year *Roe* was decided. According to the study, sixteen states still have on their books outright abortion bans or other laws that are unconstitutional or unenforceable under *Roe* and its successor cases. Altogether, states have passed hundreds of laws to restrict abortion access, including not only prohibitions of state funding for abortion but also bans on abortion counseling and referrals. States have also imposed waiting periods, enacted PARENTAL NOTIFICATION or PARENTAL CONSENT laws for minors, mandated state-sponsored lectures urging against abortion, required "abstinence only" education programs for teenagers, and passed laws to punish pregnant women who use alcohol or drugs.

Even with the decline, though, abortion remains the single-most-performed surgical procedure in the United States—and one of the safest. One death occurs for every 150,000 legal abortions, about one-tenth the risk of bearing a child. Early abortions are safer still, with one death reported for every 530,000 abortions at eight or fewer weeks of gestation. Abortions performed after twenty-one weeks are the most dangerous, with one death for every 6,000 performed. Serious complications, including hemorrhage, pelvic infection, or the need for major surgery, occur in less than one percent of abortions.

For all the attention focused on late-term abortions, the vast majority of abortions are performed early in pregnancy. Eighty-eight percent are performed in the first twelve weeks of pregnancy; 99 percent before twenty weeks' gestation. Only 1 percent take place after twenty-one weeks' gestation.

A survey by AGI found that so-called partial-birth abortions, known medically as "intact dilation and extraction," or D&X, accounted for only about 650, or less than one-half of 1 percent, of the 1.37 million abortions in 1996. Although other estimates have put the number as high as several thousand, these procedures still represent a tiny fraction of abortions performed.

Most abortions are performed using a technique called *vacuum aspiration* or *suction curettage*. The procedure, performed on an outpatient basis with a local anesthetic, involves dilating a woman's cervix to about the width of a pencil, inserting a tube called a "cannula," which is attached to a suction machine, then suctioning out the contents of the uterus. The person performing the abortion (usually a physician, but in some cases a PHYSICIAN ASSISTANT) then uses a spoon-shaped "curette" to scrape the uterine walls to ensure all the tissue has been removed. The entire procedure takes about ten minutes, and the woman can usually go home after resting for an hour or two and being checked for excessive bleeding. Some bleeding and cramping is normal with first-trimester abortions.

Abortions after thirteen weeks are usually performed using a technique called *dilation and evacuation* (D&E). A more advanced version of the vacuum aspiration method, D&E requires that the cervix be dilated to a much greater extent, a process that can take place over a few minutes, several hours, or overnight. The physician uses a suction machine, but also forceps to dismember and remove fetal parts too large to pass through the machine's tube. That procedure is followed by curettage to ensure no portion of the fetus remains in the uterus. A D&E procedure takes from ten to thirty minutes to complete.

About 3 percent of abortions are performed by inducing labor. Labor can be induced using a saline solution, prostaglandin, or other substances. The injected substance causes contractions, and later the woman vaginally delivers the fetus.

A Brief History of the Abortion Debate

Until the mid-nineteenth century, abortion was both legal and common. Most early abortion laws were instigated by the medical profession and had at least as much to do with establishing medicine as a profession as with protecting women's health or the rights of unborn children. By 1900 abortion was illegal virtually across the country.

In the late 1960s, as the women's movement was gathering momentum, some states moved to relax their abortion laws. A major turning point was the Supreme Court's 1965 decision *Griswold v. Connecticut*, which overturned a state law prohibiting the use of contraceptives by married couples. In 1972, in *Eisenstadt v. Baird*, the Court extended the right to contraception to unmarried individuals, citing a right to privacy, "to be free from unwarranted governmental intrusion into matters so fundamentally affecting a person as the decision whether to bear or beget a child." The privacy rights expressed in *Griswold* and *Eisenstadt* would later be interpreted to encompass abortion.

Between 1967 and 1973, seventeen states rewrote their abortion laws; four, Alaska, Hawaii, New York, and Washington, repealed their bans entirely. In the two-and-a-half years immediately preceding *Roe,* some 350,000 women traveled to New York from elsewhere in the country to obtain an abortion.

Most historians date the current abortion battles to January 22, 1973, the day the Court handed down *Roe v. Wade.* That 7–2 decision, along with its companion case, *Doe v. Bolton,* struck down state laws banning abortion in Texas (in *Roe*) and in Georgia (in *Doe*), and, by extension, similar laws across the country. *Roe* declared that the right of privacy expressed in *Griswold* and other cases "is broad enough to encompass a woman's decision whether or not to terminate her pregnancy." *Roe* divided a pregnancy into three "trimesters" and declared that during the first thirteen weeks of pregnancy, the decision on whether to have the procedure should be left up to "the attending physician, in consultation with his patient." During the second trimester, states may regulate abortion to protect the woman's health (by requiring, for example, that procedures be performed in hospitals or only by licensed physicians). Only after the fetus is *viable* (able to live outside the womb, with or without artificial life support) may the state "in promoting its interest in the potentiality of human life . . . regulate, and even proscribe abortion, except where it is necessary, in appropriate medical judgment, for the preservation of the life or health of the mother."

Roe not only legalized abortion nationwide—it also had the paradoxical effect of energizing a nascent antiabortion movement. Indeed, on the policy level, the remainder of the 1970s were largely devoted to deciding whether to use public funds to finance abortions for poor women through the state-federal MEDICAID program.

In 1976 the Supreme Court in *Planned Parenthood of Central Missouri v. Danforth* struck down requirements for parents and spouses to consent to abortions, on the grounds that the laws "delegated to third parties an absolute veto power which the state does not itself possess." The decision also struck down a ban on saline amniocentesis, then the most common second-trimester procedure, on the grounds that the choice of method must be left to the physician.

Meanwhile, Congress spent the next four years tussling over what would come to be called the HYDE AMENDMENT, in honor of its leading proponent (but not, ironically, its author), Rep. Henry Hyde, R-Ill. (The author was Rep. Silvio Conte, R-Mass., longtime ranking Republican on the appropriations subcommittee that funded the then-Department of Health, Education and Welfare.) The Hyde amendment, in its various forms, restricted Medicaid funding of abortion to those procedures needed to protect the life of the pregnant woman and to those required in other special circumstances. This time the Court would go along with Congress. In 1977, in *Maher v. Roe,* the Court upheld a Connecticut law restricting Medicaid abortion funding to abortions that are "medically necessary." In 1980, in *Harris v. McRae,* the Court specifically upheld the Hyde amendment, noting that the government had no obligation to fund abortions for the poor.

With Ronald Reagan, who ran on a strong "right-to-life" platform, in the White House and Republicans in control of the Senate for the first time in a generation, in 1981 the GOP moved to keep its promise to overturn *Roe.* But in 1982 legislation that would have banned abortion by statute fell victim to a Senate filibuster. Then, on June 28, 1983, the Senate rejected a proposed constitutional amendment that said merely that "a right to abortion is not secured by this Constitution." The 49–50 vote was 17 short of the two-thirds needed to send the amendment to the states for ratification. Sen. Jesse Helms, R-N.C., voted "present" on the amendment because, he said, it did not go far enough to ban abortion.

Meanwhile, the Supreme Court continued to strike down proposed state restrictions on abortion. In 1983's *Akron v. Akron Center for Reproductive Health* the Court invalidated a city ordinance requiring that all abortions after the first trimester be performed in a hospital; that parental consent be required for abortions on girls under age fifteen; that physicians deliver a state-mandated speech including details of fetal anatomy, a list of the risks and consequences of the procedure, and a statement that "the unborn child is a human life from the moment of conception"; that women wait at least twenty-four hours between providing "informed consent" for an abortion and having the procedure done; and that fetal remains be given some sort of "humane" disposal.

However, in a companion case decided the same day, *Planned Parenthood of Kansas City, Mo. v. Ashcroft,* the Court upheld certain requirements of a Missouri law, including those mandating that a pathology report be prepared for every abortion (deemed protective of the woman's health), that minors have parental consent or judicial permission for their abortions (because the law met the requirements set out in *Bellotti v. Baird* in 1979; see PARENTAL INVOLVEMENT LAWS), and that two doctors be present at abortions after fetal viability. The Court struck down other elements of Missouri's law, including a requirement that all second-trimester abortions be performed in hospitals.

However, in a third case decided that day, *Simopoulos v. Virginia.* the Court upheld a Virginia law requiring all post–first-trimester abortions to be performed in hospitals because the law provided for the designation of freestanding ambulatory surgical facilities as "hospitals."

In 1986, in *Thornburgh v. American College of Obstetricians and Gynecologists, Pennsylvania Section,* the Court struck down provisions of Pennsylvania's 1982 Abortion Control Act requiring a state-sponsored speech designed to deter women from having abortions, obligating physicians to use the abortion method most likely to result in fetal survival unless it would cause "significantly" greater risk to a woman's life or health, mandating detailed reporting to the state on each abortion, and requiring a second physician to be present at post-viability abortions. The Court said the speech requirement was unconstitutional because the state could not "intimidate women into continuing their pregnancies." The method requirement increased

the risk to the woman, the Court held, while the two-physician requirement, unlike the one it upheld in *Planned Parenthood v. Ashcroft,* did not include an exception for emergencies.

Meanwhile, after defeat of their broader efforts to outlaw abortion, antiabortion lawmakers in Congress, with the aid of antiabortion presidents Reagan and George Bush, instead moved to an incremental strategy of rooting out federal support of the procedure wherever they could. By the end of the decade federal funding had been eliminated for all Medicaid abortions except those needed to save the woman's life; for abortions previously covered as a benefit under the FEDERAL EMPLOYEE HEALTH BENEFITS PLAN; for those performed in federal prisons; and for those performed in overseas military medical facilities on servicewomen or military dependents, even if the patient had paid for the procedure herself. In addition, abortion funding by the District of Columbia, using city tax money, had been eliminated. Congress also ratified the Reagan administration's MEXICO CITY POLICY, barring funding for international family planning organizations that used their own funds to "perform or actively promote abortion as a method of family planning," and cut off funding to the UNITED NATIONS POPULATION FUND (UNFPA), which was accused of underwriting coercive sterilization and abortion programs in China.

The next pivot point in the abortion debate came in 1989, when the Supreme Court, in WEBSTER V. REPRODUCTIVE HEALTH SERVICES, reversed course and upheld many of the restrictions it had previously struck down, including a ban on use of public employees or facilities for abortion and a restriction requiring physicians to perform tests to determine viability on fetuses of more than twenty weeks' gestation. In upholding the restrictions on a 5–4 vote, the Court signaled—but did not expressly say—that it no longer considered abortion a fundamental right. Thus, both sides agreed, it essentially invited states to pass their own laws limiting abortion.

But just as the abortion-supporting *Roe* decision had energized antiabortion forces in 1973, *Webster* mobilized abortion-rights supporters who suddenly realized that the future of legalized abortion was in real doubt. In the months immediately following the decision, both the House and Senate voted to roll back various restrictions imposed over the previous decade, including the ban on federal funding of abortion in cases of rape or incest and a restriction barring the District of Columbia from using its own tax dollars to pay for abortions. Four presidential vetoes, however, prevented any of the restrictions from being eliminated.

The Supreme Court again thwarted abortion-rights supporters with its 1991 decision *Rust v. Sullivan,* upholding Reagan administration regulations, known as the GAG RULE, barring abortion counseling and referrals in federally funded family planning clinics. Congress voted repeatedly to overturn the regulations but never mustered the veto-proof supermajority needed to accomplish the goal. The same was true for efforts to overturn a 1988 ban on research using tissue from aborted fetuses. (See FETAL TISSUE RESEARCH.)

With abortion-rights forces on the offensive, the Supreme Court threw them for another loop with its 1992 decision *PLANNED PARENTHOOD OF SOUTHEASTERN PA. V. CASEY.* At issue in the case was a Pennsylvania law imposing a series of requirements—many of them struck down by the Court in earlier cases. But this time the Court decided that it was permissible to allow Pennsylvania to mandate a twenty-four-hour waiting period and to require women seeking an abortion to be given state-sponsored material about fetal development and abortion alternatives. That decision expressly overturned two earlier cases, *Thornburgh v. American College of Obstetricians and Gynecologists* (1986) and *Akron v. Akron Center for Reproductive Health* (1983).

But unlike the decision in *Webster,* in which the Court did not openly address the continuing viability of the framework established in *Roe,* the plurality opinion in *Casey* did address the fundamental question of a woman's right to abortion. And, much to the surprise of those on both sides, it affirmed it. But Justice Sandra Day O'Connor's opinion made it clear that the right she was embracing was not nearly as unlimited as the one for which *Roe* had become known. Rather, the decision lowered the threshold for state restrictions; only those

that imposed "an undue burden" would be invalidated. Using that new standard, the justices overturned one of the Pennsylvania law's provisions that would have required a married woman to notify her husband before obtaining an abortion.

Although it significantly weakened *Roe,* the decision in *Casey* affirming even a somewhat more limited right to abortion impeded the progress of the abortion-rights movement, contributed to its failure to push through Congress the so-called Freedom of Choice Act, which would have written *Roe*'s protections into law, and blocked many of the restrictions the Court had previously upheld.

What helped abortion-rights advocates most was the election that November of Bill Clinton. On only his second full day in office, Clinton wiped out an entire series of restrictions imposed over the previous twelve years. With the stroke of a pen Clinton struck from the books the gag rule barring abortion counseling and referrals at federally funded family planning clinics; canceled an "import alert" barring individuals from bringing into the country the French abortion pill RU486; lifted the moratorium on research using tissue from aborted fetuses; ended the ban on self-paid abortions in overseas military medical facilities; and canceled the Mexico City policy banning U.S. aid to international family planning programs that used their own funds to promote or perform abortions.

Congress would later that year undo several other restrictions. Various appropriations bills restored the ability of the District of Columbia to use locally raised funds to pay for abortions for poor women, permitted federal employee health plans to offer abortion as a covered benefit, and restored funding for the UNFPA. Moreover, an NIH reauthorization bill (PL 103-43) codified language allowing fetal tissue research.

Congress also restored Medicaid funding for abortions in cases of rape or incest, but that development was considered a loss for abortion-rights groups. They had hoped to eliminate the Hyde amendment restrictions altogether but were outmaneuvered by abortion opponents, and support for abortion rights turned out to be not as strong as some had thought. Similarly, Congress again failed to act on the Freedom of Choice Act, even though President Clinton had supported it on the campaign trail.

The years 1993 and 1994 turned out to be the high-water marks for abortion-rights supporters. In 1995 the new Republican majority in Congress moved quickly to reinstate the 1980s' restrictions relaxed during Clinton's first two years in office. Despite President Clinton's vehement opposition, the bans on military abortions, D.C. abortions, prison abortions, and those performed as federal employee benefits were reinstated through various appropriations measures, and the UNFPA was defunded. The Republican-led Congress also effectively blocked a requirement that doctors training to be obstetrician/gynecologists be taught to perform abortions unless they have a moral or religious objection (see AC-CREDITATION COUNCIL ON GRADUATE MEDICAL EDUCATION), and imposed an explicit ban on research using human embryos (see EMBRYO RESEARCH).

Abortion opponents, however, were less successful than they had previously been at moving stand-alone abortion bills, including a ban on so-called partial-birth abortions and a measure to make it a crime to take a minor across state lines for an abortion in contravention of her home state's parental involvement law. (See CHILD CUSTODY PROTECTION ACT.) President Clinton also managed to fend off a reimposition of the Mexico City policy for international family planning groups, although only by allowing significant funding reductions to the international family planning aid program.

In addition to caring for patients, academic health centers like the Mayo Clinic, in Rochester, Minnesota, conduct basic and applied research and instruct medical students in the most advanced health practices. Source: Scott Cohen, Reuters

Academic health centers

The term describes entities consisting of a medical school and the hospitals with which it is affiliated. These roughly 400 hospitals that are affiliated with one of the nation's 125 medical schools deliver some of the most advanced medical care in the nation. They include many familiar names in medicine—the Mayo Clinic, Johns Hopkins University Medical Center, and the Cleveland Clinic Foundation, to name a few. Sometimes referred to as academic medical centers, academic health centers (or AHCs) carry out a threefold role. Like other hospitals, they provide care, both to inpatients and outpatients. They also teach the next generation of doctors, often those pursuing the most advanced and high-tech specialties. Finally, AHCs are the locus of significant biomedical research, both basic and applied.

Because of what they do, AHCs attract many sicker-than-average patients who are much more expensive than average to treat. (Virtually all teaching hospitals incur higher-than-average expenses per patient because their teaching role by definition requires multiple doctors in various stages of their training to treat each sick person, and this style of treatment often results in more tests and other procedures as part of the training process.) In recent years, however, AHCs have experienced significant financial stresses as MANAGED CARE has become the predominant force in the nation's health care system. Before the rise of managed care, AHCs tended to finance their research and teaching operations in three major ways. The first way was through "practice plans," in which members of the faculty charge premium rates, then return a portion of their fees to the institution. AHCs also charged insurers higher hospitalization rates, using the excess to underwrite their noncare missions. Finally, the government, primarily through MEDICARE and MEDICAID, provided AHCs with extra payments in recognition of their multiple roles—spending approximately $7 billion annually.

But as managed care plans have sought to lower costs, they have steered all but the sickest patients away from AHCs to less advanced—and less expensive—community hospitals, depriving AHCs of income from both the physician-faculty members and the hospital fees. At the same time, the federal government has been cutting back in its effort to rein in the cost of Medicare and Medicaid. The 1997 Balanced Budget Act was estimated to reduce payments to AHCs by 28 percent following a five-year phase in.

Accreditation Council on Graduate Medical Education (ACGME)

This body sets the standards for the nation's seventy-four hundred medical residency programs in more than one thousand institutions that train doctors to perform various specialties. The ACGME sets guidelines for what residency programs should teach, then evaluates and accredits programs to ensure that no matter where a doctor trains, he or she completes that training with a consistent body of knowledge and experience. The ACGME is composed of representatives of the American Board of Medical Specialties, American Hospital Association, AMERICAN MEDICAL ASSOCIATION, Association of American Medical Colleges, and Council of Medical Specialty Societies. Standards are proposed by "residency review committees" (RRCs), composed of

physician educators in each of the twenty-six recognized medical specialties. The RRCs, staffed by up to two hundred volunteers, evaluate each residency program on average every three and a half years and render decisions on accreditation. Standards for each specialty are updated approximately every five years to account for new discoveries, techniques, and changes in practice patterns.

In 1995 the ACGME came under fire in Congress for a change to the standards for training obstetrician/gynecologists that required residents without moral or religious objections to learn how to perform ABORTIONS. The chairman of the ACGME testified before Congress that "it is the opinion of the obstetricians serving on the Residency Review Committee for Obstetricians and Gynecology and the medical organizations that reviewed and approved these standards that specific training is necessary in order to perform abortions safely and protect the public health." But abortion opponents argued that because ACGME accreditation is required for receipt of federal funds for a variety of activities, including Medicare reimbursement and medical student loans, the new requirement represented an unwarranted federal mandate for abortion. "In effect, ACGME is drafting American obstetricians into a war on their unborn patients. It has no right to impose such a draft, with or without exemptions for 'conscientious objectors,'" said a statement from the antiabortion United States Catholic Conference. Congress ultimately overrode the ACGME ruling with a compromise crafted with the aid of the American College of Obstetricians and Gynecologists that permitted federal funding of an unaccredited Ob/gyn residency program if the program's failure to provide abortion training was "a decisive factor in its lack of accreditation."

Activities of daily living

Used to measure the degree of disability for those requiring LONG-TERM CARE or other services, activities of daily living (ADLs) include such necessities of life as bathing, getting in or out of a bed or chair, dressing, eating, and using the toilet. Individuals are generally considered *severely disabled* if they need assistance with three of five ADLs. *Instrumental activities of daily living* (IADLs) are those tasks persons must be able to perform to remain independent. They include things like cooking, cleaning, shopping, using the phone, taking medication, and bill-paying. As the baby boom generation ages, the number of Americans who will require help with one or more ADLs or IADLs is expected to balloon. An estimated one-quarter of the elderly population currently needs assistance with one or more ADLs or IADLs.

ADAMHA

The Alcohol, Drug Abuse, and Mental Health Administration (ADAMHA) is an agency of the U.S. Public Health Service that was disbanded in 1992. Under legislation enacted that year (PL 102-321) ADAMHA's three research arms, the National Institute of Mental Health, National Institute on Alcohol Abuse and Alcoholism, and National Institute on Drug Abuse, were folded into the NATIONAL INSTITUTES OF HEALTH, becoming that agency's fourteenth through sixteenth institutes. The remaining programs to provide treatment and prevention services were reconstituted as the SUBSTANCE ABUSE AND MENTAL HEALTH SERVICES ADMINISTRATION, or SAMHSA.

Adjusted average per capita cost (AAPCC)

The monthly payment MEDICARE makes to managed care plans to provide medically necessary services to Medicare beneficiaries, the AAPCC is calculated according to how much it costs to serve a Medicare beneficiary in a particular county under Medicare's FEE-FOR-SERVICE program. MANAGED CARE payments are based on 95 percent of the AAPCC, adjusted for age, sex, and disability status. Because the payments are based on geographic spending levels, there is tremendous variation around the country, and even within the same metropolitan areas. Health policy analysts, however, have long contended that even 95 percent is much too high a

payment, because it doesn't take into account the healthier-than-average Medicare population that tends to join managed care plans. In the 1997 Balanced Budget Act (PL 105-33) Congress attempted to reduce variations by imposing a 2 percent cap on the highest-paid areas, a "floor" to boost payments in the lowest-paid areas, and a "blended payment" to attempt to boost payments in areas at the lower end of the payment range. As a result, however, many plans cut back their coverage or dropped out of the Medicare managed care program altogether. (See MEDICARE+CHOICE.)

Adjusted community rate (ACR)

The adjusted community rate (ACR) is used to measure the difference between what MEDICARE pays a MANAGED CARE plan and what it costs the plan to serve its commercial enrollees. Medicare requires that if the Medicare payment is higher than the plan's projected costs, then the plan either refunds the difference to Medicare or uses it to provide additional benefits to its Medicare enrollees. Virtually all plans take the latter option, which is why so many Medicare HEALTH MAINTENANCE ORGANIZATIONS (HMOS) offer prescription drug, vision, and hearing aid coverage and annual physicals, none of which is otherwise covered by Medicare. Plans must submit their ACR plans to Medicare in advance each year, detailing what the plan will provide in the way of benefits, the premiums or other costs it intends to charge Medicare enrollees, and its projected costs and revenues.

Adolescent family life program

Created by Title XX of the Public Health Service Act, the program was enacted in 1981 budget reconciliation legislation (PL 97-35) at the urging of antiabortion lawmakers to help fund programs that seek to convince teenagers to refrain from sexual activity rather than to use contraception, and to encourage young unmarried girls who do get pregnant to carry their babies to term. The latter provision, along with another that encour-

Advanced practice nurse 11

aged religious organizations to apply for grants, resulted in a lawsuit challenging the constitutionality of the entire program.

Like the much larger federal family planning program (Title X), the adolescent family life (AFL) program has not been reauthorized by Congress since its last authority expired in 1985. Both programs have been caught up in continuing controversy over abortion-related questions. AFL received a fiscal year 1999 appropriation of $17.7 million. The program authorizes grants to public and private nonprofit entities for programs that promote abstinence. Programs may provide family planning services but may not use funds for ABORTION (also banned under the Title X program) or for abortion counseling or referrals (both of which Title X requires).

Advance directives

These legal documents express an individual's health care desires in the event that individual becomes incapacitated or otherwise unable to communicate his or her wishes. There are two basic types of advance directives, LIVING WILLS and DURABLE POWERS OF ATTORNEY FOR HEALTH CARE (also known as medical powers of attorney). All fifty states recognize the legal power of advance directives for health care, or of their discontinuation. Advance directives enable individuals to make their own medical decisions, even when they are incapacitated. The 1990 PATIENT SELF DETERMINATION ACT, part of that year's budget reconciliation bill (PL 101-508), required that all hospitals that participate in MEDICARE or MEDICAID advise all patients of their right to exercise advance directives, in an effort to encourage their use.

Advanced practice nurse

The term applies to a registered nurse (RN) who has undergone advanced training and clinical practice requirements beyond the two to four years required for an

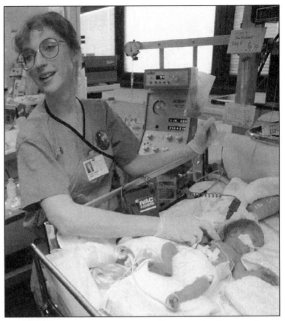

Advanced practice nurses, registered nurses who have undergone additional training, are caught in the crossfire between insurance companies, which benefit from the nurses' reasonable rates, and physicians, who argue that allowing nurses to practice without adequate supervision by doctors could endanger patients. Source: Brent Smith, Reuters

RN degree. Advanced practice nurses, who include NURSE PRACTITIONERS, CERTIFIED NURSE MIDWIVES, CLINICAL NURSE SPECIALISTS, and certified nurse anesthetists, provide many primary care and most specialized services with the supervision of a physician and, sometimes, without. Advanced practice nurses, along with PHYSICIAN ASSISTANTS and some therapists, are known collectively as mid-level practitioners. In many states turf battles have broken out between physicians and mid-level practitioners, with insurance companies arguing that the less-expensive practitioners can provide quality care at a lower cost, while physicians argue that they lack adequate skills to practice independently. However, a 1986 report by the Office of Technology Assessment found that advanced practice nurses "are more adept than physicians at providing services that depend on communication with patients and preventive actions."

Adverse selection

Adverse selection is said to occur when people likely to incur high medical costs join the same health plan. It often results from a health plan, policy, or network of specialists offering a particular benefit much more generously than does the competition, thus attracting sicker-than-average people who need that benefit.

Agency for Health Care Policy and Research (AHCPR)

Created in 1989, this federal agency examines the cost, quality, access to, and effectiveness of medical care in the United States. Its mission is to provide the government, health care professionals, and the public with information to help them obtain care that is both as appropriate and as effective as possible.

Unlike other agencies such as the NATIONAL INSTITUTES OF HEALTH, whose biomedical research efforts help discover the causes of diseases and how to cure or prevent them, AHCPR is the lead federal agency in what is known as HEALTH SERVICES RESEARCH, which examines the way the health system works and the intersection of care financing and delivery. Until 1996 AHCPR devised and issued its own clinical practice guidelines for patient care of a variety of conditions, from heart failure to children's ear infections to bedsores. Such guidelines are intended to lessen what other health services research has shown as tremendously wide variation in the treatment patients receive depending on where they live. (See SMALL MARKET VARIATION.) However, a 1994 guideline for acute low-back pain that found surgery to be relatively ineffective raised the ire of back surgeons, who set out to see the agency defunded. Although that effort failed, in 1996 AHCPR announced it was getting out of the business of developing guidelines per se. Other research had shown that doctors are most likely to follow guidelines they have helped devise, making the guideline business more local and regional. Today AHCPR collects and publishes data for others to use in developing their own guidelines,

and monitors how well its guidelines and others' are followed by practitioners. AHCPR was funded at $171 million in fiscal year 1999.

Agency for Toxic Substances and Disease Registry (ATSDR)

With a fiscal year 1999 budget of $74 million, the registry conducts public health assessments, health studies, surveillance activities, and health education training in communities around "Superfund" waste sites determined by the U.S. Environmental Protection Agency. The newest of the PUBLIC HEALTH SERVICE agencies, ATSDR was established in 1980 and is based in Atlanta, Georgia.

AIDS

AIDS, or, more formally, Acquired Immune Deficiency Syndrome, is not only a relatively new and frightening disease (it was first identified in 1981) but also one that has helped reshape the way the U.S. government addresses public health, research, and other medical and social issues. The AIDS epidemic in the United States and around the world has forced an examination of attitudes about sexual conduct (the first group affected in the United States was homosexual men), about the ability of the medical community to respond to previously unknown communicable diseases, and about the ability of well-organized lobbying groups to spur government action. AIDS activists' success in getting Congress to increase research funding helped inspire similar tactics by those pushing for more money for breast cancer, Parkinson's disease, and other, more common maladies. At the same time, AIDS activists pushed the FDA for "fast-track" approvals for drugs that could treat AIDS, even if they could not yet cure it. The fast-track procedures were later written into law for drugs for other life-threatening conditions as part of the 1997 FDA Modernization Act (PL 105-115).

Congress had addressed the AIDS epidemic in a va-

A Massachusetts woman views the 1996 AIDS quilt, a 37,000-panel memorial to American AIDS victims that was displayed on the Mall in Washington, D.C. Source: Robert Giroux, Reuters

riety of bills since it had come to public awareness in the early 1980s. Among these various legislative efforts were the following:

• As part of the fiscal year 1988 Labor-HHS appropriation, Congress adopted language, pushed by Sen. Jesse Helms, R-N.C., forbidding AIDS education funds from being used for activities that "promote or encourage, directly or indirectly, homosexual sexual activities." Helms's original amendment would have barred education efforts from "condoning" homosexual activity, but he was prevailed upon to drop that language when health officials said it could cripple their efforts to stem the spread of the disease.

• In an omnibus health bill passed in 1988 (PL 100-607) Congress authorized $270 million over three years for AIDS education efforts, and a total of $400 million over two years for anonymous blood testing and counseling. The measure also authorized $2 million in operating costs for a new national AIDS commission. At Helms's insistence, however, sponsors of the bill dropped provisions guaranteeing confidentiality of AIDS test results. Helms and other conservative Republicans argued that AIDS should be treated like every other communicable disease, with mandatory testing and reporting of names to public health authorities. But health officials, including then–U.S. surgeon general C. Everett Koop, argued that those at greatest risk for acquiring AIDS—homosexuals and intravenous drug users—would be driven underground by mandatory testing requirements, only spreading the epidemic further.

• The RYAN WHITE COMPREHENSIVE AIDS RESOURCE AND EMERGENCY (CARE) ACT was passed by Congress in 1990 and signed reluctantly by President Bush (PL 101-381). The Ryan White program has rapidly become the major source of funding for treatment and detection of AIDS and *HIV,* the AIDS virus. In fiscal year 1999 Congress appropriated $1.4 billion for the program, named for an Indiana teenager who contracted HIV from the contaminated clotting factor he took for hemophilia and whose struggle attracted national attention early in the epidemic.

• Congress passed the 1990 AMERICANS WITH DISABILITIES ACT (PL 101-336), which banned discrimination against those with actual or perceived disabilities, including those with AIDS and HIV.

• Congress in 1993 enacted NATIONAL INSTITUTES OF HEALTH (NIH) reauthorization legislation (PL 103-43), which, in addition to creating in statute an office of AIDS research within the NIH to centralize research efforts, also acknowledged in law that infection with HIV could be grounds for excluding immigrants and travelers from entering the United States. Congress had first imposed limits on immigrants with HIV in 1987 and did so again in 1990, and President Clinton had vowed to change the policy on the campaign trail. But the Senate refused to go along with the president, and the final legislation continued to give the attorney general authority to grant waivers to those entering the country for medical treatment, tourism, or other short-term visits.

• The Ryan White Act was reauthorized in 1996. It required mandatory testing of newborn babies for HIV if states did not successfully lower the "perinatal" (pregnant mother to newborn child) transmission of the virus.

• Congress passed the 1998 RICKY RAY HEMOPHILIA RELIEF FUND ACT, which authorized tax-free payments of up to $100,000 for hemophiliacs and their families who contracted HIV from contaminated clot-

ting factor before blood tests for AIDS were in wide use. The measure (PL 105-369) was the culmination of years of lobbying by the hemophilia community, an estimated half of whose members became HIV-positive from using the contaminated clotting factor, which, unlike regular blood transfusions, was derived from thousands of donors, thus substantially increasing the risk of contracting HIV.

Alternative medicine

Also referred to as complementary medicine (particularly when used in conjunction with Western medical techniques), or "integrative" medicine, alternative medicine is, in essence, any healing practice or philosophy not widely taught in medical schools or widely available in hospitals. Many alternative medicine techniques, such as chiropractic, acupuncture, and biofeedback, are widely used and have some scientific evidence to back them up. Other treatments, such as aromatherapy or magnetic field therapy, are looked on more disdainfully by the mainstream medical community.

Regardless of how doctors look at alternative medicine, however, patients are embracing nontraditional medical methods as never before. A 1998 study published in the *Journal of the American Medical Association* found that visits to alternative medicine practitioners had jumped by 47.3 percent from 1990 to 1997, and in that year the estimated 629 million visits to alternative medicine practitioners by 83 million people had exceeded the number of visits to primary care physicians by more than a third. An estimated 42.1 percent of all adult Americans had used one of sixteen alternative therapies included in the survey, up from 33.8 percent of the population seven years earlier. The most popular therapies were massage, chiropractic, hypnosis, biofeedback, and acupuncture. Americans spent an estimated $12.2 billion out-of-pocket on alternative therapies in 1997, more than they spent out-of-pocket for hospital care ($9.1 billion). Increasingly, alternative therapies are being covered, at least in part, by medical insurance (particularly for chiropractic, megavitamins, biofeedback,

Although some alternative medicine techniques have been viewed by the medical establishment with skepticism, others, such as yoga, are winning the profession's cautious support.
Source: Agence France-Presse

and acupuncture), but nine of the top sixteen alternative medical services were not covered by insurance at all in 1997.

In recognition of the fact that more and more Americans are turning to nontraditional medical techniques, the U.S. scientific community is beginning to devote efforts to attempting to validate which methods work and which do not. In 1992 Congress established within the NATIONAL INSTITUTES OF HEALTH the National Center for Complementary and Alternative Medicine (NCCAM). NCCAM's mission is "to facilitate the evaluation of alternative medical treatment modalities" to determine their effectiveness. In carrying out that mission, the center, with a budget of $50 million in fiscal year 1999, conducts and supports basic and applied research on alternative medicine topics and supplies information to the public. The center divides its studies into seven main fields: diet-nutrition-lifestyle changes, mind-body interventions, bioelectromagnetic applications, alternative systems of medical practice, manual healing, pharmacological and biological treatments, and herbal medicine.

The medical community is also addressing alternative medicine in a more serious way. In 1998 the *Journal of the American Medical Association* devoted an entire issue to alternative medicine, publishing, among other things, a half-dozen rigorously-scientific studies of various alternative medicine treatments. The studies' results were mixed. One found, for example, that chiropractic manipulation was relatively ineffective in treating tension headaches, while another found that yoga techniques showed promise in treating carpal tunnel syndrome, a painful wrist condition, and still another demonstrated that Chinese herbs may be effective in treating the symptoms of irritable bowel syndrome.

American Association of Health Plans (AAHP)

The AAHP is the leading organization representing the MANAGED CARE industry. The group's one thousand members are HEALTH MAINTENANCE ORGANIZATIONS (HMOS), PREFERRED PROVIDER ORGANIZATIONS (PPOS), and other network-based plans. Those plans collectively cover approximately 140 million Americans. The AAHP was officially formed in 1996 through the merger of the Group Health Association of America and the American Managed Care and Review Association. In addition to advocating for its members before federal and state regulators and lawmakers, the AAHP has moved to respond to the consumer backlash against managed care by stiffening its own standards. In 1996 the organization formally adopted a code of conduct for its members aimed at improving communications among health plans and patients and physicians. In 1997 the AAHP board voted to require health plans to comply with the code of conduct in order to continue their membership in the association.

American Association of Retired Persons (AARP)

Formally renamed in 1998 just by its acronym (in recognition of the fact that a third of its members are

President Bill Clinton addresses a 1998 forum on Social Security cosponsored by the American Association of Retired Persons (AARP), one of the nation's most powerful special interest groups. Source: Jeff Taylor, Reuters

still working), AARP is considered one of the most influential special interest groups in the nation's capital. The nonprofit, nonpartisan association, with more than 30 million members, concentrates its legislative efforts on health care and pension issues, emphasizing MEDICARE and Social Security. AARP's leaders in Washington were burned in 1988 and 1989, when the organization helped develop and strongly supported the MEDICARE CATASTROPHIC COVERAGE ACT, only to see local AARP chapters and others protest the measure

to the point that Congress was forced to repeal it even before it took effect. AARP also came under fire after Republicans took over Congress following the 1994 elections. Republican senator Alan Simpson of Wyoming, perceiving the organization as having a Democratic tilt, launched a series of hearings looking into AARP's tax status. No legislation or evidence of wrongdoing emerged from those hearings, however, and AARP has remained an important voice representing the interests of America's over-fifty population.

American Medical Association (AMA)

Founded in 1847, the AMA calls itself the "voice of medicine" and lists as its core purpose "to promote the art and science of medicine and the betterment of public health." Although the organization, with its roughly three hundred thousand members, represents less than half of the nation's medical doctors, it remains one of the most powerful lobbying organizations in Washington, D.C. A significant portion of the AMA's clout comes through its American Medical Political Action Committee, or AMPAC, which has traditionally been one of the largest contributors to political campaigns for the House and Senate. In the 1996 election cycle AMPAC contributed $2.4 million to federal candidates, ranking fourth among all political action committees. The AMA is probably best known for its opposition to national health insurance in the 1950s, to the creation of MEDICARE in 1965, and to President Bill Clinton's health reform plan in 1993–1994. In 1995 and 1996 the AMA was one of the leading organizational backers of the Republican congressional leadership and one of the few health organizations to support GOP attempts to rein in spending on Medicare and MEDICAID. In 1998, however, the AMA broke with the GOP to support President Clinton's proposed PATIENTS BILL OF RIGHTS, a measure to impose federal rules on MANAGED CARE and other health insurance plans.

Americans with Disabilities Act (ADA)

Signed by President George Bush on July 26, 1990, the Americans with Disabilities Act (ADA, PL 101-336) extended to people with disabilities protections from discrimination in employment and public accommodations similar to those afforded women and racial and ethnic minorities by the 1964 Civil Rights Act. The measure also required that public transportation systems, other public services, and telecommunications systems be accessible to the estimated 43 million Americans with disabilities.

Discrimination against the disabled was already prohibited in federally funded activities by the 1973 Rehabilitation Act and in housing by the 1988 Fair Housing Act amendments. But the disabled were not among those protected under the 1964 Civil Rights Act, which barred discrimination in employment and public accommodations on the basis of race, sex, religion, or national origin.

But although the measure was approved overwhelmingly by Congress—the conference report passed in the House, 377–28, on July 12 and in the Senate, 91–6, a day later—it was not without controversy. Some business interests worried that the measure would expose them to unwarranted lawsuits and cost them thousands of dollars to comply with its requirements. Restaurateurs were worried that they would be required to permit workers with contagious diseases to remain in food-handling jobs. (Backers of the measure pointed out it already included an exemption from the anti-discrimination provisions for individuals "who posed a direct threat to the health or safety of others.") Hovering over the entire two-year debate over the measure was the specter of the ongoing and escalating AIDS epidemic, and some legislators attempted to exclude AIDS or HIV, the AIDS virus, from the ADA's protections.

One major impetus for the measure was a group of members of Congress who themselves had overcome disabilities or who had a close family member with a disability. Among the lead sponsors were Sen. Tom Harkin, D-Iowa, whose brother was deaf; Sen. Lowell Weicker, R-Conn. (sponsor of the original measure before his defeat in 1988), who had a child with a severe birth defect; Sen. Bob Dole, R-Kan., who had limited use of his right arm from an injury incurred during World War II; and House majority whip Tony Coelho, D-Calif., who had epilepsy. The measure was also strongly backed by President Bush, who spoke of it repeatedly during his 1988 campaign and who endorsed it again two days before his 1989 inauguration, calling it "simple fairness to provide the disabled with the same rights afforded other minorities."

The law defined an *individual with a disability* as a person with a physical or mental impairment "that substantially limited one or more major life activities, had a record of such an impairment, or was regarded as having such an impairment." The last part of the definition was to prevent discrimination against someone on the basis of a perceived disability, such as someone who had been disfigured by a birth mark or burn scars but who was not actually hindered from performing major life activities.

Among its key provisions was a ban on discrimination against "qualified individuals with a disability" by employers with more than fifteen workers. Employers were prohibited from discriminating in job application procedures, in hiring, advancing, training, compensating, and discharging employees, and in fulfilling other terms, conditions, and privileges of employment. Employers were required to make "reasonable accommodations" to workers with disabilities as long as doing so did not cause an "undue hardship," defined as an action requiring significant difficulty or expense. Reasonable accommodations could include job restructuring, providing qualified readers or interpreters, or acquiring or modifying equipment or devices.

Title II of the ADA prohibited public entities from discriminating against individuals with disabilities and stipulated that such individuals were not to be excluded from or denied the benefits of the "services, programs, or activities of a public entity." Public entities included not only state and local governments but also Amtrak and commuter rail authorities. Title II ensured accessibility to public transportation systems for those with disabilities, requiring "paratransit" systems for those unable to use fixed-route public transit.

Title III, the ADA's "public accommodation" section, applied to a much broader array of private entities than did the 1964 Civil Rights Act. Not only did it require access by those with disabilities to the restaurants, lodging, places of entertainment, and gasoline stations covered by the earlier law, but it also mandated their access to museums and sports stadiums, doctors' offices and hospitals, dry cleaners, pharmacies, grocery stores, and all other retail and service establishments. Owners of such public accommodations were required to make new and renovated facilities accessible to the disabled and to make whatever "readily achievable" modifications in existing facilities were needed to accommodate the disabled. The law also required all new purchased or leased buses and rail cars to be accessible to the disabled but did not mandate retrofitting of existing vehicles.

Finally, Title IV of the bill required that interstate and intrastate telecommunications relay services be available "to the extent possible and in the most efficient manner" to hearing- and speech-impaired individuals. Title IV also ordered that television public service announcements funded in whole or in part by the federal government be closed-captioned for the hearing impaired.

But for all its overwhelming support, the ADA's trip to passage was tortuous, taking more than two years and traveling through four separate House committees. Among the sticking points was the potential cost to business of complying with the measure's requirements. One of the final sticking points concerned coverage of people with AIDS and HIV.

Supporters of the ADA assumed all along that it would cover both those with full-blown AIDS and those with earlier stages of HIV infections. They based those claims on a complicated framework of court decisions, legislative history, and administrative interpretation. The underpinning of the framework was a 1987 Supreme Court decision, *School Board of Nassau County, Fla., v. Arline,* which had held that a person with a contagious disease (in that case, tuberculosis) was handicapped as defined by amendments to the 1973 Rehabili-

tation Act. Although that definition almost certainly covered AIDS, it left open the question of whether asymptomatic HIV protection would also trigger the ADA's protections. The House in 1988 seemed to indicate that it would, when it specifically rejected, by 63–334, an amendment that would have sent a fair housing bill back to committee with instructions to eliminate protections for HIV. In October 1988 the Justice Department weighed in, agreeing that those with HIV as well as AIDS were covered under the Rehabilitation Act. "The surgeon general advises us that the impairment of HIV infection cannot be meaningfully separated from clinical AIDS, and that it is medically inappropriate to think of this disease as composed of discrete conditions," said a Justice Department official in announcing the change. "Because HIV infection may limit the likelihood of bearing a healthy child and may adversely affect intimate sexual relations, we believe that an individual proving these facts to a court could fairly be found to be an individual with handicaps for purposes of the [rehabilitation] act."

But it took a 1998 Supreme Court decision, *Bragdon v. Abbott,* to resolve the matter conclusively. On June 25 the Court, in a 5–4 decision, ruled that HIV infection alone, without symptoms, still entitled individuals to the ADA's protections. In the case an HIV-positive Maine woman, Sidney Abbott, sued a dentist for refusing to provide her treatment. Abbott's attorneys argued that she had a disability in that her HIV status hindered her ability to have children, and the Court majority agreed. "Reproduction falls well within the phrase 'major life activity,'" wrote Justice Anthony Kennedy in the majority opinion. "Reproduction and the sexual dynamics surrounding it are central to the life process itself."

In 1999, however, the Supreme Court acted to limit the number of people who could qualify for the ADA's protections. In a 7–2 ruling in separate cases handed down on June 22, the Court ruled that persons with disabilities that could be corrected (such as with medication or eyeglasses) were not entitled to sue for discrimination under the ADA. One of the cases, *Sutton v. United Airlines,* involved a nearsighted set of identical twins who were rejected for pilot jobs with the airline because of their eyesight. The other, *Murphy v. United Parcel Service*, involved a mechanic fired by UPS because of an inability to control his high blood pressure.

On the same day, the Court did hand one victory to advocates for the disabled. In a 6–3 ruling in *Olmstead v. L. C.*, the justices said that states must place disabled individuals in community-based settings rather than institutions if the individuals are capable of living outside institutions and desire such placement. That case involved two mentally retarded women in Georgia who were kept institutionalized even after their doctors said such care was no longer needed.

Assignment (Medicare)

Physicians who accept "assignment" under MEDICARE agree to accept the program's predetermined fee as payment-in-full. That means that patients are responsible for their 20 percent copayment but no more. Physicians who sign an annual agreement to accept assignment for all patients for all services are known as PARTICIPATING PHYSICIANS and receive a 5 percent bonus from Medicare. Physicians may charge more than Medicare's approved rates, up to certain limits. (See BALANCE BILLING.) In 1997 96.5 percent of Medicare claims were assigned, the highest rate in the history of the program, and up from only 80 percent in 1990.

Assisted suicide

See SUICIDE, ASSISTED

B

Balance billing (Medicare)

Also known as "extra billing," balance billing refers to an amount a physician charges a MEDICARE patient over and above Medicare's approved fee. As part of the 1989 budget reconciliation bill that overhauled Medicare's physician payment system (PL 101-239), Congress limited physician charges to no more than 115 percent of the Medicare-approved amount. Thus, if Medicare allows $100 for a procedure, a physician may charge a patient no more than $115. The patient, however, would be responsible for paying $35: the $20 required "coinsurance" payment (because Medicare covers only 80 percent of allowed physician fees) plus the $15 "balance bill." Four of the ten standardized private MEDIGAP INSURANCE policies cover some or all of a physician's balance bills.

Baseline

This term is used in federal budgeting to measure the effect of proposed changes in tax and spending law. The CONGRESSIONAL BUDGET OFFICE (CBO), the official arbiter of cost estimates for federal legislation, periodically estimates how much the federal government will spend on various programs over the ensuing five years assuming no legislative changes are made. This estimate is the official "baseline." CBO then uses that baseline to estimate how much a proposed change would add to or subtract from that projection. Programs that would increase federal spending (such as new benefits covered under MEDICARE or a tax cut) are counted as "cost" provisions; those that would reduce spending (such as reductions in inflation updates for doctors or hospitals under Medicare) are counted as "savings" provisions.

Beneficiary

In health care parlance, a person entitled to benefits is known as a beneficiary. For example, those "entitled" to MEDICARE or MEDICAID are beneficiaries. Legally, beneficiaries are also those designated by wills or trusts.

Blue Cross/Blue Shield Association (BCBSA)

This trade association comprises the fifty-five independent Blue Cross and Blue Shield member plans, which were originally (but are no longer exclusively) not for profit. The "Blues," as they are known, collectively covered 71.1 million people in all fifty states, the District of Columbia, and Puerto Rico in 1998. The Blue Cross/Blue Shield plan covering 3.7 million federal workers and dependents is the largest privately underwritten health contract in the world. Although they are traditionally associated with offering FEE-FOR-SERVICE care, Blue Cross/Blue Shield plans are also collectively the nation's largest provider of MANAGED CARE services, with 67 percent of subscribers belonging to a managed care network of some sort. (The Blues operate eighty-eight HEALTH MAINTENANCE ORGANIZATIONS, sixty-eight PREFERRED PROVIDER ORGANIZATIONS, and eighty-one POINT-OF-SERVICE PLANS.) The thirty-five Blue Cross/Blue Shield Medicare managed care plans covering an estimated 900,000 MEDICARE beneficiaries made them the second-largest provider in that program in 1998 (after the California-based PacifiCare). The Blues are also the largest processor of Medicare claims, a service provided under contract to the federal government. In 1997 Blues plans processed 569 million claims and paid $143 billion on behalf of Medicare beneficiaries.

The BCBSA owns the names *Blue Cross* and *Blue Shield,* licenses their use to member plans, and enforces quality and financial standards, although each plan is independently owned and operated.

Among the nation's oldest health insurers, the Blues were founded in 1929, when Dallas's Baylor University devised the first Blue Cross plan to guarantee school teachers twenty-one days of hospital care for $6 per year. Blue Cross plans were largely begun by hospitals because the depression had left hospital care out of financial reach of most Americans. Although the early plans were offered by individual hospitals in competition with each other, ultimately the American Hospital Association stepped in to facilitate community-wide plans (it registered the Blue Cross trademark). Blue Shield plans, created to cover physician services, were begun in the Pacific Northwest, where employers, often in remote areas such as logging camps, contracted with groups of doctors to provide health services to their workers. As provider-sponsored plans, the Blues pioneered payments based on "usual and customary" charges, which Medicare would emulate upon its creation.

In many but not all cases, Blue Cross and Blue Shield plans have merged to provide comprehensive health care coverage. California is a notable exception, where Blue Cross of California and Blue Shield of California compete against each other, although both plans offer hospital and physician care. The Blue Cross and Blue Shield associations merged in 1982, forming the current group.

Originally not-for-profit, the Blues benefited from special statutes passed by many states, which granted them preferential tax treatment in exchange for their agreeing to perform certain community service roles, such as insuring individuals or groups that commercial insurers would not cover, and for their adopting COM-MUNITY RATING policies, so that people would pay the same premium regardless of their health status. The federal government also made the Blues tax-exempt, although that exemption was ended with passage of the 1986 Tax Reform Act (PL 99-514), in recognition of the fact that many Blues plans were taking on characteristics of commercial insurers, including, in some cases, conversion from nonprofit status. (The largest conversion so far was that undertaken by Blue Cross of California, which became WellPoint Health Networks in 1996. A California law requiring built-up assets to be left in a nonprofit entity as part of the conversion process led to the creation of two foundations, to which Blue Cross left $3 billion. Overnight, the foundations became the nation's sixth-largest philanthropies.)

In 1990 Blue Cross and Blue Shield of West Virginia became insolvent, leaving some 51,000 individuals with $42 million in unpaid claims and 280,000 subscribers scrambling for new coverage. That crisis led to a high-profile congressional investigation that found significant mismanagement and even fraud in a number of the plans. "The problem pattern . . . undermined the Plans' ability to perform their essential insurance functions for policyholders and providers, as reflected in dramatically increased premiums, poor claims service, and diminished coverage," said a report from the Senate Permanent Subcommittee on Investigations, which led the probe. That investigation ultimately led to the sacking of the head of the association, and it has since taken a significantly lower profile.

Boren amendment

Originally passed in 1980 and named for its sponsor, Oklahoma Democratic senator David Boren, the Boren amendment sought to ensure that states provide adequate payments to nursing homes and other LONG-TERM CARE facilities, including intermediate care facilities for the mentally retarded. In 1981 budget reconciliation legislation (see BUDGET RECONCILIATION LEGIS-LATION AND HEALTH CARE), Congress extended the requirement to hospitals. It required not only that payment be "reasonable and adequate" to cover the costs of an "efficiently and economically operated facility" but also that the care provided meet applicable state and federal laws, regulations, and quality and safety standards. In 1990 the Supreme Court, in *Wilder v. Virginia Hospital Association,* upheld the right of health care providers to sue states under the Boren amendment for insufficient payment levels.

As part of the 1997 Balanced Budget Act (PL 105-33), Congress repealed the Boren amendment. In its place it required a public process under which proposed rates, methodologies underlying them, and reasons for them would be published and made available for public comment. The law also required the secretary of the Department of Health and Human Services to evaluate the effects of state rate-setting methods and report back to Congress in the year 2001.

Budget reconciliation legislation and health care

Since 1980 budget reconciliation bills have been a principal way—if not *the* principal way—Congress has shaped health policy in general and made alterations to the MEDICARE and MEDICAID programs in particular. Technically, the purpose of the budget reconciliation bill is literally to "reconcile" the terms of the annual budget resolution with existing law for permanently authorized programs such as Medicare and Medicaid. In most cases fulfilling that purpose means changing the terms of the programs to reduce their cost. But sometimes the budget resolution "assumes" additional spending, as in the case of expansions in Medicaid eligibility or new preventive benefits for Medicare.

Making policy using reconciliation is not ideal, say lawmakers who have been involved in crafting the bills. They note that such policy changes are driven by the numbers—usually savings targets imposed by the budget resolution. More than once, say congressional aides, at the end of a difficult reconciliation bill, staff would "run the numbers," see how far from their savings target they were, then "back-fit" a cut to meet the target, with more attention to the savings achieved than to the policy objective involved. Reconciliation is also "obsessed with the short-term," as one lawmaker put it, giving legislators little chance to think about big-picture health policy issues.

On the other hand, reconciliation has had some significant advantages. Sometimes, note aides, it has enabled legislators to make decisions that represented good policy but not-so-good politics, like trimming reimbursements to health care providers that are also major contributors to legislators' campaign war chests. A reconciliation bill is also protected legislation, with amendments significantly limited in the House, and both amendments and debate time limited in the Senate (it is one of the very few bills that cannot be filibustered under Senate rules). Reconciliation is also a must-pass bill for the Congress and usually a must-sign bill for the president (although President Clinton proved the exception to that rule in his 1995 standoff with Congress. Clinton vetoed that bill, largely because of changes Republicans wanted to make to Medicare and Medicaid. That measure eventually died, although pieces of it were included in the next reconciliation bill, the 1997 Balanced Budget Act.) Thus, getting a policy initiative into a reconciliation bill all but guarantees it will become law.

Reconciliation is all about meeting budget targets that add to or subtract from a budget BASELINE, or estimate of what a program will cost in the future barring legislative changes. Legislators over the years have developed a series of budget "tricks" to meet reconciliation targets. (Budgeteers have closed some—though not all—of the loopholes allowing these practices. But the practices are included here to illustrate why many of the reconciliation bills were shaped as they were.) On the savings side the techniques include:

• The *golden goose,* a provision that Congress extends only as long as required to achieve savings in a particular budget cycle, usually a single year. If such a cut were permanent, it would be factored into the baseline and could not be used to show savings in future years. Thus the nickname, which comes from the provision's ability to lay annual "golden eggs" of savings. Probably the most-often-used golden egg was the continuing reimposition of the requirement that Medicare Part B premiums be set to cover 25 percent of the program's costs. During years of high health care inflation, the provision had the effect of boosting premiums for beneficiaries and thus saving federal dollars. (Without the provision the Part B premium would have reverted to a level dictated by underlying law, under which it would have risen by either the amount needed to cover 50 percent of the program's cost or the percentage cost-of-living allowance (COLA) increase in Social Security benefits, whichever was lower.) Ironically, by the 1990s, when health inflation slowed, the 25 percent rule became a money loser, since the premium at 25 percent of program costs would have been lower than the premium as increased by the Social Security COLA. In 1997, in the Balanced Budget Act (PL 105-33), Congress made the 25 percent rule permanent.

• The *noncut cut,* the practice of holding inflation increases for doctors, hospitals, and MANAGED CARE plans below the predicted inflation rate. For example, hospital payments are updated annually according to price increases in a typical market basket of goods and services hospitals purchase. In a reconciliation bill Congress would typically provide an increase on the order of "market basket minus one percentage point," so if that year's market basket increase was scheduled to be 3.5 percent, hospitals would receive a 2.5 percent increase instead. Because they had reduced the baseline, these were "scored" as cuts, even though providers still received payment increases. It was just these sorts of cuts that led Republicans in 1995 to insist that they were not cutting Medicare by $270 billion at all, as Democrats had charged, but merely decreasing scheduled increases. Such noncut cuts sometimes gave rise to "reverse pork," in which an interest group sought to minimize its losses compared with those of other groups. Rural hospitals, for example, which are more financially dependent on Medicare than are other hospitals, frequently managed to obtain smaller decreases in their inflation increases.

• *Payment shifts,* a technique much favored in the early years of reconciliation (and which were essentially blocked in the 1987 "fix" to the Gramm-Rudman-Hollings budget enforcement bill (PL 100-119)). This technique pushed payments due in one fiscal year to the next. In the 1982 Tax Equity and Fiscal Responsibility Act (TEFRA, PL 97-248), for instance, Congress suspended hospital payments for the last six weeks of fiscal years 1983 and 1984, pushing those outlays into the subsequent year. Similarly, Congress on more than one occasion ordered the HEALTH CARE FINANCING ADMINISTRATION, which oversees Medicare and Medicaid, to slow claims payments, pushing some bills into the next year.

Just as lawmakers had techniques to make savings look larger, they also developed ways to make new spending look smaller. Those included:

• The *three-quarters rule,* designed to make outlays for new programs look as small as possible. Starting a new program one, two, or three quarters into a fiscal year minimizes outlays in that year and hence, for the purposes of that year's budget, scores lower. For example, the fiscal year 1988 bill, the Omnibus Budget Reconciliation Act of 1987 (OBRA '87, PL 100-203) authorized states to offer Medicaid coverage to pregnant women and young children with incomes of up to 185 percent of the poverty threshold, but not beginning until July 1, 1988, the first day of the last quarter of the fiscal year. That ensured that Medicaid's federal matching money would not begin to flow until the year's final quarter. In extreme cases lawmakers have resorted to the "September 30 option," in which a new program is begun on the final day of a fiscal year, thus raising the baseline by only one day's worth of spending.

• The *stretch-out,* or phasing in of a program, which can make it appear less costly. When Congress in the fiscal year 1988 law required states to increase payments to hospitals that serve a disproportionate share of Medicaid and low-income patients, for example, it required that the higher rates (with their higher federal match) be phased in over three years. (See DISPROPORTIONATE SHARE HOSPITAL.)

• The *option-mandate,* a spending-reducing technique that transforms this year's voluntary program into next year's requirement. In Medicaid, for instance, allowing rather than requiring a state to extend coverage for a particular service or to a particular population is less expensive, since not all states will exercise the option. And if that option later becomes a mandate, it will still look less costly, since the cost for states that have already exercised it on their own will have already been factored into the baseline. The option-mandate technique was the key to Medicaid expansions for low-income pregnant women and children throughout the 1980s.

Here is a thumbnail history of reconciliation bills, including their nicknames and some of the most important health policy changes in them:

• *1980. Unnamed, fiscal year 1981 (PL 96-499)*. Although less sweeping than reconciliation bills that would follow, this measure, among other things, authorized Medicare reimbursement for outpatient surgery and diagnostic tests performed subsequent to hospitalization. It also first employed the payment-shifting technique of achieving budget savings by postponing Medicare payments to hospitals—in this case by six weeks.

• *1981. Unnamed, fiscal year 1982 (PL 97-35)*. In addition to making the largest Medicaid cut of the Reagan era ($2.9 billion over three years), this bill created the so-called Section 2176 waiver, which allowed states to obtain permission to use Medicaid to fund home- or community-based services for those who would otherwise require institutional care.

• *1982. Tax Equity and Fiscal Responsibility Act (TEFRA), fiscal year 1983 (PL 97-248)*. Although TEFRA, one of two budget reconciliation measures passed in 1982 (the other made spending reductions in agriculture, veterans', and other programs), produced the most dramatic Medicare savings of any reconciliation bill in the 1980s ($13.3 billion over three years), it also included the most sweeping structural expansions. The bill first authorized contracts between Medicare and HEALTH MAINTENANCE ORGANIZATIONS (HMOs) to enroll Medicare beneficiaries, allowed for the first time Medicare payment for HOSPICE services for the terminally ill, required federal employees to pay the Medicare payroll tax, and replaced the often-criticized Professional

Standards Review Organization program with physician-run PEER REVIEW ORGANIZATIONS. The bill was also the first to require that the Medicare Part B premium be set to cover 25 percent of the program's costs, a provision that would be reenacted a half-dozen times before it was made permanent in 1997.

• *1984. Deficit Reduction Act (DEFRA), fiscal year 1984 (PL 98-369)*. Although DEFRA achieved fully a third of its $6.1 billion in Medicare savings by freezing physician fees, it also created the participating physician (PAR) program to encourage physicians to agree to accept Medicare's approved fee as payment in full for all Medicare patients' covered services. DEFRA was also the first of a series of reconciliation bills to expand eligibility for Medicaid, in this case by requiring states to extend pregnancy-related services to single, poor women pregnant with their first child (who were previously ineligible because they had no "dependent children") as well as to provide basic coverage to children up to age five in two-parent families with incomes at or below the state's welfare eligibility level.

• *1986. Consolidated Omnibus Budget Reconciliation Act of 1986 (COBRA), fiscal year 1986 (PL 99-272)*. COBRA, held up by non–health-related issues and thus not enacted until more than halfway through fiscal year 1986, broke ground on several fronts. It ordered creation of the PHYSICIAN PAYMENT REVIEW COMMISSION (PPRC, replaced in 1997 by the MEDICARE PAYMENT ADVISORY COMMISSION), an independent board to make recommendations on Medicare physician payment issues. It also ordered all state and local employees hired after March 31, 1986, to pay the Medicare payroll tax. It barred PATIENT "DUMPING" by threatening hospitals with expulsion from Medicare if they failed to provide emergency department care to those without the ability to pay. And it took the first steps to address the problem of the UNINSURED by requiring employers to continue existing group health coverage for eighteen months for laid-off employees and to allow spouses and dependents who would otherwise lose coverage because of death or divorce from a worker to purchase coverage at the group rate through the employer. In Medicaid, COBRA required states to provide pregnancy-related services for women in two-parent families in which the principal wage earner was unemployed (such coverage had been optional).

• *1986. Omnibus Budget Reconciliation Act of 1986 (OBRA '86), fiscal year 1987 (PL 99-509).* In the second of two reconciliation bills approved in 1986, Congress responded to a report from its organ-transplant task force by requiring hospitals, as a condition of participation in Medicare or Medicaid, to "routinely request" organ donations from the next of kin of a deceased patient and authorized a year's worth of antirejection drugs for Medicare beneficiaries who have organ transplants. OBRA '86 also created "maximum allowable actual charge" limits (known as MAACs) for nonparticipating physicians in Medicare. The limits were aimed at preventing physicians from avoiding a Medicare fee freeze by passing fee increases along to patients, while at the same time allowing physicians who had been undercharging patients relative to their colleagues to begin to raise their fees. For Medicaid, it gave states the option of covering pregnancy-related services for pregnant women as well as programs for senior citizens and children up to age five (a year at a time) in families with incomes below poverty.

• *1987. Omnibus Budget Reconciliation Act of 1987 (OBRA '87), fiscal years 1988 and 1989 (PL 100-203).* The use of reconciliation to advance non–budget-related proposals reached a pinnacle when congressional conferees appended to this measure a bill overhauling federal regulation of nursing homes that served Medicare and Medicaid patients. Also included in OBRA '87 were provisions to implement a 1986 law (PL 99-660) creating a no-fault compensation system for families of children with severe adverse reactions to vaccines to prevent childhood diseases. The bill allowed states to extend Medicaid coverage to pregnant women and infants in families with incomes of up to 185 percent of poverty.

• *1989. Omnibus Budget Reconciliation Act of 1989 (OBRA '89), fiscal year 1990 (PL 101-239).* OBRA '89 outdid even OBRA '87 in its reach. It included a complete overhaul of Medicare's physician payment system, replacing a system based on doctors' historical charges with one based on the skill, time, and training needed to

provide specific services, as well as volume controls to brake the then-fastest-growing portion of the program. The bill also imposed the first of two efforts to prevent physician "self-referrals," the practice of doctors' sending patients to laboratories or other facilities in which the doctor had an ownership interest (see SELF-REFERRAL CURBS). In addition, the measure created the federal AGENCY FOR HEALTH CARE POLICY AND RESEARCH (AHCPR) to research and promote quality and effectiveness in the health care system. In Medicaid, the bill required states to provide coverage to pregnant women (for pregnancy-related services) and to infants up to age one in families with incomes of up to 133 percent of the federal poverty line. That requirement represented an increase from that included in the 1988 MEDICARE CATASTROPHIC COVERAGE ACT (PL 100-360) for coverage of those populations in families with incomes at or below poverty. The measure also spelled out minimum requirements for coverage under Medicaid's EARLY AND PERIODIC SCREENING, DIAGNOSTIC, AND TREATMENT (EPSDT) program for children up to age twelve. The bill required that states cover treatment for conditions discovered through EPSDT screenings, even if the state's Medicaid program did not otherwise cover such services. And the measure required state Medicaid programs to cover services provided by FEDERALLY QUALIFIED HEALTH CENTERS and to pay those centers 100 percent of their "reasonable costs."

• *1990. Omnibus Budget Reconciliation Act of 1990 (OBRA '90), fiscal year 1991 (PL 101-508).* OBRA '90, the bill that emerged from the famous "budget summit" between Congress and the Bush administration after which President George Bush renounced his "no new taxes" pledge, included the largest-yet Medicare reductions—an estimated $44.2 billion over five years. But that reduction was smaller than the amount originally negotiated by summiteers—the first effort was rejected in the House, and the measure hastily rewritten. The bill also included a major benefit expansion for Medicare; for the first time, the program would cover a strictly preventive service, mammograms to detect breast cancer. The measure also required Medicare and Medicaid providers to inform patients about their rights under state law to execute LIVING WILLS or other ADVANCE DIRECTIVES about their care should they become unable to express their wishes. Also included in the measure was a major overhaul of federal regulation of MEDIGAP INSURANCE policies to supplement Medicare coverage. In Medicaid, the measure initiated a program requiring drug manufacturers to grant the same discounts to Medicaid as they provided for other bulk purchasers, such as managed care organizations and the Department of Veterans Affairs. And the bill capped off a half-dozen years of Medicaid coverage expansions by requiring states to cover, a year at a time, all children born after September 30, 1983, in families with incomes under the federal poverty line. The bill expanded mandatory Medicaid help with Medicare cost-sharing for more low-income elderly, and authorized two new, optional programs to help states pay for home- and community-based care for the frail elderly and for the mentally retarded and others with developmental disabilities.

• *1993. Omnibus Budget Reconciliation Act of 1993 (OBRA '93), fiscal year 1994 (PL 103-66).* The pivotal bill that passed with only Democratic votes in the summer of the first year of Bill Clinton's presidency included the largest-yet cuts in Medicare—$55.8 billion over five years. The measure contained the second round of prohibitions against physician self-referrals, as well as made it harder for individuals to divest themselves of their assets in order to qualify for Medicaid-covered nursing home care. It also created a new—and controversial—$1.8 billion child immunization program that effectively federalized the provision of vaccines for low-income and uninsured children.

• *1997. Balanced Budget Act of 1997, fiscal year 1998 (PL 105-33).* The reconciliation bill to end all reconciliation bills—the first to anticipate a balanced federal budget—dramatically changed both Medicare and Medicaid. In addition to making cuts in Medicare nearly as large as all previous cuts combined—$115 billion over five years—the measure ordered the Health Care Financing Administration to create updated payment systems for HOME HEALTH CARE, nursing home care, and hospital outpatient services. It created a new Medicare Part C, called MEDICARE+CHOICE, to encourage beneficiaries to join private managed care and other health plans. And it added a raft of new preventive benefits to Medicare in an effort to begin to update the program's meager benefit package. For Medicaid, the program continued a crackdown on what federal lawmakers said was state abuse of a program allowing special payments to hospitals that serve a disproportionate share of Medicaid and low-income patients. (See DISPROPORTIONATE SHARE HOSPITAL PAYMENTS.) The measure also made it easier for states to move Medicaid beneficiaries into managed care plans. And it created a $48 billion program to help cover up to half of the nation's estimated 10 million uninsured children (see CHILDREN'S HEALTH INSURANCE PROGRAM).

C

Cafeteria benefits plans

Such plans permit employees to select from a list of benefits provided by an employer and allow them to customize their noncash compensation to their individual needs. For example, a worker with no dependents might not need life insurance but might prefer tuition aid or other educational assistance. Child or elder-care benefits are often offered under cafeteria plans, as well as health care coverage. Cafeteria benefits are most likely to be offered by larger employers; in 1991 36 percent of employees at large and medium-sized firms were able to choose from a list of benefits, up from 5 percent in 1986. But in 1992 only 14 percent of workers in firms with less than one hundred employees were eligible for cafeteria-style benefits.

CalPERS

The California Public Employee Retirement System, or CalPERS, provides pension and health coverage to more than a million state and local employees, retirees, and dependents, making it, after the FEDERAL EMPLOYEE HEALTH BENEFITS PLAN, the nation's largest single purchaser of health care. CalPERS' health program, begun in 1962 to cover state workers and expanded in 1967 to cover local government employees as well, is considered a national model of group health negotiating and purchasing. It was one of the first large groups to adopt MANAGED COMPETITION, giving workers a broad choice of plans (sixteen in 1999: ten HEALTH MAINTENANCE ORGANIZATIONS (HMOs) and six PREFERRED PROVIDER ORGANIZATIONS (PPOs)) and negotiating with plans to increase quality and decrease premiums. With twelve hundred participating public employers and $1.7 billion in premiums paid annually, CalPERS has significant bargaining power over plans and has not been shy about using it.

Capitation

From the Latin for "head," capitation in health care refers to the practice of paying for medical care on a preset, per head basis. Under capitation systems a physician or medical group generally receives a per-month payment intended to cover all of a patient's medical care for that period. If the patient needs more care, the "capitated" entity has to make up the difference itself; if the patient needs less or no care, the entity gets to keep the difference. *Partial capitation* is a payment mechanism in which the payer makes the medical providers responsible for only a subset of all medical care; a typical example is making a group of doctors financially "at-risk" for all physician care but not for hospital or other care. *Global capitation,* on the other hand, makes the capitated entity liable for all care. The theory behind capitation is that the payments for patients who need little care will offset the losses for those who need more than the capitated amount, while eliminating the incentive for practitioners to do more than may be necessary in order to increase their income. Critics of capitation point out that although it eliminates the incentive to overserve, it simultaneously creates one to underserve since the capitated entity gets to keep money not spent on patient care.

Carrier (Medicare)

Carriers are private insurance companies that contract with MEDICARE to administer Medicare PART B services. Carriers make coverage and payment decisions under guidance from the HEALTH CARE FINANCING ADMINISTRATION (the agency of the federal HEALTH AND HUMAN SERVICES DEPARTMENT that oversees Medicare). Carriers also act as beneficiaries' first contact with questions or complaints and help police the Part B program for fraud. Medicare PART A services are handled by INTERMEDIARIES.

Carve-out organizations

These organizations contract with MANAGED CARE plans to provide a specialized set of services. *Carve-outs,* as they are called, may themselves be managed care entities or may provide services on a FEE-FOR-SERVICE basis. The term comes from the fact that the services are "carved out" of coverage by the patient's insurance plan, which delegates the care in question (for a fee, of course) to the carve-out organization. Carve-outs, which maintain their own networks and administrative operations, are most common in mental health, where MANAGED BEHAVIORAL HEALTH CARE plans in 1997 covered an estimated 169 million Americans, and in pharmacy benefits.

Catastrophic illness

Definitions vary widely for what type of illness can be considered "catastrophic," but policy analysts agree that it is the cost, not the nature of the malady, that makes a medical event catastrophic. One definition labels as catastrophic the average medical expenses incurred by the top 1 percent of the population. Others say it is any illness or condition that requires a family to spend more than 10 percent of its annual take-home income out-of-pocket for health care expenses, regardless of whether it has insurance or not. Families with insur-

ance that could still leave them at-risk for having to spend more than 10 percent of their income for a serious illness are considered UNDERINSURED. (See MEDICARE CATASTROPHIC COVERAGE ACT.)

Categorical eligibility

This phrase used in MEDICAID describes people who are eligible for the program because they are members of a specific group or "category," such as children, the elderly, or the disabled. It is because of Medicaid's categorical eligibility standards that the program only covers roughly half of all Americans who live in poverty. For example, a single, childless man who is not disabled cannot generally qualify for Medicaid no matter how poor, because he does not fit into any of the program's categories. A pregnant woman with income below 133 percent of poverty, on the other hand, is categorically eligible for Medicaid.

Centers for Disease Control and Prevention (CDC)

Renamed in 1992 legislation (previously it was merely the Centers for Disease Control), the Atlanta, Georgia–based CDC is the agency of the U.S. Public Health Service responsible for promoting health and preventing disease, injury, and premature death. With a workforce of 7,100 and a fiscal year 1999 budget of $2.7 billion, the CDC is the nation's preeminent public health agency.

The CDC dates back to 1946, with the establishment of the Communicable Disease Center in the Office of Malaria Control in War Areas in downtown Atlanta. CDC's original mission was to combat malaria (still common in the southern United States at that time), typhus, and other communicable diseases. A year later CDC officials provided disaster relief in the wake of chemical explosions in Texas that killed hundreds, after which the agency was designated as the Public Health Service agency to respond to disasters or epidemics. In

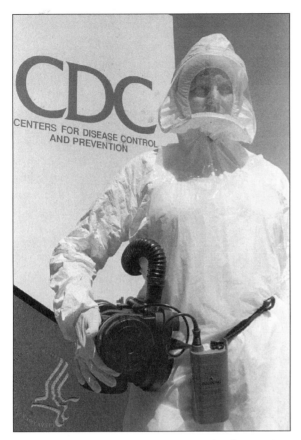

A staffer from the Centers for Disease Control and Prevention (CDC) models equipment developed by the agency to combat the Ebola virus in Zaire. Fighting communicable diseases around the world is just one of CDC's many public health responsibilities. Source: John Kuntz, Reuters

• Administration of the Preventive Health Services Block Grant ($150 million in fiscal year 1999), which provides grants to states for a broad range of public health activities, from rape prevention and treatment to rodent control and water fluoridation.

• Operation of the federal childhood immunization program, which provides funds to states for planning, developing, and conducting childhood immunization activities. The CDC also maintains a stockpile of childhood vaccines and conducts surveillance (of adverse reactions or disease outbreaks that could indicate vaccine failure), investigations, and research into the safety and efficacy of new and presently used vaccines.

• Development of a stockpile of antidotes, antibiotics, and vaccines needed to respond to acts of bioterrorism.

• Oversight of state and local efforts to identify, prevent, and treat HIV and AIDS.

• Operation of programs to prevent, identify, and treat tuberculosis and sexually transmitted diseases.

• Administration of a program authorized in 1992 to provide breast and cervical cancer screening services to low-income women.

• Operation of the National Institute for Occupational Safety and Health (NIOSH), which conducts and funds applied research and develops standards for occupational health and safety.

• Operation of the National Center for Health Statistics, which collects, interprets, and disseminates data on the health status of the U.S. population and its use of health services.

1951 CDC established its most famous operating unit, the Epidemic Intelligence Service (EIS), which draws young physicians from around the nation and deploys them around the world to track down the source of communicable disease outbreaks.

In 1999 the CDC had eleven operating units performing research, education, and disease surveillance activities. Like the NATIONAL INSTITUTES OF HEALTH, CDC funds research in universities and other laboratories around the nation, including efforts to reduce the incidence of lead poisoning and injuries. Among its other principal programs and activities are the following:

Certified nurse midwife

An ADVANCED PRACTICE NURSE who provides routine gynecological and low-risk obstetrical care, including prenatal, labor-and-delivery, and post-partum care, a certified nurse midwife (CNM) may prescribe drugs in thirty-three states. An estimated 7,400 CNMs practice in the United States, according to the American Nurses Association. In 1990 they delivered nearly 150,000 babies, representing 3.6 percent of that year's births. CNMs study an average of 1.5 years beyond nursing school.

Certified registered nurse anesthetist (CRNA)

This type of ADVANCED PRACTICE NURSE specializes in anesthesia. CRNAs practice the oldest of the advanced nursing specialties. An estimated twenty-five thousand CRNAs, who have completed two to three years of advanced training beyond the required four-year bachelor's degree, work in hospitals, dental offices, and outpatient surgery centers and administer nearly two-thirds of all anesthetics given to patients in the United States. They are the sole providers of anesthesia in 85 percent of rural hospitals. In most, though not all, cases, CRNAs work under the direct supervision of a physician-anesthesiologist. Whether CRNAs should be able to work independently has been a source of dissension in the medical community in recent years. Physicians say CRNAs are not well enough trained to deal with emergencies that occur with anesthetized patients; CRNAs respond that physicians are motivated by the potential loss of income.

CHAMPUS

The Civilian Health and Medical Program of the Uniformed Services (CHAMPUS) provides health coverage for military active-duty and retired personnel and their dependents. CHAMPUS is being replaced by a new, MANAGED CARE–based system called TRICARE.

Child Custody Protection Act

First introduced in Congress in 1998, the act (which failed to clear Congress that year) would have made it a crime for a person to accompany a minor across state lines for an ABORTION in contravention of the girl's home state PARENTAL INVOLVEMENT LAWS. Violators could have been subject to fines of up to $100,000 and a year in prison. Critics of the measure pointed out that it even made it illegal for a parent to accompany the girl if the home state law required notification or consent of both parents (which several state laws did).

The measure was inspired by a case in Pennsylvania, where a woman named Rosa Hartford was convicted of violating that state's "Interference with Custody of a Minor Act" by taking her eighteen-year-old son's thirteen-year-old girlfriend across state lines to Binghamton, New York, for an abortion. Pennsylvania law required at least one parent's consent or a judge's permission for a minor to have an abortion; New York had no parental involvement law.

The measure was also intended to be abortion opponents' follow-up to the "Partial Birth Abortion Ban Act," which had over the previous three years successfully shifted the locus of the abortion debate from issues on which the public largely supported abortion rights to those on which sympathies were against the procedure (see PARTIAL-BIRTH ABORTION). Parental involvement in a minor's abortion decision had long been an area of overwhelming public support.

Proponents of the measure insisted that regulating interstate activities was the federal government's natural role and pointed to Yellow Pages ads for clinics proclaiming "no parental consent required" in states without parental involvement laws. Opponents said that the act, however, would endanger, not protect, minors with unintended pregnancies. The bill, opponents complained, would force young women to travel alone to another state or go much farther away from home in their own state—causing unnecessary delays that increased the risks to their health.

Other opponents, including the Clinton administration, pointed out that the law made no exceptions for other adult family members to accompany a girl to have an out-of-state abortion. During debate on the measure in the House and Senate Judiciary Committees, amendments to allow other close relatives to be exempt from the ban were defeated.

In spite of strong opposition, however, the measure did enjoy significant support. Even President Bill Clin-

Although public opinion on abortion is divided, concerned citizens on both sides of the debate agree that parents should be involved in their child's abortion decision. Public support for parental involvement buoyed sponsors of the 1998 Child Custody Protection Act, which, despite significant support, drew fire from the Clinton administration and failed to clear Congress. Source: R. Michael Jenkins

ton said he would sign it if "it is carefully targeted at punishing nonrelatives who transport minors across state lines for the purpose of avoiding parental involvement requirements." It passed the House on July 15, 1998, by a vote of 276–150. But that vote was short of the two-thirds "supermajority" needed to override the veto promised by the president.

President Clinton, however, did not get a chance to veto the measure in 1998. The Senate took up the bill in September, but it got caught up in an unrelated fight over Senate Republicans' blocking from floor consideration legislation to regulate the practices of MANAGED CARE plans (see PATIENTS' BILL OF RIGHTS). When Democrats tried to append their managed care measure to the abortion-travel bill, sponsors of the measure balked. On September 22 a vote to cut off debate on the abortion bill failed by 54–45, six votes short of the total needed for "cloture." With the session approaching its conclusion and most of the appropriations bills still awaiting consideration, Senate majority leader Trent Lott, R-Miss., pulled the bill, killing it for the rest of the year. Backers of the bill came right back in 1999. The

House on June 30 passed the CHILD CUSTODY PROTECTION ACT by a vote of 270–159. The Senate was scheduled to take up the bill later that year.

Children's Health Insurance Program (CHIP)

Passed in 1997 as part of the Balanced Budget Act (PL 105-33), CHIP represented the largest one-time expansion of public health insurance coverage since the inception of MEDICARE and MEDICAID thirty-two years earlier. The program provided $48 billion over ten years to states to help insure an estimated one-half of the eight to ten million children who lacked coverage.

The "kids first" concept of extending health care coverage began in the late summer of 1994 as it became increasingly clear that legislation to guarantee insurance for all Americans was not going to happen. But only as the economy began to improve did the concept take on political and economic feasibility. Indeed, covering children was not even President Bill Clinton's top health

A six-year-old cancer patient at Boston's Dana Farber Cancer Institute receives a teddy bear from a visitor. Bipartisan support for legislation expanding children's health care coverage led to the creation in 1997 of the Children's Health Insurance Program (CHIP). Source: Jim Bourg, Reuters

care priority in 1997—instead, he had been pushing hard for a plan to provide short-term coverage for those temporarily unemployed. But a coalition of mostly senators, including Sen. Jay Rockefeller, D-W.Va., a long-time crusader both for childrens' and health care issues, and Sens. Edward Kennedy, D-Mass., and Orrin Hatch, R-Utah, who earlier had teamed up successfully to push through Congress both child care legislation and a bill to provide treatment funds for AIDS, brought the issue front and center.

It helped that states were already moving to cover children on their own. Pioneering programs in Florida, New York, and Pennsylvania were singled out and "grandfathered" in the legislation, not only to permit them to continue and expand but also to encourage other states to copy them.

In retrospect it should have been obvious to policy makers that children's coverage should be expanded. Not only are children generally healthy and, hence, inexpensive to insure, but they are also politically popular with politicians from both parties. Kennedy and Hatch made their plan more irresistible still by proposing to finance the majority of the increased coverage through a boost in the cigarette tax. That plan would have the doubly beneficial effect, they noted, of not only deterring smoking in general but also deterring it particularly among younger smokers, who are most sensitive to price increases.

But the program still nearly did not come about, as lawmakers sparred over how it should be structured and how much flexibility states should be given in spending the money. Democrats and some moderate Republicans favored funneling much of the money through the existing Medicaid program, since each state already had an administrative mechanism in place and the program guaranteed a comprehensive package of benefits. More conservative Republicans, however, wanted states to be allowed to offer less generous packages in an effort to cover more children. They also noted that many states were not enamored of Medicaid and its myriad rules and regulations.

In the end Congress split the difference, allowing states to choose between expanding Medicaid or creating (or expanding) new, stand-alone programs to cover uninsured children under age nineteen who are not eligible for Medicaid and who live in families with incomes generally under 200 percent of the federal poverty line. States whose Medicaid coverage already extended above 150 percent of the poverty threshold (including Hawaii, Tennessee, and Vermont) would be permitted to extend coverage to those in families with incomes fifty percentage points higher than their existing Medicaid limits.

States choosing to create new programs could offer plans with benefits either identical to those of one of three types of "benchmark" plans (the Blue Cross/Blue Shield plan available to federal employees, any plan broadly available to state employees, or the HEALTH MAINTENANCE ORGANIZATION (HMO) plan offered in the state with the largest commercial enrollment) or "actuarially equivalent" to those of one of those plans. States were also allowed either to provide a plan with the same benefits as those offered in the Florida, New York, or Pennsylvania plans or to devise their own plan and apply to the federal government for approval. Generally, the insurance had to cover inpatient and outpatient hospital care, physician care, laboratory and X-ray services, and well-baby and well-child care, including immunizations. Plans were also required to include at least 75 percent of the actuarial value of four additional benefits—for mental health, vision, hearing, and prescription drug services—but only if the benchmark plan offered any of those benefits.

Although the federal government was providing funds at a more favorable rate under the new program than it did under Medicaid, states were still required to come up with a significant share of the funding for the program. Generally, states were provided funds at rates fifteen percentage points higher than their Medicaid matching rates, up to a ceiling of 85 percent federal funds. For example, if under Medicaid a state had received sixty-five cents from the federal government for every thirty-five cents it spent, under CHIP it generally took in eighty cents from the government for every twenty cents spent. Although the program was optional for the states, the vast majority were quick to jump at it. As of January 1999 the HEALTH CARE FINANCING ADMINISTRATION had approved plans from fifty-two states and territories. Together, the CHIP plans had enrolled 982,000 children, putting the program on target to enroll 2.5 million children by the end of the year 2000. As of the end of 1998, fourteen states were operating separate CHIP plans, twenty-six had expanded Medicaid, and twelve used a combination of the two.

Clinical Laboratory Improvement Act (CLIA)

Congress passed CLIA (PL 100-578) in 1988, largely in response to news reports detailing how substandard laboratory practices had led to deaths and suffering, particularly for women whose Pap smears to detect cervical cancer were misread. A 1987 series in the *Wall Street Journal* documenting testing inaccuracies, lax regulations, and outright fraud won a Pulitzer prize and helped prompt legislative action. The far-reaching law, which took effect in 1992, put under federal purview nearly every clinical laboratory in the United States. (A previous federal law, also called CLIA, was passed in 1967, but it regulated only independent labs involved in interstate commerce.) In 1996 the HEALTH CARE FINANCING ADMINISTRATION (HCFA), which runs the CLIA program, implemented quality assurance standards for more than 150,000 laboratories, 90,000 of them located in physician offices.

CLIA requires federal registration of all laboratories—defined as "any facility which performs laboratory testing on specimens derived from humans for the purpose of providing information for the diagnosis, prevention, treatment of disease, or impairment of, or assessment of health." However, laboratories that perform only the most rudimentary tests are exempt from CLIA's inspection, proficiency testing, and training requirements. Such tests include nonautomated urine dipstick tests, tests to detect blood in the stool, urine pregnancy tests, and certain simple blood tests. Waived laboratories pay a fee of around $100.

Laboratories that perform tests of moderate or high complexity must meet a range of federal standards and undergo periodic inspections every two years, either by HCFA or a private accrediting organization. CLIA is funded by user fees; the average fee for a physician office laboratory is around $1,000, according to the American College of Physicians. Laboratories must meet quality-control and assurance standards and be subject to proficiency testing for every examination or procedure they are certified to perform. The law also sets separate standards for cytology testing (including the evaluation of Pap smears), such as a maximum number of slides an individual may examine in a twenty-four-hour period, a program of rescreening to ensure accuracy, and periodic retesting of personnel.

CLIA has been controversial since its inception—the federal government extended its reach to all laboratories, regardless of whether they participate in federal health programs. Doctors have complained that the rules are so burdensome that many physicians have stopped doing many types of tests, thus inconveniencing patients. A 1995 study commissioned by a coalition of physician groups found that two-thirds of physician office laboratories had dropped some or all of their on-site testing between 1991 and 1995.

But federal officials maintain that the program has worked well, noting that the total number of deficiencies found by inspectors had dropped by some 40 percent between the first round of inspections and the second. Physician groups, though, still say evidence that CLIA has improved the quality and accuracy of tests is lacking, and have urged Congress to repeal CLIA's oversight of in-office laboratories. Despite such powerful legislative champions as House Ways and Means Committee chairman Bill Archer, R-Texas, as of the end of the 105th Congress, CLIA critics had yet to prevail.

Clinical nurse specialist (CNS)

This type of ADVANCED PRACTICE NURSE specializes in a specific area of medicine (such as mental health, gerontology, or cancer care) or in research, education, or administration. The most numerous of advanced practice nurses (the American Nurses Association estimates there are more than fifty-eight thousand CNSs in practice), clinical nurse specialists have master's or doctoral degrees and provide PRIMARY CARE and psychotherapy, as well as perform health assessments, make diagnoses and provide treatment, and develop quality control methods.

Clinical practice guidelines

According to the INSTITUTE OF MEDICINE of the National Academy of Sciences, clinical practice guidelines are "systematically developed statements to assist practitioner and patient decisions about appropriate health care for specific clinical circumstances." Guide-

lines, which recommend specific therapies, often referred to as "algorithms," are intended to literally guide decision-making on the treatment of medical conditions ranging from backaches to ear infections to congestive heart failure. They are a key element of EVIDENCE-BASED MEDICINE, the attempt to make medical care more of a science than an art by employing therapies and techniques scientifically shown to work best and most cost effectively.

Guidelines are developed by a wide variety of entities, ranging from professional medical societies to public or private organizations, to government agencies, to health care organizations or plans. During its early years, development of clinical practice guidelines was a major part of the work of the AGENCY FOR HEALTH CARE POLICY AND RESEARCH. However, its 1994 guideline on treatment of acute back pain, which suggested that surgery was not necessarily the most effective therapy, so outraged spine surgeons that they nearly succeeded in having the agency defunded. In 1996 the agency announced it would cease developing guidelines of its own. However, the agency in 1998 did launch a World Wide Web–based National Guideline Clearinghouse in conjunction with the AMERICAN ASSOCIATION OF HEALTH PLANS and the AMERICAN MEDICAL ASSOCIATION.

Clinton health care plan

See HEALTH SECURITY ACT.

Cloning, human

The 1997 announcement of the "cloning" of Dolly, a sheep, from another adult sheep's cells, raised for the first time the near-term possibility that a human could be created by a method other than by the union of a sperm cell from a man and an egg from a woman. The mere possibility of human cloning touched off a heated debate in Congress about how such ethically far-reaching research should be regulated. Several bills were in-

The 1997 birth of Dolly, the first genetically reproduced sheep, touched off a heated debate in Congress on human cloning research. Scientists at the Roslin Institute in Roslin, Scotland, created Dolly by "fertilizing" her mother's egg cell with a cell from another sheep's mammary gland. Source: Jeff J. Mitchell, Reuters

troduced in 1997 aimed at banning public, and in some cases even private, research on the cloning of humans, and President Bill Clinton on March 4 of that year issued a directive barring any federal agency from supporting, funding, or undertaking any research related to human cloning. The president also urged a private moratorium on such research, so "we can ensure that as we move forward on this issue, we weigh the concerns of faith and family and philosophy and values, not merely of science alone."

But the hand of President Clinton and Congress was forced by the announcement in January 1998 of a Chicago scientist, Richard Seed, that he intended to raise private money to pursue the cloning of human beings. That announcement led Republicans to rush to the Sen-

ate floor with a hastily rewritten version of the 1997 bill introduced by Sen. Christopher Bond, R-Mo. That measure, rewritten with the input of Sen. Bill Frist, R-Tenn., the chamber's lone physician, would have banned the use of "human somatic cell nuclear transfer technology."

But some biotechnology organizations complained that the Republican bill would go further than intended, banning not only human cloning research but also other types of potentially breakthrough research into a wide array of diseases. Instead of the bill, biotechnology groups rallied around a measure offered by Sens. Dianne Feinstein, D-Calif., and Edward Kennedy, D-Mass. That bill would have placed a ten-year moratorium on the implantation of human embryos created using the somatic cell nuclear transfer technique, whereby the nucleus of a female egg cell is removed and replaced with the nucleus of another cell from an adult male or female. The bill would have ordered the National Bioethics Advisory Board to report back to Congress and the president periodically about the scientific, ethical, and social issues surrounding human cloning and to recommend whether the ban should be continued. Antiabortion groups, however, opposed the Feinstein-Kennedy measure because, they said, it would encourage the creation, experimentation, and killing of human embryos.

In the end, however, the politics of research trumped the politics of abortion. After several days of debate the Senate on February 11 failed to break a filibuster on the GOP bill by a vote of 42–54, thus sending the measure back to committee. No further action was taken in the 105th Congress.

COBRA

Short for Consolidated Omnibus Budget Reconciliation Act of 1985, the term for this massive bill now refers, in health policy parlance, to a single—and at the time considered minor—provision regarding health insurance continuation. Despite its name, COBRA didn't become law until 1996 for reasons unrelated to its health provisions. The provision in question, formally known as "COBRA continuation," originally required employers with more than twenty employees to permit workers who would otherwise lose coverage (and/or their spouses and dependents) to continue under the employer's group health insurance plan for up to eighteen months in certain situations if they pay for the coverage themselves. Events that qualify for COBRA continuation include voluntary resignations from a job, dismissal (except for cases of "gross misconduct"), or, in the cases of workers' families, the death of the worker or a divorce or legal separation from that worker. Also eligible for COBRA are spouses of workers who become eligible for MEDICARE and dependent children who "age out," or get too old to qualify under their parents' coverage or cease to be dependents. Congress has since enlarged and otherwise expanded COBRA provisions; in a 1989 budget reconciliation bill, Congress added eleven months to the eligibility period for workers who become disabled, to enable them to keep coverage until Medicare kicks in under SOCIAL SECURITY DISABILITY INSURANCE rules. In 1990 Congress allowed states to use their MEDICAID programs to make COBRA continuation premiums. Congress also revised the penalty for employers who fail to comply—originally those firms faced loss of deductibility of their health insurance costs; in 1988 Congress imposed an excise tax penalty instead.

Under COBRA rules the former workers and their families must pay the entire premium, including the portion, if any, formerly paid by the employer, plus an extra two percent to cover administrative costs. Even so, COBRA is often a good deal because group rates tend to be lower than those for individuals, and plans cannot exclude or charge more for those with PREEXISTING CONDITIONS. Some employers, however, particularly small employers, complain that COBRA participants are "self selecting" to be sicker than average (because those most likely to need coverage are those who purchase it), and can end up raising PREMIUMS for an entire group.

Coinsurance

The portion of a health care fee that must be paid by an insured patient is known as coinsurance. In the few remaining FEE-FOR-SERVICE plans as well as in Part B of MEDICARE, coinsurance is set at 20 percent. Thus, if a bill for a physician visit is $50, the patient would be responsible for $10 of that amount, with insurance making up the rest. In MANAGED CARE plans coinsurance is often called a "copay" and is usually a flat fee rather than a percentage; $10 or $20 is common.

Commissioned Corps of the U.S. Public Health Service

See PUBLIC HEALTH SERVICE, COMMISSIONED CORPS

Community health centers

The nation's six-hundred-plus community health centers (CHCs) are the cornerstone of the federal government's efforts to provide PRIMARY CARE services to the UNINSURED, those with low-incomes, and others with difficulties obtaining health care, whether due to cultural or economic factors or geographic barriers.

Founded in the 1960s as part of the federal government's War on Poverty, in fiscal year 1995 CHCs and other clinics that are part of the federal government's Consolidated Health Centers program (including migrant health centers, sites providing health care for the homeless, and those offering care to residents of public housing) provided services to an estimated 8.1 million Americans at some twenty-two hundred sites, roughly half urban and half rural. CHCs are by definition located in areas characterized by both a lack of health services and a large percentage of the population with low incomes. They also cater to those with nonfinancial barriers to care, providing transportation, translation, case-management, and other services to those who may have the means to pay for care but nonetheless may lack access.

CHCs provide all of the services offered by a typical private clinic—from preventive care to treatment of acute and chronic conditions to laboratory tests, imaging, and pharmacy services. But in recognition of their vulnerable patient base—virtually all patients have incomes under 200 percent of poverty—CHCs also provide a wide array of social services, including health education, nutrition guidance, and counseling.

CHCs receive about two-thirds of their funding from federal grants (32 percent in fiscal year 1995) and MEDICAID payments (31 percent). State, local, and private grants provide another 16 percent, private insurance and MEDICARE about 14 percent, and direct payments from patients the remaining 7 percent. In fiscal year 1999 Congress appropriated $925 million for the health centers program, an increase of more than 12 percent from the previous year's appropriation.

Community rating

The insurance practice of charging the same rate to every member of a specified population (with allowances only for family size, benefits package, or geographic location), community rating tends to produce savings for those who consume more-than-average amounts of health care services, and to cost healthier people more. Where it exists, community rating is often required by law, with proponents arguing that without it, sicker-than-average people would not be able to afford insurance. Opponents of community rating, however, say it boosts premiums for healthy people so high that they do not purchase coverage, leaving the entire insured pool sicker than it would have been and boosting costs for everyone left. This type of ADVERSE SELECTION can result in what insurers refer to as the "death spiral," in which the more healthy people leave, the more rates climb because the insured pool is sicker, with the higher prices continuing to drive out all but the sickest. In order to avoid both extremes some insurers and governments have adopted *modified community rating* schemes, in which rates can vary by factors such as age and gender but only within certain limits.

Confidentiality of medical records

See MEDICAL RECORDS CONFIDENTIALITY.

Congressional Budget Office

Created as part of the 1974 Congressional Budget and Impoundment Control Act, the Congressional Budget Office (CBO) is the official "scorekeeper" for federal legislation. CBO's mission is "to provide the Congress with objective, timely, nonpartisan analyses needed for economic and budget decisions and with the information and estimates required for the Congressional budget process." CBO is best known for "scoring" bills, or estimating if they would cost the federal government more money or reduce spending over the ensuing five years. When CBO and the executive branch budget agency, the Office of Management and Budget, disagree (as they frequently do), it is CBO's estimate that prevails, under budget law. CBO measures its estimates of what a bill would cost against a BASELINE, its projection of federal spending absent legislative changes.

Although it is nonpartisan, CBO is far from nonpolitical. In health policy lawmakers have complained that CBO does not take into account savings from prevention strategies. Thus most estimates of legislation to provide immunizations or other screening tests do not reflect enough in savings from preventing ailments or catching them before they become serious.

In 1994 CBO played a major role in the demise of President Bill Clinton's HEALTH SECURITY ACT. CBO, then under the directorship of a Democrat, Robert Reischauer, said that contrary to the administration's claims, the proposal would not save money but rather would add $74 billion to the federal deficit over the first six years of its existence. CBO analysts also said that the requirement in the bill that employers pay for health insurance for their workers should be treated as a tax for federal budget purposes.

Conscience clause

Generally applying to ABORTION, a conscience clause is any statutory language allowing an individual health care provider to refuse to perform a service he or she finds morally or religiously objectionable. Conscience clauses have also been used to exempt certain health care entities (such as Catholic hospitals) from providing services (such as distributing contraceptives for family planning) that violate their beliefs.

Congress passed its first conscience clause only weeks after the Supreme Court had legalized abortion nationwide with its ROE V. WADE decision. The so-called Church amendment, named for Sen. Frank Church, D-Idaho, gave individuals and medical facilities the right to decline to provide abortion or sterilization services. By the end of 1974, according to the Alan Guttmacher Institute, which studies reproductive health issues, nearly half the states had enacted similar laws, and by 1978 nearly all states had done so.

With the rise of MANAGED CARE and its blurred distinction between payers and providers, some states began taking another look at conscience clauses. In 1997 several states passed laws that in effect allowed entire health plans to opt out of providing certain services. In addition, services subject to conscience clauses were broadened from abortion and sterilization to family planning and other services.

In the 1997 Balanced Budget Act (PL 105-33), Congress included a conscience clause provision allowing MEDICARE and MEDICAID managed care plans to decline to provide any counseling or information on moral or religious grounds, including information about abortion, family planning, sterilization, and AIDS treatment.

Advocates of the language said it was needed to protect religiously based health plans, particularly those owned by the Catholic Church, from having to contract with health care providers that provide services the church does not recognize as acceptable. Opponents of the language, however, argued that a health plan cannot have a "conscience" and that moral or religious objections should be exercised only by those who perform the services, not by those who pay for them.

Congress also added a conscience clause exception to a requirement imposed in 1999 that health plans serving federal employees cover all five of the FDA-approved reversible contraceptive methods. (See following entry.)

Contraceptive coverage

This major initiative for abortion-rights forces in the 105th Congress (1997–1999) had two objectives. First, it was meant to encourage contraception and prevent the need for ABORTION. Second, it was intended to "change the subject," to steer the focus away from efforts to ban a specific abortion procedure in an attempt to win back some of the public support lost in the battle over so-called PARTIAL-BIRTH ABORTIONS.

The centerpiece of the effort was the "Equity in Prescription Insurance and Contraceptive Coverage (EPICC) Act," introduced in the House and Senate by two abortion-rights-supporting Republicans, Sen. Olympia Snowe of Maine and Rep. Jim Greenwood of Pennsylvania. The measure would have required that health insurance plans that offered prescription drug coverage also offer coverage of the five prescription methods of reversible contraception approved by the FDA—birth control pills, Norplant (a time-release device implanted under the skin of a woman's arm), Depo Provera (a long-acting, injectable medication), the diaphragm, and the intrauterine device (IUD).

Although most insurance plans covered prescription drugs in 1998, many did not cover prescription contraceptives or covered only some of them. One survey found that fewer than one in five FEE-FOR-SERVICE and PREFERRED PROVIDER ORGANIZATION (PPO) plans covered all five FDA-approved methods of contraception. For HEALTH MAINTENANCE ORGANIZATIONS (HMOs) the coverage was only slightly better—about 40 percent. And many plans drew a distinction between contraceptives and other prescription drugs or devices. For example, though 97 percent of fee-for-service plans routinely covered prescription drugs, only 33

Sen. Olympia Snowe, R-Maine, sought to encourage contraception by sponsoring the 1997 Equity in Prescription Insurance and Contraceptive Coverage Act. A centerpiece of the 105th Congress's contraceptive coverage initiative, the act would have required that some health insurance plans cover FDA-approved contraception methods. Source: Lisa Berg, Congressional Quarterly

quired partial coverage. Texas, for example, required plans that covered prescription drugs to also cover prescription birth control pills.

Although the EPICC legislation did not get voted on by the House or Senate in 1997 or 1998, in 1998 Congress did take a first step by requiring that plans serving federal workers provide contraceptive coverage. Among the plans serving more than 9 million federal workers and dependents, coverage of contraception was even less generous than it was in the private sector. Only an estimated 19 percent of plans covered all five methods, and 10 percent provided no coverage whatsoever.

The requirement, however, almost did not happen. The House in July approved the mandate as part of the appropriations bill funding the Postal Service, Treasury Department, and other federal agencies—after defeating an amendment by antiabortion lawmakers to exclude from the requirement any contraceptives that also act as "abortifacients," including the IUD and, in some cases, birth control pills. The Senate also approved the coverage in its version of the bill. But the requirement was dropped in conference when abortion foes complained. Backers of the original amendment blocked final approval of the Treasury-Postal appropriations bill in protest, and the measure had to be rolled into a huge year-end omnibus spending bill. At the insistence of the White House, the contraceptive coverage language was restored, along with a CONSCIENCE CLAUSE permitting religious-based health plans, as well as individual practitioners with moral or religious objections to some or all of the methods, to opt out.

percent covered oral contraceptives. Similarly, whereas 83 percent of HMOs covered medical devices in general, only 44 percent covered Norplant. Yet a cost estimate commissioned by the Alan Guttmacher Institute found that requiring full contraceptive coverage would cost employers only an additional $17.12 annually, and workers an additional $4.28 per year.

In 1998 Maryland became the first state to require insurers to cover all five FDA-approved contraceptive measures, and also required that women not have to pay higher cost-sharing fees for contraceptive drugs or devices than for other prescriptions. Seven other states re-

Cost shifting

This term refers to the overcharging by a health care entity of a patient or set of patients to make up for underpayments from other payers. For generations, hospitals underwrote care for the UNINSURED and indigent by padding the bills of those with insurance. Doctors and hospitals often also charged higher rates to private patients to offset relatively low reimbursements provided by government insurance plans. MANAGED CARE companies, however, have largely put an end to cost shifting by demanding lower prices. That, in turn, has threatened the ability of health care providers to care for those who cannot afford to pay.

CPT codes

The acronym stands for Current Procedural Terminology, a system devised by the AMERICAN MEDICAL ASSOCIATION (AMA) in 1966 to code procedures performed in hospitals and physicians' offices for reimbursement purposes and for research, allowing comparisons across various parts of the country. For example, a "brief" office visit would have one code, an "intermediate" visit another, and so forth. CPT codes have in many cases been augmented by ICD-9 CODES, which code actual diagnoses to facilitate research into appropriateness of care. MEDICARE began requiring use of CPT codes in 1983; MEDICAID adopted the standard in 1986. Revisions to CPT (currently in its fourth edition) are made by a panel of sixteen physicians: eleven nominated by the AMA and one each nominated by the BLUE CROSS/BLUE SHIELD ASSOCIATION, the HEALTH INSURANCE ASSOCIATION OF AMERICA, the HEALTH CARE FINANCING ADMINISTRATION (HCFA), the American Hospital Association, and the chairman of the HCFA Common Procedure Coding System.

CRNA

See CERTIFIED REGISTERED NURSE ANESTHETIST.

Crowd out

Also known as "substitution," this term describes the replacement of publicly funded health insurance with private insurance. In designing the CHILDREN'S HEALTH INSURANCE PROGRAM (CHIP), which was part of the 1997 Balanced Budget Act (PL 105-33), for example, Congress was worried that if the federal government began paying for children's coverage, employers would stop offering it, thus transferring a cost previously borne by the private sector to taxpayers. In effect, lawmakers worried that public coverage would "crowd out" private insurance.

D

Deductible

The amount a patient must pay, usually each calendar year, before insurance coverage begins is called the deductible. MEDICARE has two main deductibles. The Part B deductible is $100, so the first $100 of covered costs incurred each year must be paid by the patient. Medicare's hospital deductible in 1999 was $768 per "benefit period," which begins when a patient enters a hospital and ends when the patient has not been in a hospital or skilled nursing facility for sixty days. Thus, if a patient leaves the hospital and needs to be readmitted within sixty days, no new deductible is required.

Defined benefit

The term refers to a benefits scheme (it can also apply to pensions) under which the employer or other grantor of benefits guarantees a certain level of benefits. MEDICARE is a defined benefit program in that the federal government guarantees patients a certain level of services (for instance, the first sixty days of hospital care) regardless of how much it costs. In a defined benefit scheme, the benefits payer is "at risk" for increases in the cost of the benefits.

Defined contribution

In contrast to a DEFINED BENEFIT plan, a defined contribution scheme assigns the risk of inflation to the recipient of the benefits in question. Under a defined contribution plan, the benefit grantor promises to pay only a set amount, or a percentage of an amount, towards a benefit. If inflation deflates the value of the benefit over time, the additional cost is shifted to the recipient. Many employers have moved from defined benefit to defined contribution schemes for pensions, in an effort to hold down future costs. Health insurance may also be provided as a defined contribution to encourage workers to opt for less expensive policies. Employers are using defined contributions increasingly to pay for health benefits for retirees (see RETIREE HEALTH BENEFITS).

Diagnosis-related group (Medicare)

Under Medicare's PROSPECTIVE PAYMENT SYSTEM, a diagnosis-related group (DRG) is any of 496 different categories that help determine hospital payments. Payments are based on each patient's diagnosis and prescribed treatment (such as bypass surgery for coronary artery disease), and what it would cost to care for the average patient with that diagnosis. The idea is to reward efficiency—if the hospital can treat the patient for less than the average for that diagnosis, it can keep the difference. But if the patient costs more than the average, the hospital has to absorb the extra cost. (Actual payments are adjusted for a variety of factors, including labor costs, the type of hospital, and, in some cases, the severity of the patient's illness.) The DRG payment covers only the hospital's own costs; physician care is billed separately under MEDICARE Part B, according to its own fee schedule.

Dietary supplement rules

Congress in 1994, on the last day of the session, passed legislation to limit the federal government's authority to regulate vitamins, minerals, and herbal remedies. The "Dietary Supplement Health and Education Act" (PL 103-417), signed by President Bill Clinton on October 25, was the culmination of more than two years of arguing back and forth between the FOOD AND DRUG ADMINISTRATION (FDA) and makers and users of dietary supplements, who deluged Congress with complaints about the FDA's alleged heavy-handed regulatory attacks on their products. Supplement manufacturers and advocates argued that FDA was trying to cut off access to alternative medical treatments; officials responded that they were merely trying to protect the public from potentially dangerous products that in some cases were being promoted as substitute drugs. Sales of dietary supplements grew throughout the 1990s, reaching nearly $12 billion in 1997.

As signed into law by President Clinton, the legislation allowed manufacturers leeway to explain a product's function on its label, with a disclaimer noting that the product did not promise to cure or treat disease. The bill did permit FDA to halt sales of a supplement if it could be shown that a product caused "a significant or unreasonable risk." (In 1990 the agency ordered the supplement L-Tryptophan pulled from store shelves after contaminated pills caused a rare muscle disorder called Eosinophilia Myalgia Syndrome that sickened at least fifteen hundred people and killed thirty.)

The measure also permitted FDA to enforce existing labeling regulations for four years, during which a seven-member, independent commission would decide what labeling regulations were needed. Manufacturers could sell new supplements without prior FDA approval, but they were required to submit evidence of a product's safety to the FDA seventy-five days before putting it on the market. If the FDA was not satisfied that the information was adequate to ensure that the new product was safe, it could block the marketing. Finally, the measure established an Office of Dietary Supplements within the NATIONAL INSTITUTES OF HEALTH to "promote

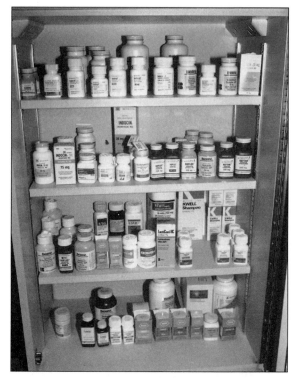

Congress drew fire from supplement manufacturers when it passed 1990 legislation to limit health claims and standardize nutrition labels for food and other products. In 1994, in response to complaints from supplement makers and consumers, Congress passed a separate bill to scale back the government's regulatory authority. Source: R. Michael Jenkins, Congressional Quarterly

scientific study of the benefits of dietary supplements in maintaining health and preventing chronic disease and other health-related conditions." In 1999 the Office of Dietary Supplements unveiled a new database to enable the public to locate "credible, scientific literature on dietary supplements."

But passage of the 1994 bill hardly ended the struggle between the supplement industry and the FDA. In December 1998 the Supreme Court declined to take a case in which supplement makers argued that the FDA's approval requirement for product labels was an unconstitutional violation of their First Amendment rights to free speech. The Court left intact a lower court ruling that found the requirements reasonable to protect the public health.

Direct medical education payments

These payments are made by MEDICARE to teaching hospitals to reimburse them for the direct costs of caring for Medicare patients. Those costs include salaries of residents, teachers, nurses, and allied health professionals in training. Medicare made approximately $2.2 billion in direct medical education payments to teaching hospitals in fiscal year 1997. Medicare also makes additional payments to teaching hospitals for the "indirect costs" of caring for BENEFICIARIES. (See INDIRECT MEDICAL EDUCATION PAYMENT.)

Disproportionate share hospital (DSH) payments (Medicare and Medicaid)

Both MEDICARE and MEDICAID have provisions to make extra payments to hospitals that serve a disproportionate share of low-income or UNINSURED patients, although DSH (pronounced "dish") payments are best known for their role in running up Medicaid spending in the late 1980s and early 1990s.

Medicare's DSH program, begun in 1986, is by far the smaller of the two. It was formally begun in 1986 budget reconciliation legislation (COBRA, PL 99-272), with language requiring additional payments to hospitals that serve a disproportionate share of low-income patients. Payments are generally available to hospitals with more than 15 percent of beds occupied by low-income patients, calculated on the basis of the number of Medicare patients receiving federal SUPPLEMENTAL SECURITY INCOME (SSI) benefits and the number on Medicaid.

But it is the Medicaid DSH program that has engendered the most attention, and most controversy. The program dates back to adoption of the so-called BOREN AMENDMENT in 1980 and 1981 budget reconciliation legislation, which required states to make "reasonable and adequate" payments to Medicaid providers. That legislation required that states "consider special payment needs for hospitals that serve a large portion of Medicaid and uninsured patients." The reasoning was

that hospitals serving large numbers of Medicaid patients lost money because payments were often below costs, and that those serving both Medicaid and uninsured patients had fewer privately insured patients from whom they could "cost shift." (See COST SHIFTING.)

The 1987 budget reconciliation legislation (OBRA 87; PL 100-203) defined DISPROPORTIONATE SHARE HOSPITALS (those with Medicaid inpatient utilization rates one standard deviation above the mean for the state or those with a low-income utilization rate of 25 percent) and required states to submit to the federal government their plans for making the additional payments. But what really set off the DSH explosion was a 1985 rule from the HEALTH CARE FINANCING ADMINISTRATION (HCFA) allowing states to receive "donations" from private health care providers. Using such programs, states could solicit payments from hospitals, collect federal Medicaid matching funds, then return the hospital donation, plus a portion of the federal match, and retain the rest of the matching funds for whatever purpose the state wanted. Similarly, some states imposed "provider taxes" that essentially worked the same way, with the money from providers being returned with "free" federal money. States, in effect, did not have to put up any of their own funds.

In the early 1990s, with a recession going on, states strapped for cash, and Medicaid caseloads rising because of congressional mandates for increased eligibility, Medicaid DSH spending exploded, rising from $1.4 billion in 1990 to $17.5 billion in 1992—accounting in that year for 15 percent of total Medicaid spending. The number of states with provider tax or voluntary donation programs grew from six to thirty-nine during the same two years. Some states found the new funds irresistible—in Louisiana DSH spending accounted for 43 percent of its Medicaid program, and in New Hampshire, 35 percent.

Congress responded with passage of the 1991 Medicaid Voluntary Contribution and Provider-Specific Tax Amendments of 1991. The measure (PL 101-234), negotiated among Congress, the Bush administration, and the National Governors Association, effectively banned provider donation schemes, required provider taxes to be "broad based" (to prevent a few providers from gaming the system), and capped DSH payments at roughly their 1992 levels.

Although the 1991 legislation did start DSH payments on a downward trend, policymakers were still worried that states were abusing the program by providing payments to hospitals that did not truly serve a disproportionate share of Medicaid and uninsured patients. As part of 1993 budget reconciliation legislation (PL 103-66), Congress cracked down again, this time limiting DSH payments to facilities that had 1 percent or more of their caseloads covered by Medicaid, and limiting payments to no more than the amount of the shortfall the hospital incurred from serving Medicaid and uninsured patients.

Congress again addressed the DSH issue in the 1997 Balanced Budget Act (PL 105-33). Still worried that states were using DSH money inappropriately, lawmakers eliminated the formula adopted in the 1991 bill and put a firm cap of 12 percent on state DSH payments. It also limited, to one-third, the percentage of each state's DSH allotment that can go to long-term care facilities for the mentally ill.

Researchers at the Urban Institute calculated that the 1997 changes would lower DSH spending by $5.8 billion between 1998 and 2002, an 11 percent decrease in spending. But by 1996 DSH spending had already dropped precipitously, falling by 19.6 percent from the year before. The reduction helped to keep that year's overall Medicaid spending increase to a historic low of 2.3 percent.

"Do-Not-Resuscitate" orders

Recognized in every state, "Do-Not-Resuscitate" (DNR) orders are legal directives for health care personnel not to perform cardiopulmonary resuscitation (CPR) on certain patients whose hearts stop. DNR orders are generally sought by patients with terminal illnesses for whom CPR is likely to be of limited use or who are in intractable pain. DNR requests can be written into LIVING WILLS or other forms of ADVANCE DI-

RECTIVES detailing a patient's health care desires if he or she becomes unable to communicate.

Drive-through deliveries

This term refers to the practice of sending new mothers and infants home from the hospital only twenty-four hours—and sometimes even sooner—after deliveries. Lawmakers who disapprove of the practice have likened it to the "drive-through" service at a fast food restaurant. (Many lawmakers have mistakenly referred to it as "drive-by" delivery, as in a random shooting.) Barring such practices was the first major legislative response to the growing backlash against MANAGED CARE. In fact, the trend towards shorter hospital stays for new mothers and newborns predated the rise of managed care. But the managed care industry, which made shortening hospital stays one of its preeminent cost-cutting practices, was seen as the primary force behind the trend.

The movement to restrict the practice began in 1994, when the media began carrying "horror stories" about babies who died or were disabled by jaundice or other conditions that didn't show up until more than twenty-four hours after delivery. Then physician groups, led by the American Academy of Pediatrics and the American College of Obstetricians and Gynecologists, weighed in, calling on legislatures to guarantee minimum hospital stays. The legislatures responded. By the end of 1996 thirty states had maternity length-of-stay laws on the books, according to the Medical Group Management Association.

Congress joined the act, too. In 1996, as part of an unrelated spending bill for the Department of Housing and Urban Development and the Department of Veterans Affairs (PL 104-204), Congress required insurers to pay for stays of at least forty-eight hours after a vaginal birth and four days following a cesarean, unless the woman and her doctor agree to a shorter stay. The federal legislation was needed, its backers said, not only to protect citizens of states without their own maternity stay laws but also to reach the companies that "self-insure" by paying for health benefits on their own, rather than purchasing insurance coverage. An estimated 40 percent of workers belong to self-insured plans that are exempt from state insurance laws under the federal EMPLOYEE RETIREMENT INCOME SECURITY ACT, known as ERISA.

Drug Price Competition and Patent Term Restoration Act of 1984

See GENERIC DRUGS.

Dual eligibles

The estimated 10 million Americans simultaneously eligible for both MEDICARE and MEDICAID are known as "dual eligibles." Roughly 6 million elderly and disabled individuals are currently enrolled in both programs; another 3–4 million are eligible, although not enrolled in one or another of the programs. Medicaid coverage can be critical for dual eligibles, who are likely to be sicker and poorer than other Medicare beneficiaries. Medicaid provides not only Medicare's hefty cost-sharing requirements (PREMIUMS, DEDUCTIBLES, and copayments) but also services Medicare does not cover, such as prescription drugs and long-term care. Dual eligibles also consume substantially more health care services than typical beneficiaries of Medicare or Medicaid. In 1995 they constituted about 16 percent of Medicare's caseload but consumed an estimated 30 percent of Medicare spending. Medicaid dual eligibles represent about 17 percent of that program's population but consume 35 percent of program payments.

Some dual eligibles qualify only for limited aid from Medicaid, rather than full program benefits. QUALIFIED MEDICARE BENEFICIARIES (QMBs) are those with incomes below 100 percent of the federal poverty line ($8,240 for an individual and $11,060 for a couple in 1999) and resources (savings and other assets) of less than $4,000 for an individual and $6,000 for a couple, but with still too much income and assets to qualify for full Medicaid benefits. QMBs (pronounced "quimbies") are eligible to have Medicaid pay all their Medicare cost-sharing, including the Part B premium and all required deductibles and copayments (although states may pay providers at Medicaid, rather than the higher Medicare, rates). *Specified low-income Medicare beneficiaries* (SLMBs, pronounced "slimbees"), those with incomes between 100 and 120 percent of poverty, are eligible for Medicaid to pay their Part B premiums but must pay deductibles and other cost-sharing expenses themselves.

The QMB program was created in the 1988 Medicare Catastrophic Coverage Act (PL 100-360), then left intact when the rest of that law was repealed in 1989. SLMBs were added under the 1990 Omnibus Budget Reconciliation Act (PL 101-508). As of 1998 about 4.5 million individuals were enrolled in the QMB program, just over three-quarters of those potentially eligible. But only 270,000 of 1.6 million eligible individuals, about 16 percent of those who could receive aid, had enrolled in the SLMB program.

Although states and the federal government share the costs of the QMB and SLMB programs to the same extent they do in Medicaid in general, the 1997 Balanced Budget Act (PL 105-33) has expanded coverage for low-income Medicare beneficiaries further still with a limited pool of fully federal funds. Those with incomes between 121 and 135 percent of poverty may apply, on a first-come, first-serve basis, to have Medicaid pay their Medicare Part B premium under a program known as "Qualifying Individuals-1," or QI-1. Those with incomes between 136 percent and 175 percent of poverty are eligible, again on a limited basis, to have Medicaid pay a portion of their Medicare premiums as part of the "Qualifying Individuals-2," or QI-2, program. The law made available $250 million for fiscal year 1999, $300 million for fiscal year 2000, $350 million for fiscal year 2001, and $400 million for fiscal year 2002, to be allocated to states based on the number of potentially eligible individuals.

Durable power of attorney for health care

A legal document that invests the power in someone to make medical decisions on another person's behalf, a durable power of attorney is a form of ADVANCE DIRECTIVE for health care. Also known as a health care "proxy," it can take effect whenever the person who has exercised it is incapacitated. It grants the agent the ability to make all medical decisions, including whether to undertake heroic measures to keep the individual alive. Agents named in durable powers of attorney for health care are generally family members or trusted friends, but legally can be anyone except a health care professional who has a financial interest in providing health care services to the patient. (See LIVING WILLS.)

E

Early and Periodic Screening, Diagnostic, and Treatment (Medicaid)

States must offer this required benefit to all MEDI-CAID beneficiaries under age twenty-one. Under EPSDT states must provide screening, vision, hearing, and dental services "at intervals which meet recognized standards of medical and dental practice." Screening services must include at least a comprehensive health and developmental history (including physical and mental conditions), a comprehensive physical exam, appropriate immunizations and laboratory tests, and health education. The most controversial aspect of the EPSDT program requires states to treat any conditions discovered through the required screening examinations, even if the treatment or condition is not otherwise a covered service under the state's Medicaid program. In practice, however, EPSDT screening rates have been low, and providers have considerable discretion to determine how the program is implemented.

Embryo research

This research has been explicitly banned by Congress since 1995, when antiabortion legislators appended to the LABOR–HEALTH AND HUMAN SERVICES APPROPRIATION bill language barring funding for "the creation of a human embryo or embryos for research purposes; or research in which a human embryo or embryos are destroyed, discarded, or knowingly subjected to risk of injury or death greater than that allowed for research on fetuses in utero." Prior to that, embryo research was largely banned by default, as part of a broader ban on research using human fetuses. (See FETAL TISSUE RESEARCH.) Regulations promulgated in 1975 theoretically allowed such research if approved by an ethics advisory board, but no board was ever able to convene, largely because of abortion-related controversies.

By 1998 scientists were reporting potential breakthroughs using stem cells from embryos (research performed using private funds). Stem cells have an unlimited capacity to divide and are capable of turning into almost any cell or tissue in the human body. One scientist told a Senate hearing that because stem cells are so malleable, they could potentially be used to grow new heart muscle for those with heart failure, insulin for those with diabetes, and nerve and brain cells to treat those with Parkinson's or Alzheimer's disease. Among those urging Congress to lift the research funding ban was Harold Varmus, director of the NATIONAL INSTITUTES OF HEALTH (NIH). Those who argued that the ban should be lifted expressed concerns that if all the research is done with private funds, patents and licenses could hinder the dissemination of potentially critical therapies for previously untreatable ailments.

But abortion opponents argued that research on embryos should not be allowed, except on those that are the products of spontaneous abortion (miscarriage). "Existing law explicitly applies to human embryos, and destroying or discarding an embryo in the laboratory is the moral equivalent of abortion," testified Richard Doerflinger of the National Conference of Catholic Bishops before the Senate Appropriations Labor-HHS subcommittee. "Members of the human species who cannot give informed consent for research should not be the subjects of an experiment unless they personally may benefit from it, or the experiment carries no significant risk of harming them," he told the subcommittee.

Among the supporters of embryo research was Harold Varmus (left), director of the National Institutes of Health (NIH), who advocated research using embryo cells to treat heart failure, diabetes, and Alzheimer's disease.
Source: Scott J. Ferrell, Congressional Quarterly

In January 1999 Varmus announced that NIH had decided to fund embryonic stem cell research after receiving a legal opinion that such activities did not violate the ban on embryo research. Both opponents and proponents of stem cell research in Congress vowed to take any action needed to disallow or allow the research.

Emergency contraception

Also known as the "morning after" pill, emergency contraception is the use of high doses of standard birth control pills that can prevent pregnancy in most cases if taken within seventy-two hours after unprotected sex. Long used by rape crisis centers and university health services, many advocates called it "the best-kept secret in America." A survey by the Kaiser Family Foundation found that a third of women between ages eighteen and forty-four had never heard of the practice. It is estimated that only 1 percent of women have used the procedure, which involves taking one dose within seventy-two hours after unprotected sex and another dose

twelve hours later. Yet emergency contraception using birth control pills can reduce the likelihood of pregnancy after unprotected sex by 75 percent.

Insertion of a copper intrauterine device within five days after unprotected sex (a less-used form of emergency contraception) is 99 percent effective in preventing pregnancy. As many as 1.7 million of the more than 3 million unintended pregnancies in the United States could be prevented by emergency contraception, experts estimate, including some 800,000 unintended pregnancies that currently result in ABORTION.

To encourage its use the Food and Drug Administration, in a relatively unprecedented move, in 1997 declared the use of birth control pills to prevent pregnancy after unprotected sex "safe and effective," and published guidelines for the use of ten separate brands of pills for emergency contraceptive purposes. The agency also invited manufacturers to package their products in a more user-friendly way. Until the approval of the first emergency contraceptive kit in September 1998, a physician had to prescribe a full month's supply of pills, then explain to women which pills to take.

The Food and Drug Administration in 1997 issued a statement supporting emergency contraception, the use of birth control pills after unprotected sex to prevent pregnancy. Emergency contraception has long been recommended by counselors at rape crisis centers and university health services. Source: R. Michael Jenkins, Congressional Quarterly

Antiabortion groups have been cautious about emergency contraception, which is different from RU486 or other drugs that cause abortions early in pregnancy. Emergency contraception does not work in women with already established pregnancies. The high-dose birth control pills can work either by preventing ovulation or by preventing implantation of an already fertilized egg. Because some consider the latter method tantamount to abortion, the NATIONAL RIGHT TO LIFE COMMITTEE "advises women faced with these situations to consult one or more physicians. If, in the best medical judgment of the physicians, the drug or drugs will cause an abortion, NRLC strongly opposes the taking of the drug. If the drug(s) will prevent fertilization, the National Right to Life Committee takes no position."

In 1998 South Dakota passed a law allowing pharmacists to opt out of dispensing medication if they have reason to believe it would be used to cause an abortion or "destroy an unborn child." The law was triggered by the case of a pharmacist who objected to dispensing birth control pills for emergency contraception.

Emergency Medical Treatment and Active Labor Act (EMTALA)

See PATIENT "DUMPING."

Employee Retirement Income Security Act (ERISA)

This 1974 law (PL 93-406) is one of the most complicated statutes governing health policy—and one of the most pivotal. After some highly publicized failures of pension plans, ERISA was originally passed to protect the pensions of workers (by imposing financial and fiduciary standards) and to make it easier for employers with workers in multiple states to offer a single retirement plan without having to meet fifty different state standards. But late in the process (legend defines late as "in the middle of the last night of the conference on the measure," although that timeframe is disputed by those who were in the room), health benefits were added to its purview. To this day, experts and courts still argue about the impact of ERISA on health insurance coverage, and its reach has blocked several states from imposing far-reaching health reforms for state residents. As of 1997 the Supreme Court had rendered sixteen different decisions on the relationship between ERISA and state laws regarding health benefits.

ERISA regulates different health plans in different ways. The ERISA "universe" consists of more than 2.5 million private sector, employer-sponsored health plans that cover some 125 million workers and their dependents, according to the U.S. Department of Labor. The only health plans not covered to some extent by ERISA are MEDICARE, MEDICAID, CHAMPUS, plans covering state and local employees, those sponsored by churches or fraternal organizations, individually-purchased plans, and those purchased by groups outside of an employer-employee relationship.

ERISA prescribes a list of "remedies" for plans that fail to meet its requirements, and states are generally "preempted" from imposing laws regarding remedies (this is why ERISA blocks most people in employer-sponsored plans from suing for damages for benefit denials). Generally ERISA remedies for benefit denials consist of the cost of the denied benefit and, in some cases, attorney fees. Thus, if an ERISA plan denies a laboratory test, with the result that an undetected cancer becomes incurable, only the cost of the test can be recovered.

ERISA does *not,* however, block individuals in ERISA plans from filing medical malpractice suits, or from collecting damages, due to actions taken by health care professionals. Nevertheless, in most cases MANAGED CARE plans and UTILIZATION REVIEW firms can avoid malpractice liability under ERISA. Legislative proposals, such as the PATIENTS' BILL OF RIGHTS pushed by congressional Democrats in the 105th Congress, would permit lawsuits for damages arising from benefit denials and their consequences.

In what is known as ERISA's *savings clause,* the law permits states to regulate the "business of insurance," as ordered under the 1945 McCarran-Ferguson Act. But ERISA also includes what is commonly called the *deemer clause,* which prevents states from deeming employee welfare plans (plans that offer benefits other than pensions) to be in the business of insurance and therefore subject to state regulation. The deemer clause puts employer plans that are "self-funded" (meaning the company pays for the benefits, rather than taking out insurance) under the exclusive reach of ERISA and out of reach of state regulation. As a result, states cannot impose premium taxes or mandated benefits on self-insured plans. An estimated 40 percent of workers; some 48 million people, are in ERISA self-insured plans. Alternatively, if an ERISA plan buys an insurance product making the insurer "at risk" for the cost of the care, the state can regulate that insurance.

End-stage renal disease (Medicare)

Some 234,000 Americans suffering from kidney failure are enrolled in MEDICARE. Eligibility for those suffering from end-stage renal disease (also known as ESRD) was included in the 1972 Social Security amendments with little debate. It was added to the bill (which also made eligible for Medicare those who qualified for SOCIAL SECURITY DISABILITY INSURANCE) as a floor amendment in the Senate and included in the final bill with less than ten minutes' discussion. ESRD patients are eligible for Medicare if they are fully insured for Social Security Old Age and Survivor Insurance Benefits (meaning they have worked forty quarters at a qualifying job), if they are entitled to monthly Social Security benefits, or if they are spouses or dependents of individuals who meet the above requirements. The requirements make eligible more than 90 percent of the population suffering from kidney failure so severe as to require kidney dialysis or a kidney transplant—in 1994 only 7.7 percent of dialysis patients, and 9.3 percent of those requiring transplants, did not qualify.

Like Medicare in general, the ESRD program has been substantially more expensive than was projected when it was passed. At the time it was estimated that by 1995 enrollment would level out at about 90,000 individuals—a threshold passed in 1985. Between 1998 and 1993, enrollment in the program grew an average of 8.6 percent annually. In fiscal year 1996 the cost per ESRD enrollee averaged $32,998, compared with $5,000 for the average Medicare beneficiary. The most significant trend in the program has been an increase in the number of older patients (the fastest growth has been among people over age seventy-five, followed by those aged sixty-five to seventy-four) and in the number of patients whose kidney failure is the result of diabetes, which makes it more difficult to treat. Medicare's ESRD program pays both for dialysis (which remains the predominant treatment) and for kidney transplant surgery. In 1994 Medicare paid for 11,312 kidney transplants.

Entitlement

A benefit for which eligibility is automatic if a person meets specific requirements—and which the government has a legal obligation to provide is called an entitlement. MEDICARE and MEDICAID are the major health care entitlement programs. Entitlements are also referred to as *mandatory spending programs* (as opposed to discretionary), in that Congress must provide funding for them, and their spending levels can only be changed by altering eligibility requirements or benefits.

EPSDT

See EARLY AND PERIODIC SCREENING, DIAGNOSTIC, AND TREATMENT (MEDICAID).

ERISA

See EMPLOYEE RETIREMENT INCOME SECURITY ACT (ERISA).

Evidence-based medicine

This term encompasses therapies or treatments whose effectiveness has been demonstrated scientifically. Among the most highly respected are so-called double-blind studies in which one group of patients, called the "control" group, is given a "placebo," or inactive drug, or else treated with a known therapy, while the other group is provided the treatment being studied. Neither the patients nor the treating health professionals know which patients are in which groups—thus the term "double-blind."

Experience rating

The insurance practice of setting premiums according to the health status of a group—that is, according to the insurer's "experience"—is called experience rating. Thus a group whose members have incurred significant medical bills in the past will pay more in the future.

External review

The process by which health care disputes are mediated by outside entities independent from the parties that disagree is known as external review. External review is used to resolve disagreements—often regarding payment or clinical issues—between patients and health care organizations.

MEDICARE has had an external review process since 1989, operated by the Center for Health Dispute Resolution (CHDR, pronounced "cheddar"). Medicare's program, which automatically forwards to CHDR cases denied by "internal" review mechanisms, is rarely used; for every one thousand Medicare beneficiaries in MANAGED CARE plans, about two cases go to Medicare's external review mechanism each year.

State laws mandating that managed care plans establish external review processes are also gaining in popularity. In 1998 eighteen states had such laws; five of them passed in the first six months of the year. The laws vary widely, however. Some simply specify the existence of an outside review entity, while others prescribe more specifically how that outside review should occur, how quickly, how much expertise outside reviewers should have, and who should pay the costs.

A 1998 study by the Georgetown University Institute for Health Care Research and Policy found that external reviews uphold coverage or medical decisions made by health plans nearly as often as they overturn them, siding with the patient between 32 and 68 percent of the time. The study also found the state external review mechanisms were used even more rarely than Medicare's. Health plan officials say the low usage rate reflects the high quality of care provided and the efficiency of internal appeals mechanisms. But state regulators worried that many people denied care do not use external reviews because they don't know of their availability, or because they are too sick or die before they can appeal.

F

False Claims Act

The False Claims Act is a Civil War era statute (it was signed by President Abraham Lincoln in 1863) that has been used frequently in the 1980s and 1990s in the effort to fight health care fraud. The original law was used to prosecute defense contractors who failed to supply the Union Army with promised goods or who delivered goods that were shoddy. A key element of the law was the ability of individual citizens to bring "whistleblower" lawsuits against those who had defrauded the government. These lawsuits are referred to as *qui tam* actions, Latin for "one who sues on behalf of the king as well as for himself." If successful, the whistleblowers could collect up to 50 percent of any recoveries. Congress updated the law in 1986, again in an effort to fight fraud by defense contractors. The new version (PL 99-562) increased penalties against those who defrauded the government, clarified the standards and procedures for bringing fraud suits, provided new incentives for private citizens to report suspected fraud, and protected whistleblowers who reported fraud cases. It also raised the percentage of recovery for individuals who brought *qui tam* suits against fraud perpetrators. In 1943 Congress had lowered the percentage to 10 percent; the 1986 law raised it to a potential 30 percent.

In the late 1990s, the federal government began using the False Claims Act to fight Medicare fraud. The much publicized investigation against the giant hospital firm Columbia/HCA was initiated by a False Claims Act whistleblower suit filed by a hospital accountant from Montana.

FDA

See FOOD AND DRUG ADMINISTRATION.

Federal Employee Health Benefits Plan

The Federal Employee Health Benefits Plan (FEHBP) is the nation's largest employer-sponsored health benefits program, serving more than 9 million federal workers, retirees, and dependents. Established by Congress in 1959, the FEHBP began covering enrollees in 1960. In 1998 federal workers could chose from some 300 different plans. The federal government paid 72 percent of the weighted average cost of all plans in the program, up to a cap of 75 percent. The enrollee paid the remainder of the premium. (The formula is a new one for 1999; it replaced a formula under which the government premium was determined by the cost of the six most popular plans.) Although the FEHBP has had its own problems with ADVERSE SELECTION, when in the late 1980s one of its most popular plans dropped out after it got too many sick enrollees, and with premiums that have fluctuated, sometimes considerably, the program has worked well overall. Many see it as a model program that provides a broad choice of plans at affordable premiums with excellent comparative information to help enrollees choose among the plans. Participants in FEHBP can change plans once a year during a month-long "open season."

Federal Food, Drug and Cosmetic Act

Originally passed in 1906 as the Pure Food and Drug Act, the 1938 Federal Food, Drug and Cosmetic Act (FFDCA) is the governing statute of the FOOD AND DRUG ADMINISTRATION. It includes statutory language relating to human and animal drugs and biologic products, food, cosmetics, and medical devices. According to the House Commerce Committee, which oversees the FFDCA, the act "is intended to assure the consumer that foods are pure and wholesome, safe to eat, and produced under sanitary conditions; that drugs and devices are safe and effective for their intended uses; that cosmetics are safe and made from appropriate ingredients; and that all labeling and packaging is truthful, informative, and not deceptive." The most recent overhaul of the statute was the 1997 FDA Modernization Act (PL 105-115).

Federal Medical Assistance Percentages

Federal Medical Assistance Percentages, known as FMAPs, are the rates at which the federal government reimburses states for spending on MEDICAID, the joint federal-state health program for the poor. FMAPs are determined annually using a formula that compares each state's per capita income with the United States as a whole. Wealthier states are matched at a rate of 50 percent, whereas states with lower per capita incomes get a larger share from the federal government, up to 83 percent. Overall, the federal government paid about 57 percent of Medicaid costs in 1997. In 1999 ten states (Colorado, Connecticut, Delaware, Illinois, Maryland, Massachusetts, Nevada, New Hampshire, New Jersey, and New York) had FMAPs of 50 percent. Mississippi had the highest FMAP at 76.8 percent, meaning that for every dollar the state spent on Medicaid, it contributed only 13 cents. Other states with FMAPs higher than 70 percent in 1998 were Arkansas (72.85), Idaho (70.15), Kentucky (70.55), Louisiana (70.32), Montana (72.3), New Mexico (72.32), North Dakota (70.42), Oklahoma (71.09), Utah (71.55), and West Virginia (74.78). *(For a complete list of FMAPs, see table on p. 112.)*

Federally qualified health centers

Federally qualified health centers (FQHCs) include federally funded COMMUNITY HEALTH CENTERS, MIGRANT HEALTH CENTERS, health clinics run by Indian tribes, tribal organizations, or urban Indian organizations, as well as certain primary care clinics that meet the requirements for community health centers but do not receive federal funding. To meet those requirements such clinics must provide PRIMARY CARE services to people living in the clinic's service area, regardless of their insurance status or ability to pay, or be clinics recognized by the HEALTH RESOURCES AND SERVICES ADMINISTRATION (HRSA) as an FQHC as of January 1, 1990. Until passage of the 1997 Balanced Budget Act (PL 105-33), Medicaid was required to reimburse FQHCs for care provided to Medicaid patients, and to pay them 100 percent of the facility's reasonable costs for providing the services. Under the 1997 law, however, that payment requirement will be phased down, beginning in the year 2000, to a 95 percent reimbursement of the FQHC's costs, declining to 70 percent in 2003, and removing any minimum payment requirements after that.

Fee-for-service

Fee-for-service is a system under which physicians or other health care providers bill for each service individually as it is provided to a patient. Critics of fee-for-service systems note that they are inherently inflationary, giving providers an incentive to provide more services, since the more services given, the more money the provider can make. Insurance plans that cover fee-for-service care are known as *indemnity plans,* because the insurer "indemnifies" the patient from most of the cost of care. Generally, although not all the time, fee-for-service insurance plans permit patients to seek care from any licensed health care professional and cover a set portion of the costs after the patient has met an annual DEDUCTIBLE.

Fetal tissue research

Fetal tissue research is an abortion-related science controversy that has continued for more than two decades. The first foray came in 1974, when, as part of a reauthorization of NATIONAL INSTITUTES OF HEALTH (NIH) training programs (PL 93-348), Congress placed a moratorium on federally funded research on "the living human fetus, before or after abortion," unless the purpose was to assure the fetus's survival. The 1974 action came in response to horror stories about unregulated and ethically questionable research on fetuses dead and alive and on other living human subjects. The law also created a two-year National Commission on the Protection of Human Subjects of Biomedical and Behavioral Research, which was to recommend whether or how such research was to proceed.

That commission concluded that such research could be ethically acceptable if certain safeguards were imposed. Regulations of 1975 stipulated that research on live fetuses that would pose more than a "minimal risk" to the woman or fetus would be permissible only if performed to meet the health needs of that specific fetus or pregnant woman. Research on aborted fetuses was also acceptable, but only if it did not alter the timing or method of the planned abortion.

For much of the 1980s, however, virtually all fetal research was banned by default, because the Ethics Advisory Board, which was to consider and approve individual projects on in vitro research or research that would impose more than a "minimal risk" but not benefit the specific woman or fetus, was disbanded in 1980 (in favor of a separate President's Commission for the Study of Ethical Problems in Medicine and Biomedical and Behavioral Research). The controversy continued throughout the 1980s, with various commissions unable to reach consensus, or even to establish themselves, due to continuing dissent over abortion-related issues. In 1985 and 1988 legislation, Congress blocked the agency's ability to waive the "minimal risk" standard for fetal research.

In 1988, a group of researchers applied to use federal funds to transplant fetal tissue in an attempt to treat Parkinson's disease. Fetal tissue, the scientists said, grows faster, is more adaptable, and is less likely to be rejected by a transplant recipient's immune system than other forms of tissue. Such use of fetal tissue, they argued, could help produce breakthrough treatments or even cures for such intractable ailments as Parkinson's disease, juvenile diabetes, epilepsy, and Alzheimer's disease. ABORTION opponents, however, argued that such treatments, if proven successful, could encourage more abortions.

Rather than approving the project, Assistant Secretary for Health Robert Windom of the HEALTH AND HUMAN SERVICES DEPARTMENT (HHS) ordered a review of the ethical, legal, and scientific questions it posed. Two subsequent advisory panels found such research "acceptable public policy" as long as safeguards were adopted to protect against commercialization or inappropriate encouragement of women to have abortions in order to provide the tissue. But the Bush administration decided to reject the recommendations of the commissions and to keep Windom's moratorium in place. Windom's successor, James O. Mason, told a House subcommittee that such research objectives "conflict with administration policy that seeks to ensure the protection of all human life." Even the NIH director, Bernadine Healy, who sat on both of the advisory panels that recommended letting the research go forward and who supported that view, agreed that the ban should remain when she assumed the NIH helm in 1991, presumably a condition for being given the job.

The moratorium was a narrow one—it affected only fetal tissue transplants, and only tissue from "elective" abortions, not from ectopic pregnancies (in which the fetus grows outside the uterus, requiring termination in order to save the woman's life) or spontaneous abortions (miscarriages). But researchers insisted that the moratorium nevertheless blocked all their efforts, since tissue from miscarriages or other naturally occurring processes tended to be diseased or otherwise unusable, as well as being available only randomly. And although the moratorium did not block privately funded research, scientists argued that federal rules were needed to ensure that tissue was not inappropriately induced from women or bought and sold.

Congressional efforts to overturn the moratorium began in 1990, when the House Commerce Committee approved a reauthorization bill for the NIH that included language eliminating the ban. But that measure never got to the House floor for a vote. In 1991 the House did pass an NIH bill overturning the ban—over a veto threat from President George Bush. But the margin, although strong (272–144), was nevertheless short of the needed two-thirds to override the promised veto. The Senate did not act until 1992, but when it did, it acted more definitively, approving the measure by a veto-proof 85–12. Among the senators speaking in favor of lifting the fetal research ban were such antiabortion stalwarts as Strom Thurmond, R-S.C. (who spoke of the potential for the research to benefit his daughter, Julie, who had diabetes), and Mark Hatfield, R-Ore., a long-time backer of biomedical research efforts.

As promised, Bush vetoed the NIH bill in June 1992 over the fetal tissue issue as well as other matters. The bill, he said in his veto message, "is unacceptable to me on almost every ground; ethical, fiscal, administrative, philosophical and legal." On the matter of fetal research, Bush said, "I believe this moratorium is important in order to prevent taxpayer funds from being used for research that many Americans find morally repugnant, and because of its potential for promoting and legitimizing abortion." In an effort to head off a veto override, Bush ordered the establishment of a "tissue bank" to collect tissue from ectopic pregnancies and miscarriages. "This approach truly represents the pro-research and ethical alternatives that will allow this research to go forward without relying on a source of tissue that many find to be morally objectionable," the president said.

Many scientists insisted that the tissue bank was unworkable, but it apparently scored politically. Although the Senate voted to override by a vote of 73–26 on October 1, the House failed to override it by 10 votes on October 2, 266–148.

Just three months later, President Bill Clinton ended the five-year saga abruptly on January 22, 1993. On his second full day in office, Clinton signed a series of executive orders repealing a number of abortion restrictions

Bringing to a close five years of contentious debate on the merits and dangers of fetal tissue research, President Bill Clinton in 1993 signed an executive order lifting the research moratorium.
Source: Win McNamee, Reuters

left over from the Reagan-Bush era, including the fetal tissue research moratorium.

Congress ratified Clinton's decision with passage in May of the oft-delayed NIH reauthorization bill (PL 103-43). That bill specifically authorized funding for "the transplantation of fetal tissue for therapeutic purposes" and instituted a series of safeguards. It required a woman providing tissue to sign a statement declaring that she was donating fetal tissue for research, that she understood she could not designate the recipient of the tissue, and that she was not aware of the recipient's identity. The physician performing the abortion was to certify that the woman gave her consent to have an abortion before she was asked about fetal tissue donation. The physician also had to disclose any financial or other interest in the subsequent research as well as any known medical risks. The measure barred the sale or purchase of human fetal tissue from induced abortions and any donation intended for a specific person, including a relative of the donor. This was intended to prohibit a woman from getting pregnant in order to have an abortion to donate the tissue to a family member. Violators could face up to ten years in prison.

Despite the antiabortion shift in Congress following the Republican takeover in 1994, the fetal-tissue controversy seemed settled by the late 1990s. In 1997, during Senate consideration of the fiscal 1998 LABOR-HHS APPROPRIATION bill, Sen. Daniel Coats, R-Ind., a leading antiabortion opponent, offered an amendment to reinstate the fetal tissue transplant research funding ban. Coats's amendment was defeated, 30–60. Instead, antiabortion forces turned most of their research efforts toward the human cloning issue (see CLONING, HUMAN).

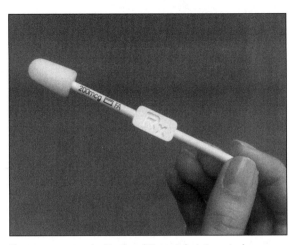

Foremost among the Food and Drug Administration's responsibilities is certifying that drugs have been proven safe and effective before they are marketed. Before approving Actiq, a drug in lollipop form that alleviates cancer pain, the agency took steps to ensure that the drug would not accidentally fall into the hands of children. Source: Anesta Corporation, Reuters

First dollar coverage

Those with true "first dollar coverage," the most generous form of health insurance, pay no DEDUCTIBLES or copayments for their health care. Economists argue that first dollar coverage is inherently inflationary, because individuals, with none of their own money at risk, have no financial incentive to limit their consumption of health care services. If individuals pay all or a portion of the premiums, the coverage is more inflationary still, because they may feel they are wasting their money if they don't consume health care. First dollar coverage, however, is increasingly rare, as more and more employers have either moved workers to managed care plans (which have other ways to limit spending) or else instituted higher cost-sharing for employees.

FMAP

See FEDERAL MEDICAL ASSISTANCE PERCENTAGES.

Food and Drug Administration

Born in the early 1900s at least partly in response to public outrage at the meatpacking methods detailed in muckraker Upton Sinclair's *The Jungle,* in 1999 the Food and Drug Administration (FDA) regulated products accounting for one of every four dollars spent in the United States. The FDA is charged with ensuring that the food Americans eat is prepared and packaged in a safe and sanitary manner, and that packaged food displays truthful and informative labels; that prescription and over-the-counter drugs and medical devices are safe and effective for their intended uses; and that cosmetics are safe and unadulterated. In 1998, the FDA's nearly 9,000 employees (including some 1,100 inspectors and 2,100 scientists) monitored the manufacture, import, transport, storage, and sale of $1 trillion worth of products.

The FDA is probably best known for its role in the drug approval process. The original 1906 Pure Food and Drug Act made it illegal to market misbranded or adulterated drugs, but it gave the federal government no authority to approve drugs prior to their introduction. Passage of the 1938 FEDERAL FOOD, DRUG AND COSMETIC ACT for the first time required that drugs be proven safe before they could be marketed. In 1962, the Kefauver-Harris amendments added the requirement that drugs be proven not only safe but also effective in meeting their intended purposes.

By the 1980s, though, manufacturers were turning out new drugs faster than the FDA could review them. In 1992, in response to complaints from drugmakers that the agency was taking too long to approve applications for new drugs, Congress passed the PRESCRIPTION DRUG USER FEE ACT (PDUFA, PL 102-571, pronounced "padoofa"). The law, which required drug companies to pay extra to have the FDA review their drug applications (the FDA does not actually test drugs but only renders judgment on research conducted or commissioned by the companies themselves), cut drug approval times in half. In 1997, Congress renewed PDUFA as part of a broader FDA Modernization Act (PL 105-115). That measure codified many actions the agency had previously taken to speed drugs for life-threatening diseases to market and to make experimental drugs more available to patients with few or no other treatment options. In an effort to shorten the timeframe for review of those applications, the measure also expanded a program to test whether outside "third parties" could safely review applications for certain new medical devices.

In 1996, the FDA asserted authority to regulate a previously unregulated area of U.S. commerce—the sale of tobacco products. Regulations issued on August 28, intended to deter smoking by children and teenagers, claimed that the FDA had authority over cigarettes and smokeless tobacco because they fall under the Federal Food, Drug and Cosmetic Act's definition of "drugs" and "devices." In 1998, however, a three-judge federal appeals court panel ruled that the agency had overstepped its authority, although in 1999 the Supreme Court agreed to consider the case. Congress in 1998 failed to pass legislation to implement the GLOBAL TOBACCO SETTLEMENT reached between tobacco companies and state attorneys general that would have given the FDA explicit authority to regulate tobacco products.

Formulary

A formulary is a list of prescription drugs and their appropriate dosages covered by a particular insurance plan. Hospitals, government agencies (including the Veterans Administration), and individual insurers develop their own formularies, generally by appointing a group consisting of physicians and pharmacy experts. Their task is to select the drugs considered to be most effective and cost-effective. According to the Academy of Managed Care Pharmacy, "a well-developed and managed formulary improves quality of care by assuring that only those drugs determined by clinical experts to be the most safe and effective for patients with certain medical conditions are dispensed on a regular basis." Some plans will not pay for drugs not on the formulary; others charge extra for nonformulary prescriptions. Consumer advocates and even some doctors have charged that some insurers limit their formularies to only the least expensive drugs, or to one or two drugs to treat conditions for which patients' needs differ. Their arguments were buttressed by a controversial 1996 study by researchers from the University of Utah medical school who found that tightly controlled formularies actually raised overall medical costs, in some cases twice as high as plans without formularies. The researchers, whose study was published in the *American Journal of Managed Care,* theorized that by using the lowest cost drugs, patients got sicker, saw the doctor more, were hospitalized more often, and ended up using more medications to cure their ailments.

Freedom of Access to Clinic Entrances Act (FACE)

The Freedom of Access to Clinic Entrances Act (PL 103-259) was the principal piece of abortion-rights legislation enacted by the 103rd Congress. It was prompted by a 1993 Supreme Court decision, *Bray v. Alexandria Women's Health Clinic,* which invalidated the use of a reconstruction-era civil rights law to stop antiabortion protesters from harassing women seeking to enter abortion clinics. It also came in response to escalating violence among antiabortion extremists, including the shootings in 1993 of two physicians who performed the procedure. Supporters of the measure argued that local laws were inadequate to address the problem and successfully framed the issue as one of law enforcement rather than one of abortion. That helped win the support of even some strong abortion opponents, despite complaints from antiabortion groups that the law would impinge on the free speech rights of abortion foes.

The Supreme Court, however, in 1994 upheld the law, and the right in general of governments to restrict protesters in order to ensure access to abortion clinics, in *Madsen v. Women's Health Center, Inc.*

As cleared by Congress on May 12, 1994, the measure made it a federal crime to use force, or the threat of force, to intimidate abortion clinic workers or women seeking abortions. Violators faced criminal penalties of jail time and fines. The bill also allowed affected individuals to sue for compensatory damages or court injunctions to restrain blockaders.

Both the House and Senate originally passed the bills in 1993, but the Senate had made changes to its version during floor debate in November that prevented a final measure from clearing before the end of the year. One key amendment, offered by Sen. Orrin Hatch, R-Utah, extended the bill's reach to protect not just those seeking abortions, but "any person lawfully exercising or seeking to exercise the First Amendment right of religious freedom at a place of worship." During conference with the House, Hatch cited several instances in which churchgoers had been harassed by protesters for various causes. House conferees agreed to the provision after clarifying that it would not create a new legal recourse for those praying while simultaneously demonstrating outside an abortion clinic. House negotiators also accepted an amendment added to the Senate bill by Edward Kennedy, D-Mass., to impose lower maximum criminal penalties for nonviolent obstruction, such as lying down in front of a clinic door. Whereas those found guilty of violent offenses could be subject to fines of up to $100,000 and a year in prison for a first offense, and up to $250,000 and three years in prison for a second offense, nonviolent offenders could be fined only up to $10,000 and imprisoned for six months for a first offense, and up to eighteen months and $25,000 for a second offense.

Freedom of Choice Act

The Freedom of Choice Act, also known as FOCA, was drafted by abortion rights backers in 1989 who said they wanted to write into statute the protections for the procedure guaranteed by the Supreme Court in the 1973 case *ROE V. WADE*. But opponents insisted that the bill would go much further, invalidating even some restrictions the court had deemed permissible under the *Roe* framework, such as state laws requiring parental notification or consent for a minor's abortion, or bans on using public funds for the procedure.

House and Senate Democratic leaders had vowed to bring the bill to the floor in 1992 just before the Republican National Convention, to highlight disagreement within the GOP over abortion rights. They also hoped that President George Bush's opposition to abortion rights would help Democratic candidates in the fall elections.

But disarray within Democratic ranks, combined with a lack of public outcry over the Supreme Court's decision upholding such provisions of a controversial Pennsylvania law as a twenty-four-hour waiting period and a requirement that women hear a state-sponsored lecture on abortion prior to having the procedure, ultimately derailed the effort. Democratic vote-counters in both houses said they could produce margins for passage, but doubted they could fend off amendments adding restrictions like those in the Pennsylvania law. Although the Democrats knew all along that they lacked the votes to override a promised veto from President Bush, they had hoped outrage over the Court's decision would propel the bill to passage. That outrage, however, never materialized, since the central holding in the case, *PLANNED PARENTHOOD OF SOUTHEASTERN PENNSYLVANIA V. CASEY*, upheld the central tenet of *Roe*, the right of a woman to have an abortion.

In 1993, with a president who had supported the bill while on the campaign trail, backers of the FOCA thought they would have smooth sailing. But they badly underestimated the depth of ambivalence on the abortion issue in both the House and Senate, as well as the public at large. And although both the House and Sen-

Demonstrating in front of the Supreme Court Building, supporters of the Freedom of Choice Act await the Court's decision in Planned Parenthood of Southeastern Pennsylvania v. Casey *(1992), which upheld a woman's right to abortion. Source: R. Michael Jenkins, Congressional Quarterly*

ate Judiciary Committees would ultimately approve the measure, it never made it to the floor of either chamber.

Congress balked at a number of the bill's possible effects, such as prohibiting restrictions on third-trimester abortions, overturning several states' requirements that teenagers obtain the consent of one or both parents before having an abortion, and prohibiting requirements

for a twenty-four-hour waiting period before a woman could obtain an abortion. And, with the budget, health reform, and the North American Free Trade Agreement occupying much of his time, President Bill Clinton proved unwilling to spend political capital on the divisive abortion issue, leaving the bill to languish.

G

Gag clauses (in managed care)

Gag clauses are jargon for language in contracts between managed care plans and physicians that limits what physicians may tell patients about their treatment options. Some of these so-called gag clauses are "explicit," such as prohibitions on telling patients about specialists or other providers not covered under the health plan, or barring physicians from discussing procedures considered "experimental," or otherwise not covered. Others are less overt, such as language requiring doctors not to "disparage" the health plan or requiring physicians to consult the health plan before having certain discussions with patients.

A 1997 report from the General Accounting Office that examined 1,150 contracts used by 529 HEALTH MAINTENANCE ORGANIZATIONS (HMOs) found no explicit gag clauses, buttressing the arguments of managed care advocates and legislators who opposed federal regulation of managed care practices. But the report did find that 60 percent of the contracts included language "that some physicians might interpret as limiting communication about all treatment options," such as forbidding physicians from denigrating the health plan or encouraging patients to choose another plan. The report also noted that even without explicit contract language, the ability of managed care plans to terminate doctors and thereby deprive them of a significant portion of their patients "can bring significant pressure to bear on physicians to modify their practice patterns or discussions with patients."

As of June 1998, forty-five states (all except Alabama, Illinois, Mississippi, South Carolina, and South Dakota) had passed laws barring managed care plans from blocking physicians from discussing all potential treatment options with patients, whether covered by the plan or not. In the 1997 Balanced Budget Act (PL 105-33), Congress also by statute barred gag clauses in managed care contracts serving Medicare and Medicaid beneficiaries (President Bill Clinton had earlier issued orders decreeing such clauses impermissible in December 1996 for Medicare and in March 1997, for Medicaid). But that left unprotected not only those in states without laws but also the estimated 48 million Americans in "self-insured" health plans that under the federal EMPLOYEE RETIREMENT INCOME SECURITY ACT (ERISA) were exempt from state regulation.

Efforts to enact separate legislation to protect those left uncovered, although drawing strong bipartisan support since members began pushing them in 1996, still were unsuccessful as of the close of the 105th Congress in 1998.

In July 1996, the House Commerce Committee approved the Patient Right to Know Act, sponsored by Rep. Greg Ganske, R-Iowa, a physician who would later become one of a handful from his party to endorse the Democrat-backed PATIENTS' BILL OF RIGHTS, and Edward Markey, D-Mass. Under the measure, doctors who provided complete information to their patients could not be removed from a health plan's list of authorized health care providers. The health plan also could not break the doctor's contract or refuse to pay the costs of treatment. The bill included civil penalties of up to $25,000 per offense for an entity that, through written or oral communications, attempted to restrict doctors from disclosing medical information to patients. The full House, however, never took up the bill.

The Senate also acted on the gag clause issue in 1996. During consideration of that year's Treasury-Postal Service appropriation act in September, fifty-one senators voted for an anti-gag clause amendment offered by Sen. Ron Wyden, D-Ore. But because the Congressional Budget Office had estimated that the proposal would increase health care costs for the federal government, sixty votes were needed to overcome a budget "point of order." Wyden quickly rewrote his amendment to render it revenue-neutral, but Senate GOP leaders managed to block it from reaching the floor for the remainder of the 104th Congress.

In 1997 the issue picked up still more support. The Ganske-Markey Patient Right to Know Act attracted 302 cosponsors, more than two-thirds of the House. And both Republicans and Democrats included anti-gag clause language in broader bills to regulate the managed care industry in 1998. But none of those broader bills was enacted, and the issue languished into 1999.

Gag rule (in abortion)

Gag rule is the name family planning advocates attached to regulations proposed during the Reagan administration to bar abortion counseling and referrals in federally funded family planning facilities. The battle raged almost nonstop from September 1987, when the rules were first proposed, until January 22, 1993, when, on his second full day in office, President Bill Clinton officially struck them from the books. In between were veto fights that held up the massive LABOR-HHS APPROPRIATION bill and a Supreme Court case, in which the rules were upheld by a single vote.

From its inception in 1970 (three years before the Supreme Court legalized abortion nationwide in ROE V. WADE) the federal family planning program, TITLE X of the Public Health Service Act, prohibited funding of programs "where abortion is used as a method of family planning." (Title X funds a broad array of family planning and other primary health care services.) Officials in the Department of Health, Education and Welfare (later, Health and Human Services) first interpreted the law to permit abortion counseling and referrals; in 1981, the department required that women be given, upon request, information on all options for an unplanned pregnancy, including abortion.

The gag rule was officially published in the *Federal Register* in September 1987 and made final in February 1988. It barred Title X recipients from performing abortion counseling or referrals; required that Title X clinics "physically separate Title X-funded activities from abortion-related activities," and forbade recipients from using nonfederal funds for lobbying, distributing information, or in any way advocating or encouraging abortion.

While the rules were making their way through the federal courts (Planned Parenthood, among others, had filed suit blocking their implementation), Congress entered the fray. As part of the fiscal 1988 Labor-HHS appropriation bill, the Senate voted to block the rules; however, conferees dropped the language under a veto threat from President Reagan. In 1990, the Senate, acting on a Title X reauthorization bill, voted 62–36 for an amendment to codify the 1981 guidelines requiring that pregnant women be provided "non-directive counseling, and referral upon request" about alternatives including prenatal care and delivery, infant foster care or adoption, and pregnancy termination. But that bill was pulled after sponsors could not cut off debate (and after antiabortion forces prevailed on a vote to require parental notification before minors could receive an abortion at facilities that also received Title X funds).

On May 23, the Supreme Court threw the issue directly back to Congress. In a 5–4 ruling, the majority in *Rust v. Sullivan* said that the rules did not violate Title X recipients' free speech rights. Rather than trying again to reauthorize Title X, a move guaranteed to tangle the Senate in other abortion-related issues, opponents of the rule instead moved a free-standing measure to overturn it that passed that chamber by a voice vote on July 17. The House of Representatives, however, appended its language blocking the rule to the fiscal 1992 Labor-HHS appropriation bill. President George Bush made good on his promise to veto the measure, and the House failed to override by a dozen votes.

In March of 1992, the Bush administration issued a directive on the implementation of the rules stipulating that "nothing in these regulations is to prevent a woman from receiving complete medical information about her condition from a physician." But opponents of the rules argued that the directive was effectively meaningless, since the vast majority of counseling in family planning clinics was delivered not by physicians, but by nurses, nurse practitioners, physician assistants, and social workers. That directive touched off another legal battle—Title X recipients went back to court, arguing that allowing physicians to counsel about abortion after all amounted to an "arbitrary, capricious and irrational" action in violation of requirements for public notice and comment on federal rule changes. A federal district court judge agreed with the plaintiffs in May, again blocking enforcement of the rules. A federal appeals court judge disagreed and lifted the stay on July 30, clearing the way for implementation to begin October 1.

In the end the five-year battle concluded with more of a whimper than a bang. On October 2, the House fell ten votes short of an override on the Senate-passed freestanding bill to block the counseling rules. But in the end it was the courts that put the rules on ice. A three-judge appeals court panel reversed the July appeals court ruling on November 3, blocking implementation that began only a month earlier. In January, Clinton ended the saga, at least for the rest of the 1990s, by repealing the rules by executive order.

Gatekeeper

Gatekeeper is a term used for a primary care physician or other health care professional who controls the access of a patient in an HMO to other forms of care. In a system using gatekeepers, that practitioner must provide a REFERRAL in order for the patient to see a specialist, obtain laboratory tests or other ancillary care, or enter the hospital. The idea behind a gatekeeper (managed care plans rarely use the term, preferring *case manager, primary care physician,* or some other description) is that a single health practitioner can best coordinate

care for an individual patient. A 1997 study by the Robert Wood Johnson Foundation's Center for Studying Health System Change found that nationwide, 40 percent of Americans with health insurance are in some type of gatekeeper arrangement, and more than 90 percent of primary care physicians surveyed said they acted as a gatekeeper for at least some of their patients. In practice, however, patients resent having to seek permission to see specialists with whom they may have pre-existing relationships, and studies have shown that busy primary care practitioners dislike the additional administrative burden. For those reasons, many managed care plans are moving away from gatekeepers and seeking alternative ways to control utilization of health care services.

Generic drugs

Generic drugs are copies of brand name medications determined by the FOOD AND DRUG ADMINISTRATION (FDA) to be safe and effective for their intended use. Generic copies of brand name drugs cannot be sold until after the expiration of the brand name product's patent. In 1984, with the price of prescription drugs spiraling, Congress sought to encourage competition in the drug industry with passage of the Drug Price Competition and Patent Term Restoration Act, PL 98-417. The FDA estimated that passage of the measure could save consumers $1 billion over the ensuing twelve years, because the generic copies sold for 50 to 80 percent less than the "innovator" (brand name) drugs they replicated. At the same time, so as not to punish makers of brand name drugs, the bill also extended by up to five years their patents, during which no generic copies could be marketed. Makers of brand name drugs had been complaining for years that the lengthy process for FDA approval robbed drugs of most of their seventeen years of patent life before they even made it to market.

The measure ordered the FDA to use an abbreviated approval system for generic copies of brand name drugs already on the market. Instead of having to demonstrate safety and efficacy, the standard for a new drug, the generics only had to prove they were "bioequivalent" to the product of which they are a copy.

In the 1984 act, however, Congress failed to anticipate the tremendous financial advantage for the first generic copy to make it to market after the expiration of the brand name drug's patent. Because that first copy often ended up with as much as half the generic market, some manufacturers took illegal means to ensure that their drug was the first approved under the abbreviated process. In 1992, in response to a series of scandals involving the bribing of FDA officials and even the substitution of samples of actual brand name drugs for generic copies to assure passage of the bioequivalence tests, Congress passed the Generic Drug Enforcement Act (PL 102-282).

The bill required the secretary of the HEALTH AND HUMAN SERVICES DEPARTMENT (HHS) to bar applications for generic drugs from corporations convicted of a felony in connection with the generic drug approval process for at least one year and up to ten years. Any subsequent violation of the process would result in mandatory, permanent debarment. Also subject to permanent exclusion from applying for generic drug approvals were individuals convicted of any felony related to the development or approval of any prescription drugs, brand name or generic. The HHS secretary was given permissive authority to exclude both companies and individuals in certain cases, such as those convicted of misdemeanors related to the drug approval process. The law provided for civil penalties of up to $250,000 for individuals and up to $1 million for companies guilty of abusing the approval process, and required the revocation of approval for drugs whose approval was "obtained, expedited or otherwise facilitated" through illegal means.

Genetic discrimination

One of the many areas in which scientific advances have outstripped public policy is the new ability to identify the genetic basis of certain diseases and potentially determine if a person will develop a particular ailment, perhaps years before the ailment manifests itself clinically. Much of this new knowledge is itself the product of government effort, or at least government funding, through the National Human Genome Project, which is in the process of identifying the exact locations of the roughly 80,000 genes that comprise each human's genetic makeup.

Some employers and insurance companies have been accused of discriminating against persons whose medical records reveal a genetic predisposition to illness. The Genetic Information Nondiscrimination in Health Insurance Act, introduced in the 105th Congress, would have prohibited disclosure of genetic information without an individual's written consent. Source: Congressional Quarterly

Research on the genetic basis of disease has already produced tests that can identify a person's predisposition for diseases, from certain types of breast cancer and colon cancer to some forms of glaucoma or kidney cancer. But although knowing in advance the likelihood of developing a disease can be of significant benefit—closer screening can identify ailments at earlier stages when they are most treatable—many people have avoided getting tested for fear that a positive result could be used against them by a prospective employer or insurer. In testifying before the Senate Labor and Human Resources Committee in 1998, Dr. Francis Collins, Director of the National Human Genome Research Institute stated, "Discrimination in health insurance, and the fear of potential discrimination, threaten both society's ability to use new genetic technologies and improve human health and the ability to conduct the very research we need to understand, treat, and prevent genetic disease."

By 1998, more than half of the states had enacted legislation to bar insurers from using genetic information to discriminate in providing coverage or setting rates. But those states could not reach the estimated 48 million Americans in "self-insured" plans that, under the federal EMPLOYEE RETIREMENT INCOME SECURITY ACT, were exempt from state regulation.

Congress, in the 1996 HEALTH INSURANCE PORTABILITY AND ACCOUNTABILITY ACT (HIPAA), PL 104-191, did bar insurers from discriminating on the basis of genetic information for those enrolled in group plans. Under that law, insurers cannot use genetic information to deny coverage to a member of a group plan nor to charge higher premiums, and it explicitly prohibits insurers from using genetic information as a "preexisting condition" unless the actual condition had been diagnosed.

But HIPAA left significant gaps, many complained. It only covered members of groups, leaving unprotected those who purchase their own coverage. And although it prohibited an insurer from charging one member of a group higher premiums because of a genetic predisposition, it left open the possibility that the insurer could raise rates for the entire group based on a single group member's genetic information. Finally, the law did not limit insurers from requiring individuals to undergo genetic testing in order to obtain coverage, nor did it protect what insurers did with that information.

The Genetic Information Nondiscrimination in Health Insurance Act, introduced in the 105th Congress by Rep. Louise Slaughter, D-N.Y., and Sen. Olympia Snowe, R-Maine, would have closed those loopholes. It would have prohibited insurers from denying or canceling health insurance coverage on the basis of genetic information, forbidden insurers from requiring individuals to disclose genetic information, and barred the disclosure of that information without prior written consent.

Although the measure did not become law in the 105th Congress, it did enjoy wide bipartisan support. President Bill Clinton called on Congress to pass it in 1997. "It's wrong when someone avoids taking a test that could save a life just because they're so afraid that the genetic information will be used against them," the president said. And Senate Republicans included provisions of the measure in their managed care regulation bill, which also did not pass.

But insurance companies argued that the legislation was unnecessary and could result in higher rates, particularly in the price-sensitive individual insurance market. Insurers also argued that there was little solid evidence that insurers were discriminating on the basis of genetic information.

Global tobacco settlement

Global tobacco settlement is the term for an agreement reached in June 1997 between attorneys general for forty states and the five major tobacco companies. The settlement would have had the companies pay a total of $368.5 billion over twenty-five years and accept new government regulation of tobacco products in exchange for immunity from future lawsuits. The settlement never took effect, because Congress failed to pass needed legislation to implement its provisions. However, forty-six states reached a more limited settlement with the tobacco companies in November 1998.

The original settlement arose from a series of lawsuits charging that tobacco products, by causing disability and disease, cost state governments billions of dollars in expenses through Medicaid and other public health programs. The tobacco companies, who had previously prevailed in virtually every other lawsuit filed against them, were moved to settle when documents that were highly damaging to the industry were disclosed in some of the trials. These documents included strategy memos on how the companies sought to attract underage smokers.

Under the settlement, $60 billion of the fees paid by the companies would have been "dedicated as punishment for past industry wrongdoing." Half of that amount would have been used for health care for uninsured children (Congress would later boost cigarette taxes by 15 cents per pack to pay for a separate CHILDREN'S HEALTH INSURANCE PROGRAM [CHIP].) The remainder of the company payments would have been parceled out by a presidential commission to reimburse states, provide free smoking-cessation programs, fund antismoking education efforts, and enforce the settlement.

The provisions of the settlement also permitted the FDA to regulate nicotine as a drug, but not ban it until 2009, and then only if it could show that a ban would not produce a black market in tobacco products. On the advertising front, the settlement would have banned all outdoor advertising of cigarette products, eliminated human images from advertising, ended vending machine sales, banned brand name sponsorship of sporting events, and restricted ads in magazines with "significant youth readership" to text. The industry also would have placed new and larger warnings on their products, including such bluntly worded messages as "cigarettes are addictive," and "smoking can kill you."

The settlement would have ended both the lawsuits filed by states to reimburse them for smoking-related health costs, as well as twenty-three pending class action suits in seventeen states filed by groups of smokers. Under the plan, individuals could still have sued the industry, but only those who became ill after the accord took effect would have been able to collect punitive damages.

In November 1998 four major tobacco companies agreed to settle lawsuits pending against them in forty-six states by paying state governments $206 billion over twenty-five years. Among the parties to the settlement was RJR Nabisco, maker of Camel cigarettes. Source: Chris Helgren, Reuters

Many aspects of the settlement, however, particularly the provisions related to the FDA, needed to be approved by Congress. But pressed by public health advocates who thought the settlement let the companies off too lightly and limited the FDA too much, antitobacco senators built the proposal into a $516 billion behemoth that would have raised cigarette prices by at least $1.10 per pack, granted the FDA authority to regulate nicotine as a drug, and imposed severe financial penalties on tobacco companies if the rate of underage tobacco consumption did not fall by 60 percent over ten years. As approved 19–1 by the Senate Commerce Committee on April 1, 1998, the Senate bill did not grant actual immunity to tobacco companies for lawsuits, but did cap at $6.5 billion the amount companies would have to pay out in court judgments. In exchange, companies would voluntarily limit advertising and marketing to young people. The latter was a key point, because there was significant question whether Congress could limit advertising activities without violating the Constitution's guarantee of free speech.

The tobacco companies balked at the Senate's alterations, however, and launched an aggressive effort to kill the bill. In the end, though, the measure simply proved so immense that it basically fell of its own weight. After four weeks of debate on the Senate floor and numerous amendments on unrelated matters, such as child care and eliminating the so-called "marriage tax," leaders finally pulled the measure in June after the Senate failed to grant a waiver of a "budget point of order."

Instead, in November 1998, forty-six states agreed to settle pending suits against the tobacco companies for a payment of $206 billion over twenty-five years. The four states that did not participate in the settlement—Florida, Minnesota, Mississippi, and Texas—had previously settled their tobacco suits for a total of $40 million. The much less sweeping agreement (with no congressional legislation needed to implement it) would require the four companies involved to end the use of billboards in advertising, to stop using cartoon characters that could appeal to children (like Joe Camel), to limit sponsorship of sporting events to one per year, and to fund a $1.5 billion campaign to deter youth smoking. Although the settlement did not grant the FDA new authority to regulate nicotine or require increases in the prices of tobacco products, it also did not grant the companies immunity from future lawsuits, merely settled those already filed.

Graduate medical education

Unlike most other professions, medicine requires in most cases that doctors undergo significant periods of training after they graduate from medical school. Doctors-in-training spend from three years (for most "primary care" roles) to seven or eight years (for specialized surgery slots) in "residency" programs, where they practice under the supervision of more experienced physicians. In 1997, according to the American Medical Association, there were 98,143 residents in accredited specialty programs.

Graduate medical education (GME) is financed from a variety of sources, including the federal government, state and local governments, and revenues from hospital patient care. The federal government, through MEDICARE and MEDICAID, is by far the largest source of funding for graduate medical education. In 1997, Medicare contributed some $6.8 billion for the cost of graduate medical education.

Unlike many other aspects of health policy, the federal government's explicit role in training the next generation of doctors was no accident. When it began the Medicare program in 1965, Congress was warned that there might not be enough physicians to treat all the newly eligible beneficiaries. That helped prompt a major subsidy program that still exists. Medicare makes two types of special payments to teaching hospitals. DIRECT MEDICAL EDUCATION PAYMENTS help underwrite the actual salaries and teaching expenses for interns and residents who treat Medicare patients. INDIRECT MEDICAL EDUCATION PAYMENTS (IME payments)—about twice as large as the direct payments—help compensate teaching hospitals for the inefficiencies associated with their teaching missions— the need for more supervision and the fact that inexperienced doctors may order more tests, for example. IME payments, calculated under a formula based on a hospital's number of residents and its number of beds and "added on" to Medicare's per-diagnosis hospital payment, also account for the fact that teaching hospitals tend to attract sicker, and thus more expensive, patients.

But many analysts say Medicare's open-ended financing of graduate medical education has taken what was a potential shortage of physicians and turned it into a glut. A 1995 report from the Pew Health Professions Commission predicted that by the year 2000, the United States would have 150,000 more physicians than it needs and called for the closure of up to 25 percent of the nation's medical schools. The report also called for a restructuring of graduate medical education programs so that half of all residencies would be in the PRIMARY CARE areas of family practice, general internal medicine, and pediatrics, by the year 2000. Although in general the United States is on a path to having too many doctors, it may be facing a shortage of physicians practicing front-line primary care. Between 1982 and 1993, the percentage of residents pursuing primary care careers fell from 36.1 percent to 19.3 percent.

Among the major contributors to the oversupply of

specialists, say analysts, are the hospitals, which have more slots for residents than there are graduates of U.S. medical schools each year. Those extra slots—about 26 percent more in 1997—are filled by "international medical graduates," Americans or foreigners who attended medical schools outside the United States. Because, at least in part, of Medicare's generous subsidies, it can cost hospitals less to staff their facilities with residents than with less highly trained personnel. A resident working a twenty-four-hour shift, for example, can take the place of three eight hour shifts of a NURSE PRACTITIONER or PHYSICIAN ASSISTANT. But when residents complete their training, they may not be able to find a job in the specialty for which they trained. A 1998 study published in the *Journal of the American Medical Association* found that just over two-thirds of physicians completing their residencies in 1996 (67.3 percent) were able to find positions in their own fields. Just over 7 percent were unemployed; the remainder went on to pursue additional studies (some because they could not find an appropriate position), took academic positions, or found work in another specialty.

Congress, in the 1997 Balanced Budget Act (PL 105-33), attempted to address the medical education issue, although lawmakers vowed that what that measure included was merely a first step. As part of overall efforts to reduce Medicare spending, the bill reduced Medicare's indirect medical education payments by an estimated $7.9 billion over five years. At the same time, however, responding to complaints from teaching hospitals that managed care companies were getting subsidies for medical education, then failing to send patients to teaching facilities, the measure "carved out" Medicare education payments from managed care payments (to the tune of $4 billion over five years) and redirected them back to the teaching hospitals.

The bill also began to address analysts' complaints about the oversupply of physicians, particularly of specialists. It capped the number of residents used to calculate DME and IME payments for individual teaching hospitals at their 1997 levels (which will be adjusted in future years). Although the secretary of the HEALTH AND HUMAN SERVICES DEPARTMENT has some authority to make exceptions to the cap, one hospital's increase can be made only if slots are reduced somewhere else. The measure also provided hospitals with incentives to shrink their residency programs by providing additional funds (critics call them bribes) to help hospitals make the transition from resident staffing to more permanent employees. The CONGRESSIONAL BUDGET OFFICE estimated that these provisions together would reduce the number of residents being trained by approximately 3 percent.

Over the long-term, analysts and interest groups involved in medical education (such as the AMERICAN MEDICAL ASSOCIATION and the Association of American Medical Colleges) have called for a system that would provide a stable, predictable source of funding for graduate medical education. Because much of medical education is funded by "cross subsidies" from medical school faculty "practice plans" that have been hard hit by the rise of managed care, and because government in general has been looking to decrease its health care spending, many fear that the educational and research missions of the nation's academic health centers could be compromised. As part of the 1995 Balanced Budget Act, passed by Congress but vetoed by President Bill Clinton, Congress proposed establishment of a $15-billion-per-year "Teaching Hospital and Graduate Medical Education Trust Fund," from which Medicare medical education payments would have been made.

More recent proposals have called for an "all-payer" system to finance graduate medical education costs, with payments coming from both public and private health insurers, on the theory that the entire health care system benefits from the research and education efforts undertaken at teaching hospitals and academic medical centers. Although such a system would likely increase insurance premiums, taxpayers are paying much of the graduate medical education bill already.

Guaranteed issue

Guaranteed issue, a requirement that insurance companies sell policies to all who agree to pay the required premiums and meet other requirements, can be mandated by states or by the federal government and can apply to different segments of the market (individuals, small groups, or everyone). The HEALTH INSURANCE PORTABILITY AND ACCOUNTABILITY ACT (HIPAA) included a modified form of guaranteed issue, requiring that insurers sell policies to all individuals, regardless of their medical condition, who have been continuously covered for at least eighteen months and meet certain other requirements. Guaranteed issue alone, however, does not regulate prices. Thus, as has happened, companies can respond to guaranteed issue rules by selling to all comers but at higher (sometimes much higher) premiums to groups they perceive as likely to be more expensive.

Guaranteed renewability

Although similar to GUARANTEED ISSUE, guaranteed renewability forbids insurers from declining to renew policies because of a change in health status of a group or a member of a group (or an individual in the case of individual coverage). The HEALTH INSURANCE PORTABILITY AND ACCOUNTABILITY ACT (HIPAA) of 1996 (PL 104-191) requires that insurers renew policies, except in cases of failure to pay premiums or of fraud, as long as the insurer continues to serve anyone in that market. In other words, an insurer may drop out of the small group or individual market completely but may not renew coverage for some groups or individuals but not others. Legislation in 1990 to tighten federal regulation of the Medicare supplement insurance market (MEDIGAP INSURANCE) also required insurers to guarantee renewal of those policies, again, as long as premiums continue to be paid and there is no "material misrepresentation."

H

Health and Human Services Department

The U.S. Department of Health and Human Services was officially created on May 4, 1980. Formerly called the Department of Health, Education and Welfare, its name was changed after the Department of Education Organization Act in 1979 created a free-standing Department of Education. The forerunner agency, HEW, was created under President Dwight D. Eisenhower, debuting on April 11, 1953. HHS, as it is known, lost another large piece of its portfolio in 1995, when the Social Security Administration became an independent agency.

Nevertheless, HHS has the largest budget of any agency in the federal government—more than $387 billion in fiscal 1999. (By comparison, the Defense Department received an appropriation of $262.6 billion that same year). Often referred to as the "people's department," HHS and its nearly 60,000 employees administer more than 300 programs that touch the life of virtually every American. HHS is also the federal government's largest grant-making agency, making more than 60,000 grants per year.

HHS is home to the U.S. PUBLIC HEALTH SERVICE

Secretaries of HEW and HHS, 1953–2000

Secretary	Department	Dates of service
Oveta Culp Hobby	HEW	April 11, 1953–July 31, 1955
Marion B. Folsom	HEW	August 1, 1955–July 31, 1958
Arthur S. Flemming	HEW	August 1, 1958–January 19, 1961
Abraham Ribicoff	HEW	January 21, 1961–July 13, 1962
Anthony J. Celebrezze	HEW	July 31, 1962–August 17, 1965
John W. Gardner	HEW	August 18, 1965–March 1, 1968
Wilbur J. Cohen	HEW	May 16, 1968–January 20, 1969
Robert H. Finch	HEW	January 21, 1969–June 23, 1970
Elliot L. Richardson	HEW	June 24, 1970–January 29, 1973
Caspar W. Weinberger	HEW	February 12, 1973–August 8, 1975
David Mathews	HEW	August 8, 1975–January 20, 1977
Joseph A. Califano, Jr.	HEW	January 25, 1977–August 3, 1979
Patricia Roberts Harris	HEW/HHS	August 3, 1979–January 20, 1981
Richard S. Schweiker	HHS	January 22, 1981–February 3, 1983
Margaret M. Heckler	HHS	March 9, 1983–December 13, 1985
Otis R. Bowen	HHS	December 13, 1985–January 20, 1989
Louis W. Sullivan	HHS	March 1, 1989–January 20, 1993
Donna E. Shalala	HHS	January 22, 1993–

Note: Until May 4, 1980, the Health and Human Services Department (HHS) was known as the Health, Education and Welfare Department (HEW). Created April 11, 1953, HEW was reorganized in 1979 by authority of the Department of Education Organization Act. In addition to creating a new Education Department, the act renamed HEW the Department of Health and Human Services.

Health and Human Services Department

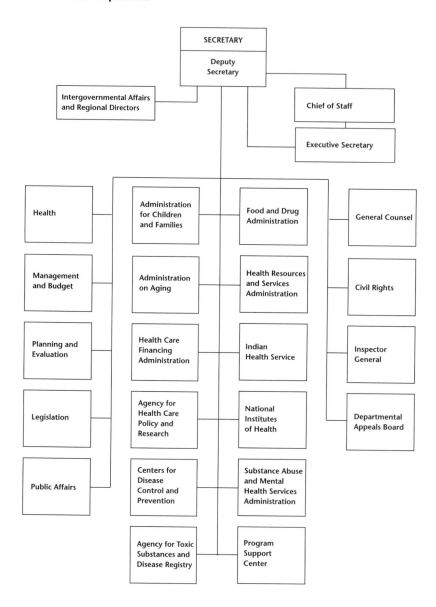

(PHS), which includes eight research and health delivery agencies, including the NATIONAL INSTITUTES OF HEALTH, CENTERS FOR DISEASE CONTROL AND PREVENTION, and the FOOD AND DRUG ADMINISTRATION. Outside of the PHS purview is the HEALTH CARE FINANCING ADMINISTRATION, which runs MEDICARE and MEDICAID.

In regard to human services, HHS encompasses the Administration for Children and Families, which operated $38 billion worth of programs in fiscal 1999, including the popular Head Start for preschoolers, Temporary Assistance to Needy Families (TANF), the successor program to the former federal-state welfare program Aid to Families with Dependent Children (AFDC).

HHS secretary Donna Shalala, appointed January 22, 1993, by President Bill Clinton, testifies on the Clinton health care plan before the House Energy and Commerce Committee. Source: R. Michael Jenkins, *Congressional Quarterly*

HHS also has programs to provide child care, adoption assistance, help with paying energy bills, and to collect child support payments. The Administration on Aging, with a budget of $883 million in fiscal 1999, runs an array of programs for the elderly, including the popular Meals on Wheels and counseling services for health insurance and other programs.

Health Care Financing Administration

The Health Care Financing Administration (HCFA) was created by the former secretary of the U.S. Department of Health, Education and Welfare Joseph Califano in 1977 to administer MEDICARE and MEDICAID for the department. Prior to HCFA's creation, Medicare was overseen by the Social Security Administration and Medicaid by the Social and Rehabilitation Services Administration. HCFA, based in Baltimore, has about 4,000 employees to administer Medicare, Medicaid, and the CHILDREN'S HEALTH INSURANCE PROGRAM (CHIP) passed by Congress in 1997 as part of the Balanced Budget Act (PL 105-33).

Medicare has remarkably low administrative expens-es of about 3 percent of spending; that of most private firms is 15–25 percent. Yet HCFA has long been the subject of criticism from health care providers, members of Congress, and the General Accounting Office (GAO). HCFA has particularly been whipsawed over the issue of fraud and abuse, which cost Medicare an estimated $20.3 billion in fiscal 1997. When the agency writes rules to prevent inappropriate use of Medicare funds that are too burdensome, hospitals and physicians complain— often to their members of Congress. But when its oversight is too lax, it costs the taxpayers money and it is criticized by the GAO and other members of Congress.

HCFA's workload has increased dramatically in the 1990s, particularly since 1996. The agency oversaw the processing of 853 million claims in fiscal 1997, and supervised the spending of nearly half a trillion dollars through Medicare and Medicaid for more than 70 million beneficiaries. The 1996 HEALTH INSURANCE PORTABILITY AND ACCOUNTABILITY ACT (HIPAA) required HCFA to take on a raft of new antifraud activities as well as become the default insurance regulator for states that failed to pass laws to conform to the new federal rules. The 1997 Balanced Budget Act (PL 105-33) gave HCFA 300 more new tasks to accomplish. At the same time, HCFA was scrambling to ensure that Medicare's computers and payment systems wouldn't shut down on January 1, 2000, because of the Y2K problem.

Many analysts have expressed concerns about HCFA's ability to accomplish the new workload imposed by the 1997 law. Among the new roles HCFA is expected to assume are creating new payment systems for home health and nursing home care, overseeing the implementation of MEDICARE+CHOICE, and approving state plans for the new Children's Health Insurance Program. Yet at the same time HCFA's workload was increasing, its budget, in real terms, was declining—by 11 percent from 1993 to 1997. And in 1998 its total workforce was down slightly from that of 1977.

Health care fraud and abuse

By some estimates, health care fraud and abuse account for one of every $10 spent in the United States on health care each year. Technically, health fraud, according to the National Health Care Anti-Fraud Association, is "an intentional deception or misrepresentation that an individual or entity makes knowing that the misrepresentation could result in unauthorized benefit to the individual, the entity, or to some other party." The most common type of health care fraud, according to the association, involves billing for services or treatments not supplied or making false statements, misrepresentation, or deliberate omission critical to the determination of benefits.

Health care abuse includes acts that are not motivated by an intent to commit fraud but are nonetheless not technically necessary for the patient's health. Examples of abuse can include "unbundling," in which, in order to gain a larger reimbursement, a physician or hospital bills separately for services normally paid as part of a package rate, and "upcoding," indicating a service was a more complicated or expensive one than what was actually provided. The line between fraud and abuse is a fuzzy one; often the same act can fall into either category.

Because fraud cases are difficult to prove and have not until recently been the focus of efforts of state or federal law enforcement officials, much of the responsibility for detecting misuse of health care dollars has fallen to private insurance companies. With the rise in electronic bill processing, computer-based fraud detection has become more cost-effective. In 1995, according to the HEALTH INSURANCE ASSOCIATION OF AMERICA, companies reported that antifraud efforts saved $262 million, up from $94 million in 1993.

As the amounts of money involved have risen, prosecuting health care fraud has become a booming business for prosecutors around the country as well. MEDICARE and MEDICAID fraud has been a particular emphasis, through the Clinton administration's "Operation Restore Trust," which began in 1995 as a five-state experiment to coordinate fraud-fighting efforts among federal, state, and private enforcement agencies, focusing on fraud in the home health care, nursing home, and durable medical equipment industries. In its first two years, the program identified $188 million owed to the federal government, a return of $23 for every $1 spent on the program. After the program went nationwide in 1997, federal "fraud busters" returned nearly $1 billion to the Treasury and expelled 2,700 providers from the programs. Between 1993 and 1997, the antifraud efforts of the Health and Human Services Department (HHS) recovered more than $20 billion and increased convictions for health care fraud by 240 percent.

But fraud and abuse remain a serious problem in Medicare; an audit by the HHS inspector general released in 1998 found that in fiscal 1997 the program made net "improper" payments of about $20.3 billion, representing 11 percent of the total Medicare nonmanaged care budget. Those payments included not only outright fraud but also inadvertent mistakes, charges not properly documented, or billings for care that was not medically necessary or care not covered by Medicare. The total, however, did represent a decrease of about $3 billion from the previous year. The 1999 report of fiscal 1998 spending showed even more progress: the error rate declined to 7.1 percent, representing improper payments of $12.6 billion.

Congress has revisited the fraud and abuse issue frequently. The current round of fraud-fighting dates back to 1987. Legislation passed that year (PL 100-93) widely expanded the HHS secretary's authority to bar unfit or incompetent health care providers from Medicare and Medicaid, as well as from participation in the MATERNAL AND CHILD HEALTH SERVICES BLOCK GRANT and Social Services Block Grant programs.

The legislation required that the secretary exclude from the programs for at least five years any individual or entity convicted of a criminal offense related to the delivery of services under any of the programs, unless a state requested otherwise because the individual or entity was the sole community physician or sole source of essential specialized services in the community.

The secretary could, but was not required to, exclude individuals or entities convicted under federal or state laws of criminal offenses relating to fraud, theft, embezzlement, breach of fiduciary responsibility or financial abuse if the offense was committed either in connection with the delivery of health care or with respect to a health care program financed in any part by the federal government or any state or local government. Also optionally excludable were individuals or entities convicted of interfering with the investigation of health care fraud or offenses related to controlled substances; individuals whose license to practice was revoked or otherwise lost for reasons bearing on an individual's professional competence, conduct, or financial integrity, or who voluntarily surrendered a license while a formal disciplinary proceeding was pending; individuals or entities suspended or excluded from any other state or federal health care program for reasons related to professional competence, professional performance, or financial integrity; HMOs that "failed substantially to provide medically necessary services;" or an entity owned or controlled by an individual, or who had been an officer, director, agent, or managing employee, who was convicted of program-related offenses, or who had had a civil penalty assessed, or who had been excluded from participation in any of the programs.

The measure also permitted the imposition of civil penalties of up to $2,000 per item plus twice the amount claimed for services not actually provided, and authorized criminal penalties of up to $25,000 in fines or five years in prison for provision of services by an unlicensed physician.

Congress's next major antifraud foray came as part of the 1996 HEALTH INSURANCE PORTABILITY AND ACCOUNTABILITY ACT (HIPAA), PL 104-191. That bill not only increased penalties for fraud and abuse, it created a self-funded program to be operated jointly by the Departments of Justice and HHS. The program was to coordinate not only federal antifraud efforts but also state and local efforts aimed at finding misconduct in both public and private health plans. The program was to be funded by the fines, forfeitures, and damages collected.

The HIPAA also authorized a separate "Medicare integrity program" to let contracts to private firms to find Medicare fraud and abuse. The program included provisions allowing "bounties" to be paid to Medicare beneficiaries who identify fraud or misconduct and whose reports result in saving the government money.

The HIPAA also included a controversial provision some Democrats and the Clinton administration complained could actually increase fraud. It required the Justice Department to issue "advisory opinions" on whether certain business arrangements violated federal anti-kickback laws. The Justice Department complained that because the law is "intent-based," advisory opinions could cripple the department's ability to prosecute such cases. The law also called for an expanded list of "safe harbor" guidelines for acceptable business practices that might otherwise be considered violations.

Among the increased penalties were imposition of mandatory exclusions for some crimes in the "voluntary" section of the 1987 law, including convictions for any felony related to health care fraud or controlled substances, and an increase in civil fines from $2,000 to $10,000 per violation. Also made explicitly illegal was the dispersal of assets by an individual in order to qualify for Medicaid.

The HIPAA also changed the legal standard for prosecution of health care fraud, from merely knowing the activity was illegal to knowing and acting with "reckless disregard or deliberate ignorance" of the law.

Finally, in order to make fraud detection easier, and to simplify administrative burdens at the federal and state level and in private plans, the law called for every health care provider to be issued a "unique identifier." In 1998, the Department of Health and Human Services proposed an eight-digit alphanumeric code that would allow for 20 billion separate identifiers.

Congress addressed the fraud and abuse issue again the following year. As part of the 1997 Balanced Budget Act (PL 105-33), Congress beefed up penalties one more time, imposing a permanent exclusion of providers from federal health programs after conviction of a third health-related felony ("three strikes and you're out"), and requiring a ten-year exclusion for a second conviction. The law gave the HHS secretary authority to bar those convicted of any felony from participation in federal health programs if the inclusion "would be inconsistent with the best interest of program beneficiaries," and to exclude entities controlled by a family member of someone who has been excluded, as well as authority to impose civil fines for persons who contracted with an excluded provider.

To help beneficiaries identify fraud, the law required that providers issue a detailed, itemized bill on request and that a toll-free telephone number for reporting potential fraud be printed on all Medicare beneficiary benefit notices. The measure also broadened the advisory opinion provision from the HIPAA to include SELF REFERRAL CURBS, potential violations of rules against physician "self-referrals."

Some say the government has gone too far in its antifraud efforts. Groups representing health care providers, mostly doctors and hospitals, have complained that the government is cracking down so hard it is prosecuting people for making inadvertent mistakes, or punishing them for failing to understand highly complex rules and regulations. Even fraud-fighters concede that when done appropriately, antifraud efforts still cannot help but increase paperwork and administrative headaches for those who deliver health care, adding yet another layer of bureaucracy to the system.

Health care spending

Health care spending has been a major source of concern for the past three decades. An aging population, new (and expensive) technology helping people live longer, and an economically comfortable society wanting more and more health care services have combined over the last several decades to put health spending on a trajectory to consume an ever-larger share of the nation's economic output. Although health spending has slowed in the years since the defeat in Congress of major health system overhaul in 1994, long-term estimates issued in 1998 showed health care spending likely to increase faster as the massive baby boom generation reaches its highest health cost years, beginning in approximately the year 2010.

The big news in 1998 was the slowdown in health cost inflation. In 1997, according to the HEALTH CARE FINANCING ADMINISTRATION (spending statistics lag by about a year), health care spending rose by 4.8 percent, the slowest increase in forty years. Analysts attributed the slowdown to a number of factors, including the continuing migration of people with employer-sponsored health insurance from traditional to lower-premium managed care plans, low inflation both in health care and in the economy as a whole, and excess capacity in the health care sector, which boosted competition. But health care spending still topped the trillion dollar mark ($1.1 trillion), with per person spending averaging $3,925.

In 1997, health care spending accounted for 13.5 percent of the nation's gross domestic product (GDP), down from 13.6 percent the previous year. Before 1994, when the current deceleration began, the percentage of the nation's economy devoted to health care had been growing rapidly, doubling from 1968 to 1993. Actual spending grew much faster, doubling from 1984 to 1993.

Personal health expenditures (what is spent on actual medical services, not including administration, research, and public health activities) reached $969 billion in 1997. Of that amount, the largest portion, $371.1 billion, or 38 percent, went to pay for hospital care. Hospital care, however, grew at a slower rate than for any oth-

National Health Expenditure Amounts, Percentage Distribution, and Average Annual Percentage Change, by Source of Funds: Selected Calendar Years, 1970–2007[1]

Item	1970	1980	1990	1992	1994	1996	1998	1999	2000	2001	Projected 2002	2003	2004	2005	2006	2007
Amounts in billions																
National health expenditures	$73.2	$247.3	$699.5	$836.6	$945.7	$1,035.1	$1,146.8	$1,216.7	$1,295.2	$1,384.1	$1,483.2	$1,591.2	$1,710.7	$1,841.0	$1,981.0	$2,133.3
Private	45.5	142.5	415.1	478.1	521.8	552.0	606.4	649.6	696.5	746.6	802.3	860.3	923.5	992.5	1,066.0	1,145.9
Public	27.7	104.8	284.4	358.5	423.9	483.1	540.4	567.1	598.7	637.4	680.8	731.0	787.2	848.7	914.9	987.4
Medicare	7.7	37.5	112.1	141.4	169.8	203.1	231.1	241.2	252.9	267.8	285.0	306.2	330.2	356.1	384.0	415.6
Medicaid	5.3	26.1	75.4	106.4	131.0	147.7	165.5	175.6	188.0	203.2	220.0	238.7	260.0	283.6	309.4	337.0
Other	14.7	41.1	96.9	110.8	123.1	132.3	143.8	150.4	157.9	166.4	175.8	186.1	197.1	209.0	221.5	234.9
Exhibit: Total federal	17.8	72.0	195.8	257.0	304.1	350.9	393.8	412.5	434.5	461.3	491.8	527.9	568.5	612.6	660.3	712.9
Total state/local	9.9	32.8	88.5	101.6	119.8	132.2	146.6	154.7	164.3	176.1	189.0	203.1	218.8	236.1	254.7	274.5
Percentage distribution																
National health expenditures	100.00	100.00	100.00	100.00	100.00	100.00	100.00	100.00	100.00	100.00	100.00	100.00	100.00	100.00	100.00	100.00
Private	62.2	57.6	59.3	57.1	55.2	53.3	52.9	53.4	53.8	53.9	54.1	54.1	54.0	53.9	53.8	53.7
Public	37.8	42.4	40.7	42.9	44.8	46.7	47.1	46.6	46.2	46.1	45.9	45.9	46.0	46.1	46.2	46.3
Medicare	10.5	15.2	16.0	16.9	18.0	19.6	20.1	19.8	19.5	19.3	19.2	19.2	19.3	19.4	19.4	19.5
Medicaid	7.3	10.6	10.8	12.7	13.9	14.3	14.4	14.4	14.5	14.7	14.8	15.0	15.2	15.4	15.6	15.8
Other	20.1	16.6	13.8	13.2	13.0	12.8	12.5	12.4	12.2	12.0	11.9	11.7	11.5	11.4	11.2	11.0
Exhibit: Total federal	24.3	29.1	28.0	30.7	32.2	33.9	34.3	33.9	33.5	33.3	33.2	33.2	33.2	33.3	33.3	33.4
Total state/local	13.5	13.3	12.7	12.1	12.7	12.8	12.8	12.7	12.7	12.7	12.7	12.8	12.8	12.8	12.9	12.9
Average annual percentage change from previous year shown																
National health expenditures	—	12.9	11.0	9.4	6.3	4.6	5.3	6.1	6.5	6.9	7.2	7.3	7.5	7.6	7.6	7.7
Private	—	12.1	11.3	7.3	4.5	2.9	4.8	7.1	7.2	7.2	7.5	7.2	7.3	7.5	7.4	7.5
Public	—	14.2	10.5	12.3	8.7	6.8	5.8	4.9	5.6	6.5	6.8	7.4	7.7	7.8	7.8	7.9
Medicare	—	17.2	11.6	12.3	9.6	9.4	6.7	4.4	4.8	5.9	6.4	7.4	7.8	7.9	7.8	8.2
Medicaid	—	17.3	11.2	18.8	11.0	6.2	5.9	6.1	7.1	8.1	8.2	8.5	8.9	9.1	9.1	8.9
Other	—	10.8	8.9	6.9	5.4	3.7	4.3	4.6	5.0	5.4	5.7	5.8	5.9	6.0	6.0	6.0
Exhibit: Total federal	—	15.0	10.5	14.6	8.8	7.4	5.9	4.7	5.3	6.2	6.6	7.3	7.7	7.8	7.8	8.0
Total state/local	—	12.7	10.4	7.1	8.6	5.1	5.3	5.5	6.2	7.2	7.3	7.5	7.7	7.9	7.9	7.8
Gross domestic product (GDP, billions)	$1,035.6	$2,784.2	$5,743.8	$6,244.5	$6,947.0	$7,636.0	$8,384.1	$8,735.2	$9,119.2	$9,531.6	$9,980.5	$10,469.0	$11,002.4	$11,579.1	$12,202.2	$12,865.5
U.S. population (millions)[2]	214.8	235.1	260.0	265.3	270.4	275.3	280.2	282.6	284.9	287.2	289.4	291.7	293.9	296.1	298.3	300.5
National health expenditures per capita	$341	$1,052	$2,691	$3,154	$3,497	$3,759	$4,093	$4,306	$4,547	$4,820	$5,124	$5,456	$5,821	$6,218	$6,642	$7,100
National health expenditures (percentage of GDP)	7.1	8.9	12.2	13.4	13.6	13.6	13.7	13.9	14.2	14.5	14.9	15.2	15.5	15.9	16.2	16.6

Source: Health Care Financing Administration, Office of the Actuary, September 28, 1998. See *www.hcfa.gov/stats/NHE-Proj/tables/t01.htm.*

Notes: Numbers and percentages may not add to totals because of rounding.

1. Spending projections for 1997 to 2007 were based on the 1996 release of the National Health Expenditures (NHE). Subsequent releases of the NHE may not be consistent with these projections and should not be substituted for the 1996 historic estimates.

2. Social Security area population estimates as of July 1, 1998.

er category of personal health spending, mostly because the continuing oversupply of hospital beds allowed managed care plans to negotiate low rates. Despite a 10 percent reduction in inpatient capacity—community hospitals closed 88,000 staffed beds between 1990 and 1997, according to HCFA—the decline in inpatient use was sharper still, and occupancy rates in community hospitals fell from 64.5 percent in 1990 to 59.6 percent in 1997.

Americans spent $218 billion on physician services in 1997, up 4.4 percent from the previous year. Again, said analysts, managed care was likely an important cause of the slowdown in spending on doctors. In 1997, HCFA reported, 92 percent of physicians had contracts with at least one managed care plan, up from 88 percent in 1996. Physicians with managed care contracts earned 49 percent of their income from managed care, up from 46 percent the previous year.

Home health care spending rose to $32.2 billion, an increase of 3.7 percent. As recently as 1990, home health care was rising as fast as 28 percent per year. Analysts attributed the slowdown to payment changes imposed by Medicare, which finances about 40 percent of all HOME HEALTH CARE SERVICES.

One of the few areas where prices are going up more rapidly than in the recent past is prescription drugs. Spending on drugs reached $78.9 billion in 1997, up 14.1 percent. Prescription drug spending has been rising at double digit rates since 1995. Again, analysts pointed to multiple factors such as FOOD AND DRUG ADMINISTRATION (FDA) reforms that are speeding up the approval of new medications (some of which are blockbusters, like the anti-impotence drug Viagra), "direct-to-consumer" advertising by drug companies that is spurring patients to urge their physicians to write prescriptions, and increased insurance coverage for prescription drugs that make them more affordable for the average patient.

Also growing more rapidly than in the past is actual out-of-pocket spending by consumers, reaching $187.6 billion in 1997, up 5.3 percent from spending in the previous year. In the early 1990s, the share of out-of-pocket spending overall fell, as people moved from traditional fee-for-service plans, which required payments of annual DEDUCTIBLES as well as "copayments" of 20 percent or more, to managed care plans that required no deductibles and minimal copayments. But more recently, managed care plans have been raising the amounts they require patients to contribute. In 1993, only 34 percent of HMO enrollees were required to make copayments of $10 or more to visit a physician; in 1997, those payments were required of 70 percent of enrollees.

But the slow growth was likely to end abruptly, analysts predicted. By 1998 managed care plans that cut rates in the early 1990s to attract a greater share of the market were raising premiums—often at double digit rates—as their patient care costs outstripped their income. In addition, the strong economy was boosting demand for health care services that more people could afford, and the labor shortage in the economy as a whole was prompting employers to be more generous with their health benefits. By the year 2008, according to HCFA projections in 1999, health care spending will reach $2.2 trillion and will consume an estimated 16.2 percent of the nation's GDP.

Health Insurance Association of America

The Health Insurance Association of America (HIAA), based in Washington, D.C., is a trade association that represents mostly small and mid-sized health insurance companies. In 1999, the HIAA had 269 members who provided health, long-term care, disability, and supplemental MEDICARE coverage to more than 115 million Americans. Although in the early 1990s the HIAA endorsed the concept of universal coverage to be achieved by requiring employers to cover their workers (the so-called employer mandate), the organization ended up as one of the highest-profile opponents of President Bill Clinton's health reform plan, the HEALTH SECURITY ACT. HIAA-funded commercials featured a pair of actors named Harry and Louise, who sat around their kitchen table puzzling over the complexities of the proposal and worried about whether it would cost them more. The commercials, which appeared more frequently in news reports about the opposition than in paid spots, were considered emblematic of the problems the plan posed. In 1998, the HIAA became one of the leaders in the fight against legislation to regulate the practices of managed care companies.

Health Insurance Portability and Accountability Act (HIPAA)

On August 21, 1996, President Bill Clinton finally got to do what he had hoped for throughout 1993 and 1994—sign a bipartisan overhaul of health insurance into law. But the Health Insurance Portability and Accountability Act, also known as Kassebaum-Kennedy, for the names of its two principal Senate sponsors, was hardly the sweeping overhaul Clinton had in mind when he took office. Although HIPAA (PL 104-191) did represent the most comprehensive federal regulation of private health insurance ever enacted, it addressed only

a very small portion of the population—those already insured who wished to move from one group plan to another or who wanted to move from a group to an individual plan. And although the measure sought to improve the availability of insurance, it did nothing to make it more affordable—an omission that would come back to haunt the measure only two years later, when analysts reported that insurers were avoiding some of the law's requirements by charging premiums up to six times higher for persons eligible because of HIPAA than they charged other customers.

At the insistence of Republicans in the U.S. House of Representatives and the Senate, the measure also went well beyond its original modest intentions. In addition to provisions seeking to reduce the ability of insurers to exclude individuals from coverage because of "PRE-EXISTING CONDITIONS," the final measure also included a major antifraud effort and a four-year experiment with the MEDICAL SAVINGS ACCOUNT (MSA), a tax-preferred account combined with a high-deductible

Flanked by Sens. Ted Kennedy, D-Mass., and Nancy Kassebaum, R-Kan., principal sponsors of the Health Insurance Portability and Accountability Act, President Bill Clinton arrives at the White House to sign the measure, the most comprehensive federal regulation of private health insurance ever enacted. Source: Stephen Jaffe, Reuters

"catastrophic" insurance policy that gave individuals much more responsibility for their personal health care spending. It also included several other health-related tax provisions, including an increase in the percentage of premiums that the self-employed could deduct from their income taxes and new tax deductions for LONG-TERM CARE services and long-term care insurance premiums.

Specifically, the measure sought to improve the "portability" of benefits by making it easier for workers to move from job to job without risk of being locked out of insurance or having to wait for coverage of preexisting medical problems. The bill did not permit workers to take their specific health plans with them when they changed jobs (what many people mistakenly thought "portability" meant), and it did not require employers to offer insurance or to offer any specific benefits if they did provide coverage. But the new law did address the problem of "job-lock," the fear many workers had of not being able to re-acquire insurance if they gave up their current job—and the insurance that came with it. The General Accounting Office estimated that up to 25 million Americans could benefit from the measure's portability provisions.

A majority of states had already passed insurance portability laws—forty states acted between 1990 and 1994, according to the General Accounting Office. But because many plans that fell under the federal EMPLOY-EE RETIREMENT INCOME SECURITY ACT (ERISA) were exempt from state regulation, those state laws could not reach some 40 percent of the population with employer-provided insurance. For that reason, even though insurance regulation has traditionally been left to states, only a federal law could impose requirements on "self-insured" ERISA plans.

The bill also prohibited insurers from discriminating against workers based on their or a member of their family's health status or medical history, including mental illness, a history of being a victim of domestic violence, or because genetic tests had detected a likelihood that the person would develop an ailment sometime in the future.

It required insurers to sell insurance to all small groups that seek it if they offer any coverage in the small group market, and accept every eligible individual in each group. Members of groups could not be excluded from coverage or denied the chance to renew coverage based on their health status, nor could any individuals in groups be charged higher premiums based on health status.

Insurers were also prohibited from imposing pre-existing condition exclusions exceeding twelve months for conditions for which medical advice, diagnosis, or treatment was received or recommended within the previous six months. For individuals who had been continuously covered for more than twelve months, no preexisting condition exclusions were allowed, and waiting periods were required to be shortened for every month of continuous coverage. For example, if a person had been covered for six months with no break in coverage of more than sixty-three days, the maximum waiting period for coverage of a preexisting condition could be no more than six months.

The measure also sought to guarantee that those leaving group coverage could obtain coverage as individuals. But it benefited only a small subset of individuals; those who were covered continuously under a group plan for eighteen months, who exhausted their extended COBRA CONTINUATION coverage, if available, and those who had no other available insurance. The law permitted states to establish health insurance coverage "high-risk pools," mandatory group conversion policies, open enrollment of some plans, or other means to accomplish the availability of insurance to these individuals. If the state did not impose some mechanism, however, insurers were required to sell coverage to qualifying individuals. Insurers, though, had significant leeway to offer only certain plans, and the law essentially imposed no limits on what insurers could charge.

The law's Medical Savings Account provision called for establishment of up to 750,000 policies combining high-deductible "catastrophic" insurance plans with tax-preferred accounts from which individuals would pay their own routine and minor medical expenses. MSAs were limited to the self-employed, small employers (those with fifty or fewer employees), and the uninsured. Policies were to be available from January 1, 1997, until January 1, 2001, after which Congress would have to vote to permit the policies to continue their preferred tax status.

On taxes, the measure increased, over ten years, the percentage of premiums the self-employed could deduct. The deduction, at 30 percent when the measure was signed into law, would rise to 40 percent in 1997; 45 percent in 1998 through 2002; 50 percent in 2003; 60 percent in 2004; 70 percent in 2005; and 80 percent in 2006 and thereafter. It also made tax deductible to the same extent as other medical expenses the cost of long-term care services, and provided the same tax preferences for long-term care insurance as for other health insurance.

To curb fraud and abuse, the measure established a joint program between the HEALTH AND HUMAN SERVICES DEPARTMENT (HHS) and the Justice Department, with a dedicated funding mechanism and orders to coordinate with state and local law enforcement efforts. It also called for establishment of a "whistle-blower" program that would pay "bounties" to Medicare beneficiaries who identified fraud or abuse, it increased fraud and abuse penalties, and it provided for mandatory expulsion from Medicare and Medicaid of individuals convicted of a felony related to health care fraud or misuse of controlled substances. A controversial provision in the measure required the HHS secretary to issue "advisory opinions" to health entities as to whether proposed business plans violated federal anti-kickback laws.

Finally, the measure included "administrative simplification" provisions calling for the development of uniform standards for the electronic transmission of health information, including health claims, premium payments, injury reports, and enrollment information. The measure also called on Congress to pass legislation designed to protect the privacy of medical records by August 1, 1999, or else standards to be proposed by the HHS secretary within six months would take effect.

The bill's early movement made it look like its passage would be all smooth sailing. On August 2, 1995, the Senate Labor and Human Resources Committee unani-

mously approved the measure under the stewardship of its sponsors, Committee Chairman Nancy Landon Kassebaum, R-Kan., and ranking member Edward Kennedy, D-Mass. That the measure proved noncontroversial was no accident—Kassebaum and Kennedy had specifically set out to craft a bill that included only the elements of the failed health reform effort that were common to both Democratic and Republican bills.

The only naysayer on the measure—at least at the beginning—was the insurance industry. Insurers worried that requiring that policies be provided to individuals who had previously been covered by group plans (a form of GUARANTEED ISSUE) would dramatically increase premiums for everyone in the individual market, because only those most likely to need insurance would purchase it. With poorer risks in the small and price-sensitive individual pool, the companies argued, the premiums would go up, thus driving the healthiest individuals out and making the pool an even poorer risk, until the market would end up so expensive that no one could afford coverage. Sponsors of the measure, however, noted that the provisions were so specific and affected so few individuals (only those who had previously been covered for at least eighteen months) that premiums would be affected only slightly, if at all.

At the behest of insurers, several conservative Republicans in the Senate placed holds on the bill, blocking floor action for the remainder of the year (which was consumed, in any case, by the budget fight that precipitated a major government shutdown). President Clinton attempted to get the issue reignited in his 1996 State of the Union speech, urging Congress to "start by passing the bipartisan bill sponsored by Senator Kennedy and Senator Kassebaum that would require insurance companies to stop dropping people when they switch jobs, and stop denying coverage for pre-existing conditions. Let's all do that."

President Clinton's endorsement spurred Republicans in the House, who decided to proceed with their own bill, which included not only the core of the Kassebaum-Kennedy measure but also other provisions designed to put a "Republican stamp" on health reform efforts, according to House GOP leaders. The resulting measure, passed by the House on a largely party-line vote of 267–151 on March 28, included not only portability provisions but also authority for creation of MSAs, limits on noneconomic damage awards in MEDICAL MALPRACTICE suits, tax-credit provisions, and antifraud efforts. It also would have allowed small groups to band together into "association health plans," that would be exempt from state regulation.

Meanwhile, in the Senate, the measure did not get to the floor until April. Despite efforts of the original backers of the Kassebaum-Kennedy measure to fend off unrelated amendments like those approved by the House, Senate GOP leaders, led by Sen. Bob Dole, R-Kan., who was running for president, decided to put together an amendment package including MSAs and health-related tax credits. Although Kassebaum and Kennedy managed to strip from the GOP package the MSA provisions on a 52–46 vote (with Vice President Gore present in the chamber to cast his vote in case of a tie), the remainder of the GOP amendment package was added to the bill. The measure ultimately passed the Senate by a rare recorded unanimous vote of 100–0 on April 23.

But even with strong support from both the House and Senate and the backing of President Clinton, it still took another three months to iron out the bill's details. Not only did President Clinton vow to veto the measure if it included MSAs, malpractice damage awards, and "association health plans," but Republicans, with an eye toward the November presidential election, were anxious to call President Clinton's bluff. Members also had to decide what to do about a surprise amendment added during Senate consideration of the measure that would have required MENTAL HEALTH PARITY, that is, insurance coverage for mental health equivalent to that for physical ailments.

In the end, neither Republicans nor Democrats wanted to give up the chance for enactment of a health insurance bill, minimal though it was. President Clinton ultimately accepted a limited MSA experiment, whereas Republicans dropped the association health plans and malpractice provision. Also dropped was the mental health amendment, although a stripped-down version of that was approved two months later, as part of an un-

related spending bill for the Department of Housing and Urban Development and the Veterans Administration (PL 104-204). By 82–15, senators approved the language requiring the same annual and lifetime limits on mental health ailments as on all other ailments.

Unfortunately, implementation of HIPAA's requirements did not go as smoothly as lawmakers had hoped. By 1998, five states—California, Massachusetts, Michigan, Missouri, and Rhode Island—had failed to enact legislation necessary to implement the HIPAA requirement. That left the federal Health Care Financing Administration (HCFA) as the fallback enforcement agency under the act. HCFA, however, had little expertise as an insurance regulator, and a fiscal 1999 supplemental funding request to hire more personnel was denied by Congress. HCFA did, however, find cases in which insurers were seeking to evade the law's requirement by delaying the processing of applications, or by providing commissions to agents artificially low so as to deter them from marketing to HIPAA-eligible individuals or small groups. A February 1998 report from the General Accounting Office found that some insurers were charging premiums "140 percent to 600 percent of the standard rate" to HIPAA-eligible individuals.

Health jurisdiction in Congress

One reason Congress seems to have such difficulty making health policy is that major responsibility for health issues is divided over seven separate committees in the U.S. House of Representatives and the Senate. (Another dozen committees have limited health jurisdictions—largely over specific populations, such as veterans, federal employees, and Indians, or specific subject areas. The House and Senate Judiciary Committees, for instance, oversee antitrust law as it relates to health care, as well as MEDICAL MALPRACTICE). Divisions among subject areas are relatively common in Congress—for example, responsibility for most subject areas is shared by an authorizing committee and the appropriations committee in each chamber. That's true for health policy, too, with most major annual spending decisions made by the Labor-Health and Human Services-Education Appropriations Subcommittee in the House and Senate. An important exception is the FOOD AND DRUG ADMINISTRATION (FDA). Although it is part of the HEALTH AND HUMAN SERVICES DEPARTMENT (HHS), for historical reasons its funding is contained in the annual appropriations bill for the Department of Agriculture (and decisions about its budget are made by that subcommittee, rather than Labor-HHS).

Where health policy differs from many other subject areas is that it is also handled by multiple authorizing committees. In the Senate, the Finance Committee has the largest single responsibility over things health-related, with full jurisdiction over MEDICARE, MEDICAID, and the new CHILDREN'S HEALTH INSURANCE PROGRAM (CHIP), authorized in 1997, as well as health-related tax policies. The Senate Health, Education, Labor and Pensions Committee (known until 1999 as the Labor and Human Resources Committee) oversees most of the other health programs run by HHS, including the vast PUBLIC HEALTH SERVICE (which comprises agencies including the NATIONAL INSTITUTES OF HEALTH and the CENTERS FOR DISEASE CONTROL AND PREVENTION), the FDA, and employee-benefit issues (by virtue of its labor jurisdiction).

In the House, primary jurisdiction over health is divided three ways. The tax-writing Ways and Means Committee has considerably less jurisdiction than the Finance Committee on the Senate side, the result of a 1974 committee overhaul intended to lessen the then-vast power of Ways and Means. Although Ways and Means shares Finance's power over health-related tax policies and has exclusive jurisdiction over Part A of Medicare (because it is funded by a payroll tax), it shares jurisdiction over Part B with the Commerce Committee. Commerce, in addition to its shared responsibility for Medicare, has exclusive jurisdiction over Medicaid. The Commerce Committee also has jurisdiction in the House parallel to that of the Senate Labor and Human Resources Committee for the Public Health Service and FDA. Health care issues related to employee benefits, however, are handled in the House by the Education and Workforce Committee.

Health maintenance organization

The oldest and most tightly organized type of MANAGED CARE PLAN, health maintenance organizations (HMOs) have become less popular during the 1990s as patients have demanded more freedom to choose their health care providers and to obtain care outside of their health plans.

Traditionally, there have been four major types of HMOs—staff model, group model, IPA model, and network model.

The oldest type is the staff model, in which the HMO directly employs the physicians and other health care professionals, who in turn care exclusively for the HMO's patients. In staff-model HMOs, the HMO itself bears risk for the cost of care. Staff-model HMOs offer patients the least choice of provider, and the HMO maintains the most control over costs and care; these HMOs are often referred to as *closed-panel* systems.

In the group-model HMO, physicians who practice as a group contract with the HMO to provide care. Kaiser-Permanente is probably the best-known group-model HMO; physicians work for the Permanente group, which in turn provides exclusive services to Kaiser Foundation health plans. For the patient, the difference between a group- and staff-model HMO is essentially invisible; the primary distinction is who bears the risk for the cost of care. In group-model HMOs, the physician group is at risk for most of the cost of the care its patients need. It receives a set fee for each patient (known as CAPITATION), intended to cover all the costs of primary and specialty physician care. In some cases the physician group is also at risk for some or all of the cost of hospital care, on the theory that physicians control hospital use.

In an IPA-model HMO, the HMO contracts with a group of physicians who have banded together into an independent practice association, or IPA. Physicians in IPA-model HMOs can assume risk with the HMO by receiving capitation or can be paid a discounted rate for each patient visit, with year-end bonuses for meeting cost or other utilization targets. Unlike physicians in staff- and group-model HMOs, physicians in IPA-mod-

Henry J. Kaiser (with arm over front seat), founder of Kaiser-Permanente, a group-model health maintenance organization (HMO), accompanies President Franklin D. Roosevelt on a 1942 visit to Kaiser's shipyards. Since 1945, when Kaiser opened his company's health care plan to the public, the plan has grown to become one of the nation's largest nonprofit HMOs.
Source: Kaiser-Permanente, AP

el HMOs may have contracts with other HMOs or other types of health plan.

Finally, network-model HMOs combine elements of the above. As mentioned earlier, by the mid-1990s, so many managed care plans were adopting so many variations on organization and payment that the term *HMO* was well on its way to being rendered essentially meaningless.

Health plan

Health plan is the umbrella term for an individual insurance product offered to a group of individuals or businesses. Health plans may be types of managed care plans (Health Maintenance Organizations (HMOs), Preferred Provider Organizations (PPOs), and the like) or traditional FEE-FOR-SERVICE plans. A single insurance or other company may offer multiple health plans. As distinctions have broken down in managed care plans (many HMOs have adopted practices more typi-

cal of PPOs or indemnity plans and vice versa), many analysts and health care companies have adopted the term *health plan*, as has the managed care industry's trade group, the AMERICAN ASSOCIATION OF HEALTH PLANS, which until the mid-1990s was known as the Group Health Association of America.

Health professional shortage area

A health professional shortage area (HPSA) is an area determined by the federal government to have a smaller supply of primary care health care professionals than is needed to maintain the health of the area's population. Although most HPSAs are in rural areas, some are also located in inner cities, where residents with low incomes may find it virtually impossible to access health care services. The secretary of the U.S. HEALTH AND HUMAN SERVICES DEPARTMENT (HHS) may also designate an individual public or nonprofit private health care facility an HPSA. The Public Health Service

Act stipulates that HPSAs "need not conform to the geographic boundaries of a political subdivision" as long as they represent "a rational area for the delivery of health services." HPSAs are eligible for placement of members of the NATIONAL HEALTH SERVICE CORPS, and health professionals practicing within such areas are eligible for special programs to encourage them to remain there. As of December 1995, HHS had designated 2,617 primary medical HPSAs that would require placement of 5,280 primary care physicians to alleviate the shortage. More than 26.6 million Americans lived in those designated shortage areas.

Health Resources and Services Administration (HRSA)

The Health Resources and Services Administration is the agency within the U.S. HEALTH AND HUMAN SERVICES DEPARTMENT most directly involved with the actual provision of medical services to patients, primarily those who, because of their incomes or where they live, would have little or no other access to health care. With a budget of $4.3 billion in fiscal 1999, HRSA provides PRIMARY CARE services through the Consolidated Health Centers Program, which includes COMMUNITY HEALTH CENTERS, MIGRANT HEALTH CENTERS, the Health Care for the Homeless program, and the Health Care for Residents of Public Housing program. It administers the TITLE X program (of the Public Health Service Act), which provides funds to family planning clinics, and the MATERNAL AND CHILD HEALTH SERVICES BLOCK GRANT and Healthy Start programs, which are aimed at lowering infant mortality rates and improving the health of the nation's youngest citizens. HRSA also oversees programs for individuals with specific health conditions. It administers the RYAN WHITE COMPREHENSIVE AIDS RESOURCES AND EMERGENCY (CARE) ACT, which underwrites treatment and prevention efforts to fight HIV and AIDS, as well as a much smaller federal program to treat those with Hansen's Disease (leprosy), and it oversees the nation's organ transplant program. HRSA also oversees

the federal government's efforts to train future health care practitioners, including doctors, nurses, and other health professionals, with an eye toward expanding the number of primary care providers and improving the geographic distribution of health care professionals. HRSA's NATIONAL HEALTH SERVICE CORPS combines the agency's missions of delivering services and training practitioners by providing scholarships or loan repayments to primary care practitioners who agree to serve for a period of time in areas with few or no other health care providers.

Health Security Act

The Health Security Act is the official name of the legislation proposed by President Bill Clinton to restructure the nation's health care system. When Clinton was sworn in as president on January 20, 1993, the country appeared ready for a major overhaul of its health system. On the one hand, HEALTH CARE SPENDING appeared out of control. In 1993, health care spending reached $903 billion, more than double the amount spent as recently as 1987. The costs were afflicting all health payers, from the federal government via the fast-growing MEDICARE program, to the states, who shared responsibility with the federal government for MEDICAID, to employers, who provided health insurance to their workers. At the same time, the number of Americans with no insurance was rising nearly as rapidly as health care spending. In 1992, on any given day, about 38.5 million Americans were uninsured, about 17 percent of the population under sixty-five.

Even health care providers were ready for a change. In 1990, the AMERICAN MEDICAL ASSOCIATION, which had helped sink several previous efforts to enact national health insurance, endorsed a requirement that employers provide insurance for their workers. Also backing an "employer mandate" was the HEALTH INSURANCE ASSOCIATION OF AMERICA.

But what really put health reform on the agenda was a surprise in a special Senate election in Pennsylvania in 1991 to fill the unexpired term of Republican John

Heinz, who had died in a helicopter crash that spring. Republican Dick Thornburgh, who had served two terms as Pennsylvania's governor, was a prohibitive favorite to defeat the little-known Harris Wofford, a political neophyte who had been appointed to fill the seat by Gov. Robert Casey. But Wofford (whose campaign was run by James Carville, who would go on to advise Bill Clinton) latched onto the health care issue. "If criminals have the right to a lawyer, I think working Americans should have a right to a doctor," Wofford said in what came to be a famous television ad. Wofford went on to defeat Thornburgh, and both Republicans and Democrats set out to do something about health care.

Bill Clinton was not the Democratic candidate in 1992 with the deepest background in health policy. Clinton was better known in Washington for his work on the 1988 welfare reform bill, the Family Support Act, and for efforts on education and child care initiatives. During the primaries, Sen. Tom Harkin (D-Iowa), Sen. Bob Kerrey (D-Neb.), and former California governor Jerry Brown all were more aggressive than Clinton about spotlighting the need for comprehensive health care reform. But once elected, Clinton quickly elevated health care to the top of his agenda, irritating those who supported Clinton's other major domestic priority, welfare reform.

But the process of turning a campaign outline in favor of a concept called MANAGED COMPETITION into an actual legislative proposal—all while trying to put together the first Democratic administration in twenty-four years—proved a daunting task. Clinton appointed a task force headed by his wife, Hillary Clinton, who turned out to be a lightning rod for criticism. The task force staff was headed by political neophyte Ira Magaziner, who turned what was already an unwieldy task into a monumental one. Magaziner assembled more than five hundred health policy experts from around the country in various nooks and crannies of the White House and executive office buildings. These experts worked literally around the clock on what would become the Health Security Act.

Unveiled in a speech on September 22, 1993, the Health Security Act had already earned more than its share of enmity and derision. Groups who should have been inclined to support it, such as the American Medical Association, which had already endorsed an employer mandate, instead felt shut out of the secretive process. In an effort to gain public sympathy, the president and first lady had made another misstep by painting insurance companies and drug-makers as greedy enemies of reform, thus ensuring their opposition. On Capitol Hill, health policymakers were annoyed that the president was putting together such a detailed proposal, insisting that it was *their* job to flesh out the specifics.

But for all the grief heaped on the 1,342-page document, Clinton's Health Security Act was actually a more elegant proposal than many gave it credit for. Although its enormity and complexity made it a hard sell politically, most health policy analysts—even those who opposed it for ideological reasons—conceded that it probably would have worked as intended had it been enacted into law.

The Health Security Act sought to build on the existing health care system by requiring employers to provide most workers and their families with health insurance and to pay most of the costs. To address complaints from small employers that the costs would drive them out of business, the plan proposed generous subsidies. Also subsidized would be low-income families and individuals, who would otherwise have had difficulty paying their share of the premiums. Overall spending would have been controlled primarily by competition between health plans, but also by fallback limits on the amount premiums could rise each year. These "premium caps" were a clever device that allowed the Clinton administration to claim (correctly) that it was not imposing price controls on medical services. But the caps would have forced just such eventualities—or else outright rationing—by the insurance companies themselves.

At the heart of the proposal were regional "health alliances" that would pool premiums from businesses and individuals and negotiate with insurance companies. (These were originally called *health insurance purchasing cooperatives* by those who devised the concept of managed competition, but Clinton administration officials discarded the term as sounding "too communistic," in the words of one aide.)

According to administration number crunchers, because the majority of new costs would be borne by employers, the remainder of the program could have been financed by a combination of a seventy-five-cents-per-pack increase in the cigarette tax; a one percent tax on the largest corporations (those with more than 5,000 workers) if they opted not to join the alliances; reductions of $124 billion in Medicare, $65 billion in Medicaid, and $40 billion in other federal health programs; and increased revenues that would flow to the federal treasury through reduced health care costs. Not only would that financing leave a $45 billion cushion in case the subsidies were more costly than anticipated, administration budget officials insisted, but the plan would also produce another $58 billion to lower the deficit.

Not surprisingly, the CONGRESSIONAL BUDGET OFFICE (CBO) didn't share that opinion of the measure. Over the first six years, said CBO, not only would the plan fail to reduce the deficit, it would add $74 billion to it. The CBO also opined that the mandatory employer contributions toward their workers' health coverage should be treated as a tax. Nevertheless, much of the rest of the CBO report on the Health Security Act was favorable. Analysts said the plan would likely cover everyone, as advertised, and, after the year 2004, would actually reduce national health care spending. It also defended the plan's scope. "A major reason for its complexity . . . is that the proposal outlines in legislation the steps that would actually have to be taken to accomplish its goals. No other proposal has come close to attempting this. Other health care proposals might appear equally complex if they provided the same level of detail as the administration on the implementation requirements," the report said.

Unfortunately for the administration, its staff proved more skilled at devising the plan than at selling it. In retrospect, though, the battle was probably lost long before it was truly engaged. Democrats were badly split on health reform—a significant minority favored a SINGLE PAYER plan like Canada's, whereas another faction favored a less sweeping version of managed competition

that included no employer mandate, no premium caps, and would not have guaranteed coverage to every American. Republicans, who had early in the debate rallied around a proposal for an "individual mandate," by later in 1993 were emboldened by polls showing declining support for the Clinton plan. They would ultimately back away from support for any far-reaching proposal.

And at center stage were the opponents, led by the NATIONAL FEDERATION OF INDEPENDENT BUSINESS, the small business lobby, which vehemently opposed the employer mandate, and the HEALTH INSURANCE ASSOCIATION OF AMERICA, whose "Harry and Louise" ads picturing a couple at their kitchen table puzzling over the complexity of the Clinton plan came to epitomize the opposition.

Congress continued to go through the motions—during the early months of 1994, nearly a dozen committees in the House and Senate worked on various aspects of a health reform plan. The Senate actually took up a bill on August 9, postponing its traditional summer recess in an attempt to rescue the floundering proposal. (House debate never reached the floor). But after two weeks of debate with little to show for it, the Senate left for a delayed vacation, and leaders conceded that a comprehensive bill could not be passed. By the end of September, it became clear that even a scaled-back proposal was not in the cards. And in November, voters told Congress what they thought of the entire escapade by giving control of both the House and Senate to Republicans for the first time in forty years.

The fact that no legislation emerged from the wrenching debate of 1993–1994 has colored the fact that Congress did come closer to enacting a national health insurance scheme than in any of its earlier tries in the 1930s, 1940s, and 1970s. In 1994, four major congressional committees (House Ways and Means, House Education and Labor, Senate Finance, and Senate Labor and Human Resources) reported five broad bills (House Education and Labor produced two measures, including a single payer proposal reported to the floor without recommendation). Four of those bills would have guaranteed "universal coverage" for all Americans. But in the end the Health Security Act, like so many national health insurance proposals before it, was consigned to a historical footnote.

Health services research

Health services research, according to the Association for Health Services Research, is defined as "a field of inquiry using quantitative or qualitative methodology to examine the impact of the organization, financing and management of health services on the access to, delivery, cost, outcomes and quality of services." Like biomedical research, health services research is conducted by university-affiliated researchers, policy research organizations, and health care providers, particularly MANAGED CARE companies, who want to examine things like technology assessment. Such assessments can help determine if new treatment is really more effective and/or less expensive than an older procedure. Health services researchers also examine the outcomes of various medical interventions to help determine which work best, and they explore health system organizational issues, such as the supply of health professionals, the number of uninsured, and the consequences of being uninsured. At the federal level, the AGENCY FOR HEALTH CARE POLICY AND RESEARCH (AHCPR) helps coordinate health services research efforts.

HEDIS

HEDIS stands for Health Plan Employer Data and Information Set, a set of measures used by employers and other purchasers of health care to assess the quality of care provided by a health plan. HEDIS was developed by the NATIONAL COMMITTEE FOR QUALITY ASSURANCE (NCQA) with the input of employers and MANAGED CARE plans to facilitate comparisons between plans. The fifty-three separate measures included in the latest iteration of HEDIS, known as HEDIS 1999, examine the effectiveness and availability of care (such as the percentage of children receiving immunizations or the percentage of women screened for breast and cervical cancer), satisfaction (as measured by a survey), health plan stability (as measured by turnover rates for patients and providers), use of services (such as the rate of childbirth by cesarean section and well-child visits), and cost of care (as measured by rate trends). More than 90 percent of health plans use HEDIS, according to NCQA; plans seeking NCQA accreditation must report ten of the measures, as well as the consumer satisfaction survey. Consumer advocates, however, have complained that because HEDIS statistics are self-reported by the plans, they are not as reliable as they could be. Previous versions of HEDIS have also focused more on inputs to care (such as immunization rates) rather than outcomes. New measures in HEDIS 1999 examine such intermediate outcome measures as whether patients hospitalized with heart problems have had their cholesterol levels checked and brought under control and whether patients being treated with antidepressant medications are being monitored frequently enough.

Hill-Burton Act

The Hill-Burton Act is the colloquial name of the Hospital Survey and Construction Act (PL 79-725). Passed in 1946 and named for its sponsors, Sen. Lister Hill of Alabama and Harold Burton of Ohio, the act was intended to boost the building and rehabilitation of hospitals that had fallen into disrepair during the Great Depression and World War II. Since its inception, the Hill-Burton Act has provided more than $4.6 billion in grants and $1.5 billion in loans to nearly 6,800 health care facilities in more than 4,000 communities. In exchange for the federal aid, facilities must agree to provide free or low-cost care to those without insurance or otherwise unable to pay their bills. In 1972 Congress placed a twenty-year limit on the free care obligations; however, 1975 amendments to the Hill-Burton Act establishing federal grants, loans, and interest subsidies required that uncompensated services be provided in perpetuity. From 1996 to 1998, the HEALTH RESOURCES AND SERVICES ADMINISTRATION (HRSA), which oversees the Hill-Burton program, had assured an estimated $700 million in free or reduced-price care for some 2 million people.

Home health care

Home health care is the provision of health-related services inside a patient's home. Home health care can range from highly technical medical services provided by a registered nurse, to Meals on Wheels deliveries, to help with household chores or such "activities of daily living" as dressing and bathing. Both MEDICARE and MEDICAID cover the provision of some, but not all, home health services.

Medicare covers services only to those who are homebound or too ill or frail to leave home on a regular basis or without considerable effort (such as requiring crutches or a wheelchair) but not disabled enough to require institutional care. Patients must require either skilled nursing or skilled physical, speech, or occupational therapy services (as opposed to less complex care such as simple bandage changing), as certified by a physician, but only on a part-time or intermittent basis. If a doctor certifies the need for care, Medicare will nevertheless also pay for less skilled care provided by a home health aide in addition to the skilled care.

In recent years, Medicare spending on home health care has risen dramatically. In 1989, it accounted for 2.5 percent of all Medicare spending; by 1996 that had risen to 9.3 percent. Both the number of beneficiaries using the benefit (which requires no deductibles or copayments) and the number of visits have been rising. In an attempt to stem that rise, Congress in the 1997 Balanced Budget Act called for creation of a PROSPECTIVE PAYMENT SYSTEM for home care that would base payments on the estimated cost according to a patient's condition, rather than on what the home health provider actually spent. Congress imposed an interim system of payments until the new system could be devised and implemented. When the HEALTH CARE FINANCING ADMINISTRATION announced in 1998 that it would not be able to meet the October 1, 1999, deadline for that new payment system, however, Congress was forced to revise the interim system, after beneficiaries and home health providers alike complained that it was forcing some providers out of business. Indeed, in 1999 the MEDICARE PAYMENT ADVISORY COMMISSION (MEDPAC) found that in the first year of the new payment system, Medicare spending for home health services actually declined in 1998. MedPAC also found that fewer Medicare beneficiaries were receiving home health services and the number of agencies participating in the program declined. The General Accounting Office, however, found that despite the payment changes, there was little evidence that beneficiaries' access to home health care was being threatened.

Hospice

Hospice care is a form of care for dying patients that emphasizes comfort over cure, focusing on managing pain and relieving symptoms rather than on trying to extend a patient's life. Hospice care can be provided in a stand-alone facility or in a terminally ill patient's home. Hospice services focus on preparing both the patient and the family for an impending death, using an interdisciplinary team of health care and social services providers, including doctors, nurses, home health aides, mental health professionals, and members of the clergy. MEDICARE covers hospice services, provided a physician certifies that a patient is terminally ill—defined as having a life expectancy of six months or less. Unlike traditional Medicare, Medicare's hospice benefit does cover the cost of outpatient prescription drugs (to treat pain and other symptoms) and "respite care" to provide a break for a family member providing care.

Hospital Insurance (HI)

The formal name of Part A of MEDICARE, the Hospital Insurance (HI) program covers not only hospital, but also home health, nursing home, and hospice care. Although fewer beneficiaries use it, Medicare's Part A is the larger of the traditional program's two parts; with

During a tour of Truman Medical Center, in Kansas City, First Lady Hillary Clinton comforts a cerebral palsy patient who lacks health insurance. Participants in Medicare's Hospital Insurance program are entitled not only to home health, nursing home, and hospice care but also to hospital services. Source: Colin Braley, Reuters

benefit payments totaling $128.6 billion in 1996. That is because the services Part A covers—particularly hospital and skilled care in a nursing home—are among Medicare's most expensive. About 22 percent of Medicare's 38 million Part A beneficiaries received services covered by the program in 1996.

Part A is funded by a dedicated portion of the Social Security tax, specifically 1.45 percent of income paid by both employers and workers. Unlike the Social Security tax, however, which is assessed only up to a floating income level ($68,400 in 1998), workers and their employers continue to pay the Medicare tax on all earnings. Congress raised the cap to $125,000 of income in 1990 and eliminated it altogether in 1993 in order to help boost the ailing financial status of the HI trust fund. Income taxes on Social Security payments that some recipients must pay also go to shore up the Medicare trust fund.

Hospitalist

A recent trend in health care delivery is the use of a hospitalist, a physician who specializes in overseeing care for patients in the hospital, working with, or sometimes in place of, the patient's primary care doctor. The National Association of Inpatient Physicians, formed in 1997 to foster the spread of the hospitalist movement, estimates that in 1998, 2,500 to 3,000 such doctors were practicing in hospitals across the United States. Backers of the hospitalist trend say it can benefit both patients and their regular physician caregivers. Hospitalists are more familiar with the workings of their institution and better able to navigate procedural hurdles, are on-site all day (while most hospitalized patients' primary care doctors are back in their offices seeing other patients) and better able to respond to emergencies or even discharge patients who are ready to go home, and are more accustomed to seeing sicker patients than the average office-based physician. On the other side of the coin, however, some primary care practitioners worry that patients would be better off with a physician who knows them, their families, and their medical histories. Office-based doctors are also worried that if they no longer see hospitalized patients, their skills in caring for the sickest may decline.

House Appropriations Committee

The House Appropriations Committee oversees the "discretionary" portion of the federal budget. The committee writes thirteen separate spending bills each year that are required for the government to run. Through the Labor-Health and Human Services-Education ap-propriation, the committee sets spending levels for most of the HEALTH AND HUMAN SERVICES DEPART-MENT (HHS), with three major exceptions. MEDICARE and MEDICAID, as "entitlement" programs, are funded according to estimates of how much they will cost; leg-islative changes to affect those costs must be initiated by "authorizing" committees. Additionally, for historical reasons, the FOOD AND DRUG ADMINISTRATION, although part of HHS, is funded as part of the Agricul-ture appropriations bill. The Appropriations Commit-tee also sets spending levels for other health-related programs, including the INDIAN HEALTH SERVICE (funded in the Interior bill), health care for veterans (funded in the VA-HUD-Independent agencies bill), health care and insurance for the military (through the Defense bill), health care for those incarcerated in feder-al prisons (through the Commerce-State-Justice bill), and health insurance for federal employees (through the Treasury-Postal Service bill).

House Commerce Committee

After the SENATE FINANCE COMMITTEE, the House Commerce Committee has the broadest health jurisdiction in Congress, and exercises it regularly. The Commerce panel oversees the FOOD AND DRUG AD-MINISTRATION (FDA), the PUBLIC HEALTH SERVICE, and all of the MEDICAID program. The Commerce Committee also shares jurisdiction with the Ways and Means Committee over Part B of MEDICARE (Ways and Means has exclusive jurisdiction over Medicare Part A, because it is financed by a payroll tax, and over taxes in the House). During the 1980s, under the chairmanship of John Dingell, D-Mich., and Henry Waxman, D-Calif., who chaired the panel's Health and Environment Subcommittee, Commerce led efforts to broaden Medi-caid substantially and break its ties with cash assistance programs. Commerce also initiated laws to strengthen federal standards for clinical laboratories (see CLINICAL LABORATORY IMPROVEMENT ACT), and to speed up FDA approval of prescription drugs by imposing user

fees (see PRESCRIPTION DRUG USER FEE ACT). Under GOP leadership since 1995, Commerce took the lead on the 1997 FDA Modernization Act and the new CHIL-DREN'S HEALTH INSURANCE PROGRAM (CHIP) included as part of the 1997 Balanced Budget Act (PL 105-33).

House Education and Workforce Committee

Formerly the House Education and Labor Commit-tee, the House Education and Workforce Committee has health jurisdiction related to employee benefits. The committee oversees the EMPLOYEE RETIREMENT IN-COME SECURITY ACT as well as legislation that would require employers to provide health coverage. Tradi-tionally populated by very liberal Democrats and very conservative Republicans (largely for the purpose of pushing or opposing legislation of interest to organized labor), during the health reform debate in 1994 the pan-el reported legislation (albeit "without recommenda-tion") that would have created a SINGLE PAYER health system funded by the federal government.

House Ways and Means Committee

The House Ways and Means Committee exercises significant influence over health care policy through its oversight of the MEDICARE program. Ways and Means has exclusive jurisdiction in the U.S. House of Repre-sentatives for Medicare Part A, and shares jurisdiction over Part B with the Commerce Committee. Ways and Means also exercises control over health policy through its jurisdiction over taxes. The U.S. system of employer-provided insurance grew up largely because health ben-efits were made tax deductible for employers who gave them and the benefits were excluded from taxation from the workers who receive them. In recent years Ways and Means has used its tax power to increase the deductibility of premiums for self-insured individuals, to make private long-term care insurance more finan-cially viable, and to fund a program to compensate children who suffer adverse reactions to required vaccines against childhood illnesses by imposing an excise tax on those vaccines. Ways and Means' health jurisdiction used to be more sweeping still but was scaled back in a 1974 overhaul intended to dilute the panel's vast power. Ways and Means, however, remains so influential that it is still referred to almost reflexively as the "powerful Ways and Means Committee."

Hyde amendment

The term *Hyde amendment* actually refers to a series of amendments on various appropriations bills barring federal funding of abortion in most cases. The amendment, which has been altered over the years as abortion-related majorities in Congress and the White House have shifted back and forth, is named for Rep. Henry Hyde, R-Ill., one of the best-known abortion opponents in Congress. But Hyde was not in fact the author of the original Hyde amendment. That distinction belonged to Rep. Silvio Conte, R-Mass., a moderate who was the ranking Republican on the Labor-Health and Human Services-Education (Labor-HHS) Appropriations Subcommittee.

Congress first engaged the question of whether it should fund abortions in 1974, just a year after the Supreme Court legalized the procedure nationwide in the landmark case ROE V. WADE. That year the House and Senate took positions opposite of those they would take for the next decade-and-a-half. The House voted no on the first amendment to the fiscal 1975 Labor-Health, Education and Welfare bill that would have cut off abortion funding (offered not by Hyde, but by Rep. Angelo D. Roncallo, R-N.Y.). Meanwhile, the Senate later that year approved an amendment offered by Dewey F. Bartlett, R-Okla., to bar funding for abortions or to encourage abortions "except to save the life of the mother." It was passed by voice vote after a tabling motion failed by 34–50. The amendment, however, was dropped in conference.

The House first passed a funding restriction offered by Hyde on June 24, 1976. As approved by the chamber on a vote of 207–167, it forbade the use of funds in the

Named for Rep. Henry Hyde, R-Ill., one of Congress's best-known abortion opponents, the Hyde amendment sought to bar federal funding of the procedure in most cases. Source: Scott J. Ferrell, Congressional Quarterly

bill "to pay for abortions or to promote or encourage abortions." The Senate, however, unlike two years earlier, was not inclined to go along. At the instigation of Sen. Bob Packwood, R-Ore., who would go on to become one of that chamber's leading abortion-rights advocates, the Senate voted 57–28 to strike Hyde's amendment from the bill.

The measure was in conference for more than eleven weeks, with both sides refusing to back down and each rejecting dozens of compromise proposals. Finally, on September 15, conferees agreed to a compromise offered by Conte barring abortion funding "except where the life of the mother would be endangered if the fetus were carried to term."

That 1976 agreement, however, left many issues unclear. Conte himself said that in his view, some psychological factors, such as suicidal tendencies of a pregnant woman, could constitute enough of a threat to a woman's life to justify an abortion. And conferees in their report said they did not intend that the language bar federal funding for the "treatment of rape or incest victims."

The 1976 language did not actually take effect until August 1977, after the Supreme Court held in three separate rulings that states were not required to use public funds for elective abortions. That prompted a federal judge to lift the injunction on the federal restrictions and the funding ban took effect for the first time, reducing MEDICAID abortions from about 300,000 per year to a few thousand.

Meanwhile, even as the funding case continued in the courts the debate in Congress raged on. The House continued to insist on its no-exceptions funding ban and the Senate stuck just as steadfastly to exceptions for life of the woman, rape, incest, and abortions considered "medically necessary" for the woman's health. The standoff persisted for five months, through twenty-five roll call votes in the two chambers until a compromise was reached. The final language, crafted primarily by Sen. Edward Brooke, R-Mass., and the then-House minority whip Robert H. Michel, R-Ill., was seen at the time as a defeat for both sides. It permitted federal funding of abortions in cases of life endangerment, rape, and in-cest, and "in those instances where severe and long-lasting physical health damage to the mother would result if the pregnancy were carried to term when so determined by two physicians." The battle continued through 1978, with the same language ultimately adopted.

For the next three years, abortion-related controversies prevented completion of regular Labor-HHS funding bills, with Congress moving gradually to narrow the exceptions to the funding ban. Buttressed by the Supreme Court's 1980 decision upholding the right of Congress to deny funding and by a right-to-life movement picking up considerable political momentum, Congress stiffened its funding ban in each succeeding year. In 1979, Senate conferees ultimately agreed to drop the exception permitting funding for abortions necessary to prevent severe health damage. The following year, the continuing resolution to keep the departments running required rape victims to report the crime within seventy-two hours and permitted states to ban abortion funding if they wanted to. By 1981, the Senate agreed to drop the rape and incest exceptions altogether, resulting in the language (forbidding all abortion funding except to save the life of the woman) that would be the law of the land for the next twelve years.

After some minor skirmishing from 1982 through 1988, in 1989 the Hyde amendment again took center stage in the nation's abortion debate. Following the Supreme Court's decision in WEBSTER V. REPRODUCTIVE HEALTH SERVICES OF MISSOURI, upholding a series of state restrictions previously considered unconstitutional under the framework of *Roe v. Wade,* abortion-rights forces in Congress and in the country mobilized in fear that the court might overturn the right to abortion entirely. Their principal goal that year was to reinstitute the rape and incest exceptions to the Hyde funding ban. Although the Senate had periodically voted for rape and incest exceptions during the 1980s, in October of that year, the House voted for the first time in eleven years to relax the Hyde restrictions. The 211–206 tally represented a swing of fifty votes from 1988, when members voted 216–166 to maintain the more restrictive language.

The language ultimately did not change—President Bush vetoed the Labor-HHS appropriation and the

House failed to override the veto by fifty-one votes. In 1990, the issue was barely addressed. The Senate adopted an amendment to grant the rape and incest exception, but antiabortion lawmakers appended to that another amendment, requiring abortion providers who received funds under the bill to notify the parents of a minor forty-eight hours before the abortion could be performed. Because it was procedurally impossible to separate the rape-incest language from the parental notification requirement, abortion rights advocates dropped the entire matter.

In 1991 and 1992, abortion-rights forces focused on other matters, notably unsuccessful attempts to block the so-called GAG RULE barring federally funded family planning clinics from counseling or referring for abortion.

In 1993, it appeared for a time that all abortion funding restrictions could be dropped. But even with abortion-rights majorities in both Houses and abortion-rights supporter President Bill Clinton in the White House, it was not to be. During House floor consideration of the Labor-HHS bill, abortion opponents used a parliamentary maneuver involving a precedent from 1908 to insert into the bill language to ban funding, but, because they recognized the reality of the situation, they allowed rape and incest exceptions. "I didn't think the votes were there anymore for a straight ban on abortion funding," Hyde said at the time. The Senate, although traditionally more supportive of abortion rights than the House, nonetheless rejected its Appropriations Committee's recommendation to lift the funding ban entirely and adopted the House-passed language. Part of the impetus was the odd way the Medicaid statute was drafted—in the absence of language banning funding of abortions, coverage would have been mandatory for the states—overturning the laws of at least thirty-one states.

Although the fiscal 1994 Labor-HHS bill, as signed into law, represented the first time since 1977 that Congress had actually loosened an abortion restriction, that relaxation was seen as a major loss by abortion-rights backers, who had hoped to eliminate the Hyde language entirely. It was also seen as a major victory for abortion

foes, who found themselves in the odd position of offering as an amendment language that until 1993 they had ardently opposed.

The Republican-controlled 104th Congress attempted to strengthen the Hyde language once again, with the House passing language seeking to make it optional for states to fund abortions in cases of rape and incest. (The previous ban mandated such coverage because of the way the Medicaid law is drafted.) The Senate refused to relent, however, and in the end the language was left unchanged from the previous year. The issue was not engaged in 1996 on the fiscal 1997 bill.

In 1995, Republicans attempted for the first time to codify the Hyde language into permanent Medicaid law. Because appropriations bills apply only for a single year, the ban had to be renewed each year. But as part of legislation vetoed by President Clinton, the Republican-backed Balanced Budget Act would have written the then-existing Hyde language—preventing funding for abortions except for those needed to save the life of the woman, or in cases of rape or incest—directly into the Medicaid statute.

In 1997, antiabortion forces decided it was time for an "update" of the Hyde language to take into account the fact that a significant portion of Medicaid recipients were being moved into managed care plans. Worried that plans could offer abortion services without technically running afoul of the funding ban, Hyde wrote language to add that no federal funds could be used to pay premiums for plans that provided abortions. Abortion-rights forces, however, complained that Hyde's language was so broad that it could end up forcing managed care plans to drop abortion coverage for their non-Medicaid enrollees. Hyde and Rep. Nita Lowey, D-N.Y., negotiated the issue for weeks, finally coming up with a compromise. The new language also refined the "life of the woman" exception, noting that abortions would be allowed to be funded only if the endangerment was "a physical disorder, physical injury, or physical illness, including a life-endangering physical condition caused by or arising from the pregnancy itself." The compromise was included in the fiscal 1999 bill as well.

Also in 1997, abortion foes again sought to codify the

Hyde language during consideration of that year's Balanced Budget Act (PL 105-33), which did become law. That measure wrote into permanent law for the new CHILDREN'S HEALTH INSURANCE PROGRAM (CHIP) Hyde-type language barring federal funding of abortion except in cases of rape or incest or to save the life of the woman. Dropped from the bill, however, was language to rewrite the definition of "medically necessary" to specifically exclude abortion, which would have amounted to a permanent codification of the Hyde amendment for all of Medicaid.

I

ICD-9 codes

The ninth revision of the International Classification of Diseases, clinical modification, referred to as ICD-9-CM, is a standardized list of codes to identify specific medical diagnoses. Although the AMERICAN MEDICAL ASSOCIATION had developed Current Procedural Terminology Codes (known as CPT CODES) to standardize the reporting of medical procedures, ICD-9 codes help identify what ailments those procedures are actually treating. Such information is invaluable in "outcomes" research, determining which treatments work best for which conditions.

The current system is maintained by a joint effort of two agencies of the HEALTH AND HUMAN SERVICES DEPARTMENT: the National Center for Health Statistics and the HEALTH CARE FINANCING ADMINISTRATION. The agencies coordinate annual code revisions, which are published each year in the *Federal Register*. The Central Office on ICD-9-CM, which maintains the system, is itself a public-private partnership that also includes the private-sector American Hospital Association and American Health Information Management Association.

Incidence

Often confused with PREVALENCE, which is the total number of people with a disease, incidence is the frequency of new cases of a particular disease.

Income-related premium

The income-related premium is a proposal for requiring wealthier MEDICARE beneficiaries to pay more for their coverage under the program's Part B, which helps pay physician and other outpatient costs. Under the original Medicare law, premiums for the Part B program were to cover half the program's costs; in the 1997 Balanced Budget Act (PL 105-33), Congress permanently fixed the premium at 25 percent of the program's cost (after having set it at that level periodically since 1982). That means that 75 percent of Part B costs are subsidized directly from federal general revenues (as opposed to Part A of the program, funded from the 1.45 percent payroll tax paid by both employers and workers). For the past decade, a significant minority of lawmakers and other interest groups have pressed to lower or eliminate the subsidy for those who can afford it.

Medicare's first experience with an income-related premium came with passage of the 1988 MEDICARE CATASTROPHIC COVERAGE ACT (PL 100-360). That measure required those BENEFICIARIES with income tax liabilities greater than $150 to pay a "supplemental premium" (starting at $22.50) along with their income taxes. Although even the top premium ($800) was smaller than the existing Part B subsidy at the time (which was just over $1,000), beneficiaries rebelled at the new costs for new coverage they said they didn't want, and Congress repealed the entire program in 1989.

President George Bush, in his fiscal 1992 budget, proposed to reverse the subsidy for Medicare Part B for individuals with incomes over $125,000 and couples with incomes over $150,000, affecting about 600,000 of

Medicare's 34 million beneficiaries. For those above the income threshold, their Part B premiums would be three times higher, requiring them to pay 75 percent of their Part B costs, with the government subsidizing only 25 percent. Critics charged that the proposal would undermine Medicare's popularity as a "universal" program and suggested that such a radical change should be made only if the program was otherwise substantially restructured (presumably to provide more benefits). The proposal was not accepted by Congress, still wary after the catastrophic debacle two years earlier.

President Bill Clinton next floated the concept. As part of his HEALTH SECURITY ACT, Medicare premiums would have tripled for individuals with incomes over $100,000 and for couples with incomes over $125,000. But in exchange, Medicare beneficiaries would have gotten a much-desired outpatient prescription drug benefit. That proposal died along with the rest of health reform.

Income-related Medicare premiums next surfaced as part of the new Republican Congress's 1995 Balanced Budget Act. That measure, which President Clinton vetoed, would have begun charging beneficiaries higher premiums at income levels of $60,000 for individuals and $90,000 for couples. Unlike previous proposals, which would have cut the Part B subsidy to 25 percent for the wealthiest beneficiaries, the GOP plan would have phased out the subsidy completely for individuals with incomes of $110,000 and couples with incomes of $150,000 or more.

In 1997, the issue arose yet again during consideration of the 1997 Balanced Budget Act (PL 105-33), which did become law. The Senate passed an amendment that would have begun charging higher premiums to individuals with incomes over $50,000, and couples with incomes above $75,000. As with the failed GOP proposal from 1995, those with incomes above $100,000 and couples with incomes above $125,000 would have had to pay the full actuarial cost of Part B, eliminating the federal subsidy altogether. Although President Clinton was careful not to oppose the concept of the income-related premium (since he had himself proposed such an increase only three years earlier), the administration did

complain that the structure of the Senate plan would have been administratively unworkable, since the Internal Revenue Service and the HEALTH CARE FINANCING ADMINISTRATION would essentially have had to track each Medicare beneficiary's monthly income to determine the appropriate premium. The administration and advocacy groups for the elderly also complained that phasing out the subsidy entirely for those with the highest incomes (as opposed to merely replacing the current 75 percent subsidy with a 25 percent subsidy) could lead more affluent beneficiaries to drop out of Medicare altogether, potentially leaving the program with a sicker risk pool and driving premiums up for everyone left. The provision was ultimately dropped. (See also MEANS TESTING.)

Indian Health Service

Established in 1924 and transferred from the Interior Department to the HEALTH AND HUMAN SERVICES DEPARTMENT in 1955, the Indian Health Service (IHS) provides care to an estimated 1.4 million of the nation's 2 million American Indians and Alaska natives who are members of 557 federally recognized tribes in thirty-four states. The Indian Health Service has approximately 14,500 employees (in addition to a tribal and urban Indian health workforce of 10,000) who care annually for 90,000 hospitalized patients and make 7 million outpatient visits, 4 million community health representative client contacts, and 2.4 million dental visits in 37 hospitals, 60 health centers, 3 school health centers, and 46 health stations.

The original authority for the Indian Health Service is the Snyder Act of 1921, which authorized funds "for the relief of distress and conservation of health [and] for the employment of . . . physicians . . . for Indian tribes throughout the United States." The Indian Self-Determination and Education Assistance Act (PL 93-638) provided tribes the option of operating their own health care systems or retaining the services of the IHS. The IHS also helps fund sanitation improvements, such as water and sewerage facilities, solid waste disposal systems, and technical assistance for operations and maintenance. Based in Rockville, Maryland, the IHS operated with a budget of $2.6 billion in fiscal 1999.

Indirect Medical Education Payments

The Indirect Medical Education (IME) payment is an additional payment made by MEDICARE to teaching hospitals to compensate them for the additional costs incurred in caring for Medicare beneficiaries. Indirect costs include the extra demands placed on the hospital staff as a result of teaching activities or extra tests or procedures ordered or performed by physicians-in-training. Teaching hospitals also tend to attract sicker-than-average patients and maintain higher staff-to-patient ratios, thus increasing their costs. In fiscal 1997, Medicare made an estimated $4.5 billion in IME payments to teaching hospitals; however, provisions of the Balanced Budget Act (PL 105-33), passed in 1997, will gradually reduce IME payments by an estimated $5.6 billion by the year 2002. Medicare makes separate payments for direct medical education costs, such as the actual salaries paid to training physicians. (See DIRECT MEDICAL EDUCATION)

Infertility clinic regulation

Responding to complaints and scandals involving clinics set up to help infertile couples become pregnant, Congress in 1992 enacted legislation (PL 102-624) re-

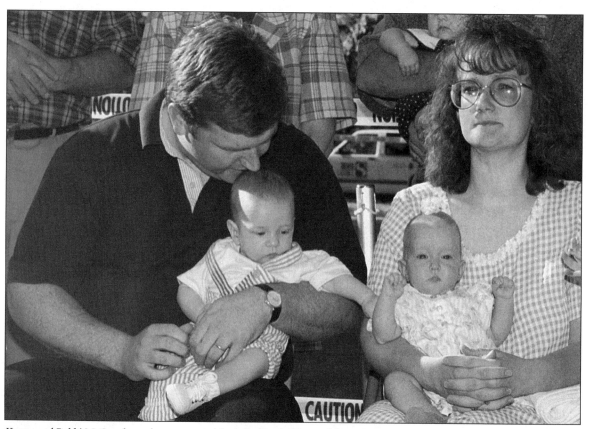

Kenny and Bobbi McCaughey, who were treated for infertility, hold two of their septuplets, born in November 1997. Source: Mark Davitt, Reuters

quiring stricter infertility clinic regulation, including annual publication of individual clinic success rates.

An estimated 2.4 million couples were infertile in 1992, and couples seeking fertility assistance, particularly in vitro fertilization, spent nearly $1 billion in 1991—much of it not covered by health insurance. Experts in the field charged that to maximize clientele, infertility clinics specializing in fertilization procedures often exaggerated pregnancy success rates, giving couples false hopes.

The legislation required clinics to report their pregnancy success rates to the HEALTH AND HUMAN SERVICES DEPARTMENT, and that the department issue each year a consumer guide noting the rates, as well as which clinics failed to report their success rates, and the names of the embryo laboratories each clinic used. The law also ordered establishment of a procedure for inspecting and certifying embryo laboratories.

In the first report, the CENTERS FOR DISEASE CONTROL AND PREVENTION found that in 1995, 11,315 live births resulted from 60,000 cycles of assisted reproductive technology. The live birth rate for nondonor eggs was 19.6 percent; for donor eggs it was 30 percent.

Critics, however, have questioned whether the 1992 law had unintended consequences. In order to ensure success rates, some fertility experts have charged, some clinics have impregnated women with dangerously high numbers of embryos, resulting in multiple births that endanger both the women and the babies.

Institute of Medicine

The Institute of Medicine, or IoM, as it is called by health policymakers, is an arm of the National Academy of Sciences, which was chartered by Congress in 1863 to advise the federal government on scientific issues. The National Academy of Sciences in turn chartered the IoM in 1970, "to enlist distinguished members of the appropriate professions in the examination of policy matters pertaining to the health of the public." Congress frequently asks the IoM to study and report on contentious issues in science and health policy. Recent issues addressed by the IoM include a study of priority setting at the NATIONAL INSTITUTES OF HEALTH, a study of ways to improve civilian responses to chemical and biological terrorism, and an examination of ways to prevent mother-to-child transmission of HIV. Members of the IoM are elected based on their professional achievements; under the institute's charter, to maintain a multidisciplinary focus, one-fourth of the members must be from professions other than those directly related to medicine or health.

Instrumental activities of daily living

See ACTIVITIES OF DAILY LIVING.

Intermediary (Medicare)

A Medicare intermediary is a private company (usually an insurance company) that processes claims for Part A services under contract to the HEALTH CARE FINANCING ADMINISTRATION (HCFA). Part A covers inpatient hospital care, care in a skilled nursing facility, HOME HEALTH CARE, and HOSPICE care. Intermediaries also handle hospital outpatient claims that are technically covered by Medicare Part B. Intermediaries assist providers and beneficiaries, determine coverage, and make payments according to guidance from HCFA, conduct reviews and audits, and help police the program for fraud. Medicare Part B claims are handled by entities called carriers. (See CARRIER.)

J

Joint Commission on the Accreditation of Healthcare Organizations (JCAHO)

The JCAHO is a private, nonprofit organization that formerly inspected and accredited hospitals. Today it has repositioned itself as an evaluative body for integrated delivery networks, nursing homes, and organizations that provide home care, behavioral health care, laboratory, and ambulatory care services. Founded in 1951, the JCAHO is the nation's oldest and largest standards-setting and accrediting body in health care, having evaluated more than 18,000 health care organizations and programs.

Judicial bypass

The process by which a minor can get permission for an abortion from a judge rather than seek the involvement of her parents is called a judicial bypass. The Supreme Court in the 1979 decision *Bellotti v. Baird* ruled that teenagers must be able to seek judicial permission rather than involve their parents if they so desire. As part of the proceeding, the minor must either demonstrate to the judge that she is mature enough to make the decision on her own, or else the judge must find that the abortion would be in the girl's best interest. If the minor is sufficiently mature to make the decision, said the court, the judge must allow the abortion even if the judge does not find the abortion to be in her best interest.

K

Kennedy-Kassebaum bill

Kennedy-Kassebaum bill is the colloquial name for the HEALTH INSURANCE PORTABILITY AND AC-COUNTABILITY ACT (HIPAA) of 1996, identified by its principal senate sponsors, Sen. Nancy Landon Kasse-baum, R-Kan., chairman of the Senate Labor and Human Resources Committee, and Sen. Edward Kennedy, D-Mass., the committee's ranking Democrat. Technically, the measure should be known as Kassebaum-Kennedy, since Kassebaum was the chairman of the committee and the Republicans controlled the Senate at the time the bill was passed. However, the measure enjoyed its strongest support from Democrats, who preferred to use Kennedy's name first.

Kerr-Mills bill

A predecessor of the MEDICAID program for the poor, the Kerr-Mills bill (named for its sponsors, Sen. Robert Kerr, D-Okla., and Rep. Wilbur Mills, D-Ark., chairman of the House Ways and Means Committee) was passed in 1960. It created a program called Medical Assistance for the Aged, which provided federal matching funds for states that covered care for "medically needy" aged individuals; those with incomes above the levels required for cash aid but who still required help to pay their medical bills. By 1965, the year Medicaid was established, forty states had established Kerr-Mills programs, and spending on it and a smaller program to pay the medical bills of cash welfare recipients totaled $1.3 billion.

L

Labor–Health and Human Services– Education Appropriation

Typically the largest of the thirteen regular spending bills that fund discretionary (as opposed to mandatory) portions of the federal government, the appropriation for the Departments of Labor, Health and Human Services, Education, and related agencies is responsible for funding nearly all of the major federal health agencies. (A major exception is the FOOD AND DRUG ADMINISTRATION, which, although part of the HEALTH AND HUMAN SERVICES DEPARTMENT (HHS), is traditionally funded through the Agriculture spending bill.) In reality, though, appropriators have almost no say over how more than 70 percent of the total is spent.

The bulk of the bill's funding goes for mandatory programs, such as MEDICARE Part B (Part A is funded via a dedicated portion of the Social Security payroll tax), MEDICAID, and unemployment insurance. Those programs' spending levels can be altered only by making changes to the underlying law that governs them, a task reserved to "authorizing" committees. In fiscal 1999, the Labor-HHS bill appropriated $291.9 billion, $78.7 billion of which was for discretionary programs over which appropriators determined funding levels, and $208.6 billion of which was for mandatory programs.

The Labor-HHS bill (as it is often referred to) has traditionally been one of the most difficult spending bills to get through Congress each year, and not because of its enormous size. In the era of tight budgets and spending limits, any increases in popular social programs must be offset by cuts in other, often equally popular programs. Over the years, lawmakers have sparred repeatedly over whether to rob education funds to increase funds for health care, or vice versa. "Robbing Peter to pay Paul" is a phrase heard more than once during consideration of the bill nearly every year.

But the measure has traditionally been hamstrung by fights over some of the most sensitive social issues, particularly ABORTION. Since 1977, the measure has carried what has come to be known as the HYDE AMENDMENT, language prohibiting the use of federal funds to pay for abortion except in very limited cases. The Labor-HHS bill has also been the venue for fights over parental involvement in family planning programs, EMBRYO RESEARCH and FETAL TISSUE RESEARCH, and school busing and vouchers.

Late-term abortion

Late-term abortion is a widely misused phrase in the debate over the procedure abortion opponents call PARTIAL-BIRTH ABORTION and abortion rights supporters call intact dilation and extraction. The phrase is generally understood to refer to abortions performed after fetal viability—when the fetus can live outside the mother's womb. Others use *late term* to refer to the final trimester of pregnancy—the start of which may or may not be after viability. It is during the final trimester that the Supreme Court, in *Roe v. Wade,* said states could limit or even ban abortions other than those needed to protect the life or health of the woman. Still others, however, use the term loosely to refer to any abortion after roughly sixteen weeks, the time after which the simplest abortion techniques can no longer be used. Using that definition, it is correct to refer to partial-birth abortion as a late-term procedure. The vast majority of those abortions, however, both sides concede, occur be-

Dr. Pamela Smith of Mt. Sinai Hospital in Chicago (displaying a model of a fetus) and Dr. Mary Campbell, medical director of Planned Parenthood of Washington, deliver Senate testimony opposing 1995's Partial-Birth Abortion Ban Act. The act, passed by Congress but vetoed by President Bill Clinton, would have banned a procedure abortion opponents called partial-birth abortion. Source: Rick Wilking, Reuters

fore twenty-two weeks gestation, too early to be considered "late term" by most definitions.

Lifetime limits

Overall caps imposed by insurers on the amount of medical expenses they will cover are called lifetime limits. An estimated 60 percent of employer-sponsored plans have lifetime caps, typically $1 million. (Federally qualified HMOs are not permitted to impose lifetime caps on basic benefits, although they may impose caps on supplemental services such as prescription drugs, dental, vision, hearing, and home health services, and durable medical equipment. Plans under the FEDERAL EMPLOYEE HEALTH BENEFITS PLAN are similarly barred from imposing lifetime spending limits.) In 1995, an estimated 1,500 individuals with catastrophic medical expenses exceeded their lifetime limits, often result-

ing in their "spending down" to poverty and qualifying for MEDICAID or relying on charity care provided by public hospitals and other facilities.

As health care costs continue to rise with no increase in the limits, it has been estimated that 2,500 people will exceed the caps annually by the year 2000. Since 1995, a group of senators led by Sen. James Jeffords, R-Vt., the Senate Health, Education, Labor and Pensions Committee chairman, has pushed for legislation to require that lifetime limits be set no lower than $10 million. A cost estimate from the consulting firm Price Waterhouse LLP found such an increased limit would raise premiums on employer-sponsored plans by an average of 1.4 percent; however, insurance companies complained that the increases could be much larger. During debate on the HEALTH INSURANCE PORTABILITY AND ACCOUNTABILITY ACT (HIPAA) in April 1996, the Senate voted down the minimum cap on lifetime limits by 42–56.

NATURAL DEATH ACT DECLARATION ("LIVING WILL")

Virginia's Natural Death Act was enacted in 1983 to permit Virginians to record their wishes regarding extraordinary care in the event of terminal illness. The declaration below is the suggested form developed by the state legislators to implement the Act. Fill out this form and give it to your physician and any relatives and friends you would like to have a copy. You must sign in the presence of two witnesses, and both witnesses must sign in your presence. Blood relatives or spouse may not be witnesses.

DECLARATION

In accordance with the Virginia Natural Death Act, this Declaration was made on _____.

Month/Day/Year

I, _____, willfully and voluntarily make known my desire and do here-

Name of person making declaration

by declare:

You must choose between the following two paragraphs. PARAGRAPH ONE designates a person to make a decision for you. In PARAGRAPH TWO, you make the decision. Cross through the paragraph you do NOT want.

PARAGRAPH ONE:

If at any time I should have a terminal condition and I am comatose, incompetent or otherwise mentally or physically incapable of communication, I designate _____ to make a decision on my behalf as to whether life-prolonging procedures shall be withheld or withdrawn. In the event that my designee decides that such procedures should be withheld or withdrawn, I wish to be permitted to die naturally with only the administration of medication or the performance of any medical procedure deemed necessary to provide me with comfort care or to alleviate pain. (OPTION: I specifically direct that the following procedures or treatments be provided to me:

OR

PARAGRAPH TWO:

If at any time I should have a terminal condition where the application of life-prolonging procedures would serve only to artificially prolong the dying process, I direct that such procedures be withheld or withdrawn, and that I be permitted to die naturally with only the administration of medication or the performance of any medical procedure deemed necessary to provide me with comfort care or to alleviate pain. (OPTION: I specifically direct that the following procedures or treatments be provided to me:

_____

_____

An example of a living will—Virginia's "Natural Death Act Declaration."

Living wills

A legal document putting an individual's desires for future medical care into writing is called a living will. A living will, which does not take effect until a patient is determined to be terminally ill, may, for example, ex-press the individual's desire not to have his or her life sustained artificially, such as on a mechanical ventilator or feeding tube. Conversely, the individual may express a desire for heroic measures to be taken to keep him or her alive. A living will does *not* designate a person to make medical decisions for one who cannot; that can be done by other forms of ADVANCE DIRECTIVES, such as a DURABLE POWER OF ATTORNEY FOR HEALTH CARE or a MEDICAL POWER OF ATTORNEY. The 1990 PATIENT SELF DETERMINATION ACT, part of that year's budget reconciliation bill, PL 101-508, required that all hospitals that participate in MEDICARE or MEDICAID advise all patients of their right to exercise advance directives, in an effort to encourage their use.

Long-term care

One of many imprecise terms in health care policy, *long-term care* means different things to different people and can mean different things to the same person, depending on the context in which it is used. Generally, long-term care is the opposite of "acute" care, or care for an immediate condition. People who need long-term care are generally unable to care fully for themselves (often defined as limited in performing ACTIVITIES OF DAILY LIVING) and need assistance for a relatively long period of time. Long-term care generally takes place outside of a community hospital, but it can be delivered in a variety of locations, ranging from a patient's own home to an assisted living facility, to a nursing home, to a rehabilitation hospital. Long-term care also may consist of different types of services. Primarily medical long-term care services may include physical or occupational rehabilitation, or nursing care such as changing dressings, giving medications, or monitoring intravenous solutions. Long-term care services can also be primarily custodial, such as help in dressing, bathing, or going to the bathroom. Long-term care can also consist of providing social services, such as help with shopping or cleaning.

Of an estimated 42.7 million Americans with disabilities, about 12.7 million require long-term care, according to a 1995 study. That means that 29.7 percent of the disabled population and one in every twenty Americans need long-term care. And as the baby boom generation begins to age, the need for long-term care will only increase, since the elderly are more likely to need long-term care services. The population over age sixty-five is expected to double by the year 2030, to nearly 70 mil-

lion; at the same time, the "old-old" population, those over age eighty-five—of whom one in four needs long-term care services—is projected to rise by 143 percent. Long-term care expenditures, including nursing home and home care, are expected to rise from $123 billion in the year 2000 to $207 billion in the year 2020.

As an acute care program, MEDICARE provides relatively meager long-term care benefits. It pays for stays in nursing homes designated as "skilled nursing facilities" (with significant required copayments and DEDUCTIBLES), as well as HOME HEALTH CARE services for those with documented medical needs, although payments are not unlimited. MEDICAID does provide coverage for long-term custodial stays in a nursing home, but only after a patient has "spent down" virtually all of his or her income and assets. Together, however, Medicare and Medicaid do pay most of the nation's annual nursing home bill. In 1996, the programs funded 61.5 percent of that year's $78.5 billion nursing home bill; Medicaid accounted for 47.8 percent and Medicare for 11.4 percent. Individuals paid 31.4 percent of nursing home costs out of pocket; private insurance accounted for a meager 5.2 percent, although that did represent a fourfold increase from 1980. Congress sought to make private long-term care insurance more attractive by allowing it, as part of the 1997 Balanced Budget Act (PL 105-33), to be treated the same as other health insurance for tax purposes.

But most long-term care is not delivered in nursing homes. Only about 40 percent of the population requiring long-term care live in a nursing home or other institution; the remaining 60 percent live in the community. In fact, much of the nation's long-term care is not even delivered for money. A 1984 survey found that more than 7 million spouses, adult children, other relatives, friends, and neighbors provided unpaid aid to disabled elderly individuals; eight out of ten caregivers provided unpaid care for an average of four hours a day, seven days a week. A 1999 study estimated that in 1997, approximately 25.8 million "informal" caregivers provided an average of 19.7 hours per week of care—an economic value of $196 billion. Because it is not paid, that figure is not included in estimates of national health care spending.

Long-term care as a political issue has waxed and waned over the past two decades. In the late 1980s and early 1990s, many policymakers suddenly began to look with alarm at the lack of a national policy to help finance the cost of long-term care, particularly given the impending cost explosion that the baby boomers will bring about. A proposal for a new public program to help all Americans with long-term care costs was approved by the bipartisan PEPPER COMMISSION in 1990. But with an estimated cost of $80 billion to fully fund the need for long-term care services, most programs were slow to gather political steam, and other social issues, particularly the plight of the uninsured and the impending financial problems faced by Social Security and Medicare, pushed long-term care as an issue back down the health care agenda.

Loss ratios

A loss ratio is the percentage of premiums paid out by an insurance company for actual medical care. A plan with a high loss ratio pays out most of the money it takes in for care; one with a low loss ratio may spend more money on advertising, administration, overhead, or may keep a larger share of premiums for profits. Legislation passed by Congress in 1990 to regulate private supplemental policies for Medicare (known as MEDI-GAP INSURANCE) requires plans to maintain loss ratios of at least 65 percent for individual policies, and 75 percent for group plans.

M

Managed behavioral health care

In an effort to save money and improve care, many insurers, MANAGED CARE and otherwise, have turned to private "managed behavioral health care" firms to manage the distribution of mental health services to patients. These firms are often referred to as CARVE-OUT ORGANIZATIONS because a specialty company "carves out" a single area of care. In 1997 nearly 169 million Americans with health insurance were covered for their mental health needs by some sort of managed behavioral care system.

Managed care

At its most basic level, managed care is any system that integrates the financing and delivery of health care services. But beyond that, definitions diverge.

Managed care includes a broad spectrum of models, all the way from the staff-model HEALTH MAINTE-NANCE ORGANIZATION (HMO), in which the managed care organization owns all facilities and directly employs all personnel, to the PREFERRED PROVIDER ORGANIZATION (PPO), where the managed care organization simply contracts with hospitals and doctors to serve patients for a discounted fee.

Although managed care has been around in some form for most of this century, until the last decade its growth was severely limited by its lack of popularity among both patients and doctors. Many of the early managed care organizations were created by industry to serve patients in areas with severe shortages of medical personnel or by consumers themselves who were attracted by the idea of prepaid medical care. But managed care was slow to take hold: many patients resisted managed care because (at least in its traditional form) it severely limited their choices of physicians and hospitals. Organized medicine (led by the AMERICAN MEDICAL ASSOCIATION) also long opposed the concept of anyone other than physicians making treatment decisions for patients.

It took a combination of factors, including federal financial incentives in the 1970s and the desire of employers in the 1980s to control their health care costs, to push managed care from the health system's back benches to the front row. New and innovative forms of managed care that allow patients and providers much freer choice helped break down consumer and provider resistance. As a result, managed care enrollment has literally exploded. Between 1986 and 1995 the number of Americans in HMOs more than doubled—from 25.7 million people to 58.2 million, according to the AMERICAN ASSOCIATION OF HEALTH PLANS, the managed care industry trade association. Overall, the number of Americans in HMOs and PPOs grew to an estimated 173 million in 1997, with 83.7 million in HMOs and 89.1 million in PPOs. In 1996 more than three-fourths of all Americans with employer-provided health insurance were covered by managed care plans. Managed care is such a confusing concept, however, that many people in it don't know it. A 1998 survey by the Employee Benefit Research Institute found that only 21 percent of those in managed care knew it, while 56 percent of those currently enrolled in managed care plans vowed they had never been covered by managed care.

But as more people join managed care—many of them involuntarily, as employers shift the type of coverage they offer—and as more managed care organizations crowd into the marketplace, a backlash has been

In spite of negative media coverage, which highlighted the overly restrictive health care delivery policies of some managed care providers, enrollment in managed care programs exploded between 1985 and 1996. Source: Beth Balbierz, KRT

developing. Television, radio, magazines, and newspapers have all been full of managed care "horror" stories about care delayed or denied, and legislatures have been quick to pass laws aimed at stopping such "abuses" as requiring new mothers and infants to leave the hospital only twenty-four hours following delivery (see "DRIVE THROUGH DELIVERIES"). A survey conducted in the fall of 1996 for some of the nation's largest managed care companies found that media coverage of the industry in major national outlets has been overwhelmingly negative, with five unfavorable stories for every one favorable report.

Types of Managed Care

In many ways managed care is like a living organism that is growing and changing all the time. Labels that mean one thing one year are meaningless months later. Still, some terms are simply used incorrectly. One of the most frequent mistakes is using "managed care" and "HMO" interchangeably. That's like using "fruit" and "apple" interchangeably. An HMO is but one of many types of managed care, just as an apple is one of many types of fruit. And just as there are different types of apples, there are also different types of HMOs. The easiest

way to differentiate between the various types of managed care is to look at them on a continuum, from most to least tightly organized.

HMOS. The HMO, or health maintenance organization, is the type of managed care that most closely ties together the financing and delivery of health care services. HMOs may be independent organizations, they may be owned and operated by an insurance company, or (rarely) they may be owned and operated by groups of physicians and hospitals. HMOs typically offer patients the least choice of health care provider. If patients choose to seek care from a doctor or hospital that is not part of the HMO, generally they must pay all of the costs themselves. The hallmark of HMOs is that they offer a comprehensive package of services on a "prepaid" basis; in other words, the employer or individual pays the HMO a monthly fee, in exchange for which the HMO provides all the care needed by that person or family—with the caveat that the HMO determines what care is "necessary." This type of financing provides the opposite of the incentive offered under the traditional FEE-FOR-SERVICE system, where the more a doctor (or other health care provider) does, the more he or she is paid. Instead, the HMO has an incentive to provide the least amount of care, since it keeps the difference between the prepaid fee and the cost of care provided. Supporters of managed care also note that it gives HMOs a strong incentive to employ preventive care and other ways to keep patients from getting sick (such as offering free nutrition or smoking cessation classes or subsidizing health club memberships), since healthy patients improve the organization's bottom line. Competition with other HMOs, say supporters, will keep HMOs from providing less than the appropriate amount of care.

HMOs also employ a variety of formal mechanisms to ensure appropriate "utilization" of health care services, both prospectively (such as by limiting the brands of prescription drugs that may be dispensed) and retrospectively (such as by reviewing how often a physician refers a patient to a specialist or admits patients to the hospital.) This is the "management" part of managed care. Rules for patients also are designed to limit care only to that deemed most appropriate according to standards of EVIDENCE-BASED MEDICINE. In order to obtain care, patients in most HMOs must work through a "GATEKEEPER" doctor, generally a PRIMARY CARE PHYSICIAN such as an internist or pediatrician. That physician decides when and if the patient should see a specialist, enter the hospital, or receive other types of care.

There are four main types of HMOs, categorized by how closely the HMO is tied to those who provide health care services and by who is "at risk" for the costs of patient care. The oldest type is the *staff-model HMO,* in which physicians are employed directly by the HMO and provide care only to HMO patients. In staff-model HMOs the HMO itself bears the risk for the cost of care. Staff-model HMOs offer patients the least choice of provider and the HMO the most control over costs and care; they are often referred to as closed-panel systems.

In the *group-model HMO,* physicians who practice as a group contract with the HMO to provide care. Kaiser-Permanente is the best-known group-model HMO, with its physicians employed by the Permanente medical group. From the patient's point of view the group model is virtually indistinguishable from the staff-model HMO; physicians care exclusively for HMO patients in a closed panel, with little or no option for patients to seek reimbursed care outside the system. The main difference between the models is in who takes the financial risk for the cost of care. In group-model HMOs the physician group is at risk for most of the cost of care. It is paid a set fee for each patient (known as CAPITATION), meant to cover costs of all specialty and PRIMARY CARE by physicians. In some cases the physician group is also at risk for some or all of the cost of hospital care, on the theory that physicians control hospital utilization.

In the *IPA-model HMO,* the HMO contracts with a group of physicians who practice alone or in small groups and who have banded together into an *independent practice association,* or IPA. Physicians in IPA-model HMOs can assume risk with the HMO by receiving capitation payments, or may be paid a "discounted" rate for every patient visit, with bonuses at the end of the year if certain budget targets are met. Physicians in IPA-model HMOs may have contracts with several different organizations as well as serve so-called private pay patients.

Some HMOs mix and match the above arrangements, contracting with different groups and even employing some physicians. These are known as *network-model HMOs.*

POS PLANS. Also known as an open-ended HMO, the POINT OF SERVICE (POS) plan gets its name because it allows the patient to choose where to receive service at the time services are desired. Patients are given incentives, in the form of lower deductibles or copayments, to seek care within the HMO network, working through a gatekeeper physician for access to other services. But unlike patients in a traditional HMO, those in POS plans can also seek reimbursed care outside the network, although they will have to pay higher out-of-pocket fees.

POS plans have proved very popular with patients, giving them simultaneously the cost savings associated with HMO membership and also the option to seek an outside opinion for very serious or rare problems. POS plans, however, have been less popular among insurers because the ability of patients to seek care on their own has made cost control and patient management considerably more challenging and premiums more difficult to calculate.

PPOS. At the least-organized end of the managed care continuum is by far the most prevalent form of managed care, the PREFERRED PROVIDER ORGANIZATION, or PPO. PPOs are networks of independent physicians (and hospitals and other providers) who contract with insurers to provide care. Physicians in PPOs usually are paid on what is known as a "discounted fee for service" basis. Under this system a physician accepts a fee lower than normal in exchange (theoretically) for a higher volume of patients. The physician, however, still has the same incentive as under traditional FEE-FOR-SERVICE insurance—the more care he or she provides, the more he or she is paid. Physicians who operate outside certain parameters, however, can be dropped by the PPO. Patients in PPOs are usually free to seek care in or out of the "network" and do not need to go through a gatekeeper for access to specialty care, but, as in POS plans, patients are given financial incentives to use physicians who belong to the PPO, usually in the form of lower payments for in-network care and higher ones for care outside.

Managed competition

Coined by researchers Alain Enthoven and Paul Ellwood, the term describes a health system in which health plans compete with each other according to ground rules set by the government or other third party. The Clinton administration's failed health plan built on the Enthoven-Ellwood model. Although the two terms were often used interchangeably during the 1993–1994 debate, MANAGED CARE and managed competition are entirely different concepts. Under a managed competition model a new type of entity (Enthoven and Ellwood called it a *health insurance purchasing cooperative,* or

HIPC; President Bill Clinton called it a *health alliance*) would act as a purchasing agent for insurance buyers (employers, public agencies, and individuals) and as a quality watchdog for consumers. The central idea of managed competition is that plans, whether managed care or FEE-FOR-SERVICE, would compete on level footing, with consumers more able to compare quality and benefits. As a result, plans would have to compete on service and quality rather than on price alone.

Maternal and Child Health (MCH) Services Block Grant

This federal grant to the states provides funding to help improve the health status of low-income pregnant women and children. Created in 1981 in a consolidation of a series of smaller programs, MCH block grant funds may be used for a variety of purposes, including reducing infant mortality, reducing the incidence of preventable diseases and handicapping conditions among low-income children, increasing the availability of health services to pregnant women, making immunizations and PRIMARY CARE services more available to children, and providing services to children with disabilities or other special needs. In fiscal year 1999 Congress appropriated $700 million for the program; states must provide $3 for every $4 provided by the federal government.

Maternity stays

See "DRIVE-THROUGH" DELIVERIES.

Means testing (Medicare)

A misnomer used in reference to MEDICARE, means testing is used to determine if a person is eligible for a program aimed at those with limited incomes. For welfare or other programs, a "means test" is applied to measure an individual's or family's income and assets. If the totals do not exceed a certain level, the person or family is eligible for the program. If the "means" are too high, the person is not eligible. MEDICAID is a means-tested program, as is the Special Supplemental Food Program for Women, Infants, and Children (WIC). In Medicare, however, policymakers since the late 1980s have been discussing the possibility of charging well-off Medicare BENEFICIARIES more for their coverage, specifically by increasing the Part B premium, since 75 percent of Part B costs are subsidized from the general federal treasury. This is, in fact, not means testing but *income relating*, in which a person or family with a higher income remains eligible for the program but pays more than those who are less affluent. The MEDICARE CATASTROPHIC COVERAGE ACT (PL 100-360), passed in 1988 and repealed a year and a half later, included an INCOME-RELATED PREMIUM.

Medicaid

Medicaid, which is Title XIX of the Social Security Act, is a joint federal-state program that in 1997 spent $159.9 billion to provide health care services to an estimated thirty-six million Americans with low incomes. Like MEDICARE, with which it was established in 1965 (by PL 89-97), Medicaid is an ENTITLEMENT, meaning that those who meet eligibility requirements are legally entitled to benefits and can sue if those benefits are denied. But unlike Medicare, which is a single, federally run program nationwide, Medicaid, as a federal-state partnership, is really fifty-six different programs, one for each state, the District of Columbia, and each of the U.S. territories. Each state and territory, operating within federal guidelines and rules, can set its own eligibility standards and payment rates for medical care, decide what and how much care it will cover, and generally administer the program as it sees fit.

Even in areas in which Medicaid is uniform, though, the program serves three distinct populations with very different health care needs:

• low-income pregnant women and children, who formerly received cash welfare payments through the joint federal-state welfare program, Aid to Families with Dependent Children (AFDC), who currently receive cash payments from the new Temporary Assistance for Needy Families program (TANF), or who qualify through poverty categories.

• low-income disabled Americans who receive cash welfare payments through the federal SUPPLEMENTAL SECURITY INCOME program (SSI). (Confusingly, individuals eligible by virtue of disability for the SOCIAL SECURITY DISABILITY INSURANCE program (SSDI) are eligible, after a twenty-four month waiting period, for Medicare, not Medicaid.)

• low-income elderly people who require nursing home or other LONG-TERM CARE services, or assistance meeting Medicare's cost-sharing requirements.

Although three-fourths of Medicaid BENEFICIARIES are low-income pregnant women and children, they are actually the least-expensive recipients, accounting for about 27 percent of Medicaid spending. The elderly and disabled, who compose about 26 percent of Medicaid's beneficiaries, account for some 64 percent of Medicaid spending, primarily because they require long-term care services, which tend to be far more expensive than the acute and PRIMARY CARE required for healthier, younger individuals.

Although everyone on Medicaid has a low income, the program doesn't cover all the poor. Because of its complicated eligibility rules (see following), Medicaid in 1995 covered only about 55 percent of those with incomes under the federal poverty line. And though much has been made of efforts over the last decade to extend Medicaid coverage to those up the income scale, in 1995 Medicaid provided coverage to only 17 percent of the "near-poor," those with incomes between 100 and 200 percent of poverty level. Still, Medicaid's expansion in the 1980s and early 1990s did stem the tide of the growing ranks of the UNINSURED.

But Medicaid does account for a significant portion of medical care delivered in the United States. It covers one of every eight U.S. residents (one of every four children); in 1995 Medicaid paid for one of every three births, cared for two-thirds of nursing home residents, and provided 40 percent of public funding for individuals with AIDS. For six million low-income individuals who are also Medicare beneficiaries, Medicaid acts as a MEDIGAP INSURER, providing coverage Medicare does not, particularly for prescription drugs and long-term care services.

Eligibility

Medicaid is not only one of the nation's largest health programs but also one of its most complex. There are some twenty-five separate eligibility categories (sometimes referred to as *pathways*) by which individuals can qualify for Medicaid coverage. Part of the reason has been a purposeful policy of delinking Medicaid eligibility from eligibility for major cash assistance programs in an effort to broaden the universe of low-income Americans who can obtain health insurance. Throughout the 1980s and early 1990s Medicaid eligibility for pregnant women, children, and the elderly was extended beyond those who could get Medicaid by virtue of receiving benefits through the Aid to Families with Dependent Children (AFDC) program or Supplemental Security Income (SSI) program. In 1984 80 percent of Medicaid enrollees were also receiving cash assistance; by 1992 that figure had dropped to 60 percent. The link between welfare and Medicaid was severed completely by passage of the 1996 welfare reform law (the PERSONAL RESPONSIBILITY AND WORK OPPORTUNITY RECONCILIATION ACT of 1996—PL 104-193), which ended the fifty-year-old entitlement status of cash welfare payments, eliminating AFDC and replacing it with the TANF program (see following discussion for more detail).

In 1998 states were required to extend Medicaid coverage to groups including the following (these individuals qualify for coverage by meeting CATEGORICAL ELIGIBILITY requirements):

• pregnant women, infants, and children up to age six in families with incomes less than 133 percent of the federal poverty level

• children ages six to fifteen in families with incomes under 100 percent of the federal poverty level (coverage for children born after September 30, 1983, is phasing in one year at a time, until, by the year 2002, all children under age nineteen in families with incomes under the federal poverty level will be eligible for Medicaid coverage)

• adults and children in families who meet the income, resource, and family composition rules that would have qualified them for the Aid to Families with Dependent Children program as of July 16, 1996

• SSI recipients (in most states)

• children receiving adoption or foster care assistance under Title IV of the Social Security Act

• children and adults in families who lose cash assistance due to increased earnings from work and who may keep Medicaid coverage for a transitional period

• Medicare beneficiaries with incomes under 100 percent of the federal poverty level. (Medicare beneficiaries with incomes up to 175 percent of poverty are eligible, on various bases, for more limited aid through Medicaid—see DUAL ELIGIBLES for specifics).

States had the option of providing Medicaid to members of other groups, including:

• pregnant women and infants up to age one with incomes between 100 and 185 percent of poverty level

• children under age twenty-one who meet the July 16, 1996, state welfare eligibility standards but are not otherwise required to be covered

• institutionalized individuals who meet certain standards set by the states, although they may have incomes no higher than 300 percent of the SSI federal benefits level

• individuals who would be eligible if they were in an institution but who are receiving care under waivers allowing Medicaid coverage of home- and community-based care

• certain working and disabled individuals with family incomes less than 250 percent of the federal poverty level who would qualify for SSI if they did not work

• individuals with tuberculosis who meet the financial eligibility requirements for SSI, but who are not members of an SSI eligibility category. Such individuals

Medicaid Recipients (by eligibility category), 1998

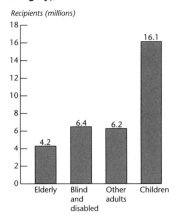

Recipients (millions)

- nurse-midwife services
- services provided by a federally qualified health center
- EARLY AND PERIODIC SCREENING, DIAGNOSTIC, AND TREATMENT (EPSDT) services for children under age twenty-one.

States can limit the scope and duration of the required services but only within limits. States must, for example, provide a level of benefits sufficient "to reasonably achieve the purpose of the benefits," and benefit limitations (such as a set number of hospital days or physician visits) may not discriminate among beneficiaries based on their medical conditions. States are also required to provide all "medically necessary" services for children eligible under EPSDT, even if those services are not otherwise covered by the state.

States can also offer thirty-four separate optional services, such as diagnostic, prescription drug, and optometrist services (including providing eyeglasses); care in an intermediate care facility for the mentally retarded (ICF/MR); nursing home care for those under age twenty-one; rehabilitation and physical therapy services; and home and community-based care.

are eligible only for services related to treatment of their tuberculosis.

- individuals deemed MEDICALLY NEEDY (see related entry)
- other individuals, under terms of several federal "waiver" programs that permit states to waive normal requirements for eligibility if they meet certain other restrictions.

Benefits

As with eligibility, states have significant flexibility in the benefits they can offer under Medicaid, with some mandatory and others optional. Required services include:

- inpatient and outpatient hospital care
- prenatal care for pregnant women
- childhood vaccinations
- physician services
- nursing home care for those aged twenty-one and over
- family planning services and supplies
- rural health clinic services
- HOME HEALTH CARE for those eligible for skilled-nursing care
- laboratory and X-ray services
- pediatric and family NURSE PRACTITIONER services

Payments and Financing

Medicaid is what is known as a *vendor payment program*, meaning that states pay providers of care. In turn, the federal government reimburses states for their share according to each individual state's FEDERAL MEDICAL ASSISTANCE PERCENTAGE, or FMAP. Overall, the federal government pays about 57 percent of Medicaid costs nationwide, with shares ranging from 50 percent in wealthier states up to 83 percent for the poorest states. In 1999 the state with the highest FMAP was Mississippi, at 76.80 percent. The federal government matches most administrative costs at 50 percent. Despite Republican-led efforts in the 1980s and 1990s to change it, Medicaid remains an *open-ended entitlement* in that there is no cap on spending. The federal government reimburses states at their FMAP rates for all mandatory services and optional services the state chooses to offer, as well as for "all necessary and proper"

Federal Medical Assistance Percentages, 1999–2000

State	Federal medical assistance percentages	State	Federal medical assistance percentages
Alabama	69.57	Nebraska	60.88
Alaska	59.80	Nevada	50.00
American Samoa	50.00	New Hampshire	50.00
Arizona	65.92	New Jersey	50.00
Arkansas	72.85	New Mexico	73.32
California	51.67	New York	50.00
Colorado	50.00	North Carolina	62.49
Connecticut	50.00	North Dakota	70.42
Delaware	50.00	Northern Mariana Islands	50.00
District of Columbia	70.00		
Florida	56.52	Ohio	58.67
Georgia	59.88	Oklahoma	71.09
Guam	50.00	Oregon	59.96
Hawaii	51.01	Pennsylvania	53.82
Idaho	70.15	Puerto Rico	50.00
Illinois	50.00	Rhode Island	53.77
Indiana	61.74	South Carolina	69.95
Iowa	63.06	South Dakota	68.72
Kansas	60.03	Tennessee	63.10
Kentucky	70.55	Texas	61.36
Louisiana	70.32	Utah	71.55
Maine	66.22	Vermont	62.24
Maryland	50.00	Virgin Islands	50.00
Massachusetts	50.00	Virginia	51.67
Michigan	55.11	Washington	51.83
Minnesota	51.48	West Virginia	74.78
Mississippi	76.80	Wisconsin	58.78
Missouri	60.51	Wyoming	64.04
Montana	72.30		

Note: Percentages were effective during fiscal year 2000 (October 1, 1999, through September 30, 2000).

administrative costs. According to the HEALTH CARE FINANCING ADMINISTRATION, which runs Medicaid as well as Medicare, 55 percent of all Medicaid spending is for populations whose coverage is optional, or for optional services.

Despite those unsuccessful efforts to cap Medicaid spending, however, in recent years the huge Medicaid increases that prompted calls for the limits have all but disappeared. In 1997 Medicaid spending grew by a mere 3.8 percent from the spending level of the year before,

the slowest growth rate in the history of the program and a major turnabout from growth rates in the early 1990s, when Medicaid spending increases routinely ran around 20 percent. (From 1990 to 1992 spending rose by more than 27 percent per year.)

Analysts attributed Medicaid's rapid growth in the late 1980s through 1992 to several different factors.

By far the most significant factor was states' use of aggressive financing mechanisms, including targeted provider taxes and so-called disproportionate share (or DSH, pronounced "dish") payments to hospitals that serve large numbers of Medicaid and other low-income patients (see DISPROPORTIONATE SHARE HOSPITAL). DSH payments exploded between 1988 and 1992, rising by 263 percent annually, from $1.3 billion to more than $17 billion. The increases led to an ugly war of words and policies between federal and state lawmakers, with federal legislators arguing that states were shifting services that previously had been exclusively state-funded into Medicaid in an effort to draw down federal funds inappropriately. Congress, in response, cracked down, outlawing most provider taxes and limiting DSH payments in separate legislation in 1991, 1993, and 1997.

But DSH payments alone did not account for the rapid Medicaid increases. Other major factors were enrollment increases, due to increased eligibility conferred by legislation, as well as inadvertent increases, such as the growth in the number of disabled children who gained eligibility for SSI (and, hence, Medicaid) following the 1990 Supreme Court decision *Sullivan v. Zebley*. The Court in *Zebley* found that the Social Security Administration had been inappropriately denying children SSI eligibility.

At the same time enrollment was growing, utilization was also rising, since some of the newer Medicaid beneficiaries also had expensive medical needs (such as those with AIDS, pregnant women, and seniors in need of significant medical care). It was also during this period that states were required to provide treatment for conditions detected through Medicaid's EPSDT program.

More recently, Medicaid spending has declined

largely because the reasons it escalated so fast have reversed themselves. DSH spending dropped by 19.6 percent in 1996, as earlier restrictions imposed by Congress started to take effect. At the same time, the rate of enrollment slowed, since many of the new populations made eligible during the late 1980s and early 1990s had already been incorporated into the program. In fact, in 1996 Medicaid enrollment actually declined slightly—worrying many analysts, who feared that the 1996 welfare reform bill, while not eliminating Medicaid eligibility for most, might be inadvertently deterring those eligible from signing up. According to the federal AGENCY FOR HEALTH CARE POLICY AND RESEARCH, as many as 4.7 million children who were eligible for Medicaid were not enrolled in 1996.

Finally, as increases in health care costs throughout the system slowed, so did Medicaid spending per enrollee. In 1996 spending increases for every major Medicaid enrollment group slowed from those of previous years.

Medicaid and the 1996 Welfare Reform Bill

The PERSONAL RESPONSIBILITY AND WORK OPPORTUNITY RECONCILIATION ACT OF 1996 (PL 104-193) made significant changes to the nation's welfare system, replacing the permanent entitlement-based AFDC program with the time-limited TANF program. But it also made significant changes to Medicaid, since Medicaid eligibility had always been tied to AFDC for qualifying populations. While Congress had, since the mid-1980s, been working to weaken the ties between eligibility for Medicaid and eligibility for the cash welfare program, the welfare reform bill severed those ties irrevocably. Although anyone who would have been eligible for AFDC benefits as of July 16, 1996 (the date the bill was passed), remained eligible for Medicaid through a newly designated eligibility category known as "Section 1931," the law did not require that those eligible for TANF automatically be enrolled in Medicaid.

The welfare law also barred legal aliens who entered the United States on or after the date of enactment (the date the law went into effect, August 22, 1996) from receiving any "federal means-tested public benefit," including SSI and Medicaid, for five years from their date of entry, affecting an estimated five hundred thousand immigrants. Congress, however, restored eligibility of some two-thirds of those legal aliens for SSI and Medicaid as part of the 1997 Balanced Budget Act (PL 105-33). Made reeligible for benefits were legal immigrants who were receiving SSI as of August 22, 1996, based on a disability, those who were receiving SSI on that date because they were elderly but who could requalify based on a disability, and those who were in the United States as of August 22 and subsequently became disabled. Disabled legal immigrants who entered the country after August 22, 1996, but before June 1, 1997, would also be eligible for benefits. Remaining legal immigrants who entered the country after August 22 would still be ineligible for SSI or Medicaid for five years, and in any case until they became citizens.

Medicaid and Managed Care

Although MANAGED CARE was slower to catch on in Medicaid than it was in the working population, when states began to enroll their low-income populations in HEALTH MAINTENANCE ORGANIZATIONS (HMOS) and other prepaid plans, the increases were dramatic. In 1991 2.7 million beneficiaries were enrolled in Medicaid managed care plans, representing 9.5 percent of the Medicaid population. By 1997 enrollment in Medicaid managed care had risen to 15.3 million, representing 47.8 percent of beneficiaries. As of mid-1997, forty states and the District of Columbia had more than 25 percent of their Medicaid populations enrolled in managed care; every state except Alaska and Wyoming had at least some Medicaid managed care program. Ten states had more than three-fourths of their Medicaid beneficiaries enrolled in managed care plans.

Medicaid managed care comes in two main forms. In *fully capitated plans*, the managed care organization assumes full financial risk for the costs of each beneficiary's care in exchange for a set monthly fee (see CAPITATION). Under *primary care case management* (PCCM), the state pays a monthly fee to a primary care "gatekeeper" physician who is not "at risk" for the cost of the beneficiary's care but who does control access by the beneficiary to specialists, hospital care, or laboratory tests. In 1996 about one-third of Medicaid managed care enrollees were in PCCM types of managed care; thirteen states used PCCM exclusively. The remaining two-thirds were in fully capitated plans; those were the ones growing fastest.

Although conventional wisdom holds that managed care restricts patients' choice of providers, for Medicaid beneficiaries the situation can often be the opposite. Because of Medicaid's traditionally low payment rates, it was often difficult for beneficiaries to find providers to serve them. In managed care, however, Medicaid patients often have a broader array of choices than they had when they were in a traditional FEE-FOR-SERVICE plan. Having a primary care physician often means that Medicaid patients stop seeking routine care in emergency rooms, previously among the only places they could get medical help. And although many analysts worried that "Medicaid-only" managed care plans would provide substandard care (which has been the case in some instances), many plans have been developed consisting of traditional safety net providers, such as COMMUNITY HEALTH CENTERS, which are attuned to the myriad health and social needs of low-income populations (see SAFETY NET FACILITIES). Evidence, however, is mixed about whether managed care actually improves access to care for Medicaid beneficiaries.

The 1997 Balanced Budget Act (PL 105-33) made a number of changes designed to further the spread of managed care in the Medicaid program. Most important, it allowed states to require Medicaid beneficiaries to enroll in a managed care plan. Previously, states had to obtain a federal "waiver" of rules requiring that beneficiaries be given free choice of medical provider. The measure also permitted states, without waivers, to enroll beneficiaries in plans that serve mostly or exclusively Medicaid beneficiaries. States could also limit the number of managed care organizations serving Medicaid patients in urban areas, thus giving themselves more bargaining leverage with the plans.

But as with Medicare enrollment, Medicaid managed care enrollment began to contract just as it was expected to explode. In 1997 and 1998 plans either froze enrollment or dropped out in at least six states. Plans blamed low reimbursement rates paid by states. But analysts worried that many managed care organizations had unrealistic expectations for Medicaid managed care. After realizing initial savings by reducing inappropriate emergency room care and other "quick fixes," many managed care providers discovered that serving Medicaid patients with complex health care needs, particularly those who are elderly or disabled, was more expensive than they had anticipated. Still under study was whether "Medicaid-only" plans would provide second-rate care or the type of care Medicaid beneficiaries truly need.

Medicaid drug rebate program

Created in 1990 by that year's BUDGET RECONCILIATION bill (Omnibus Budget Reconciliation Act of 1990, PL 101-508), the program was intended to force prescription drug manufacturers to provide the same rebates to state MEDICAID programs that they routinely granted to other "bulk" purchasers, such as large MANAGED CARE organizations, hospitals, and the Veterans Administration.

At $3.3 billion in 1988, drug costs represented a major expense for Medicaid. According to data compiled by the Senate Special Committee on Aging, whose chairman, David Pryor, D-Ark., championed the drug discount effort, Medicaid drug outlays for states that offered drug benefits rose 224 percent between 1980 and 1988, a rate three times faster than the inflation rate in the rest of the economy and significantly greater than that in other sectors of health care.

The prescription drug industry vehemently opposed the measure—Medicaid purchases accounted for some 15–20 percent of all drug sales, reported the Pharmaceutical Manufacturers Association (PMA, later renamed the Pharmaceutical and Research Manufacturers Association). The industry argued that it was already facing increased price competition as a result of 1984 legislation that made it easier for companies to market "generic" copies after patents expired on brand name products (see GENERIC DRUGS). The PMA also argued that limiting the profits of drug companies would jeopardize research into new drugs that could ultimately reduce health care costs by curing chronic ailments or serving as substitutes for surgery or other expensive procedures.

After a fierce fight, however, Congress decided to require the rebates. Originally, the rebates were set at the lower of 12.5 percent off the average manufacturer price or the "best price" at which the manufacturer sold the drug to any customer except the Department of Veterans Affairs. Discounts on drugs for which generic copies were already on the market were set at 10 percent for the first three years and 11 percent thereafter.

Medical malpractice

Medical malpractice is one form of *tort*, or wrongful personal injury by one person against another. Patients who believe they have been injured can recover damages in court if they can show that the physician or health care provider had a duty not to harm them, breached that duty by not meeting the community's prevailing "standard of care," and as a result of the breach, caused the injury. Most medical malpractice law is at the state level; however, health care providers have been pushing the federal government to get more involved.

There is widespread agreement that the system by which doctors who are incompetent or neglectful are punished does not work very well. The purpose of medical malpractice laws is twofold: to compensate those who are injured as a result of substandard medical care and to deter health professionals from providing bad or negligent care. Yet a 1991 study by researchers at Harvard University that examined medical records from hospitals in New York City found the system does not accomplish either goal. Researchers examined more than thirty thousand patient records and identified forty-seven malpractice claims. But only eight of those claims were filed for the 280 patients who the records suggested had been victims of medical negligence. In other words, lawsuits were never filed for the vast ma-

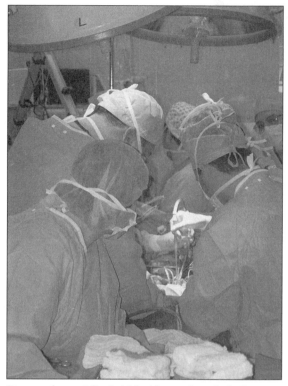

Doctors who specialize in high-risk procedures, including surgeons, are among the health care professionals most likely to be sued for malpractice. Source: Mary Agnes Carey, Congressional Quarterly

jority of cases in which malpractice likely occurred, while most of the lawsuits that were filed were for cases for which there was no evidence that any malpractice took place. A follow-up study found that the size of malpractice awards was determined more by the severity of the injury than by the extent to which the defendant in the case was responsible for that injury. It is little wonder that insurers and doctors refer to the nation's malpractice system as "a lawsuit lottery" in which a few people win multimillion-dollar judgments while the vast majority of those injured receive nothing.

Medical malpractice lawsuits cost the health system money in two different ways. One is through insurance premiums paid by doctors and other health care providers, premiums that are generally passed on to patients and insurers. These premiums may be quite high for doctors who practice high-risk procedures, particularly obstetrician/gynecologists, and surgeons, who are statistically among the most likely to be sued. It is not uncommon for ob/gyns to have malpractice premium costs in excess of $100,000 per year, and a 1992 survey found that 12 percent of ob/gyns had stopped delivering babies because they could not afford the malpractice insurance premiums. Overall, however, malpractice premiums account for about 1 percent of total health care spending.

The other way malpractice affects health care spending is through the practice of "defensive medicine," which occurs when doctors order tests or procedures not because they think they are medically indicated but because of fear of being sued, or to have a defense if they are sued. Although some estimates have put defensive medicine costs as high as 25 percent of all care, a 1994 study by the federal Office of Technology Assessment (OTA) found that defensive medicine more likely accounts for less than 8 percent of diagnostic procedures performed. The OTA study also noted that not all defensive medicine is unnecessary and may well be of benefit, even though some of it might not be performed but for physicians' concerns about potential liability.

Physicians say lawyers make too much money off malpractice suits, that patients with minor injuries cannot get compensation because lawyers won't take their cases, and that physicians are unfairly sued too often. One study by the RAND Corporation found that injured patients collect only forty-three cents of every dollar paid in damages; lawyers take home more than half of each dollar. Provider groups want Congress to impose a "cap" on so-called *noneconomic damages*—those awarded for pain and suffering, as opposed to *economic damages,* which reimburse patients for lost wages and the costs of care, or *punitive damages,* which are intended to punish particularly egregious behavior. California and several other states have imposed such caps as part of malpractice reforms; California's cap is $250,000.

Consumer and legal groups, however, say capping damages would further injure those already injured by a medical professional. The American Bar Association says that capping noneconomic damages would particularly affect women and low-income individuals, who are likely to have limited direct economic losses, as well as those with severe injuries. Consumer groups also say that the medical profession does too poor a job of policing itself for lawmakers to curb legal recourse. According to the Public Citizen Health Research Group, in 1997 state medical boards took serious disciplinary actions (suspensions, revocations, or surrenders of medical licenses) against fewer than four physicians per one thousand. The group said that other studies suggested that 1 percent of physicians should be sanctioned each year, a level more than twice the level of sanctions being imposed.

The malpractice battle between doctors and lawyers, particularly at the federal level, is reflected in campaign contributions made by each side. According to the Center for Responsive Politics, which tracks campaign finance issues, in the 1997–1998 election cycle the Association of Trial Lawyers of America's political action committee made $2.3 million in contributions to congressional candidates, 85.7 percent of which went to Democrats. Those contributions ranked the group, which opposes caps on damage awards or attorney fees, number three among all political action committees (PACs) (behind the tobacco company Phillip Morris and the International Brotherhood of Electrical Workers, a labor union). By contrast, the American Medical Association, the leading proponent of malpractice reforms, gave $1.59 million, 67 percent of which was directed to Republican candidates. That donation ranked it thirteenth among PAC givers.

The "crisis of availability" in malpractice insurance in the 1980s prompted federal officials to take a closer look at the issue. In 1991 President George Bush proposed that states make several malpractice reforms. Included in the proposal, which did not become law, were caps on noneconomic damages, and "alternative dispute resolution" mechanisms, such as binding arbitration and mediation, that would keep malpractice cases out of court. Bush proposed to withhold 2 percent in administrative payments made under Medicaid from states that failed to pass malpractice reforms meeting the requirements.

President Bill Clinton, as part of his Health Security Act in 1993, proposed a variety of malpractice reforms, although not a cap on damages. The centerpiece of the act's malpractice proposals was a concept called "enterprise liability," which would have made entire health plans, rather than individual physicians, liable for malpractice. Physician groups opposed that concept, noting that it would give health plan administrators even more control over doctors' actions. Clinton in his plan also proposed alternative dispute resolution techniques: requiring claims to be awarded a "certificate of merit" from a "qualified specialist" verifying the claim's legitimacy; limiting attorney fees to one-third of awards; and allowing physicians to use as a defense their following of clinical practice guidelines.

Since the Republicans took over Congress after the 1994 elections, the House has passed legislation to cap noneconomic damages five times. The House appended its malpractice proposal to three bills that did not become law: the "Common Sense Product Liability and Legal Reform Act"; the 1995 Balanced Budget Act, which was vetoed by President Clinton; and the 1998 "Patient Protection Act," which passed the House but not the Senate. The House included the provisions again in its versions of what would become the HEALTH INSURANCE PORTABILITY AND ACCOUNTABILITY ACT (HIPAA, PL 104-191) and the 1997 Balanced Budget Act (PL 105-33). In both laws the malpractice provisions were dropped in conference at the insistence of the Senate and the White House.

Medical necessity

A critical term in MANAGED CARE and health insurance, it determines what care will and will not be covered. Most insurance policies pay only for "medically necessary" care. That category of care is intended to exclude things like cosmetic surgery or other "lifestyle" treatments. But the boundaries of the category often depend less on written definitions and more on who makes the determination of whether care is necessary or not. In the past, anything a physician ordered was gen-

erally deemed medically necessary by an insurer. But today, most insurance companies, particularly managed care companies, have their own definitions of medical necessity. Managed care officials say making medical necessity determinations helps them improve care, often by steering a treating physician toward a treatment that research has shown to be more effective. But doctors, led by the AMERICAN MEDICAL ASSOCIATION, say that health plans use medical necessity as a tool to save money, even if it means denying care a patient truly needs. The PATIENTS' BILL OF RIGHTS legislation backed by President Bill Clinton would bar health plans from "arbitrarily interfering with or altering" a treating doctor's judgment if the care in question is otherwise covered and is "consistent with generally accepted principles of professional medical practice."

Medical power of attorney

See DURABLE POWER OF ATTORNEY FOR HEALTH CARE

Medical records confidentiality

How to protect the confidentiality of medical records is one of the most contentious issues in health policy. On the one hand, the increasing ability to transmit information electronically has an enormous potential to improve health care—theoretically emergency room personnel can access critical medical information on a person who has a heart attack or is in an automobile accident thousands of miles away from home. And researchers using information in medical records can uncover untold new discoveries, not to mention finding which treatments are most cost-effective or have fewest side effects. But the increasing dissemination of personal medical information—bits of data are almost continuously traveling between doctors' offices, hospitals, pharmacies, and insurers and other third-parties—has its downside as well. The leaking of sensitive or embarrassing information—such as a history of a mental illness or sexually-transmitted disease—can be emotionally devastating. And there is anecdotal evidence that patients are becoming reluctant to share pertinent medical information with their health providers for fear they will suffer job or insurance discrimination (see GENETIC DISCRIMINATION).

As part of the 1996 HEALTH INSURANCE PORTABILITY AND ACCOUNTABILITY ACT (HIPAA, PL 104-191), Congress ordered the secretary of Health and Human Services (HHS) to make recommendations to Congress on ways to protect "individually identifiable" medical information and to set penalties for wrongful disclosure of such information. In that law Congress set itself a deadline of August 1999 (which it missed) by which to either enact a law governing the confidentiality of medical records or authorize HHS to promulgate its regulations, which were presented by Secretary Donna Shalala in September 1997.

Privacy advocates, health care providers, insurers, and researchers all want federal legislation. As health care becomes increasingly a multistate endeavor, with patients, providers, and insurers frequently living and working across jurisdictional lines from each other, everyone involved in health care is struggling to cope with fifty different sets of requirements. But not everyone agrees on exactly how to protect personal medical information, who should have access, and what the penalties should be for misuse.

In announcing the HHS proposal—which applied only to electronic information, not paper records—on September 11, 1997, Shalala said the recommendations "strike a balance between the privacy needs of our citizens and the critical needs of our health care system and our nation." Specifically, the HHS proposal would impose confidentiality rules on anyone who provides or pays for health care, or who receives health information from a provider or payer, either with permission of the patient or as authorized under the legislation. Recipients of "identifiable" patient information would be required to ensure its confidentiality by creating audit trails, using administrative and management techniques, and leveling sanctions against employees who use information improperly. Stronger state laws, such as

those specifically protecting mental health information or information related to HIV/AIDS, would still apply and would not be preempted.

Consumers would be given the right to see their medical records, to copy them, and to propose corrections. Those who collect information would have to inform patients how the information will be used, kept, and disseminated, and patients would be permitted to see a written history of who has accessed their personal health information. Providers could not condition treatment on a patient's consenting to disclose health information (as is commonplace currently, when patients sign "blanket authorizations" in order to receive care), unless the information is required for treatment, coverage, or payment purposes. (Although privacy advocates acknowledge the need for some information to be provided if care is to be covered, they ask that mandatory disclosures be limited as much as possible.) In cases of wrongful disclosure, federal criminal penalties would apply, and patients would have the right to file a civil suit, known as a "private right of action," against the party who wrongfully disclosed the information,

The HHS proposal did allow for some exceptions to the confidentiality rules. Information would be available for overseeing the health care system (for conducting audits, fraud investigations, quality assurance activities, and health professional licensing programs). Information would also be released for emergencies affecting life or safety, for public health purposes, for research, and for state health data systems. Other exceptions to the confidentiality rules concerned medical records requested by law enforcement authorities for court proceedings in which the patient is a party, and for other court proceedings in which records had been sought under a specific court order.

Not surprisingly, the HHS recommendations proved controversial. Patient advocates criticized the proposal for not taking stronger measures to protect identifiable medical information from law enforcement authorities—a blanket exception reportedly imposed on HHS by the Justice Department. Insurance groups argued that allowing stronger state laws to remain in force

Privacy advocates have lobbied for tight restrictions on the use of medical records. Marines John Mayfield (left) and Joseph Vlacovsky faced court martial in 1996 for refusing to provide the military with DNA samples and for questioning the use of their genetic information.
Source: James M. Thresher, Reuters

would undermine the entire concept of creating a single uniform standard.

But by far the most contentious issue is whether patients should have to consent to each use of personally identifiable medical information. Privacy advocates say yes, but researchers say such a requirement could cripple their ability to do their jobs. At one congressional hearing in March 1998, a researcher from the Mayo Clinic said that if a Minnesota privacy law had been in effect two years earlier, Mayo researchers would not have been able to access the information used to demonstrate the relationship between the diet drug "phen-fen" and heart valve damage. The Mayo study resulted in the drug being pulled from the market.

Medical savings accounts (MSAs)

These tax-preferred vehicles enable people to "self-insure" for their own routine medical expenses while simultaneously saving money for themselves. Individuals with MSAs carry a "catastrophic" insurance policy with a high deductible (usually $1,500 or more) that kicks in if severe illness strikes. The theory behind MSAs is that by making individuals responsible for their own routine medical expenses, the savings accounts will make those individuals more price-conscious, thereby holding down overall health spending. Because individuals can keep any money in the MSA that they don't spend on health care (although they must pay taxes on funds not spent for medical care), they have an incentive to spend only for care that is necessary and at the best price possible, the reverse of the situation under FIRST DOLLAR COVERAGE insurance, in which individuals have no incentive to economize. Political conservatives have been the biggest boosters of MSAs, arguing that they return choice and responsibility to individuals.

But MSAs are also among the most controversial entities in health policy. Detractors argue that individuals with MSAs are likely to forgo needed preventive care, because they would prefer to save the money to spend on non–health care items. They also argue that MSAs could undermine the insurance market as a whole. Because they appeal more to healthier people (who are most likely to have money left over at the end of the year in their MSA), MSAs could draw the healthiest people out of the insurance pool, leaving the sick behind and raising premiums. MSAs are also more attractive to wealthy individuals—since any difference between the amount in an MSA and the amount of the deductible will have to be made up out-of-pocket, they can better afford the risk involved. Higher-income people also benefit more from the tax advantages of an MSA, since their own contributions are tax-deferred, as are amounts deposited by an employer.

Congress in 1996 and 1997 authorized two separate MSA programs. Although federal legislation was not technically needed for MSAs to exist (many employers have been offering them for years), only the federal government could grant the tax advantages needed to make the program attractive to large numbers of people.

As part of the 1996 HEALTH INSURANCE PORTA-BILITY AND ACCOUNTABILITY ACT, Congress authorized a demonstration program, to last until 2001, during which 750,000 policies could be sold. The program was limited to the self-employed and firms with fifty or fewer workers; deductibles for catastrophic insurance coverage were required to be between $1,500 and $2,250 for individuals and between $3,000 and $4,500 for families; and contributions to the MSA could not be more than 65 percent of the deductible for individuals and 75 percent for families. MSA contributions have two tax advantages: no federal taxes are due on the money deposited, and the interest that accumulates in the account is also tax-free. Still, the program was slow to catch on. As of June 30, 1998, only 54,702 policies had been sold; only 17,688 had been purchased by people who were previously uninsured. MSA advocates argued that the program was structured in such a way as to make MSAs unattractive; however, legislative efforts to lift the enrollment caps, lower the limits on deductibles, and allow both workers and employers to make contributions to the MSA were not successful as of the end of 1998.

As part of the 1997 Balanced Budget Act (PL 105-33), Congress also authorized an MSA demonstration program for MEDICARE beneficiaries. Under the law, up to 390,000 Medicare beneficiaries could open an MSA and purchase catastrophic coverage until the year 2002. However, for the first year of the program, 1999, no

MSAs were available because no plan had signed up to offer them. Medicare MSA beneficiaries would be eligible to receive payments equal to those provided to managed care plans in their counties. Medicare would purchase the BENEFICIARY's high-deductible catastrophic policy (with an annual deductible limited to $6,000), then deposit the remainder into the individual's MSA. Beneficiaries could use MSA funds without tax penalty for "qualified medical expenses," as defined by the Internal Revenue Service, or to pay premiums for LONG-TERM CARE or other health insurance. Individuals could also withdraw funds for nonhealth purposes, paying regular income taxes, as long as the withdrawals left at least 60 percent of the catastrophic insurance deductible in the MSA. Account balances could be left to heirs under the same tax treatment as that of other tax-preferred retirement accounts.

The Medicare MSAs presented opponents yet another argument—that scarce Medicare dollars could theoretically be used for nonmedical purposes. But many analysts also predicted that seniors, being much more risk-averse than younger consumers, would be slow to sign up for MSAs in any case.

Medical underwriting

The term refers to a process by which insurers determine how much an individual or group is likely to incur in the way of medical bills, and, thus, how much that person or group should pay in premiums. Medical underwriters look at demographic factors, such as age and gender, as well as individual medical histories. In some cases, the underwriting process results in an insurer's declining to offer coverage at all, or offering coverage that excludes certain conditions.

Medically needy

This optional federal program allows a state to provide MEDICAID coverage, either in full or in limited form, to certain individuals who have incomes or assets too high to permit them to qualify under the state's eligibility rules, but who have "spent down" their income and assets to medically needy eligibility levels by paying for health care services. Except for their income and asset levels, medically needy individuals must otherwise be members of groups eligible for Medicaid. States may offer benefits to those in its medically needy program that are less comprehensive than those offered in its regular Medicaid program, but if they offer coverage to any medically needy populations, they are required to offer it to certain groups and provide coverage for certain services. (In other words, states cannot merely offer LONG-TERM CARE coverage for the elderly under a medically needy program). Mandatory medically needy groups include children under age nineteen and pregnant women, and states must cover prenatal and delivery care for pregnant women and outpatient care for children. In 1996 forty-two states provided care under a medically needy program; the remaining states provided separate optional Medicaid coverage to institutionalized individuals with incomes up to 300 percent of the level needed to qualify for SUPPLEMENTAL SECURITY INCOME (SSI).

Medicare

The federal program that provides health insurance to thirty-nine million elderly and disabled Americans, Medicare is something of a policy paradox. It is simultaneously one of the most beloved programs run by the federal government and one that provides considerably less in the way of benefits than do most private plans. It also remains financially unprepared for the impending eligibility of the massive baby boom generation beginning in the year 2010.

History

President Lyndon B. Johnson signed the legislation to implement Medicare (PL 89-97) on July 30, 1965, following a fight that lasted nearly a generation, dating from President Harry S. Truman's failed effort to enact national health insurance in 1949–1950. Johnson signed the bill in Independence, Missouri, Truman's hometown, as a tribute. Backers based their case for creating a government program for health care for the elderly on the low economic status of the over-sixty-five population—in 1962, 47 percent of senior citizens had incomes below the federal poverty line, compared with 13 percent of the rest of the population. At the same time, although older people have more health problems, individual insurance was largely unavailable—only about 56 percent of seniors had HOSPITAL INSURANCE in 1965. And the average senior citizen in 1966, the year Medicare began, spent 15 percent of his or her income for health care services.

Still, President John F. Kennedy was unsuccessful in getting Medicare legislation—one of his top domestic priorities—through a reluctant Congress. It was not until the Democratic landslide in the 1964 elections that Congress was finally willing to make Medicare a reality. But the legislation creating Medicare remained a political compromise.

Engineered by powerful HOUSE WAYS AND MEANS COMMITTEE chairman Wilbur Mills, D-Ark., the measure consisted of three parts. One was Medicare's HOSPITAL INSURANCE (HI) program, also known as Part A. This is a "social insurance" program funded by broad-based taxes (in 1999 a 1.45 percent add-on to the Social Security tax paid by all active workers and employers on all of their earnings), and available to all those eligible for Social Security benefits. This universal program was strongly backed by Democrats and organized labor. The second element was SUPPLEMENTARY MEDICAL INSURANCE (SMI), also known as Part B of Medicare. This optional program, available to all over age sixty-five willing to pay its monthly premiums (originally matched one-for-one by federal dollars), was based on a proposal offered by Republicans and the AMERICAN MEDICAL ASSOCIATION, mostly in an effort to avoid creation of Medicare's Part A. Finally, the measure created a separate MEDICAID program for the poor elderly and others with very low incomes.

Medicare, which grew quickly, was expanded further in 1972, when certain disabled individuals and those with END-STAGE RENAL DISEASE (ESRD) were made eligible for coverage, although seniors are still Medicare's predominant population. In 1998 the program covered 34 million individuals over age sixty-five and 5 million disabled persons (about three hundred thousand of whom have ESRD).

In 1997 Congress created a Medicare Part C, formally called MEDICARE+CHOICE. This program consists of private plans (mostly—but not exclusively—MANAGED CARE plans) that provide Medicare beneficiaries with services covered under both Part A and Part B. Many managed care plans, in order to attract customers, also offer benefits Medicare does not normally cover, such as outpatient prescription drugs, foot care, eyeglasses, and hearing aids. Medicare+Choice plans receive premiums directly from Medicare under a complex formula based on average spending in the county where the plan is offered.

Eligibility

Anyone age sixty-five or older who is eligible for Social Security or Railroad Retirement benefits is automatically eligible for Medicare Part A. A worker and spouse become eligible after working forty calendar quarters (ten years) in a qualifying job. Also automatically eligible for Part A are individuals under age sixty-five who have been receiving SOCIAL SECURITY DISABILITY INSURANCE payments for twenty-four months. (Recipients of a related program for the disabled, SUPPLEMENTAL SECURITY INCOME, or SSI, are eligible for Medicaid, not Medicare.) Those over age sixty-five who have worked thirty to thirty-nine eligible quarters can purchase Part A coverage if they also enroll in Part B (see below). In 1999 the premium was $170 per month. Those with fewer than thirty quarters can purchase Part A coverage for $309 monthly.

Part B is available on a voluntary basis to anyone who is eligible for Part A, and to anyone over age sixty-five regardless of his or her Part A eligibility. (Those who purchase Part A coverage must also enroll in Part B.) The monthly premium in 1999 was $45.50. For those also receiving Social Security payments, the premium is deducted automatically from their checks. Because it is an excellent buy, and because most supplemental insurance policies require Part B enrollment, the vast majority of Part A beneficiaries (more than 95 percent) also enroll in Part B. Beneficiaries who wish to enroll in a private Part C (Medicare+Choice) plan must also enroll in Part B and must continue to pay the Part B premium.

Led by Speaker Newt Gingrich (right), R-Ga., the House in 1995 approved radical changes in the Medicare program, some of which were later implemented in the 1997 Balanced Budget Act. Prior to the House vote, New York residents Roslyn Wolf and Gene Bedsole urged Gingrich to "save" the financially troubled program. Source: Mike Theiler, Reuters

Benefits

To overcome initial resistance to Medicare from the medical community—doctors and hospitals—lawmakers designed Medicare to resemble the type of insurance that was typical in the 1960s—insurance that paid for people when they got sick rather than paying to keep them well. Since most insurance plans of that era did not pay for such items as preventive services, outpatient prescription drugs, or hearing or vision care, neither did Medicare.

Medicare's benefit package, typical by 1965 standards, today looks quite meager. Although it pays for most "medically necessary care" (see MEDICAL NECESSITY), it excludes most preventive measures, virtually all LONG-TERM CARE expenses (other than rehabilitative care in nursing homes following a hospital stay), most coverage of hearing, vision, dental, and foot care, and, perhaps most important, almost all costs for outpatient prescription drugs. Medicare also includes no "stop-loss" or "catastrophic" coverage. Most private plans limit the amount a patient must pay for his or her share of covered medical bills each year, often to between $1,000 and $3,000. Congress approved a program to cap Medicare costs in 1988, but it was to be financed by BENEFICIARIES themselves. When beneficiaries objected, the program was repealed even before it fully took effect in 1989. (See MEDICARE CATASTROPHIC COVERAGE ACT.)

Medicare has improved its benefits somewhat over the years. In the late 1980s and early 1990s, Congress gradually added coverage of annual shots to prevent flu and pneumonia, as well as mammograms to detect breast cancer in women. As part of the 1997 Balanced Budget Act (PL 105-33), Congress beefed up preventive coverage still more, adding more frequent mammograms, pap smears to detect cervical cancer, as well as screening for prostate and colorectal cancer and coverage of costs for managing diabetes.

Even with improved benefits, however, Medicare still requires beneficiaries to pay a significant amount out of pocket for their medical care. In 1999 Part A required a deductible of $768 for each "benefit period" requiring hospitalization. After the first sixty days in the hospital,

---

Medicare Beneficiary Amounts for 1999

Inpatient hospital insurance (Part A)
- Deductible—$768 (per benefit period requiring hospitalization)
- Coinsurance—(1) $192.00 a day for the 61st through 90th days of each benefit period; (2) $384.00 a day for the 91st through 150th days ("lifetime reserve period")
- Skilled nursing facility coinsurance–$96.00 a day for the 21st through 100th days of each benefit period

Hospital insurance (Part A) premium
- $309.00 per month (paid only by individuals who are not otherwise eligible for premium-free hospital insurance)
- $339.90 (paid by those who must pay a premium surcharge for late enrollment)
- Part A premium of $170 (paid by indivuals having thirty or more quarters of coverage—they must pay a premium plus a surcharge of $187.00 for late enrollment)

Supplementary Medical Insurance (SMI) Part B
- Deductible—$100.00 per year
- Copayment—20 percent of cost of all Medicare-covered services

Part B monthly premium
- $45.50 (1999)
- $43.80 (1997 and 1998)

---

patients paid $192 per day for days sixty-one through ninety, and $384 per day during a "lifetime reserve" period of sixty days. Medicare-covered nursing home stays were fully paid for twenty days; after that, patients were required to contribute $96 per day.

Part B required a $100 annual deductible and, after that, a 20 percent copayment for all covered services. For example, if a doctor charged $100 for a service, the patient was responsible for $20 of that amount, assuming Medicare allowed the entire $100 bill under its fee schedule.

Because of Medicare's cost-sharing requirements, in 1996 beneficiaries spent an average of $2,605 per person on health care, about 21 percent of their income. About

Medicare Expenditures per Beneficiary (by Decile of Least Costly to Most Costly, 1996

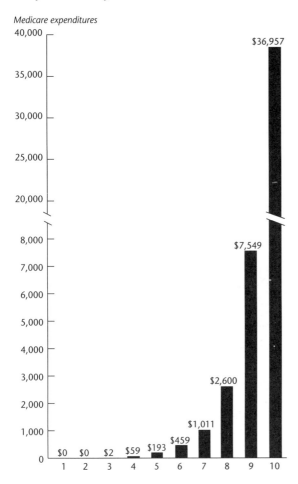

Medicare expenditures

Source: Marilyn Moon, *Restructuring Medicare's Cost-Sharing,* The Commonwealth Fund, December 1996.

half that amount went to pay Medicare and private MEDIGAP INSURANCE premiums; the remaining half was split between Medicare-required copayments and payments for services not covered by Medicare or Medigap. By contrast, nonelderly Americans spent about 8 percent of their incomes on health care. In 1997 Medicare paid about 53 percent of its beneficiaries' health care costs, ranking it in the bottom 10 percent of insurance plans.

Cost-cutting efforts

Not long after Medicare's inception, its costs began to spiral. Part of the reason was the increase in medical costs overall, particularly as technological advances made more things possible, from organ transplants to joint replacements to new treatments for cancer and other formerly fatal diseases. But a big part, too, was Medicare's "cost-plus" reimbursement, intended to entice providers to serve beneficiaries by paying hospitals, doctors, and other health care purveyors essentially whatever they charged. Between 1975 and 1994 Medicare spending per enrollee grew by an average of 17 percent per year.

Efforts to slow Medicare's rapid spending spiral began as early as 1972, when Congress created Professional Standards Review Organizations (PSROs) to review and control use of Medicare services by beneficiaries. In 1974 Congress imposed the first tentative price controls on Medicare hospital payments.

In 1982 Congress in the Tax Equity and Fiscal Responsibility Act (TEFRA, PL 97-248) imposed a ceiling on hospital payments, prompting outrage from hospitals, which claimed the limits were unfair given their individual circumstances. That paved the way for creation, as part of the 1983 legislation to "rescue" Social Security (PL 98-21), of a new PROSPECTIVE PAYMENT SYSTEM (PPS) for hospitals that based payments on a patient's diagnosis rather than on what the hospital happened to spend to treat that patient. The system created 467 DIAGNOSIS-RELATED GROUPS and set a payment according to what the average hospital would spend to treat a patient with that condition. With some allowances for geographic variations and other hospital characteristics (such as whether the hospital has a teaching program), hospitals are paid the same to treat patients with the same condition. The new system reversed the previous incentives, according to which the more services a hospital provided (and the longer a patient stayed), the more the hospital got paid. Under PPS hospitals were given an incentive to become more efficient, because they could keep the excess if care cost less than the predetermined payment, whereas they would have to make up the difference if care cost more.

The new system rapidly brought hospital spending under control, but at the same time, physician spending began to balloon. Throughout the 1980s Medicare physician spending rose at an average of 15–18 percent per year. That increase led to legislation in 1989 (part of that year's budget reconciliation bill, PL 101-239) to revamp physician spending. Central to the new system was implementation of something called a RESOURCE-BASED RELATIVE VALUE SCALE (RBRVS), devised under 1986 orders from Congress by a group of researchers from Harvard University and refined by the PHYSICIAN PAYMENT REVIEW COMMISSION. The RBRVS measured the time, training, and skill required to perform a given service and was adjusted for overhead costs and geographical differences. It was intended to redress Medicare's tendency to overcompensate for surgery, diagnostic tests, and other procedures and to underpay for PRIMARY CARE services that involved examining and talking to patients rather than doing things to them.

But controlling the price of physician services was only half the battle. To prevent doctors who stood to see lower prices from simply increasing the number of services they provided, the new system also imposed volume controls via an annual Medicare Volume Performance Standard (MVPS), which was to set targets for total spending increases based on the change in the number of beneficiaries, inflation, changes in volume and technology, and other factors. Inflation increases in future years were to be adjusted according to whether the previous year's target was met.

Even with the new hospital and physician payment systems, though, many health care analysts argued that the only way to slow Medicare spending overall was to move away from the program's traditional FEE-FOR-SERVICE orientation and put more beneficiaries into managed care. Congress took the first tentative steps in 1982 budget reconciliation legislation, allowing beneficiaries to join what it called Medicare "risk" plans, HMOs that agreed to provide all medically necessary care for a preset monthly fee. That fee, known as the ADJUSTED AVERAGE PER CAPITA COST, or AAPCC, was based on 95 percent of the cost incurred by the average Medicare

beneficiary in the county where the plan is located. Enrollment grew slowly at first because the plans, like most HMOs, required beneficiaries to give up their free choice of doctors and hospitals and use only providers in the plan's "network." But managed care enrollment took off in the mid-1990s, when plans began to offer attractive new benefits traditional Medicare did not cover, particularly coverage of prescription drugs. By 1998 about 17 percent of beneficiaries had joined managed care plans.

In theory, Medicare managed care would appear to save money. Because the payment is 95 percent of the cost of the average beneficiary, the program should be saving 5 percent for every beneficiary who enrolls. But numerous studies have shown that beneficiaries who join managed care are healthier than average, thus costing Medicare money over the long run. As part of the 1997 Balanced Budget Act (PL 105-33), Congress moved to slow increases in managed care payments; among other things, it imposed a 2 percent annual cap on payment increases for most plans. As a result, more than forty plans dropped out of the program for 1999; more than fifty others stopped offering coverage in certain counties. In July 1999 a similar number of plans announced they would leave Medicare in the year 2000.

In addition to creating the new Medicare+Choice program, the 1997 Balanced Budget Act also set in place a series of policies designed to slow Medicare spending dramatically enough to keep the program solvent until the year 2010 (previously the Medicare Part A Trust Fund was projected to run out of money in the year 2001). The success of those efforts, even those only partly implemented, was obvious as early as 1998, when Medicare spending grew by just 1.5 percent, the slowest growth in the history of the program. It also represented the first time Medicare spending had grown more slowly than the federal budget as a whole, and the first time in recent years that Medicare had grown at a rate slower than that of private health care spending (which rose by an estimated 4 percent). As a result of the combination of more revenue in payroll taxes, due to the strong economy, and less Medicare spending, in March 1999 Medicare's trustees projected that the Hospital Insurance (HI) trust fund would remain solvent until the year 2015.

Medicare's impending financial difficulties

The efforts described above did succeed in slowing Medicare spending—a 1991 report by the CONGRESSIONAL BUDGET OFFICE estimated that the changes rendered in the 1980s reduced overall Medicare spending by 20 percent compared with what it would have been without the changes. But Medicare is still financially unprepared for the impending eligibility of the baby boomers beginning in the year 2010. Even after cutting costs, Medicare is consuming an ever larger share of the nation's health care dollar. In 1995 Medicare spending accounted for one of every five health care dollars, up from 11 percent in 1970. Even with the savings achieved by the 1997 Balanced Budget Act, Medicare is still expected to grow rapidly. Although the 1997 changes are projected to slow Medicare spending sufficiently to preserve the program's financially ailing HI trust fund until the year 2010, Medicare will continue to absorb a growing share of all national resources. (Part B spending comes from general revenues, so technically that portion of the program cannot go bankrupt unless the rest of the federal treasury does). According to the Congressional Budget Office, Medicare spending as a share of the nation's total economic output is scheduled to more than double by the year 2030, to 5.5 percent, from its 1995 level of 2.6 percent.

A major reason for the continuing increase in Medicare spending is the growing number of Medicare enrollees. In 1967 Medicare had 19.2 million beneficiaries; by 1997 that number had doubled to more than 38 million. But as the baby boom generation ages, it is threatening to literally swamp Medicare. The number of beneficiaries is expected to grow from 38 million in 1997 to 68 million in 2040; from 14 percent of the population in 1997 to 22 percent in 2030. At the same time, the proportion of working Americans who pay the tax that funds Medicare Part A is declining. In 1997, for every Medicare beneficiary, there were 3.9 workers paying the 1.45 percent payroll tax; by 2010 that figure will decline to 3.6 workers per Medicare beneficiary, and by 2030 only 2.3

workers will be paying taxes to support each Medicare recipient.

Medicare is a victim of its own success. Thanks to improvements in medical care, and access to health care made available thanks to the program, Medicare beneficiaries are living longer than ever, with the proportion of "old-old" (over age eighty-five) rising rapidly. This is important because the oldest beneficiaries need the most medical care and cost the most.

But Congress appeared unlikely to make the changes needed to keep Medicare solvent for the long-term much in advance of the impending insolvency. Not only was Congress facing a similar situation for Social Security, but also both programs have proven so politically radioactive in the past that Congress has never been able to impose major changes except in the face of a crisis.

Medicare+Choice

Medicare+Choice is the formal name of the Part C of MEDICARE created by Congress in the 1997 Balanced Budget Act (PL 105-33). The theory behind Medicare+Choice was to both save the program money by encouraging beneficiaries to join private health plans—which would accept the "risk" for the cost of their care—and provide BENEFICIARIES with health care choices that better resemble those available to workers and their families.

Since 1985 Medicare beneficiaries have been able to join HEALTH MAINTENANCE ORGANIZATIONS (HMOS); as of 1998, about 17 percent of beneficiaries had done so. Moving to managed care was attractive to beneficiaries in parts of the country where plans offered extra benefits at no extra cost, including prescription drug coverage, which traditional Medicare did not cover. But Medicare HMOs are largely the old-fashioned type, with enrollees required to seek care only from providers within the plan's "network." That requirement deterred many beneficiaries, particularly those with long-standing relationships with doctors.

Medicare+Choice sought to expand the types of

choices available to Medicare beneficiaries. It authorized Medicare PREFERRED PROVIDER ORGANIZATIONS (PPOS) and POINT OF SERVICE (POS) PLANS that permit enrollees to more easily seek care from outside a health plan's network, although at a somewhat higher cost. To encourage the development of MANAGED CARE in rural and other areas where Medicare managed care payments have traditionally been lower, the measure also authorized creation of PROVIDER-SPONSORED ORGANIZATIONS, or PSOs, groups of doctors, hospitals, or other health delivery professionals who band together to offer insurance.

At the urging of conservative members of Congress, Medicare+Choice also included authority for a variety of non–managed care private plans. Among those are private FEE-FOR-SERVICE plans that would allow enrollees to leave traditional Medicare but continue to see any doctor or use any health facility. Doctors in those plans would not have to abide by Medicare fee limits. The plans were urged by the NATIONAL RIGHT TO LIFE COMMITTEE, a leading antiabortion group that also works against euthanasia and health care rationing. The group argued that if the traditional Medicare program continues to see its budget squeezed, providers will drop out rather than accept the lower fees, and beneficiaries will not be able to receive adequate care. In the private plans, patients could continue to obtain "unrationed" care, albeit at a likely higher out-of-pocket cost.

Also authorized under Medicare+Choice were MEDICAL SAVINGS ACCOUNTS, or MSAs. Under the law, up to 390,000 beneficiaries could open the accounts between 1999 and 2002. Under the MSA provisions, Medicare purchases for beneficiaries a high-deductible "catastrophic" policy (with a deductible up to $6,000). The difference between what the policy costs and what Medicare would have paid to a managed care plan in the beneficiary's county of residence is then deposited into the beneficiary's MSA. The amount will vary depending on where the beneficiary lives, since Medicare+Choice payments are determined on a county-by-county basis. Beneficiaries can use the money in the account for any health care expenses. If their medical expenses exceed their plan's deductible in any year, the insurance will be-

gin paying 100 percent of Medicare-covered expenses (although the beneficiary would still be responsible for expenses not covered by the program). Beneficiaries are required to keep in their MSA an amount equal to 60 percent of their plan's deductible; however, they can withdraw funds in excess of that amount tax-free.

Proponents of MSAs say they will make beneficiaries more cost-conscious, since they will be paying most of their health bills themselves. But critics charge that it is fiscally irresponsible to give beneficiaries Medicare money they may be able to spend for nonhealth items on a tax-free basis.

The 1997 measure also imposed a series of consumer protections for beneficiaries who join the private plans. For example, plans were prohibited from including in contracts with doctors GAG CLAUSES that limit doctor-patient communications, and plans were required to pay for emergency room care in situations in which a "prudent layperson" would consider such care needed. The law also encouraged beneficiaries to "try out" private plans by making it easier for them to repurchase private MEDIGAP INSURANCE if they wished to return to the traditional Medicare fee-for-service program.

Not only did the law encourage beneficiaries to join private plans by allowing more types to be offered, but it also encouraged more plans to be offered in more places by altering the payment system. Because, as noted above, Medicare payments to private plans are based on historical costs within each county, payments varied widely—in 1997 they ranged from a low of $221 per beneficiary per month in Arthur County, Nebraska, to a high of $767 in Richmond (Staten Island), New York. The Balanced Budget Act (PL 105-33) sought to lessen the variation in three ways. First, it imposed a minimum payment for the lowest-paid areas ($380 in 1999). Then—to prevent plans that had been receiving high payments from dropping out—it guaranteed increases of 2 percent per year for all areas. Finally, to raise payments in relatively low-paying areas not affected by the new floor, the law called for a "blend" of regional and national payment rates to be phased in gradually.

Altogether, the government estimated that by the year 2008, 38 percent of beneficiaries would be enrolled in a private Medicare+Choice plan, more than double the percentage in 1998. By 1999, however, it remained unclear if that target would be met. One problem was the payment rates. Because of the required "floor" and the 2 percent increases, there was no money left to implement the blended rate without exceeding the total amount of funds set aside for the program. In the end, the rates in the low-paid areas remained too low to attract many new plans, while the constraints in the higher-paid areas (the 2 percent was not only a "floor" but also a "ceiling" for rate increases) prompted more than ninety plans to either drop out of Medicare altogether or reduce the number of counties in which they participated. In all, 440,000 Medicare beneficiaries found themselves required to find a new health plan for 1999, with some 50,000 living in counties with no other managed care plans from which to choose. The dropouts continued for the year 2000, with some 325,000 beneficiaries affected.

At the same time, fewer companies than expected applied to the HEALTH CARE FINANCING ADMINISTRATION (HCFA) to offer the new types of Medicare+Choice plans. By the time the program officially kicked off January 1, 1999, only one PSO had been approved (to offer an HMO product in Oregon), and no MSAs or other types of plans were available.

Medicare Catastrophic Coverage Act

In June of 1988, Congress passed the Medicare Catastrophic Coverage Act (PL 100-360). It was at the time the largest-ever expansion of MEDICARE since its inception in 1965, and would also prove to be its shortest-lived change. Not even a year and a half later, in November of 1989, after having been deluged with complaints from angry senior citizens who didn't want to pay the bill for the new benefits, Congress repealed the measure in a separate bill (PL 101-234).

The "catastrophic" measure, as it was referred to by lawmakers and lobbyists, was originally intended to fill some of Medicare's most glaring gaps—particularly its lack of any sort of cap on potential out-of-pocket costs.

Whereas typical insurance policies (both indemnity and MANAGED CARE) include annual limits beyond which the insurance will pay 100 percent of costs (typically between $1,500 and $5,000 annually), Medicare included no such "stop-loss." In fact, Medicare was designed so that the sickest people paid the most, particularly for hospital care, in which the first sixty days are covered (after payment of a deductible, $768 in 1999). Thereafter, patients are responsible for an increasing portion of the bill. In 1999 patients were required to pay $192 per day for days sixty-one through ninety and $384 per day during a "lifetime reserve" period of sixty days. After that, Medicare stops paying altogether. In the Part B program for outpatient care, patients are responsible for a 20 percent "copayment" with no limits. Thus, a $25,000 bill (easily reached for a serious illness) would leave a BENEFICIARY owing $5,000.

The original Medicare catastrophic plan, devised by Otis Bowen, secretary of the HEALTH AND HUMAN SERVICES DEPARTMENT (HHS) (and a physician and former Indiana governor), and officially proposed by President Ronald Reagan in February 1987, would have closed only the aforementioned gaps. The plan would have imposed an additional premium of $4.92 per month for unlimited hospital coverage after payment of a single annual deductible and a $2,000 annual cap on Part B out-of-pocket expenses.

But Democrats, having retaken control of the Senate in 1986, thought the Bowen plan far too meager. They noted Medicare's other major gaps—its lack of coverage of outpatient prescription drugs and paltry coverage of LONG-TERM CARE services—and decided to see if they could build a more ambitious proposal. At the same time, Democrats and some Republicans were worried that merely adding onto Medicare's existing Part B premium—a classic regressive tax, since it is a flat fee paid by all beneficiaries regardless of income—would not help the low-income beneficiaries who most needed the catastrophic coverage. Those were the people too poor to be able to afford private Medicare supplemental MEDIGAP insurance that *did* fill Medicare's gaps for the majority of beneficiaries. Thus, lawmakers wanted not only a broader benefits package (including prescription drug coverage) but also a more progressive financing method.

Some wanted to go further still, most notably House Rules Committee chairman Claude Pepper, D-Fla., a longtime crusader for the elderly and much beloved by the nation's senior citizens. Calling the Bowen plan "a pygmy step," Pepper noted—with what would prove great prescience—that Congress ought to expand Medicare as far as it could, even adding hugely expensive long-term care coverage. "If we pass up this opportunity," he said, "we may not come around to this again for another 20 years."

The one thing that held lawmakers back was the absolute unquestioned requirement that any new benefits had to be fully and openly financed. And Democrats and Republicans agreed that the payers in this case should be those who stood to benefit—Medicare beneficiaries themselves. Although groups representing the elderly initially balked at what came to be called "seniors only" financing, they ultimately made it clear that they would back such a radical change in Medicare financing only if the new benefits were worth it—and that the benefits would only be worth it if they included prescription drug coverage.

The bill signed by President Reagan in a Rose Garden ceremony on July 1 represented what everyone at the time thought would be a workable compromise. It included an array of new benefits, including unlimited hospital coverage after a single annual deductible, a cap on Part B out-of-pocket costs of $1,370 in 1990 (the first year it would take effect, to be increased thereafter to hold constant the percentage of beneficiaries who would reach the limit at 7 percent), and limited expansions of Medicare's existing nursing home, HOME HEALTH, and HOSPICE benefits. The program also included several benefits new to Medicare, including coverage of outpatient prescription drugs (ultimately Medicare would have paid 80 percent of the cost, after beneficiaries met an annual deductible starting at $600 in 1991); up to eighty hours of "respite care," paid care to give a respite to an unpaid family member or friend who lived with and cared for a "chronically dependent" Medicare beneficiary; and coverage of mammograms to

screen for breast cancer. (After the 1989 repeal of the catastrophic measure, the mammography benefit was added separately to Medicare in 1990 BUDGET RECONCILIATION LEGISLATION, PL 101-508.)

About 37 percent of the cost of the new program was to be financed by a mandatory increase in the Part B premium, starting at $4.90 per month in 1989 (the total premium was $24.80 in 1988), rising to an estimated $10.20 monthly add-on by 1993. The remainder of the program was to be financed by what those who devised the program called a "supplemental premium," a surtax assessed on the 40 percent of Medicare beneficiaries wealthy enough to owe federal income taxes of more than $150. In 1989 the supplemental premium (to be paid with 1989 taxes by April 15, 1990) was set at $22.50 per $150 in tax liability, up to a cap of $800 per enrollee.

Although only about 5 percent of Medicare beneficiaries would have had to pay the maximum premium, that message never got out to them. A combination of sloppy and incomplete reporting by the news media (one newspaper incorrectly reported that all seniors would have to pay the lower of $800 or 15 percent of their income) and aggressive direct mail campaigns by opponents of the measure (including liberal groups, who disapproved of the "seniors only" financing, and conservative, antitax organizations) led to an almost immediate backlash against the new law. Lawmakers' caution in putting the program together also led to another public relations problem. In 1989 all of the financing was being collected in order to create a "contingency reserve" for the program, but only the unlimited hospital benefit, which helped the fewest beneficiaries, was actually in effect. That led many Medicare beneficiaries to feel they were being cheated, and they wasted no time or effort telling their legislators just that.

The iconic moment in the debate came in the summer of 1989, when a protester against the measure, Leona Kozien, separated herself from a throng of sign-waving septuagenarians and draped herself across the hood of HOUSE WAYS AND MEANS COMMITTEE chairman Dan Rostenkowski's car after the congressman tried to escape a raucous meeting with angry Medicare beneficiaries in his Chicago district. As with much of the protests about the law, the confrontation with Rostenkowski was a set-up—the media had been tipped off in advance. But the pictures of a sweating, obviously uncomfortable, and unabashed defender of the program being harassed by his own constituents had a powerful effect on other members of Congress who were, unlike Rostenkowski, not as clear on the details of the program or its merits.

Ironically, repealing the program proved nearly as difficult as putting it together in the first place. Because the premiums were already being collected, repealing the program would add an estimated $6 billion to the fiscal 1990 deficit, estimated the CONGRESSIONAL BUDGET OFFICE. Under budget rules, the cost would have to me made up with cuts of that magnitude from elsewhere. And try as they did to find a way to modify the program to make it more acceptable, lawmakers ultimately came up empty-handed. The Senate tried to push a proposal advanced by Sen. John McCain, R-Ariz., that would have eliminated the surtax and left only the expanded hospital benefits. But by November it was clear the entire program had to go. The repeal measure, which waived budget rules so as to not require offsetting cuts, eliminated all of the new Medicare benefits. It left intact only a handful of MEDICAID expansions (including key expansions for pregnant women and young children, and protection from impoverishment of persons living at home whose spouses were living in nursing homes at Medicaid expense), as well as authority for the so-called PEPPER COMMISSION, a bipartisan panel charged with devising proposals to cover the UNINSURED and finance long-term care (the panel was included to pacify the House Rules Committee chairman).

Medicare Payment Advisory Commission (MedPAC)

Created by Congress in the 1997 Balanced Budget Act (PL 105-33), MedPAC advises Congress on provider payment policies and on general quality of care issues for MEDICARE beneficiaries. MedPAC was formed by merging two previous advisory bodies, the PROSPECTIVE PAYMENT ASSESSMENT COMMISSION (ProPAC),

which oversaw Medicare hospital payments, and the PHYSICIAN PAYMENT REVIEW COMMISSION (PPRC), which monitored Medicare physician payments. Like its predecessors, MedPAC is required to report to Congress each year (by June 1) with recommendations on Medicare payment policies, in light of other changes in the nation's health care system. Originally fifteen members, Congress in 1998 expanded the panel's membership to seventeen (in the Omnibus spending bill). MedPAC's first chair was former PPRC head Gail Wilensky, a health care economist who advised President George Bush on health issues and headed the HEALTH CARE FINANCING ADMINISTRATION during the development and implementation of Medicare's physician payment reforms.

Medigap insurance

Also known as MEDICARE supplemental insurance, these are private policies that fill the "gaps" in basic Medicare coverage. More than three-fourths of Medicare BENEFICIARIES have Medigap coverage, 40 percent purchased by beneficiaries privately and 37 percent obtained through a current or former employer.

Congress has regulated the sale of Medigap insurance since 1980, after a 1978 investigation by the House Select Committee on Aging uncovered numerous abuses in the marketing and sale of Medigap policies. By 1988, however, it was clear that abuses were continuing. A study by the General Accounting Office found that one-third of Medigap insurers failed to meet the 1980 target that plans return 60 percent of premium dollars in benefits for individual policies, and two-thirds failed to meet the 75 percent LOSS RATIO for group policies. (Loss ratio is the percentage of premiums paid out by an insurance company for actual medical care. The higher the loss ratio, the more money is spent on actual care, and less on administration, overhead, advertising, or profits.) Medigap insurers also sold policies that duplicated benefits covered by Medicare and that duplicated each other. Congress tightened the restrictions again in 1988 as part of the MEDICARE CATASTROPHIC COVERAGE ACT (when that law was repealed in 1989, the

Standardized Medigap Plans and Benefits

	A	B	C	D	E	F	G	H	I	J
Basic benefits Coinsurance for days 61–90 and days 91–150 in hospital and payment in full for 365 additional hospital days; 20 percent coinsurance for physician and other Part B services; three pints of blood	•	•	•	•	•	•	•	•	•	•
Hospital deductible Plan covers $768.00 in 1998.		•	•	•	•	•	•	•	•	•
Skilled nursing facility (SNF) **daily coinsurance** $96.00 per day for days 21–100 in SNF			•	•	•	•	•	•	•	•
Part B deductible Plan covers $100.00 in 1999.			•			•				•
Part B excess charges benefits Coverage for up to 115 percent of Medicare's approved charge, physicians' legal charge limit under federal law (some states' laws are stricter). Policy pays either 80 percent or 100 percent of excess charge.						100%	80%		100%	100%
Emergency care outside the United States Eighty percent of cost of emergency care during the first two months of the trip, with a $250.00 deductible and up to $50,000.00 in lifetime			•	•	•	•	•	•	•	•
At-home recovery benefit Policy pays maximum of $40.00 per visit for forty visits—$1,600 per year.				•			•		•	•
Preventive medical care Up to $120.00 per year for preventive services ordered by doctor					•					•
Outpatient prescription drugs **Basic coverage:** 50 percent of prescription drug costs that Medicare does not cover, after an annual deductible of $250.00, up to a maximum benefit of $1,250.00								•	•	
Extended coverage: 50 percent of prescription drug costs that Medicare does not cover, after an annual deductible of $250.00, up to a maximum benefit of $3,000.00										•

Medigap provisions were left in law). Then, in 1990, Congress again acted, this time to standardize the marketing and sale of Medigap policies into ten plans, labeled A–J. Congress also required insurers to sell policies to all seniors (but not disabled Medicare beneficiaries) who want them during the first six months after the seniors sign up for Medicare. After that, the federal law limits exclusions for PREEXISTING CONDITIONS to six months, and insurers can turn down seniors for coverage entirely or exclude coverage permanently for certain conditions (although some states have stricter requirements for "open enrollment").

Under the 1990 law all Medigap policies are required to cover certain benefits, including copayments for hospital stays longer than sixty days (in 1999, $192 per day for days 61–90, $384 for "lifetime reserve" days 91–150, and an additional 365 days after all Medicare hospital coverage is exhausted); the 20 percent coinsurance for Medicare Part B services (50 percent for mental health services); and the first three pints of blood required in a year. Plan A, the least expensive, covers only the minimum. Plan B covers the benefits included in Plan A, along with Medicare's annual hospital deductible ($768 in 1999). Plan C includes the above benefits plus coverage of the Medicare Part B deductible ($100). Other plans offer coverage of coinsurance for care in a skilled nursing facility ($96 in 1999), BALANCE BILLING by physicians (up to 115 percent of Medicare's approved charge), coverage of emergency care outside the United States, HOME HEALTH coverage in excess of what Medicare already provides, up to $120 in preventive benefits not offered by Medicare, and up to 50 percent of the cost of outpatient prescription drugs, to a maximum of $3,000 per year.

In 1997, as part of the Medicare overhaul in the Balanced Budget Act, Congress addressed Medigap again. One quirk of the 1990 Medigap law required insurers to sell policies to seniors without preexisting condition restrictions when they first enroll in Medicare. But if the senior drops coverage to move into a Medicare MANAGED CARE plan, then later leaves the plan, that senior may not be able to repurchase his or her former Medigap plan. Under the 1997 law seniors who leave their Medigap plan to enroll in a MEDICARE+CHOICE option and then leave again within a year to return to traditional Medicare may reenroll in their former Medigap plan, if it is still available, or in a Medigap plan labeled A, B, C, or F. None of those plans, however, offers prescription drug coverage.

Problems in the Medigap market remain, however. For most policies, premiums increase as beneficiaries age, generally a time when their income goes down. Prices have also been increasing rapidly in recent years. Some analysts say part of the problem has been the movement of healthier Medicare beneficiaries to managed care plans. Since those people drop their Medigap coverage, those left behind in the Medigap pool are less healthy, and premiums rise accordingly.

MedPAC

See MEDICARE PAYMENT ADVISORY COMMISSION

Mental health parity

For a variety of reasons, both economic and historic, most health plans offer substantially less coverage for mental health ailments than for those considered strictly "physical." One reason is that treatment of those with severe mental illness has historically been funded by states, mostly in asylums and other institutions. Moreover, in the early days of insurance, most mental health treatment for minor ailments was provided on an outpatient basis, and insurance did not cover outpatient treatment for mental or physical conditions. But as science has increasingly demonstrated the biological basis for most mental illness, those distinctions have become more and more artificial. Today the reason for less generous mental health coverage is more economic than anything else; because mental illness is so commonplace, offering full coverage would be prohibitively expensive, insurers say. According to the INSTITUTE OF MEDICINE, 23 percent of Americans ages fifteen through fifty-four suffer from a mental health problem each year. The National Alliance for the Mentally Ill estimates that one in five American families will have a member who suffers from an episode of severe mental illness (including such ailments as schizophrenia, manic depression, and major depression). Annual spending on mental health treatment reached $81 billion in 1995; according to the National Institute of Mental Health, direct and indirect spending (such as lost work time) totals $150 billion annually.

With new and more effective treatments available, advocates for those with mental illness have been lobbying insurance companies and policymakers for more equitable coverage, not only for the major mental illnesses but also for the less-serious ailments (such as anxiety disorders and mood disorders) which, though not totally disabling, can nevertheless interfere substantially with a person's ability to function. Typical mental health coverage might cover no more than thirty days in an inpatient facility or twenty outpatient visits, compared with unlimited hospital and doctor coverage for physical ailments. Often mental health copays are higher, requiring patients to pay half the cost of an outpatient visit to a mental health professional, compared with only 20 percent of the cost of a visit to a physician.

The resulting pressure for mental health "parity" led nineteen states (as of December 1998) to pass laws requiring that insurers offer the same coverage for mental illness as for physical incapacity. In September 1996 Congress also passed a limited mental health parity law that required insurers to provide the same annual and lifetime limits for mental health benefits as for other health care benefits.

The laws have had only a small impact, however, according to analysts, primarily because they are very limited in scope. Most of the state laws cover only treatment of serious mental illnesses (excluding coverage of lesser illnesses as well as sickness related to substance abuse). And many exclude small employers.

The federal law came about after the Senate unexpectedly approved a much broader parity requirement during its consideration of what would become the HEALTH INSURANCE PORTABILITY AND ACCOUNTABILITY ACT (PL 104-191). Sponsored by Sens. Pete Domenici, R-N.M., a longtime advocate for federal funding of mental health research, and Paul Wellstone, D-Minn., the amendment approved by the Senate by a vote of 68–30 would have required full mental health parity in most private insurance plans. It was dropped from the final measure after groups representing employers said it would drive premiums up so high that some employers would have to stop providing any insurance.

Instead, Domenici and Wellstone did manage to attach their stripped-down version to an unrelated spending bill for the Department of Housing and Urban Development and the Veterans Administration (PL 104-204). By 82–15 senators approved the language requiring the same annual and lifetime limits on mental health ailments as those on all other ailments. The provision, however, which was kept in the final bill, included a series of loopholes. It did not require any plan or employer to offer mental health benefits, applied only to group plans of fifty-one or more, did not include coverage for illness caused by substance abuse or chemical

dependency, and was scheduled to expire after September 30, 2001. The requirement also stipulated that it would not apply if the additional coverage would raise employer premiums by more than 1 percent. Even in its minimal form, however, many employers have still managed to skirt the requirement by changing their plans to replace dollar limits with per-visit or per-day limits. Thus, instead of a $1,000 limit on outpatient mental health visits per year, plans would simply impose a limit of fifteen visits.

A 1998 study by the SUBSTANCE ABUSE AND MENTAL HEALTH SERVICES ADMINISTRATION found that most state parity laws have had a small effect on premiums, that employers have not attempted to avoid laws by moving to SELF-INSURANCE, and that costs for mental health and substance abuse services have not been shifted from public payers to the private sector. The study projected that full mental health parity would increase premiums by an average of 3.6 percent, with lower increases for plans that tightly control utilization of mental health services and higher increases for those limited to children. Although children use mental health services at lower rates than adults do, children who need mental health care tend to cost more then adults do. Also, because children tend to be healthier than adults, the costs for mental health care are a larger percentage of costs overall.

Mexico City policy

Implemented by the Reagan administration at a 1984 U.N. population conference held in the Mexican capital, this policy denied U.S. funding for international family planning organizations that use their own funds to "perform or actively promote" ABORTIONS. At that conference, administration officials announced a reversal of a long-standing policy and challenged the assumption that population booms deterred economic development in less-developed countries. Whereas for decades U.S. policies had provided aid to international family planning efforts in an attempt to boost economic development, at Mexico City the administration argued that population expansion was inherently a "neutral" phenomenon. Although family planning could contribute to population stability, the White House said, free-market economic policies were the "natural mechanism for slowing population growth."

The Mexico City policy, which, among other things, cut off funding for the International Planned Parenthood Federation, was formally in place from 1984 until it was repealed by President Bill Clinton on his second day in office in 1993. During most of that time, family planning supporters tried but failed to overturn the policy. Supporters of the policy insisted that allowing U.S. funds to go to organizations that use non-U.S. monies to perform or advocate for abortion is tantamount to condoning the activities. Since money is "fungible," they noted, using U.S. government funds for allowable activities provides the organizations with more resources for their abortion-related work. But opponents of the ban argued that it represented an unfair restriction on the free speech rights of organizations that worked to change abortion laws in other countries, and that it was in particular aimed at defunding International Planned Parenthood, a favorite target of the antiabortion movement.

When Republicans took over Congress following the 1994 elections, they made reimposing the Mexico City policy a top priority. But although the House repeatedly voted to reinstate what opponents called "the global GAG RULE," the Senate just as steadfastly refused to go along. The fight ultimately produced a complicated and messy compromise that helped reopen the government in early 1996 after the budget standoff in 1995 closed it down. Under the compromise, the Mexico City restrictions were not reimposed, but funds for international family planning programs were reduced by 35 percent from their fiscal 1995 level of $548 million—unless a separate bill reauthorizing those programs became law by July 1 (which did not happen). In the absence of a reauthorization, the family planning programs received $356 million, a reduction of $192 million. At the same time, negotiators stipulated that even the reduced amount could only be "metered out" at a rate of 8 percent per month.

Mexico City again stymied budget negotiators working on the fiscal 1997 budget at the close of 1996. Again, the policy was not reinstated, and Congress restored some of the funds cut at the start of the year—providing $385 million. But the terms were even more stringent. Under the compromise, none of the money would be available until July 1, 1997 (more than halfway through the year) and again would be "metered out" at 8 percent per month. The measure did stipulate the funds could be made available as early as March 1, 1997, if the president issued a finding that the lack of funding was having "a negative impact on the proper functioning of the population planning program," and if both houses of Congress voted to concur with that finding.

President Clinton issued the finding on February 1, 1997, and, much to the surprise of advocates of the Mexico City policy, both the House and Senate voted to release the funds. The House voted 220–209 on February 13; the Senate officially released the money by a vote of 53–46 on March 8. Proponents of family planning successfully argued that it can reduce abortion. In Russia, said Sen. Patrick Leahy, D-Vt., contraceptive use increased 5 percent from 1990–1994. At the same time, abortions declined by eight hundred thousand.

But the fight was not over. Later in 1997, during work on the fiscal 1998 budget, the fight over Mexico City was again one of the last issues settled in the entire budget negotiation. Again, the restrictions were not reimposed, and again funds for international population aid were restricted—the level was maintained at $385 million. But this time supporters of the Mexico City policy took hostages. Dropped from the final measure were provisions the Clinton administration badly wanted to pay back dues to the United Nations (U.N.) and $18 billion in loan guarantees for the International Monetary Fund. Abortion opponents then accused President Clinton of holding important foreign policy initiatives hostage to his proabortion agenda. "We do not believe our disagreement over abortion should block action on national security issues," said a letter to the president from House Speaker Newt Gingrich, R-Ga. "We believe firmly that we should be able to meet our United Nations obligations and strengthen our international financial tools even while we disagree over taxpayer subsidies of organizations that promote abortion."

Despite the vows of Mexico City policy proponents in Congress not to leave in 1998 without getting their policy reinstated, the final result was much the same. But this time there was a different twist. As approved by the House on September 17, the Foreign Operations appropriation would have permitted funding for the minority of groups that performed abortions, though in that case the funding would have been reduced from $385 million to $356 million. The measure, however, would still have barred any organization receiving U.S. funds from advocating, lobbying for, or in any way trying to influence the abortion laws of any country in which it operated. But the administration didn't bite at what was offered as a compromise. In the end, the program again received $385 million and again "metered" out at a rate of 8 percent per month. And the administration did finally get its funding for the IMF. But no funds were paid back to the United Nations. Instead, the back–U.N. funding was included in a State Department authorization bill that also included the Mexico City language. President Clinton, as promised, vetoed that measure after Congress adjourned for the year.

Mifepristone

Formal name of the abortion-inducing drug better known as RU486. *See* RU486

Migrant health centers

These facilities provide PRIMARY CARE services to migratory and seasonal agricultural workers and their families. *Migratory workers* are those whose principal employment is in agriculture on a seasonal basis and has been for the past two years. *Seasonal agricultural workers* are those whose principal employment is in agriculture on a seasonal basis but who are not migratory workers. Migrant health centers are part of the Consolidated Health Centers Program, run by the HEALTH RESOURCES AND SERVICES ADMINISTRATION of the HEALTH AND HUMAN SERVICES DEPARTMENT. (See COMMUNITY HEALTH CENTERS.)

"Morning after" pill

See EMERGENCY CONTRACEPTION.

N

National Abortion and Reproductive Rights Action League

Better known as NARAL, the organization is the nation's best-known abortion-rights group. NARAL has had three different names since its founding in 1969 as the National Association for the Repeal of Abortion Laws. After the Supreme Court legalized the procedure nationwide in its 1973 ruling *ROE V. WADE*, NARAL changed its name to the National Abortion Rights Action League and adopted a new mission of protecting the rights *Roe* granted. In 1994 the organization changed its name yet again and added to its mission the encouragement of family planning services that can reduce unintended pregnancies and make ABORTION less necessary.

National Association of Insurance Commissioners

The organization representing the leaders of state insurance departments, NAIC writes model laws and regulations and consults with Congress and federal agen-

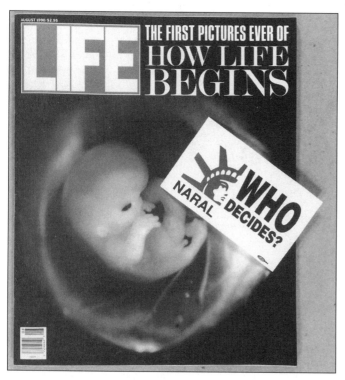

The primary mission of the National Abortion and Reproductive Rights Action League, founded in 1969, is to protect a woman's right to make the abortion decision. Source: Congressional Quarterly

Unable to reach agreement on how to prepare Medicare for the retirement of the baby boom generation, the National Bipartisan Commission on the Future of Medicare—whose members included Sen. Phil Gramm, R-Texas (left), Stuart Altman, and Rep. Bill Thomas, R-Calif.— disbanded in March 1999.
Source: Douglas Graham, Congressional Quarterly

cies on national laws and policies in an effort to establish some uniformity in insurance regulation among states.

National Bipartisan Commission on the Future of Medicare

The commission was established by the 1997 Balanced Budget Act (PL 105-33) to develop recommendations for how to shore up MEDICARE's finances in anticipation of the retirement of the baby boom generation, which was projected to more than double the program's enrollment between the years 2010 and 2030. After a year of work the panel disbanded in March 1999 without reaching agreement on the matter. The group's co-chairs, however, Sen. John Breaux, D-La., and Rep. Bill Thomas, R-Calif., who did win a majority vote from commissioners for their proposal to transform Medicare into a PREMIUM SUPPORT program, drafted the proposal into legislation that they planned to introduce themselves.

The reason the majority vote for the Breaux-Thomas proposal was not enough for the commission to make a formal recommendation dates back to the origin of the commission itself as part of the 1997 budget bill. When congressional Republicans, Democrats, and the Clinton administration proved unable to resolve during negotiations on that bill provisions to extend Medicare's financial stability beyond the next decade—particularly provisions passed by the Senate but dropped in conference to raise the program's eligibility age from sixty-five to sixty-seven and to require wealthier BENEFICIARIES to pay higher Part B premiums—they decided to refer the problem to a commission.

With each side distrustful of the other, the makeup of the commission was one of the last provisions settled in the Balanced Budget Act. Congress ultimately decided the commission should have seventeen members— eight each appointed by Republicans and Democrats (including the Clinton administration) and a chairman jointly appointed by Republicans and Democrats. To ensure that any proposals represented a consensus, negotiators on the budget bill also required that in order to receive formal consideration in Congress, the recommendation would have to be approved by eleven of the panel's seventeen members.

The panel got off to a late start when the two sides could not agree on a chairman. Breaux, a moderate Democrat who had sided with Republicans in the past on Medicare issues (and a member known for his penchant for dealmaking) was finally appointed in January 1998—just fourteen months before the panel's March 1, 1999, termination deadline. In exchange for allowing a Democrat to be appointed chairman (giving Democrats a 9–8 majority of the members), Democrats agreed to appoint Representative Thomas the commission's "administrative chairman." But many observers were already predicting the commission could only end in deadlock, as House Speaker Newt Gingrich, R-Ga., made his four appointees promise not to recommend any policies calling for tax increases.

Breaux was clearly leaning toward the premium support concept from the start. He had long advocated making Medicare resemble the FEDERAL EMPLOYEE HEALTH BENEFITS PLAN, which allowed some nine million federal workers and dependents to choose each year from a menu of different health insurance options. By the time Breaux presented the commission with his proposal in January, the partisanship on the commission had become apparent. Although Breaux's proposal was clearly favored by Republicans on the panel, giving him nine of the eleven votes he needed, Democrats held out for inclusion of a prescription drug benefit for Medicare, something it lacked. They also urged the commission to consider the proposal offered by President Bill Clinton in the State of the Union address to reserve 15 percent of the projected budget surplus to help keep Medicare financially solvent. As the commission's termination deadline neared, with Sen. Bob Kerrey, D-Neb., siding with Breaux, the search for the pivotal eleventh vote centered on two Clinton administration appointees, former Clinton economic adviser Laura D'Andrea Tyson and Brandeis University health policy professor Stuart Altman, who had worked on health issues during Clinton's transition and previously had chaired Medicare's PROSPECTIVE PAYMENT ASSESSMENT COMMISSION.

In the end, neither Altman nor Tyson, both of whom had expressed some interest in the premium support strategy, voted for the proposal. They said it did not do enough to shore up the program's finances and the proposed drug benefit did not aid enough beneficiaries. The commission's failure to find eleven votes also led Republicans to charge President Clinton with purposefully attempting to thwart the panel's work. Clinton responded that he would propose his own Medicare reform plan. That plan was unveiled in June 1999.

National Committee on Quality Assurance

A nonprofit organization supported by employers, health plans, and health foundations, the committee assesses and reports on the quality of MANAGED CARE plans in an effort to encourage health plans to compete on the basis of quality and service, rather than cost alone. About half of the nation's managed care plans (which insure more than three-fourths of Americans enrolled in HEALTH MAINTENANCE ORGANIZATIONS, or HMOs) participate in NCQA's rigorous accreditation program. That program, begun in 1991, examines the structure of a health plan to judge its potential for delivering quality care. NCQA's HEDIS measures (for Health Plan Employer Data and Information Set) examine the way plans actually provide care.

To qualify for accreditation, NCQA examines plans in five separate areas:

1. *Quality management and improvement:* how the plan ensures that patients have access to needed care
2. *Member rights and responsibilities:* how well the plan responds to member complaints and how clearly it informs members about how to use plan services
3. *Physician qualifications and evaluation for physicians in the network:* how well the plan researches the credentials of physicians
4. *Preventive health services:* how well the plan promotes the use of preventive tests and activities

5. *Utilization management:* (how fair, consistent, and prompt the plan is in making decisions)

Plans can receive full, three-year accreditation (for those judged excellent), one-year accreditation (for plans that meet most but not all of the standards), provisional accreditation (for plans that meet some of the standards), or may be denied accreditation.

A September 1998 study for the Commonwealth Fund found that plans with full NCQA accreditation actually cost about 4 percent less than other HMOs, meaning that there is no tradeoff between quality and cost. The researchers, from the consulting firm KPMG Peat Marwick, theorized lower costs are due to the fact that larger, more established plans more able to exercise clout in the marketplace are most likely to seek and obtain accreditation. The same study, however, showed that most employers still do not avail themselves of NCQA's work when choosing health plans for their workers. Only 9 percent of employers surveyed required NCQA accreditation of their health plans, and only 1 percent provided HEDIS data to help employees choose between plans.

In 1999 NCQA announced plans to begin to evaluate PREFERRED PROVIDER ORGANIZATIONS (PPOs) as well as HMOs, starting in the year 2000. An estimated eighty-nine million Americans belonged to PPOs in 1998 according to NCQA, about nine million more than belonged to HMOs. The first steps in NCQA's PPO accreditation process would consist of measuring patients' assessments of PPO quality and satisfaction. Later, the organization planned to conduct on-site review of appeals procedures, processes to evaluate providers, and quality improvement activities.

National Federation of Independent Business

The largest association representing small business owners, the NFIB has been a major player in health policy in the 1980s and 1990s. It helped successfully oppose passage of President Bill Clinton's health care plan and other attempts to "mandate" that employers provide coverage to their workers. In 1998 it helped lead a successful fight against legislation to impose federal regulations on MANAGED CARE plans. It was a founding member of the Health Benefits Coalition (HBC), which was run out of its offices in Washington, D.C. The HBC argued that requiring patient protections for managed care would raise premiums to the point that employers would be forced to drop coverage.

National Health Service Corps

Created in 1970 (its founding was chronicled in the popular political science case-study *The Dance of Legislation*), the National Health Service Corps places physicians and other health professionals in medically underserved areas, such as rural and inner-city health clinics as well as Indian reservations. Originally the program provided scholarships for medical students who agreed, upon completion of their training, to serve for a period of time in the corps, part of the PUBLIC HEALTH SERVICE'S CORPS OF COMMISSIONED OFFICERS. But by 1987, as the Reagan administration tried to phase out the program, the number of doctors and other health care professionals in the pipeline had dropped so low that Congress instituted a loan repayment program authorizing the federal government to reimburse health professionals already in practice for up to $20,000 (in 1990 raised to $35,000) per year of their educational loans. Congress appropriated $115 million for the NHSC in fiscal 1999, enough to support approximately twenty-five hundred health professionals.

National Institutes of Health (NIH)

The nation's preeminent biomedical research institution traces its origin to the 1887 establishment of a bacteriological laboratory in the Marine Hospital at Staten Island, New York, by Dr. Joseph Kinyoun, a physician and bacteriologist who had worked with Louis Pasteur. In 1891 the laboratory was moved to

National Institutes of Health Appropriations, 1989–1999

Fiscal year	Appropriation (billions)
1999	$15.6
1998	13.6
1997	12.7
1996	11.9
1995	11.3
1994	10.9
1993	10.3
1992	9.0
1991	8.3
1990	7.7
1989	7.2

Source: Congressional Quarterly; *Congressional Record.*

Since its founding in 1887 the National Institutes of Health has grown from a single laboratory to twenty-four separate institutes, centers, and divisions. NIH director Harold Varmus was appointed in 1993 to oversee the popular agency and its $15.6 billion budget. Source: Larry Downing, Reuters

Washington, D.C., and in 1902 was vested by Congress with authority to test and improve vaccines. It officially became the National Institutes of Health in 1930, with passage of the Ransdell Act, and in 1938 moved to its current campus in Bethesda, Maryland, just up the road from Washington.

In the past 110 years the NIH has grown from a single laboratory to twenty-four separate institutes, centers, and divisions and from a budget of about $300 to a fiscal 1999 appropriation of $15.6 billion. NIH has been a bipartisan political favorite over the past decade and has enjoyed major budget increases even as other domestic programs have been squeezed. In fiscal 1999 NIH received an increase of just under $2 billion from the appropriation of the year before and has seen its budget double since fiscal 1990. Indeed, the NIH's funding has gone up so fast that some policymakers (although not many) have questioned whether it can put all the money to good use.

Although NIH conducts extensive research on its three-hundred-acre campus in Maryland, the vast majority of its funds are used for its "extramural" programs, funding researchers in hospitals, universities, medical schools, and other research laboratories around the country. In fiscal 1999 NIH will fund more than thirty thousand "new and competing" grants; however, the agency still can fund only about 30 percent of the projects researchers propose each year. In fiscal 1998 the "success rate" for research grants was 30.6 percent.

NIH has eighteen separate institutes:

• *National Cancer Institute,* the oldest and largest institute, which conducts and supports basic and applied research in the detection, diagnosis, prevention, and treatment of cancer and in the rehabilitation of cancer patients

• *National Eye Institute,* which studies not only diseases of the eye but also the special needs of those who are blind or have vision impairments

• *National Heart, Lung, and Blood Institute (NHLBI),* which supports and conducts research on diseases of the heart, blood vessels, lungs, and blood. The NHLBI is also home to NIH's Women's Health Initiative, a longitudinal study of women's health conditions scheduled for completion in the year 2004 that includes a clinical trial involving some forty-six thousand women at forty different centers.

• *National Human Genome Research Institute (NHGRI),* whose mission is to locate and sequence the estimated one hundred thousand genes that constitute the human genome. (A *genome* is the total of all the genetic material in the chromosomes of an organism. The human genome is thought to consist of an estimated three billion "base pairs" of DNA on twenty-four different chromosomes.) The NHGRI is the newest NIH institute, elevated to that status in 1997. The institute also conducts and funds research into the ethical, legal, and social implications of the work, given that when successfully completed, the project could make possible the prediction of disease well before it strikes, or the alteration of human DNA to cure or prevent disease.

• *National Institute of Alcohol Abuse and Alcoholism,* which studies the biological causes of alcoholism and why people drink, as well as prevention and treatment strategies

• *National Institute of Allergy and Infectious Diseases,* which has, among other things, pioneered much of the U.S. research on AIDS

• *National Institute of Arthritis and Musculoskeletal and Skin Diseases,* whose research focus is more than one hundred forms of arthritis, osteoporosis and other bone diseases, muscle biology and muscle diseases, orthopedic disorders, such as back pain and sports injuries, and skin diseases

• *National Institute of Child Health and Human Development (NICHD),* which examines the reproductive, developmental, and behavioral processes that determine and maintain the health and well-being of children, adults, families, and populations. NICHD is also home to the National Center for Medical Rehabilitation Research, which studies better ways to support and aid persons with disabilities.

• *National Institute of Dental and Craniofacial Research,* which conducts and supports research to improve craniofacial, oral, and dental health

• *National Institute of Diabetes and Digestive and Kidney Diseases,* whose research spans the study of diabetes, endocrinology, and metabolic diseases; digestive diseases and nutrition; and kidney, urologic, and hematologic diseases

• *National Institute of Environment Health Sciences,* which supports and conducts research into how environmental exposures affect human health

• *National Institute of General Medical Sciences,* which conducts and funds the most basic forms of biomedical research, such as research in cell biology, genetics and biophysics.

• *National Institute of Mental Health,* which conducts and supports research to improve the prevention, diagnosis, treatment, and overall quality of care for persons with mental illness

• *National Institute of Neurological Disorders and Stroke,* whose research seeks to advance understanding of the brain and to improve the prevention and treatment of neurological and neuromuscular disorders, including head and spinal cord injury, epilepsy, multiple sclerosis, and Parkinson's disease

National Institute of Nursing Research, whose mission is to foster research to reduce the burden of illness and disability, improve health-related quality of life, and establish better approaches to promote health and prevent disease

• *National Institute on Aging,* which supports biomedical, behavioral, and social research related to aging

• *National Institute on Deafness and other Communication Disorders,* which studies human communication issues, including the biomedical and behavioral problems of those with communications impairments or disorders

• *National Institute on Drug Abuse,* whose research centers on drug abuse causes, prevention, and treatment

Within the NIH director's office are several other important operating divisions, including:

• *Center for Complementary and Alternative Medicine* (see ALTERNATIVE MEDICINE)

• *Office of AIDS Research,* which coordinates the scientific, budgetary, legislative, and policy elements of NIH's AIDS research program

• *Office of Dietary Supplements* (see DIETARY SUPPLEMENT RULES)

• *Office of Rare Diseases,* which coordinates and stimulates research into diseases that affect a relatively small number of patients (see ORPHAN DRUGS) and helps match persons with rare conditions with ongoing or planned clinical research projects

• *Office of Research on Women's Health,* which ensures the inclusion of women in clinical research and promotes research on conditions that primarily affect women

In some ways NIH has proven too popular. Congress has sought to micromanage its activities, often in response to lobbying efforts by those afflicted with diseases that, they say, NIH is not paying enough attention to. Both members of the House and Senate Appropriations Committees, through "earmarks" in annual spending bills, and members of authorizing committees, through periodic reauthorization legislation (most of NIH is, in fact, permanently authorized), have ordered, at various levels of insistence, that NIH take certain actions. Some of these orders have come in the form of statutory commands, written directly into an appropriations measure (for example, a statute designating a specific amount for a specific purpose). In 1997 Congress used the appropriations bill to order creation of Parkinson's disease research centers. More often, however, Congress's input into NIH activities comes in the form of "report language" in the conference report (the report resolving disagreements on a bill between the House and Senate) on the appropriations bill or in the House and Senate committee reports. Typically this sort of language urges NIH to devote more resources to a certain disease or condition, or earmarks funding, or asks for a report or study on a certain topic.

A 1998 report by the INSTITUTE OF MEDICINE on NIH's priority-setting process took Congress to task for occasionally ordering NIH to use more than the amount of that year's increase for specific purposes, in essence forcing funding to be reduced for other efforts. In fiscal year 1993, for example, Congress earmarked $77 million of funding within the National Cancer Institute

for research on breast, ovarian, cervical, and prostate cancers but provided the institute with only $28 million in additional funding. As a result, NIH was forced to cut basic research on other cancers, including leukemia, non-Hodgkin's lymphoma, and cancers of the colon, bladder, kidney, and brain.

NIH has also been a lightning rod in Congress for all manner of contentious ethical issues in science. For example, Congress, various presidential administrations, and NIH have been arguing over the propriety of research on human fetuses since 1974, when legislation imposed a moratorium on research involving "the living human fetus, before or after abortion," unless the purpose was to assure the fetus' survival. Congress in 1993 NIH reauthorization legislation (PL 103-43) lifted a ban imposed during the Reagan administration on transplants using tissue from aborted fetuses. But the Republican-controlled Congress imposed a new ban on research involving human embryos in 1995. (See FETAL TISSUE RESEARCH; EMBRYO RESEARCH.)

National Practitioner Data Bank

The data bank was created in 1986 to help facilitate the flow of information about physicians and other health practitioners who have been found to have committed malpractice or had adverse actions taken against them. As of December 31, 1996, according to the HEALTH RESOURCES AND SERVICES ADMINISTRATION, which runs it, the data bank contained reports on more than 145,000 actions and malpractice payments involving 99,925 practitioners. Creation of the data bank, which did not get up and running until 1990, was controversial because doctors complained that often malpractice cases are settled even when no malpractice has occurred—it can be easier and cheaper for the malpractice insurer to settle than to fight a case. In other cases, doctors have had their licenses to practice suspended or revoked not because they did anything wrong, but because of administrative mix-ups that were not the doctors' fault. Members of Congress who argued in favor of the data bank cited cases in which doctors who had been convicted of malpractice or had their licenses or hospital privileges revoked because of sub-standard care merely moved to another state and re-sumed practice without anyone's knowing until after other medical mistakes had been made.

Currently, medical malpractice payers must report to the data bank and to the appropriate state licensing board within thirty days of making a payment. Hospi-tals and other health care entities, including profession-al societies, must report to state medical and dental boards any adverse actions taken against a health care professional (such as license suspension or revocation or loss of hospital privileges) within fifteen days; those boards then have fifteen days in which to notify the data bank. Access to the data bank is strictly limited—its in-formation is *not* available to the general public, nor to medical malpractice payers. Those found guilty of vio-lating the confidentiality of information from the data bank can be fined up to $11,000 per incident. Practition-ers themselves may see copies of their own records, and may dispute information they think is incorrect or add

an explanation. Hospitals are *required* to check the data bank when a practitioner applies for privileges and again every two years. Information from the data bank *may* be sought by other health care entities, including state licensing boards, hospitals performing profession-al review activities, and professional societies or other entities with a formal peer-review process. Plaintiffs' at-torneys may seek information from the data bank under certain circumstances.

National Right To Life Committee

Founded in 1973, the year the Supreme Court hand-ed down its landmark decision legalizing ABORTION nationwide, *ROE V. WADE,* NRLC is the largest (with an estimated seven million members) and best-known an-tiabortion group. In addition to fighting abortion, the group also has a medical ethics division that actively op-poses assisted suicide, euthanasia, and health care ra-tioning. (See SUICIDE, ASSISTED.)

The National Right to Life Committee, an association of fifty state right-to-life organizations, supports antiabortion legislation, operates an information clearinghouse, and en-courages members to par-ticipate in the annual March for Life. The march is held each January to mark the anniversary of Roe v. Wade *(1973), in which the Supreme Court recognized a woman's right to an abortion.*
Source: Mark Wilson, Reuters

Needle exchange

Needle exchange programs are aimed at reducing the transmission of the HIV virus via the sharing of used needles by intravenous drug users. More than a third of AIDS cases (36 percent) are directly or indirectly (through sexual relations with someone who has used a contaminated needle or has had sexual relations with someone who has) associated with injection drug use, according to the CENTERS FOR DISEASE CONTROL AND PREVENTION (CDC), and half of all new infections are associated with injection drug use.

Policymakers have been arguing the merits of needle exchange programs—in which drug users trade used needles or syringes for clean ones—for most of the past decade. Public health officials say research has shown such programs can and do reduce the spread of not only HIV but also other blood-borne diseases such as hepatitis B, without increasing drug use. But antidrug officials have argued just as vehemently that such programs condone the use of illegal drugs, a position that, some analysts say, the government has no business taking.

Congress first barred federal funding of needle exchange programs in the 1990 RYAN WHITE AIDS CARE ACT (PL 101-381). That measure explicitly prohibited any of the funds it authorized from being used to distribute hypodermic needles or syringes "so that persons might use illegal drugs."

The ban was broadened in 1992 legislation overhauling substance abuse and mental health programs (PL 102-321). That measure banned any federal funding of needle exchange programs. The ban was reiterated in that year's LABOR-HHS APPROPRIATION bill, barring funding "unless the Surgeon General determines that such programs would help prevent the spread of AIDS and would not encourage the use of illegal drugs." That language headed off a more sweeping amendment proposed by Sen. Jesse Helms, R-N.C., that would have barred federal funds from going to state or local governments that used their own money to pay for needle exchange programs.

The ban on federal funding continued in roughly that form until 1997, when the fiscal 1998 Labor-HHS appropriation bill placed a firm six-month ban on funding. The secretary of the HEALTH AND HUMAN SERVICES DEPARTMENT, Donna Shalala, was permitted to lift the ban after six months if she could develop criteria to ensure that needle exchange programs prevent the spread of HIV and do not encourage the use of illegal drugs.

By early 1998 such evidence was significant, including several studies commissioned by federal health agencies. One study published by the NATIONAL INSTITUTES OF HEALTH (NIH) found that needle exchange programs reduced high-risk behaviors among injection drug users by 80 percent, with reductions in the transmission of HIV by 30 percent or more. At the same time, the panel concluded that "the preponderance of evidence shows either a decrease in injection drug use among participants or no changes in their current levels of drug use."

On April 20, 1998, Shalala announced her finding that "the scientific evidence indicates that needle exchange programs do not encourage illegal drug use and can, in fact, be part of a comprehensive public health strategy to reduce drug use through effective referrals to drug treatment and counseling." President Bill Clinton, however, at the urging of his drug czar, General Barry McCaffrey, declined to allow the funding ban to be lifted. Instead, Shalala announced, "the administration has decided that the best course at this time is to have local communities which choose to implement their own programs use their own dollars to fund needle exchange programs, and to communicate what has been learned from the science so that communities can construct the most successful programs possible to reduce the transmission of HIV, while not encouraging illegal drug use."

Although the administration did not lift the funding ban, the House of Representatives responded to even the possibility the next week, passing by a vote of 287–140 legislation to permanently ban federal needle exchange funding. During the debate, proponents of the bill pointed to other studies that did find increases in drug use in areas where needle exchange programs were in operation. The Senate, however, never acted on the measure.

Even in the absence of federal funding, needle exchange programs in the United States have proliferated. A study published in the *American Journal of Public Health* in 1999 found that between 1994 and 1996 the number of cities with needle exchange programs—legal or illegal—increased by 54 percent, and the number of states with programs increased by 38 percent. A total of eighty-four programs surveyed reported exchanging approximately fourteen million syringes, up 75 percent from the total in 1994.

Nurse practitioner

A type of ADVANCED PRACTICE NURSE, nurse practitioners (NPs) have studied and practiced above and beyond the four years required to obtain a bachelor's degree in nursing. The estimated forty-eight thousand NPs in the United States practice in a wide variety of settings, from hospitals to physician offices to clinics to nursing homes, performing many of the same functions as PRIMARY CARE PHYSICIANS do—conducting physical exams, ordering and interpreting laboratory tests and X-rays, diagnosing common illnesses, managing chronic conditions, and providing health promotion and disease prevention services. In forty-eight states NPs may prescribe certain drugs; nine states permit nurse practitioners to practice independently. NPs and PHYSICIAN ASSISTANTS (PAs) are particularly important in rural areas, where they may be the only health professionals for miles around.

Although both NPs and PAs are required to practice under a physician's supervision, frequently that physician is located far away. The AMERICAN MEDICAL ASSOCIATION (AMA), which represents the nation's physicians, has generally supported the spread of NPs but has opposed legislation in many states to expand their "scope of practice" to equal that of physicians, and has continued to insist that all "mid-level" health professionals practice under a doctor's supervision. Said AMA trustee John Nelson in 1998, "If [nurse practitioners or physician assistants] want to do more, they can go to medical school." Still, the demand for NPs is growing

as payers of health care search for lower-cost ways to offer PRIMARY CARE services.

Nursing home standards

In 1986 the INSTITUTE OF MEDICINE of the National Academy of Sciences issued a report noting that care received in too many of the nation's nursing homes was "shockingly inadequate" and "likely to hasten the deterioration of [residents'] physical and emotional health." The report laid much of the blame on a set of 1974 standards for nursing homes that focused too much on the physical ability of each facility to provide required care and not enough on the quality of the care provided. Congress responded in 1987 with a new set of standards for facilities that participate in MEDICARE and MEDICAID, standards enacted as part of that year's budget reconciliation bill (OBRA 87; PL 100-203).

Among other things, the new standards for the first time set minimum training and staffing requirements, including at least seventy-five hours for nurse aides, who deliver most of the care in nursing homes. Skilled nursing facilities were required to have a licensed nurse on duty twenty-four hours a day, and intermediate care facilities, which deliver less-advanced care, were required to have staff on duty around the clock, but not necessarily licensed nurses.

The new standards also focused more on outcomes than on the ability of a facility to provide care. For example, facilities were required to develop a standardized assessment and plan of care for each resident upon admission. Residents were also guaranteed a "patients' bill of rights" giving them the ability to choose their own physician and participate in their own treatment; to be free of inappropriate physical and chemical restraints; to receive visitors, mail, and other communications in private; to be free from physical or mental abuse, including involuntary seclusion; and to reject most involuntary transfers or discharges.

In 1995, at the behest of Republican governors and the nursing home industry, who complained the rules were too burdensome, the Republican-led Congress attempted to repeal the 1987 standards. Implementation of the standards had long been marked by disputes between state and federal officials and nursing home operators, and the rules only became final in 1994. As part of an effort to "block grant" Medicaid, the bill passed by Congress but vetoed by President Bill Clinton would have required states to develop their own standards in eight separate categories. Republicans said their efforts were part of an overall plan to lessen federal "micromanagement" of Medicaid. But backers of the original standards launched an aggressive campaign not to undo the rules. They pointed to several studies, among them one from the Program on Aging and Long-Term Care at North Carolina's Research Triangle Institute, showing that the new standards had resulted in fewer hospital admissions for nursing home patients, thus saving the Medicare program an estimated $2 billion per year. The Medicare/Medicaid changes ultimately enacted in 1997 as part of the Balanced Budget Act (PL 105-33) did not include the language to repeal the 1987 standards.

Nutrition Labeling and Education Act

Passed in 1990 (PL 101-535), this legislation was intended to cut down on unsubstantiated health claims manufacturers were making for food products and to provide consumers with more useful nutrition information. Under previous law, food labels had to list nutrition information only if a nutrition claim for the product (such as "low calorie") had been made. Even when information was provided voluntarily, there was no uniformity in labeling. As scientific evidence began to emerge that certain foods could improve health or deter disease, consumer groups found themselves at odds with manufacturers who they said were claiming products were more healthful or beneficial than they actually were. Those consumer groups pressured Congress to act to police the advertising claims, which Congress did through passage of the Nutrition Labeling and Education Act (NLEA).

As signed into law by President George Bush on November 8, 1990, the measure required that most processed food products include labels detailing specific nutritional information about a single portion of the product, including the total amount of fat, saturated fat, cholesterol, sodium, sugars, dietary fiber, protein, carbohydrates, and complex carbohydrates. Retailers were also required to provide similarly detailed information for the twenty most-frequently-consumed types of raw agricultural products as well as for raw fish and shellfish.

To standardize the information, and to free manufacturers from having to package their products differently for sale in different states, the law preempted state nutrition labeling laws. The law did not, however, prohibit states from requiring their own labeled health warnings, such as those alerting consumers to potential toxins or the danger of allergic reactions to products.

To cut down on false or misleading claims, the law required the HEALTH AND HUMAN SERVICES DEPARTMENT to define terms such as "natural," "light," or "low-fat." Manufacturers could use the terms on labels or in advertising only if the product fit the government's definition. Manufacturers were also barred from making health claims about their products—for example, saying that high-fiber diets prevented cancer—if the claims had not been fully tested or backed by the FOOD AND DRUG ADMINISTRATION. The law prohibited manufacturers from making certain nutritional claims about their products on the label—such as promoting a product as "high-fiber" or "low-sodium"—when other equally important nutritional information, such as cholesterol level, had not been mentioned.

Congress has subsequently amended the NLEA. In 1993 legislation (PL 103-80) broadened exemptions from the labeling rules for small businesses, both retailers and manufacturers. It gave them an extra three years to come into compliance with the rules. In 1994, under pressure from a massive campaign by manufacturers of vitamins, minerals, and herbal supplements and by those who used the products, Congress passed separate legislation (PL 103-417) limiting the federal government's power to regulate those substances. (See DIETARY SUPPLEMENT RULES.)

Office of Research on Women's Health

See WOMEN'S HEALTH, OFFICE OF RESEARCH ON.

Off-label use

The term refers to the prescription by a physician of a product approved by the FOOD AND DRUG ADMINISTRATION (FDA) for a use other than the one for which the product was originally approved. Off-label use has long been legal, and many drugs are used for purposes other than those for which they were first developed and approved. An estimated 80 percent of cancer treatments, for example, are off label.

As part of the 1997 FDA Modernization Act (PL 104-115), Congress made it easier for drug companies to promote off-label uses. Critics had charged that if companies were permitted to advertise or otherwise disseminate information about off-label uses, they would not bother to do the research and testing needed to have the drugs approved for the new purpose. As a result, FDA had banned most promotion of off-label uses since 1991. The compromise reached in the 1997 law permitted companies to distribute information from "peer-reviewed" journals (see PEER REVIEW) or from reference works such as medical textbooks, but only if the company agreed to conduct the research needed to have the product approved for the new use. (In certain circumstances, such as those involving off-label uses for "orphan" diseases that affect only a small number of patients for whom seeking separate FDA approval would not be cost-effective, the secretary of the HEALTH AND HUMAN SERVICES DEPARTMENT (HHS) could waive that requirement.) Also under the compromise, the FDA was required to review the information before it

could be disseminated, and could require that "balancing" information be provided along with the journal article, as well as require disclosure of conflicts of interest (such as whether the company paid for the research in question).

In July 1999, however, a federal judge struck down the off-label section of the 1997 act as an unconstitutional infringement on the free speech rights of drug makers. U.S. District Court Judge Royce Lamberth barred the FDA from enforcing the off-label requirements, calling them "a kind of constitutional blackmail—comply with the statute or sacrifice your First Amendment right to free speech." Lamberth's ruling freed drug companies to distribute any information to doctors about uses for their products.

Oregon Health Care Plan

A first-in-the-nation system of overt rationing for health coverage, the plan was devised by then–senate president (and later governor) John Kitzhaber, an emergency room physician. It took four years for the state to gain federal permission to institute its landmark system of providing coverage for more people, but for fewer services. Under the system, which Kitzhaber described as a shift "from who is covered to what is covered," MEDICAID in Oregon pays only for a set number of "diagnosis-treatment" pairs on a ranked list of 745 conditions. The list ranks services with a high likelihood of success and a high likelihood of death or disability if they are not performed (such as appendectomy for appendicitis) near the top of the list, and services that are unlikely to work or unlikely to have much of an impact (such as antibiotics for a viral infection) at the bottom.

Oregon launched the rationing debate in 1987, when, at Kitzhaber's urging, the state legislature voted to end Medicaid coverage for organ transplants, an optional service under federal law. Instead, it directed more funds to prenatal care for pregnant women and basic care for young children. Legislators knew the new law meant probable death for an estimated 30 Oregonians who would lose their chance for transplants. But the same amount of money would provide basic health and prenatal services to about 1,200 pregnant women and 1,800 children. What the legislature did not foresee was the publicity that would be generated by Coby Howard, a seven-year-old leukemia victim who needed a bone-marrow transplant. Since the boy could no longer get Medicaid assistance for the transplant, Howard's family turned to the media to help raise $100,000 to pay for the surgery. Coby died that December, before the money could be raised. Although Oregon's legislature meets only in odd-numbered years, in 1988 its emergency board convened to consider overturning the policy in light of the Coby Howard case. Kitzhaber was labeled "Dr. Death" by critics when he led the charge to maintain the no-transplant policy. Frustrated, Kitzhaber instead developed the framework for what would become the Oregon Health Care Plan.

The heart of the proposal, passed by the legislature in 1989, expanded Medicaid to cover every Oregonian with income under the federal poverty line. But to pay for the estimated 120,000 new beneficiaries, Medicaid coverage would be denied for services deemed less important by an eleven-member commission of consumers and health care providers. Using cost-effectiveness data as well as input from public hearings and town meetings, the commission devised a list of 709 medical conditions and their treatments. At the top of the list were fatal but curable ailments, with illnesses best treated by preventive care listed next, and at the bottom, conditions for which treatment prolongs life without improving its quality.

After the list was refined to prevent it from violating the AMERICANS WITH DISABILITIES ACT, the federal government granted Oregon permission to proceed with its program in March 1993 under existing "waiver"

authority written into Medicaid law. The program officially began in February 1994, with coverage of the first 606 items on the 745-item list of diagnosis-treatment pairs. In 1995, when the program began to outstrip its financing, the legislature scaled it back somewhat, imposing premiums on a sliding scale of up to $26 per month, eliminating coverage for full-time college students, requiring individuals to show their incomes have been below the poverty line for three months (up from one), and requiring them to have no more than $5,000 in liquid assets. The legislature also reduced the number of conditions treated to 574, and in 1999 was seeking to push that number to 564, eliminating, among other things, treatments for poison ivy and genital warts.

As part of the original plan, Oregon also passed an employer mandate proposal to provide coverage to most of the rest of the state's UNINSURED population. But the proposal was several times delayed by the legislature and was ultimately repealed after the state failed to obtain a needed waiver from the federal government. Oregon did reduce its percentage of uninsured residents from about 15 percent to about 11 percent, but in 1999 the state still had more uninsured residents—350,000— than enrollees in the Oregon Health Care Plan (340,000).

Organ donations

Organ donations were officially encouraged by Congress with passage of the 1984 National Organ Transplant Act (PL 98-507). The measure established a national computerized network, the Organ Procurement and Transplantation Network, which maintains a list of patients waiting for organ transplants as well as a round-the-clock computerized organ placement center that matches donors and recipients. In addition, the act provided funds to upgrade and coordinate local and regional agencies that procured human organs for transplantation. It also made selling organs for transplantation a federal crime, subject to fines of up to $50,000. Passage of the bill was delayed by a fight over whether the legislation should include authorization of funding

Despite medical advances, including improvements in organ shipment technology, the demand for organs still far outstrips the supply. Source: Ken Heinen

for drugs that can prevent rejection of transplanted organs for those who could not otherwise afford them. To the dismay of its House sponsor, Rep. Albert Gore, D-Tenn., the final measure did not include the drug coverage provision, although it was added in subsequent legislation.

BUDGET RECONCILIATION legislation in 1986 (OBRA 86; PL 99-509) expanded the federal organ donor program by requiring that hospitals that participate in MEDICARE and MEDICAID establish protocols for making "routine requests" about potential organs to be donated from the next-of-kin of patients who die in the hospital. That legislation also required that hospitals that perform transplants be members of the national network established under the 1984 law. And, for the first time, it provided under Medicare up to one year's coverage of immunosuppressive drugs for the patients who undergo transplants. Legislation passed in 1988 (PL 100-607) reauthorized the 1984 law and called for creation of a bone marrow registry to match donors with recipients. The measure also authorized a block grant to

help states provide immunosuppressive drugs to transplant patients without insurance coverage. Fiscal year 1993 budget reconciliation legislation (PL 103-66) gradually expanded Medicare coverage of immunosuppressive drugs, from one year to three years, beginning in 1998.

Medical advances, including the use of unrelated living donors and the "splitting" of livers and lungs, to provide transplants to two patients with one organ, helped make transplants more available. But the number of patients waiting for organs still far outstrips the supply. According to the UNITED NETWORK FOR ORGAN SHARING (UNOS), which runs the national network under contract to the HEALTH AND HUMAN SERVICES DEPARTMENT (HHS), the number of patients on organ waiting lists has tripled since 1990. In 1997, while 20,045 transplants were performed, 56,716 people remained on waiting lists, and 4,316 people died before receiving a needed organ. Preliminary 1998 data from UNOS showed an increase in the number of organ donors of 5.6 percent, the first substantial increase since 1995.

The chronic organ shortage has led to political strife. In 1998 HHS proposed rules designed to reduce geographic disparities in the way organs for transplant are distributed. HHS officials argued that scientific advances in shipping organs made obsolete the old system of first offering donated organs in the closest area. Instead, the new rules called for a national waiting list so donated organs would go to those who could most benefit, regardless of where they were located. But states that had been more successful in getting citizens to become organ donors cried foul, as did UNOS. Officials at UNOS charged that the proposed rules would result in too many organs going to the largest transplant centers, possibly forcing some smaller centers to close. In the Labor-HHS portion of the fiscal 1999 omnibus appropriations bill (PL 105-277), Congress imposed a one-year moratorium on the rules. But it also ordered UNOS to provide detailed data, including center-by-center statistics on survival rates, organ waste, and waiting lists. The bill also called for a study by the INSTITUTE OF MEDICINE on existing distribution policies and the potential effect of the new rules.

Orphan drugs

These prescription medications are designed to treat rare conditions, generally considered those that affect fewer than two hundred thousand people alive and living in the United States at any time. According to the National Organization for Rare Disorders, there are more than five thousand such disorders, which together affect approximately twenty million Americans. Among the better known of such rare diseases are amyotrophic lateral sclerosis (Lou Gehrig's disease), cerebral palsy, and AIDS.

Because drug development is so expensive (costing an average of $500 million and taking from twelve to fifteen years, according to the Pharmaceutical Research and Manufacturers Association), drugs that will be used by a relatively small number of patients are not cost-effective for companies to pursue. One drug approved in 1997, for example, will benefit only an estimated four hundred patients worldwide. In 1982 Congress passed the Orphan Drug Act (PL 97-414; signed into law January 4, 1983), which provided a series of incentives for companies to develop drugs to treat orphan diseases. The most significant of the incentives granted companies that developed orphan drugs seven years of "exclusivity," or the right to sell the drug in a market free of generic "copies." As of December 31, 1997, the FOOD AND DRUG ADMINISTRATION (FDA) had granted orphan status to 849 drugs and biologic products. Of those, 163 had been approved and brought to market.

Companies can also receive tax incentives for clinical research they have performed or funded. In the 1997 Taxpayer Relief Act (PL 105-34), Congress made permanent the tax credit for orphan drug research, which reimburses companies for up to 50 percent of qualified clinical testing expenses.

Outcomes

In medical parlance, outcomes are the results of a medical intervention. The ultimate "bad outcome," of course, is a patient's death. But good outcomes can be measured in various ways, including not only a lengthened lifespan but also an improvement in the quality of life even if lifespan is not lengthened. The measurement of outcomes has been a focus of HEALTH SERVICES RESEARCH for only the past few decades, but in the age of MANAGED CARE, it has taken on a new importance and prominence as a proxy for the question, "What works in medicine?" Measuring outcomes can be as specific as charting the number of complications suffered by patients of an individual surgeon or as general as looking at the childhood immunization rates of an entire metropolitan area after implementation of a new public health campaign. More and more health plans and government agencies are also measuring patient satisfaction under the broad umbrella of "outcomes research," on the theory that even if a patient is successfully cured of a condition, if the experience was unsatisfactory, there is likely room for improvement.

P

PACE program

See PROGRAM OF ALL-INCLUSIVE CARE FOR THE ELDERLY.

Parental consent

Parental consent is a legal requirement that health care professionals obtain the permission of one or both parents before rendering treatment to minors. When parental consent is applied to abortion, the Supreme Court has required that states employ a JUDICIAL BY-PASS allowing a judge to consent to the procedure if the minor does not wish to consult her parents. Twenty-one states had parental consent laws on the books in 1998, according to the National Abortion and Reproductive Rights Action League. In sixteen of those states the laws were being actively enforced (in some others, laws were blocked by courts). Some of the states also allowed a minor to seek consent from an adult family member other than a parent in certain situations. (See PARENTAL INVOLVEMENT LAWS.)

Parental involvement laws

Parental involvement laws are one of the most contentious issues surrounding the contentious issue of abortion. Proponents of such laws point out that minors need a parent's permission to go on a school field trip, to get their ears pierced, or to be given an aspirin by a school nurse, yet, according to the Supreme Court, parents do not necessarily need to be told, much less give permission, for their daughters to have an abor-

tion—a surgical procedure. They also say the government has no business—and no authority—to interfere in the raising of children. Foes of consent and notification requirements, however, say that such laws can put some minors at risk, particularly those who are victims of incest, or who fear violent reactions from parents if they tell them they are pregnant. Requiring minors to tell parents (or, for that matter, having to seek permission from a judge) also makes it more likely teens will delay seeking medical care. Adolescents are twice as likely as other women to have second-trimester abortions, which are considerably more dangerous than abortions performed earlier. Teens frightened of telling their parents about an unplanned pregnancy may also seek even more dangerous options—illegal abortions.

In fact, a majority of teenagers who have legal abortions do tell a parent. According to the Alan Guttmacher Institute, 61 percent undergo the procedure with at least one parent's knowledge; 45 percent of minors who have abortions tell both their parents.

In 1998, thirty states enforced parental consent or notification laws for minors seeking an abortion, according to the NATIONAL ABORTION AND REPRODUCTIVE RIGHTS ACTION LEAGUE. Nine other states had laws on the book that were not being enforced, in some cases because they were blocked by court orders.

The Supreme Court has made its position clear on the issue of parental involvement laws for abortion. In the 1979 decision *Belotti v. Baird*, the court struck down a Massachusetts law that required minors to seek parental consent before approaching a judge for a waiver and that permitted the judge to deny the petition if he or she found that the abortion would be against the minor's best interests. The court said a minor must be given an opportunity to approach a judge on a confidential basis instead of going to her parents, and that a judge must grant a "mature minor's" request for an abortion, regardless of whether the judge feels it would be in the minor's best interest or not.

The court expanded on its requirements for parental involvement laws in two cases decided in 1990. In *Hodgson v. Minnesota*, a 5–4 majority ruled that a state can require both parents to be notified, but only if the law also includes a judicial bypass. In a companion case, *Ohio v. Akron Center for Reproductive Health*, the court similarly upheld a one parent notification law, but also only if it had a judicial bypass. The cases represented the first time the court extended its requirement for minors to seek a judge's permission for an abortion from consent laws to those merely requiring parental notice.

Parental notification

Parental notification is the legal requirement that health care professionals treating minors notify one or both parents before treatment is rendered. In 1998, according to the NATIONAL ABORTION AND REPRODUCTIVE RIGHTS ACTION LEAGUE, eighteen states had parental notice laws on abortion on the books; thirteen of them requiring notification of one parent, five of them requiring notice to both parents. Of those, fourteen were being enforced. In eight states, minors had the option of notifying specified adults other than their parents in certain circumstances. In 1997, according to the Alan Guttmacher Institute, no state required parental consent or notice for minors seeking contraceptive services, prenatal care, sexually transmitted disease services, or treatment for alcohol or drug abuse. Indeed, many states explicitly authorized minors to receive such services on their own, in confidence. (See also PARENTAL INVOLVEMENT LAWS.)

Fights over parental notification for both abortion and family planning services have been a major factor in Congress's failure to reauthorize the federal government's family planning program, Title X of the Public Health Service Act.

The issue first emerged in 1983, when the Reagan administration issued regulations to require parental notification for minors seeking prescription contraceptives through Title X clinics. That effort fizzled when a federal appeals court threw out the rule and the administration declined to appeal.

In 1985, the Energy and Commerce Committee of the House of Representatives, by voice vote, rejected an amendment by Rep. William E. Dannemeyer, R-Calif., to require parental notification for minors seeking contraceptives. When Dannemeyer was not allowed to offer a similar amendment during floor debate, his objections helped kill the reauthorization bill. In the Senate, a compromise engineered by Labor and Human Resources Committee chairman Orrin Hatch, R-Utah, won a special demonstration program for his home state, whose parental consent requirement for contraceptive services rendered it ineligible for Title X funding. That bill, however, never made it to the Senate floor.

In 1987, with Democrats having taken the Senate back, Hatch was rebuffed in his attempt to get special treatment for Utah, with the labor committee voting 11–5 against the exception. But that reauthorization bill died, too.

The full Senate took up the issue in September 1990, when members by voice vote adopted an amendment that would have required Title X recipients who perform abortions with nonfederal funds to notify parents of minors seeking an abortion forty-eight hours before the procedure could be performed. But it was unclear exactly what the Senate's sentiment was, because the amendment was appended to an unrelated amendment on the strategic petroleum reserve. That bill, too, failed to become law after members were unable to cut off a filibuster against it. Two weeks later, abortion rights advocates failed to beat back another parental notification amendment, this time on the Labor-Health and Human Services (Labor-HHS) appropriations bill, that would have applied to all recipients of federal funds, on a 48–48 tie. The amendment, however, was dropped in conference.

That amendment, drafted by Sen. Nancy Landon Kassebaum, was notable in that it was equally opposed by those on both sides of the abortion debate. Kassebaum's proposal would have required that at least one parent consent to an abortion or be notified forty-eight hours in advance. But it also included numerous exceptions, including allowing a pregnant teen to obtain permission from a judge, physician, or professional counselor with no financial interest in the abortion.

The House, through various parliamentary sleights of hand, actually managed never to vote on parental involvement—at least until 1993. That year, as part of yet another bill to reauthorize Title X that would not become law, members rejected a motion to recommit the bill with instructions to report it back with a restrictive federal parental notice requirement for those family planning clinics affiliated with abortion facilities. The vote, however, seemed to turn less on the issue of parental involvement than on whether the federal government or the states should be the ones to determine how much involvement, if any, was appropriate. Many who rejected federal intervention said they were strong supporters of state parental notice or consent laws.

In 1996, the issue of parental notification or consent for receipt of contraception, dormant since the Title X "squeal rule" was struck down in 1983, again re-emerged. Rep. Ernest Istook, R-Okla., pushed an amendment to the Labor-HHS appropriations bill that would have required minors to have parental consent for receipt of prescription contraceptives or else to wait five business days for the provider of the services to notify a parent or legal guardian of the intent to provide contraceptive drugs or devices. The House instead adopted a substitute amendment that required clinics to provide counseling to minors on how to discourage coercion to have sex and that required them to encourage parental involvement. The year 1997 proved to be a replay of 1996. In 1998, Istook's insistence on a straight up-or-down vote on the House floor on his amendment effectively prevented the bill from ever coming up. On October 8, just days before adjournment—and after conferees on the measure had agreed among themselves not to include Istook's amendment in the final measure—House leaders brought the bill to the floor long enough to give Istook his vote. The amendment passed by a vote of 224–200, but it was not included in the final measure.

Part A (Medicare)

See HOSPITAL INSURANCE PROGRAM.

Part B (Medicare)

See SUPPLEMENTARY MEDICAL INSURANCE PROGRAM.

Partial-birth abortion

Since 1995, partial-birth abortion has been the most visible issue in the nation's ongoing debate over abortion—and one of the most confusing, with both sides disagreeing on how many procedures take place, at what point in pregnancy, and what procedures a bill, twice passed by Congress and twice vetoed by President Bill Clinton, would ban.

The bill in question, called the Partial-Birth Abortion Ban Act, would have banned a procedure it defined as "an abortion in which the person performing the abortion partially vaginally delivers a living fetus before killing the fetus and completing the delivery." It would have barred prosecution of the pregnant woman, but would have imposed fines and prison terms of up to two years for those performing such an abortion, and permitted the woman, or the parents of a minor, or her husband to sue the abortion provider for damages.

Abortion opponents hoped focusing on what everyone agreed was a horrendous-sounding procedure would help draw attention to the brutality of abortion. "We would hope that, as the public learns what a 'partial-birth abortion' is, they might also learn something about other abortion methods and that this would foster a growing opposition to abortion," Douglas Johnson of the NATIONAL RIGHT TO LIFE COMMITTEE (NRLC) told the *New Republic* magazine in 1996.

Adding to the confusion was that medically, there was no such procedure as "partial-birth" abortion; the phrase was coined by antiabortion activists to describe a procedure devised independently by an Ohio abortion-

At a September 1996 prayer service on Capitol Hill, Chicago's Cardinal Joseph Bernardin (left) and New York's Cardinal John O'Connor urged Congress to override President Bill Clinton's veto of the Partial-Birth Abortion Ban Act. Proponents of the measure hoped that public opposition to partial-birth abortion, a procedure that many found horrifying, would heighten opposition to abortion in general. Source: Stephen Jaffe, Reuters

ist and one in California. The Ohio physician, Martin Haskell, wanted to find a way to perform second-trimester abortions without an overnight hospital stay, since local hospitals did not permit most abortions after eighteen weeks. Haskell's procedure was a variation on the more common "dilation and evacuation" (D&E) method, in which the physician dismembers the fetus still in the womb in order to remove the pieces through the woman's dilated cervix. Haskell's procedure involved pulling the fetus intact through the cervix, feet first, until only the head remained. Using a scissors or other sharp instrument, the head was then punctured, and the skull compressed, so it, too, could fit through the dilated cervix. Haskell called his procedure "dilation

and extraction," or D&X; McMahon, who died in November 1995, referred to his variation as "intact D&E."

Abortion opponents discovered the procedure after Haskell presented it at a conference of the National Abortion Federation in 1992. Appalled by its apparent brutality, they dubbed it "partial-birth" abortion and set about to see it banned. The NRLC commissioned drawings to illustrate the procedure and published them in booklet form as well as placing them as paid advertisements in newspapers to build public opposition. Haskell's home state of Ohio passed the first ban on D&X abortions in 1995, but it was struck down by a federal district court, which ruled it was so vague it would also ban more common procedures used earlier in pregnancy. In 1998, the Supreme Court refused to hear Ohio's appeal of the decision striking the law down.

From the very beginning, the federal measure enjoyed more than a two-thirds majority support in the House, which first passed it by 288–139 on November 1, 1995. The Senate, however, long more supportive of abortion rights than the House, passed the bill on December 7 by only 54–44, after adding to the measure an exception to the ban for situations in which the life of the woman was endangered "by a physical disorder, illness or injury and no other medical procedure would suffice." The Senate, however, refused to adopt a separate amendment allowing the procedure to protect the woman's health, by a vote of 47–51.

That failure to include a health exception, abortion-rights proponents (and President Clinton) argued, made the measure unconstitutional under the tenets of ROE V. WADE, which held that abortion could not be banned before viability and only after that point if it allowed exceptions to protect the woman's life or health. Abortion opponents, however, correctly pointed out that the Supreme Court had defined *health* so broadly as to encompass psychological as well as physical threats. Thus, they said, adding a health exception would "gut" the measure.

President Clinton kept his promise not to sign the bill without a health exception, vetoing it on April 10, 1996, surrounded by women who had undergone the procedure and who told heart-rending stories of their badly deformed fetuses who were almost certain to die soon after birth. The procedure, they argued, not only saved their lives but also their future ability to bear children.

Republicans chose to wait to have the override vote until September, to hold the vote as close to the November elections as they could. But even the added pressure wasn't enough to enact the measure over the president's objections. Although the House voted to override 285–137 on September 19, the Senate tally of 57–41 was nine votes short. Three senators, however, who had voted against the bill in 1995 switched to support the override: Patrick Leahy (D-Vt.), Arlen Specter (R-Pa.), and Sam Nunn (D-Ga.).

In 1997, proponents of the measure picked up where they left off. In the Senate, leaders designated the measure S 1, denoting its importance. The House again went first, passing the measure in March, by its biggest majority yet; 295–136. Just days before the Senate vote in May, the AMERICAN MEDICAL ASSOCIATION (AMA) unexpectedly endorsed the measure.

Even the AMA's imprimatur, however, was not quite enough to put the measure over the top. Again, the tally was the Senate's highest yet, but the 64–36 vote was still three votes short of the number needed for an override. Again, President Clinton vetoed the bill, this time in October 1997. And again, Republican leaders waited until closer to the election to mount their override effort. The House overrode the veto on July 23, 1998, by a vote of 296–132. But the Senate again fell short, voting 64–36, on September 18, ending the effort for the 105th Congress.

And although backers of the measure hoped the 1998 elections would add the needed three votes to their side, that apparently did not happen. After the elections, both sides estimated that the net change on the partial-birth abortion issue for the 106th Congress in the Senate would be zero or one.

But the debate continued to rage, at the state level, as well. By the end of 1998, twenty-eight states had passed various procedure bans, many, but not all of them, based on the proposed federal law. However, in twenty of those states, courts or the state attorney general had blocked enforcement.

By far the biggest source of dissension about the issue—other than what a partial-birth abortion is—has been how many such abortions are performed, and at what stage of pregnancy. A 1998 study by the abortion-rights research group the Alan Guttmacher Institute (AGI) found that D&X procedures accounted for a minuscule proportion of abortions in 1996—0.03–0.05 percent; or about 650 procedures out of 1.37 million abortions. The large majority of procedures were provided at between twenty and twenty-four weeks of pregnancy. According to AGI and the CENTERS FOR DISEASE CONTROL AND PREVENTION (CDC), only 320 abortions took place after twenty-six weeks, accounting for 0.0002 percent of all abortions. Indeed, only three physicians in the United States were known to perform third-trimester abortions.

Although it claimed that the number of such abortions was more likely in the low thousands than the high hundreds, even the National Right to Life Committee didn't dispute that, despite claims to the contrary of healthy babies being aborted in the ninth month, those are the exception, not the rule. Indeed, the NRLC vehemently opposed proposals offered as an alternative to the partial-birth procedure ban that would have banned all abortions after the start of the third trimester. Such a bill, said the NRLC, "means that the vast majority of partial-birth abortions would continue without any limitation, because they occur *before* the third trimester" (their emphasis).

Even the medical community could not agree on whether the procedure should be banned. The American College of Obstetricians and Gynecologists (ACOG), firmly opposed the legislation from the beginning. "The College finds very disturbing that Congress would take any action that would supersede the medical judgment of trained physicians and criminalize medical procedures that may be necessary to save the life of a woman," said a letter to the then Senate majority leader Bob Dole, R-Kan. "Moreover, in defining what medical procedures doctors may or may not perform, HR 1833 employs terminology that is not even recognized in the medical community—demonstrating why Congressional opinion should never be substituted for professional medical judgment."

Until 1997, that was also the opinion of the nation's leading medical organization, the American Medical Association. In December 1996, the AMA's policymaking House of Delegates, noting that "ethical concerns have been raised by the intact dilatation and extraction," concluded that "the physician must . . . retain the discretion to make that judgment, acting within standards of good medical practice and in the best interest of the patient." But after negotiating with sponsors of the measure to make what both sides conceded were "cosmetic" changes to protect physicians from wrongful prosecution under the measure, the AMA endorsed the

measure in May 1997, just days before the Senate was scheduled to vote on the measure. "Although our general policy is to oppose legislation criminalizing medical practice or procedure, the AMA has supported such legislation where the procedure was narrowly defined and not medically indicated. HR 1122 now meets both those tests," said a letter to the bill's Senate sponsor Rick Santorum, R-Pa., from the executive vice president of the AMA, P. John Seward. A 1998 audit of the AMA, however, said that trustees had "blundered" in endorsing the bill, contradicted long-standing AMA policy, and "set itself up for accusations of playing politics." The audit, by Booz Allen and Hamilton, came after the AMA replaced most of its leadership in the wake of an unrelated scandal.

Participating physician (Medicare)

Participate is a term of art in MEDICARE parlance. It does *not* mean any physician who accepts Medicare payments. Rather, it is a specific program in which physicians agree to accept Medicare's rate as payment in full for all Medicare patients for all Medicare-covered services (patients remain responsible for Medicare's required 20 percent copayment). In exchange for agreeing not to "balance bill," or charge more than Medicare's set fee, physicians receive incentives, including a 5 percent payment bonus, speedier payment of their bills, and having their names published in a special directory, thus, theoretically, bringing them more business. The participating physician program was first established in 1984 budget reconciliation legislation (DEFRA - PL 98-369) and revised in the 1986 Omnibus Budget Reconciliation Act (OBRA86 - PL 99-509). As of January 1, 1998, 720,960 of the 870,768 physicians who billed Medicare had signed up as participating physicians, representing 82.8 percent of doctors who treat Medicare patients. That was up from 72.3 percent in 1995. More than 90 percent of physician services under Medicare are provided by participating physicians.

Patient "dumping"

This is jargon for hospital emergency rooms denying care or inappropriately transferring to another facility patients with medical conditions requiring emergency treatment, usually because the patient does not have insurance. As part of its 1986 budget reconciliation legislation (COBRA - PL 99-272), Congress passed the Emergency Medical Treatment and Active Labor Act (EMTALA), which required hospitals, as a condition of participation in MEDICARE and MEDICAID, to screen all patients seeking emergency care and to provide treatment needed to stabilize patients with emergency conditions. Patients in unstable condition cannot be transferred unless the benefit of the transfer outweighs the risk (such as transferring a trauma patient to a facility with a trauma center). Hospitals found to transfer patients inappropriately or refuse treatment because of an inability to pay (or, in some cases, because the hospital cannot get the patient's managed care plan to authorize care) can be expelled from the Medicare program (a serious penalty—since most hospitals get a significant portion of their revenues from the federal program for the elderly and disabled), and hospitals and doctors are subject to fines of up to $50,000 for each offense.

Advocacy groups for the poor have charged that the law is underenforced. According to a report by the Public Citizen Health Research Group, the HEALTH AND HUMAN SERVICES DEPARTMENT (HHS) cited 503 hospitals for violating EMTALA, but only 41 were actually penalized, and only 9 were dropped from Medicare. Nearly 700 hospitals were cited for violations during the first ten years the law was in effect, according to the report. In 1996–1997, the federal government settled 67 cases and collected $2.3 million in fines—more than in the previous ten years combined.

Doctors and hospitals complain that they are being squeezed unfairly by the EMTALA requirements on the one hand, and by what they say is a growing practice of managed care plans' refusing to pay for legitimate emergency treatment on the other. In 1997, Congress required health plans to pay for emergency room care for Medicare and Medicaid beneficiaries if a "prudent layperson" deemed it necessary. But legislation to extend the requirement to privately insured individuals was not enacted during the 105th Congress. In December 1998, however, HHS issued an order to hospitals to see patients presenting for emergency care without waiting for approval from a managed care plan. As part of that order, it issued guidelines recommending that hospital emergency rooms should not even ask patients about health insurance coverage until the patient's condition has been evaluated and the patient stabilized.

Patients' Bill of Rights

Patients' Bill of Rights is the name of the bill pushed by Democrats in the 105th Congress to regulate practices of managed care and other health insurance plans. Confusingly, it was also the name of the competing bill introduced by Senate Republicans. (A bill introduced by House Republicans, called the Patient Protection Act, passed that chamber in July 1998). Despite polls showing broad public support for restrictions on such alleged managed care practices as denying emergency room care and limiting access to specialists, the Senate never fully debated a patient protection bill and the issue was carried over to the 106th Congress.

By far the leading proposal to address a growing backlash against managed care, the Patients' Bill of Rights was hardly the first such measure. As far back as 1994, several lawmakers introduced their own bills. They were backed by the AMERICAN MEDICAL ASSOCIATION (AMA), which was locked in a life-or-death struggle with managed care, not only for money, but for whether doctors or administrators would exercise autonomy over the nation's health care system. The Patient Protection Act, introduced in 1994 by Sen. Paul Wellstone, D-Minn., one of the most liberal members of the Senate, and Sen. Conrad Burns, R-Mont., one of the most conservative, would have required that patients receive "clear statements about services that are covered and not covered, patient out-of-pocket costs, and financial incentives that restrict or require the use of specific physicians or services." It also would have provided appeals processes for denied claims, required plans to respond to practitioner requests for "prior authorization" within two business days, and required health care provider participation in the development of "utilization review" standards. The bill was never acted on.

Dozens more bills were introduced in the 104th Congress, most of them seeking to address a single issue, such as required coverage of emergency room care, mandatory minimum hospital stays for childbirth and for mastectomies for breast cancer, or barring GAG CLAUSES in managed care contracts limiting communications between physicians and patients. But the only provisions that became law required coverage for childbirth.

In 1996, President Bill Clinton announced the creation of a commission to examine quality issues in health care. In November 1997, the Advisory Commission on Consumer Protection and Quality in the Health Care Industry proposed a Consumer Bill of Rights and Responsibilities. It included requirements for information disclosure, choice of providers and health plans, access to specialists, access to emergency room care, patient participation in treatment decisions, confidentiality of medical information, nondiscrimination in receipt of health care services, and "an independent system of external review." The commission issued its final report in March 1998, after its members disagreed only about whether patients should be able to sue their health plans for injuries resulting from benefit denials.

The panel ultimately called for a national dialogue "regarding the current state of existing remedies for individuals in public and private plans who are injured as a result of inappropriate healthcare decisions." The panel also came to no consensus on whether its bill of rights should be implemented through legislation or voluntarily.

President Clinton and congressional Democrats had no such doubts. About six weeks after the commission issued its final report, Democrats introduced their Patients' Bill of Rights. Among the provisions in the bill were requirements that:

• patients injured as a result of being denied care be permitted to sue in state courts (this would amend the EMPLOYEE RETIREMENT INCOME SECURITY ACT (ERISA), which bars those in an employer-sponsored health plan from seeking remedies other than in federal court, where they can recover only the cost of the actual treatment denied.

• physicians, not health plans, have the final say over what care is "medically necessary" and that health plans not impose gag clauses or any other limitations on communications between physicians and patients (see MEDICAL NECESSITY).

• health plans permit patients to see specialists who are not part of the plan if the plan has no qualified practitioner to deliver the needed care.

• health plans provide drugs ordered by physicians even if the drugs are not on the plan's list of approved medications.

• health plans provide "standing referrals" to see specialists to patients with chronic conditions, so they do not have to go back through their primary care doctor every time they need to see a specialist who is caring for them regularly.

• health plans permit patients to participate in approved clinical trials to test new drugs or treatments.

• health plans permit women to designate their obstetrician/gynecologist as their primary care physician.

• health plans cover the costs of emergency room care in situations in which a "prudent layperson" would deem such care necessary and that health plans pay for post-stabilization care provided by a hospital if a patient went to a non-network hospital for an emergency medical condition.

• health plans allow women in their last trimester of pregnancy or those undergoing an active course of treatment to continue seeing their physician even if the employer changes to an insurance plan that does not include the doctor in that network.

• health plans not retaliate against doctors, nurses, or other health professionals who advocate for their patients' care, and that plans not provide financial incentives to providers to limit care.

• patients have access to a "point of service" option (at their own expense), allowing them to see doctors outside the plan's network if an employer offers only a closed-panel plan.

Responding to criticism of managed care health plans, congressional Democrats in 1998 drafted reform legislation known as the Patients' Bill of Rights. Republicans sponsored similar bills, including one introduced by Rep. Greg Ganske, R-Iowa (flanked by Richard A. Gephardt, D-Mo., and President Bill Clinton), that permitted patients to sue their health insurers under state malpractice laws. Source: Scott J. Ferrell, Congressional Quarterly

• patients be given uniform, comparable information on what is and is not covered by the plan and the plan's rules and procedures.

• health plans have in place appropriate safeguards to protect the confidentiality of patients' medical records.

• health plans maintain internal grievance procedures and provide access to an external, independent body to decide disputes. Plans would have to pay the cost of the "external appeal," and the decision would be binding.

• health plans pay for minimum hospital stays for women undergoing mastectomies for breast cancer and for reconstructive breast surgery after breast removal. (The latter provision became law in 1998 as part of the year-end omnibus appropriations bill, PL 105-277.)

Patient Self Determination Act of 1990

The Patient Self Determination Act of 1990 is the formal name of language enacted as part of the fiscal 1991 budget reconciliation act (PL 101-508) requiring hospitals participating in Medicare and Medicaid to provide written information to all patients about their rights to accept or refuse medical care, and to exercise "advance directives" about their desire for care in the event they become incapacitated. Such directives include LIVING WILLS, which express a person's desire about being kept alive by artificial means at the end of life, and DURABLE POWERS OF ATTORNEY FOR HEALTH CARE, which permit a patient to designate a person to make medical decisions in their stead. The 1990 law also requires medical personnel to document in the patient's written record whether the individual has completed an advance directive. The 1997 Balanced Budget Act (PL 105-33) required that the actual advance directive be placed in the patient's permanent medical record.

Payers

Payers can refer to anyone who pays for medical care, but the word is usually shorthand for employers, insurers, and federal, state, and local governments, who pay the majority of the nation's trillion-dollar-plus annual health care tab. As health care costs began to spiral upward in the 1980s, payers began to play a more active role in health care. Rather than routinely and unquestioningly paying bills, payers began urging providers of health care (which can also include insurers) to pay more attention to both costs and quality. In some cases payers banded together into buying groups to increase their bargaining power.

Pay or play

See PLAY OR PAY

Peer review

The practice of peer review, common in science and medicine, is that of having other experts review a study before it is published or otherwise released to the public, thus increasing its credibility. Most important medical journals, including the *New England Journal of Medicine* and the *Journal of the American Medical Association,* are "peer reviewed" in that studies proposed for publication are not accepted or printed until they have passed muster with a "peer review" panel.

Peer review organization (Medicare)

Peer review organizations (PROs) in regard to MEDICARE are bodies headed or staffed by doctors charged with reviewing services furnished to Medicare beneficiaries to determine if the services "met professionally recognized standards of care and were medically necessary and delivered in the most appropriate setting." PROs are also charged with investigating complaints from Medicare beneficiaries about potential quality problems. In 1998, the organizations conducted an estimated 14,000 Medicare reviews to evaluate the quality and necessity of care. Created in the 1982 Tax Equity and Fiscal Responsibility Act of 1982 (TEFRA - PL 97-35), PROs subsumed Medicare's former quality watchdog program, the Professional Standards Review Organizations. Although PROs largely review inpatient hospital care, they also have limited oversight of Medicare-covered ambulatory surgery, post-acute care, and services received from Medicare HMOs.

The job of the fifty-three PROs (which cover all fifty states, the District of Columbia, and U.S. territories) has changed over the years. Today, they are also known as Quality Improvement Organizations, or QIOs, in recognition of the changes made in 1992 to orient them away from the traditional fee-for-service setting in which care was delivered and more toward a health care system that is primarily managed care. The reconfiguration of the PROs into the Health Care Quality Improvement Program was an attempt to shift the organizations' activities away from reviewing records after care has been provided and more toward community-based quality improvement and consumer education. Currently, PROs and QIOs, using detailed clinical information on providers and patients, focus on nationally uniform criteria to examine patterns of care and outcomes. In addition to working on a state-by-state basis, the organizations are also working together on national quality improvement projects.

Pepper Commission

Officially the "Bipartisan Commission on Comprehensive Health Care," the commission was created at the behest of and named for its first chairman, Rep. Claude Pepper, D-Fla., a crusader for the elderly who died in 1989, before the panel could complete its work in 1990. The commission, stacked with influential members of Congress from both Houses and both parties, was charged with devising proposals to address the dual problems of individuals needing LONG-TERM-CARE services and those lacking health insurance. But it was one of many such commissions that started out with great hopes and ended essentially in failure, with members badly divided and recommendations that never saw the legislative light of day.

Pepper, who chaired the influential House Rules Committee, essentially blackmailed the commission into existence by threatening to attach to a fast-moving measure written to provide catastrophic cost protections to Medicare a larger and more expensive program guaranteeing long-term-care services. Pepper was ultimately persuaded to drop his long-term-care proposal from the bill in exchange for the commission being created instead. When the rest of the catastrophic coverage bill was repealed in 1989, the commission's authorization was left intact. (See MEDICARE CATASTROPHIC COVERAGE ACT.)

The fifteen-member commission was riven from its outset, initially unable to decide whether to prioritize its task to address long-term care or the UNINSURED. (Pepper's initial plan was to give the group six months to devise a long-term-care plan, then another six months to look at coverage issues.) Pepper was finally prevailed upon to allow both reports to be issued together in November 1989, but the commission's work was ultimately set back further by Pepper's death on May 30 of that year. Members elected as their new chairman Sen. John D. Rockefeller IV, D-W.Va., and the commission's deadlines were officially extended to March 1, 1990, as part of the fiscal 1990 budget reconciliation bill.

Members did manage to agree on proposals. By a vote of 11–4, members approved a $42.8 billion plan to create a largely federal program to provide long-term-care services to all Americans who required them, regardless of age. The program would have helped pay for HOME HEALTH CARE for all severely disabled individuals and would have paid for three months of nursing home care, as well.

The more controversial proposal to address the problem of the uninsured passed 8–7. It called for various tax incentives and subsidies over the following five years to encourage businesses to provide health insurance coverage to their employees. It also called for changes in private insurance to prevent companies from refusing to cover those most likely to need care, provisions ultimately enacted as part of the 1996 HEALTH INSURANCE PORTABILITY AND ACCOUNTABILITY ACT (HIPAA). Finally, the plan urged expanded federal health coverage of the poorest Americans. If, after five years, at least 80 percent of previously uninsured workers and dependents in small businesses still lacked health insurance coverage, the plan called for a PLAY OR PAY system requiring employers either to provide workers with health insurance or else to pay into a special fund from which insurance would have been provided.

The commission's major failing, however, was its failure to reach any semblance of a consensus on how to finance its initiatives. "I don't think we've done our job. We didn't figure out how to pay for it," said Rep. Pete Stark, D-Calif., a commission member who was then chairman of the House Ways and Means Subcommittee on Health. "There is no tax fairy out there who's going to pull it out from under a pillow."

Personal Responsibility and Work Opportunity Reconciliation Act

The Personal Responsibility and Work Opportunity Reconciliation Act (PL 104-193) is the 1996 welfare reform law that ended both welfare as an open-ended entitlement and ended one of the main "automatic" eligibility pathways for MEDICAID, the joint federal-state health program for those with low incomes. The law also restricted Medicaid eligibility for many immigrants. (See MEDICAID and the 1996 Welfare Reform law.)

Pharmacy benefit managers

Pharmacy benefit managers (PBMs) are firms that specialize in operating insurance companies' benefits programs for prescription drugs. Originally these companies were simply claims processors, paying the bills as a subcontractor to an insurance company or managed care organization. But as prescription drug prices began to rise sharply in the late 1980s, the PBMs began to act as "prudent purchasers," cutting deals with drug companies and otherwise urging doctors and patients to use certain medications and not to use others, based on both cost and effectiveness. In the early 1990s, large drug companies began to purchase the PBM companies. In 1993, Merck bought Medco Containment; Eli Lilly bought the PBM market leader PCS Health Systems (and sold it in 1999 to the Rite Aid pharmacy chain). Drugmakers' purchases of PBMs led to conflict-of-interest charges on the grounds that the PBMs would favor the medications made by their parent companies. PBMs, however, continue to be a major player in the health care industry; they now control slightly more than one-third of the market for prescription drugs.

Physician assistants

Physician assistants (PAs) are part of a new breed of mid-level health care providers who specialize in providing primary care services, frequently in areas where there is a shortage of doctors. The first PA class was organized in 1965, comprising mostly navy corpsman who had received training and experience in Vietnam but whose civilian employment prospects were bleak. As of January 1999, 34,000 physician assistants were in clinical practice, according to the American Academy of Physician Assistants. More than half work in primary care medicine, including family practice, internal medicine, obstetrics/gynecology, and pediatrics. Another 19 per-

cent specialize in surgery or surgical subspecialties.

Like doctors, PAs are licensed to practice, although only with physician supervision (which may or may not have to be on-site). PAs perform many functions also done by physicians, including performing examinations and ordering and interpreting lab and other tests, diagnosing and treating illnesses, and counseling patients. Forty-four states grant PAs drug-prescribing privileges. PAs must graduate from an accredited physician assistant program and pass exams to qualify for a license. PA training is similar to that received by medical students, except that it lasts two years instead of the four required for medical school, and PA candidates are required to have only two years of college, rather than the four needed for medical school admission. In addition, PAs, unlike physicians, do not have to complete an internship and residency before starting practice. The majority of PA students, however, have both bachelor's degrees and more than four years of previous health care experience before beginning their studies. A 1986 Office of Technology Assessment report found that PAs "perform better than many physicians in supportive care and health-promotion activities." The PA profession is growing fast—health policy analysts project that PA jobs will grow by 23 percent between 1994 and 2005.

Physician Payment Review Commission

The Physician Payment Review Commission (PPRC) is a group created by Congress in 1986 to advise lawmakers on physician reimbursement issues under MEDICARE. PPRC and a parallel advisory commission for hospitals, the PROSPECTIVE PAYMENT ASSESSMENT COMMISSION (ProPAC), were merged into a single entity, called the MEDICARE PAYMENT ADVISORY COMMISSION (MedPAC), as part of the 1997 Balanced Budget Act (PL 105-33).

Physician self-referrals

See SELF-REFERRAL CURBS.

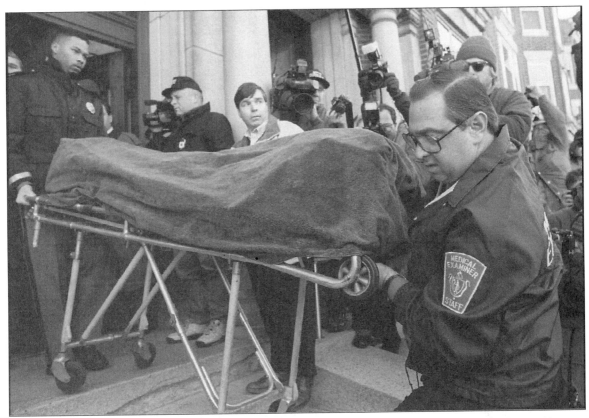

Its support for legalized abortion has made Planned Parenthood Federation of America, the nation's largest abortion provider, a frequent target of antiabortion activists. A gunman in December 1994 opened fire in a Planned Parenthood clinic in Brookline, Massachusetts, killing two people and injuring five. Source: Brian Snyder, Reuters

Planned Parenthood Federation of America

The Planned Parenthood Federation of America (PPFA) is the nation's oldest, largest, and one of its most controversial reproductive health organizations. Founded in 1916 by birth control pioneer Margaret Sanger, PPFA in 1996 provided reproductive health care and sexual health information to some 5 million women and men at 900 local health centers operated by the organization's 152 affiliates in every state except North Dakota and Mississippi. Planned Parenthood clinics performed 153,367 abortions in 1996, making it the nation's single largest provider of the service. But its contraception and family planning programs prevented an estimated 494,000 unwanted pregnancies that same year, 235,000 of which would likely have ended in abortion. Planned Parenthood clinics also provide much more than abortions and contraceptive services. The clinics provide basic primary care to women and girls with no other access to health care, infertility screening, and testing and counseling for HIV and other sexually transmitted diseases for women and men, as well as a wide array of educational services aimed at preventing disease and unwanted pregnancy and fostering reproductive health.

Planned Parenthood says it is "dedicated to the principles that every individual has a fundamental right to decide when or whether to have a child, and that every child should be wanted and loved." Sanger herself was a controversial figure. A trained nurse, she not only founded what is today's Planned Parenthood, but her single-minded writing and lobbying helped strike down the "Comstock law" in 1936 that banned the distribution of most birth control information. But her advocacy of smaller families, particularly for poor immigrants, and her support of sterilization for those with hereditary diseases, have led critics to charge her with supporting eugenics, the practice of improving humanity through selective reproduction. Family planning advocates say some of the more inflammatory statements attributed to Sanger were actually said or written by others; and that they are being spread purposefully by those opposed to contraception.

In recent years, however, the organization's advocacy of legalized abortion has made it a major target of antiabortion activists. Although Planned Parenthood does not use federal funds to provide abortion services, abortion opponents have sought to cut off funding it receives for providing family planning and other health care services. A set of regulations proposed in 1987 to bar abortion counseling and referrals in federally funded clinics (as well as barring abortion-performing facilities from being "co-located" with family planning clinics) was clearly aimed at driving Planned Parenthood clinics from the federal family planning program, abortion opponents said (see GAG RULE). In the 1990s, abortion opponents turned their efforts toward seeking to end family planning funding through the U.S. Agency for International Development for international organizations that "perform or promote" abortion, particularly the International Planned Parenthood Federation, of which PPFA is a member. (See MEXICO CITY POLICY.)

Planned Parenthood of Southeastern Pennsylvania v. Casey

Planned Parenthood of Southeastern Pennsylvania v. Casey was a pivotal 1992 Supreme Court case that simultaneously upheld the core right to abortion set forth in 1973's *Roe v. Wade* while at the same time making it significantly easier for states to impose restrictions on the procedure. Chief Justice William Rehnquist in the plurality opinion issued on June 29, wrote that the decision "retains the outer shell of *Roe v. Wade,* but beats a wholesale retreat from the substance of that case. . . . *Roe* continues to exist, but only in the way a storefront on a Western movie set exists; a mere facade to give the illusion of reality."

At issue in the case was a Pennsylvania law imposing a series of requirements—many of them struck down by the Court in earlier cases (see ABORTION). But this time the court decided that it was permissible to allow Pennsylvania to require a twenty-four-hour waiting period and to require women seeking an abortion to be given state-sponsored material about fetal development and abortion alternatives. That expressly overturned two earlier cases: *Thornburgh v. American College of Obstetricians and Gynecologists* in 1986, and *Akron v. Akron Center for Reproductive Health* in 1983.

But unlike the 1989 case *Webster v. Reproductive Health Services,* in which the court did not openly address the continuing viability of the framework established in *Roe,* in *Casey* the plurality opinion did address the fundamental question of a woman's right to abortion. And, much to the surprise of those on both sides, it affirmed it. But Justice Sandra Day O'Connor's opinion made it clear that the right she was embracing was not nearly as unlimited as the one for which *Roe* became known. The trimester framework, said the opinion, "undervalues the State's interest in potential life, as recognized in *Roe.*" Thus, the decision discarded the trimester system, and in its place substituted a rule under which only state regulation that imposed "an undue burden" would be invalidated. Using that new standard, the justices proceeded to overturn one of the Pennsylvania law's provisions that would have required a married woman to notify her husband before obtaining an abortion.

Play or pay

A health reform option that enjoyed significant popularity in the early 1990s, "play or pay" was initially endorsed by then-presidential candidate Bill Clinton. The concept, intended to produce "universal coverage," would require that employers either provide their workers with health care coverage (play) or else "pay" into a government fund from which insurance would be provided. The idea lost popularity after several studies predicted that most employers would "pay" rather than "play," with the system thus devolving into a "single payer" program. (See SINGLE PAYER.)

Point of service plan (POS)

Generally, a point of service (POS) plan is an HMO that permits patients to seek care outside the HMO's network for an additional fee. A POS plan is different from a PREFERRED PROVIDER ORGANIZATION (PPO). Although in both cases enrollees can seek care within a network at a lower fee or outside for a higher cost, in a PPO, care is generally less managed in the first place, and in a POS plan the underlying coverage is generally an HMO, with its requirements for primary care physicians to provide referrals for specialty or other care. POS plans may or may not require referrals for patients to seek covered out-of-network care.

Portability

Portability refers to the ability to maintain insurance coverage without having to undergo waiting periods or other exclusions. Often portability is mistakenly thought to be the concept of moving from employer to employer while remaining in the same insurance plan. Rather, the type of portability promised by the failed Clinton health reform plan and the 1996 HEALTH INSURANCE PORTABILITY AND ACCOUNTABILITY ACT (HIPAA) (PL 104-191) permits those in employer-sponsored plans to maintain coverage, but not necessarily the same coverage. In the case of job-to-job portability, if both the old and new jobs offer coverage, the law requires that the new coverage not impose waiting periods or preexisting condition exclusions if the worker was covered for at least eighteen months (and waiting periods must decline on a sliding scale for previous coverage of less than eighteen months). For job-to-individual coverage, the law has similar requirements. Another form of portability is so-called COBRA CONTINUATION, which guarantees those with employer-provided plans the ability to continue in that plan for eighteen months if they pay the full premium (plus a 2 percent administrative fee) themselves.

Poverty statistics

Poverty statistics are used by the federal government not only to determine how many poor people there are but also to determine eligibility for programs aimed at those with low incomes, including health programs such as MEDICAID and the new CHILDREN'S HEALTH INSURANCE PROGRAM (CHIP). The government actually has two separate poverty measures. The federal poverty threshold is the "official" measure. It is updated each year by the U.S. Census Bureau based on a formula developed by Mollie Orshansky, an economist with the Social Security Administration, in 1963. Orshansky estimated how much money it would take to feed a family using the U.S. Department of Agriculture's "economy food plan," the lowest-cost of four "nutritionally adequate" diets developed by the department. The department said the economy plan was "designed for temporary or emergency use when funds are low." Based on a finding that a family of three spent about one-third of its after-tax income on food, Orshansky estimated that income under three times the price of the economy food plan was by definition less than subsistence level, and that became the original poverty level. That original calculation was modified to develop thresholds for families of other sizes, and has been updated ever since, based on the year 1963. The Orshansky formula was formally adopted by the federal government in 1969.

Health and Human Services Department Poverty
Guidelines, 1999

Size of family unit	Forty-eight contiguous states and D.C.	Alaska	Hawaii
1	$ 8,240	$10,320	$ 9,490
2	11,060	13,840	12,730
3	13,880	17,360	15,970
4	16,700	20,880	19,210
5	19,520	24,400	22,450
6	22,340	27,920	25,690
7	25,160	31,440	28,930
8	27,980	34,960	32,170
For each additional person, add	2,820	3,520	3,240

Source: *Federal Register* 64, no. 52 (18 March 1999): 13428–13430.
    Note: The Health and Human Services Department has listed separate poverty guidelines for Alaska and Hawaii since the 1966–1970 period.

The thresholds, which lag by a year because they are based on inflation from the previous year, are used mostly for statistical measures, including calculating the percentage of the population that lives below the poverty line.

Each year the HEALTH AND HUMAN SERVICES DEPARTMENT also publishes poverty "guidelines," which are used for administrative purposes, such as to make eligibility determinations for MEANS-TESTED programs. The guidelines are by necessity based on cost increases from the previous year, but they are dated for the year in which they appear. The poverty guidelines are often referred to as the "federal poverty level," or FPL.

The poverty numbers have been controversial since their inception. Those who think they understate poverty argue that they do not account for differences in costs in different parts of the country (although there are separate, higher guidelines for Alaska and Hawaii). They also argue that the original research showing that an average family spends a third of its income on food is from the 1950s, and that spending patterns have changed considerably. Those who think the numbers overstate poverty complain that they do not take into account the value of non-cash income, particularly housing subsidies or Medicaid health insurance coverage.

PPRC

See PHYSICIAN PAYMENT REVIEW COMMISSION.

Practice guidelines

See CLINICAL PRACTICE GUIDELINES.

Preexisting condition

A medical condition, physical or mental, that existed prior to the date of health insurance coverage. Insurers frequently deny coverage for costs associated with preexisting conditions, or impose waiting periods (typically a year), although various laws have put significant limitations on insurers' ability to do that. The HEALTH INSURANCE PORTABILITY AND ACCESSIBILITY ACT (HIPAA), barred insurers from imposing preexisting condition limitations on members of group plans who had been continuously covered by another group plan for at least eighteen months and on individuals who were previously covered by a group plan. Similarly, during seniors' first six months of enrollment in MEDICARE, sellers of private MEDIGAP INSURANCE may not impose preexisting condition limitations on those wishing to purchase such coverage.

Preferred Provider Organization (PPO)

A preferred provider organization, or PPO, is a type of managed care health plan that tries to limit costs by steering patients to physicians and other health care providers who have agreed to accept discounted prices in exchange for larger patient volumes. PPOs are the most prevalent form of managed care in the United States, enrolling an estimated 89 million Americans in 1999. Patients are typically given an incentive to use providers in the plan's "network" in the form of lower copayments. Unlike those in an HMO, however, patients in a PPO can obtain covered care outside the network, usually after paying an annual deductible and a higher copayment. PPOs also typically do not require patients to select a GATEKEEPER or PRIMARY CARE PHYSICIAN who must approve all other care, including visits to specialists.

Premiums

Premiums are fees, usually paid monthly, for health insurance (or other insurance) coverage. Until the mid-1980s, premiums were invisible to most workers, with employers paying the entire monthly fee, and employees responsible only for copayments and an annual DEDUCTIBLE. As premiums rose in the 1980s, however, more employers began charging workers at least a portion, usually deducted from their paychecks. MEDICARE has always charged a premium for its optional Part B coverage, $45.50 in 1999, withheld from the Social Security checks of most Medicare beneficiaries. MEDICAID law bars charging premiums for its low-income enrollees, although in some cases Medicaid patients can be asked to participate in cost-sharing.

Premium support

Premium support is a concept developed by academics and modified as a proposal for reforming MEDICARE by the NATIONAL BIPARTISAN COMMISSION ON THE FUTURE OF MEDICARE in March 1999. The commission failed by one vote to formally recommend its premium support plan to Congress, but the concept was drafted into legislation by the panel's co-chairs, Sen. John Breaux, D-La., and Bill Thomas, R-Calif. The idea was for Medicare to encourage competition between private health plans by paying a portion of each plan's premium. Beneficiaries who wanted to purchase more expensive plans would have to pay more out of their own pockets; those who opted for plans with lower premiums could save both themselves and the federal government money. The federal government would also pay a portion of costs for Medicare's traditional "fee-

for-service" program, making it compete against private plans on the same footing. The premium support concept was similar to MANAGED COMPETITION, the failed concept on which President Bill Clinton's HEALTH SECURITY ACT was based.

Prescription Drug User Fee Act

Also known by its acronym, PDUFA (pronounced "padoofah"), the Prescription Drug User Fee Act (PL 102-571) was passed swiftly in 1992 after years of dissension over the issue among GOP presidents Ronald Reagan and George Bush, Democrats in Congress, and the prescription drug industry. With appropriations for domestic spending in general being increasingly squeezed by the growing federal budget deficit, a perennial suggestion in administration budgets sent to Capitol Hill had been to require drug companies to pay "user fees" to have their drug applications considered by the FOOD AND DRUG ADMINISTRATION (FDA). And, at least until 1992, the suggestion had been just as perennially ignored by Congress.

What changed the situation was the realization by the drug companies that although the FDA's workload was increasing, there was little prospect of new funds to help clear the backlog of drugs waiting for review. In 1992 it took an average of twelve years to bring a drug from initial discovery to market. Of that time, it took the FDA an average of twenty months to review and approve new drug applications, FDA commissioner David Kessler told Congress, and forty months to review applications for new biologics, such as vaccines or blood products. And the backlog appeared likely only to get worse. In 1980, companies filed 66 applications to begin clinical trials on potential new drugs; by 1991, that had grown to 504 applications.

The other half of the compromise was the agreement by the Bush administration that any funds raised by the user fees go back to the FDA to speed up the approval process. Earlier administration user fee proposals would have returned at least some of the fees to the treasury, prompting drugmakers to label it a "tax on innovation."

As signed into law by President Bush, the measure required makers of prescription drugs and biologics to pay both annual "facilities" fees and fees every time they submitted a drug for approval to the FDA. The facilities fees began at $60,000 and rose to $138,000 by the fifth year. The application fees started at $100,000 and rose to $233,000 in five years. Drugmakers also had to pay a separate fee for each drug marketed, starting at $5,000 and rising to $14,000. Small and start-up companies were allowed to pay reduced or no fees.

The FDA kept its promise to speed up its approvals. In 1996, the FDA took an average of 15.4 months to approve new drugs, down from 30 months in the late 1980s. The percentage of approvals made within the statutory time limits was 95 percent in fiscal 1995, compared to 40 percent before passage of PDUFA. That exceeded the measure's goal for that year, which was 70 percent.

Congress reauthorized PDUFA in 1997 as part of a broader overhaul of FDA in the FDA Modernization Act (PL 105-115).

Prevalence

In health policy, prevalence refers to the total number of people with a particular disease or condition. Prevalence is different from INCIDENCE, which is the rate of new cases of a disease or condition.

Primary care

The term *primary care* is used to describe basic medical services provided to patients and to differentiate it from "specialty care." Primary care physicians include internists, family practitioners, pediatricians, and geriatricians. Many obstetrician/gynecologists also provide primary care, as do such mid-level practitioners as PHYSICIAN ASSISTANTS and NURSE PRACTITIONERS.

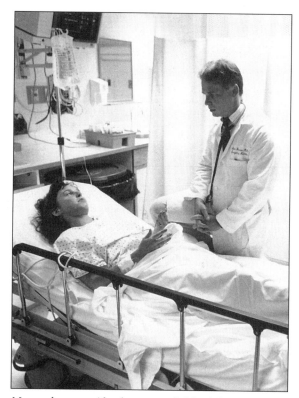

Managed care providers have expanded the definition of pri-mary care physicians. Originally limited to doctors who are not specialists, the term now embraces internists, general practitioners, pediatricians, and even specialists who act as "gate-keepers," deciding when a patient may undergo tests or enter a hospital. Source: R. Michael Jenkins, Congressional Quarterly

Primary care physician

Originally a term that referred to any physician who is not a specialist, in the age of managed care the concept of primary care physician has shifted somewhat. Internists, general practitioners, pediatricians, and doctors who have completed residencies in family practice are all primary care physicians (or PCPs, as they are sometimes called). But since in many managed care plans the primary care physician also acts as a GATE-KEEPER—coordinating all of a patient's medical care and deciding whether and when a patient undergoes tests, enters a hospital, or sees a specialist—some specialists are also acting as primary care physicians, oxymoronic as that seems. In particular, many plans permit women to designate their obstetrician/gynecologists as their primary care physician for purposes of coordinating their care.

Private Contracting (Medicare)

Private contracting for MEDICARE is an agreement between a physician and a Medicare beneficiary in which the patient agrees to pay the doctor out of his or her own pocket for Medicare-covered services, at whatever rate the doctor wants to charge, with no reimbursement from either Medicare, or, in most cases, supplemental MEDIGAP INSURANCE. Private contracting was explicitly authorized by Congress for the first time as part of the 1997 Balanced Budget Act (PL 105-33). But some who advocated for the change almost immediately sought to alter the language, arguing that the limitations placed on the practice—particularly the requirement that physicians who want to make private payment arrangements with patients opt out of Medicare entirely for two years—actually made the situation worse then it was before. Previously, the HEALTH CARE FINANCING ADMINISTRATION, which runs Medicare, had held it impermissible for a physician to "privately contract" with a Medicare beneficiary to provide a Medicare-covered service, because provisions of the 1989 BUDGET RECONCILIATION law (Omnibus Budget Reconciliation Act of 1989, PL 100-239) required physicians to file claims on Medicare patients' behalf for such services.

The 1997 change was championed by Sen. Jon Kyl, R-Ariz., who argued that it was needed to allow patients who become eligible for Medicare to continue existing relationships with physicians who do not take part in the program. Kyl was worried about highly sought-after specialists or generalist physicians in areas with few health care providers who, if they did not accept Medicare, would no longer be legally allowed to see patients who became Medicare beneficiaries. But consumer advocates, as well as the Clinton administration, worried that allowing doctors to determine for which patients, or even for which services, they wanted to accept Medicare payment would undermine the program's beneficiary cost protections. In other words, allowing doctors to pick and choose not to accept Medicare's payment rates in certain cases could expose beneficiaries to unlimited costs.

The compromise enacted in the 1997 budget law required that physicians and patients sign a written contract in advance of the treatment in question, with both agreeing not to bill Medicare for the services and the patient agreeing to pay the full amount of the doctor's bill. Patients would also have to be informed in writing that the service would be covered by Medicare if it was provided by another doctor. Private contracts are not allowed in emergency medical situations, to prevent doctors from coercing patients into paying higher-than-Medicare rates. The HEALTH CARE FINANCING ADMINISTRATION, which runs Medicare, argued that requiring doctors to drop out of Medicare entirely for two years was the only way to preclude unscrupulous physicians from billing both Medicare and patients simultaneously.

But some conservative groups, led by the 600,000-member United Seniors Association, charged that the law could actually prevent Medicare beneficiaries from paying out-of-pocket for services Medicare did not cover, such as annual physicals, or from paying for services Medicare covers in some cases, but not others, such as laboratory tests performed every three months rather than every six months. Critics also worried that the law could restrict people from paying for sensitive services—particularly mental health care—themselves to avoid notifying a third party. HCFA, however, said that nothing in the new law or old prevented a patient from paying privately for services Medicare does not cover, nor for more frequent uses of Medicare-covered services than Medicare allows. HCFA also notified doctors that it would not penalize them for not filing claims for patients who failed to provide sufficient information; thus protecting patients who wish to keep their medical affairs confidential.

HCFA also said that doctors who wanted to perform

a service they were uncertain that Medicare would cover would not need a private contract and would not be required to drop out of Medicare for two years. Rather, they could provide patients with an "advance beneficiary notice" that the service might not be paid for and ask that the patient agree to pay the claim if Medicare did not.

Unsatisfied with HCFA's interpretation, United Seniors sued in federal court to overturn the 1997 law, charging that the private contracting provisions unconstitutionally limited Medicare beneficiaries' access to medical care. On April 14, 1998, U.S. District Court Judge Thomas Hogan dismissed the case, noting that "The plaintiffs have not demonstrated that they have a constitutional right to privately contract with their physicians." United Seniors appealed the ruling to the District of Columbia Court of Appeals, which upheld the lower court ruling on July 16, 1999.

Meanwhile, relatively few physicians availed themselves of the private contracting option. HCFA reported that during the first quarter of 1998, only 278 physicians (of more than 700,000 practicing doctors) signed private contract agreements. More than half, 140, were psychiatrists.

Private fee-for-service (Medicare)

Private fee-for-service plans were authorized by Congress in the 1997 Balanced Budget Act (PL 105-33) as one of the private plan options available to beneficiaries under the new MEDICARE+CHOICE program. Allowing the plans came at the urging of the NATIONAL RIGHT TO LIFE COMMITTEE (NRLC), an antiabortion group that also worked to prevent health care rationing. The NRLC was concerned that if Congress continued to ratchet down on MEDICARE payments to doctors, hospitals, and other health care providers, they would begin to stop accepting Medicare patients. That would leave beneficiaries with no choice but to join one of the MANAGED CARE plans, which overtly ration care.

The concept behind the private fee-for-service plan is that it would allow beneficiaries to pay a premium to

a private entity that would set prices for providers high enough to entice them to participate. The private fee-for-service plan would also have to allow any provider to participate who agreed to accept the plan's fee schedule, thus giving beneficiaries essentially unfettered access to the provider of their choice. Plans would not be allowed to provide incentives for providers to limit care, nor would they be allowed to otherwise seek to control use of health care services. Beneficiaries, in addition to having to pay a premium to join the plan, would also be subject to higher cost-sharing than in the traditional Medicare fee-for-service plan. Consumer advocates worried that in rural areas or others with a limited number of providers, virtually all the providers could join together in a private fee-for-service plan and drop out of traditional Medicare, potentially leaving low-income beneficiaries with limited or no access to health care services. As of mid-1999, however, no entity had come forward to offer a private fee-for-service plan.

Program of All-inclusive Care for the Elderly

Known as PACE, the Program of All-inclusive Care for the Elderly was created as a demonstration program in 1986 BUDGET RECONCILIATION legislation (OBRA 86) and was made permanent in the 1997 Balanced Budget Act (PL 105-33). An optional program for states, PACE represents a multidisciplinary, comprehensive program of health and social services that integrates acute and LONG-TERM-CARE services in an effort to keep those who are age fifty-five or over and in frail condition out of nursing homes. PACE providers receive a capitated monthly payment from the state, for which they are responsible for all care required by PACE enrollees, twenty-four hours a day, seven days a week. PACE programs use adult day care, private homes, hospitals, and nursing homes to help manage health and social service needs, with teams providing preventive, rehabilitative, curative, and support services. PACE operates through both the MEDICARE and the MEDICAID programs, and providers must contract with PACE programs and not charge DEDUCTIBLES, copayments, or other cost-sharing.

Prospective Payment Assessment Commission

An advisory body created by Congress in 1983 to oversee the implementation of Medicare's new prospective payment system for hospitals and recommend changes, the Prospective Payment Assessment Commission (ProPAC) also proposed the amounts by which hospital payments should be adjusted annually. In the 1997 Balanced Budget Act, ProPAC and the parallel advisory commission for physician payments, the PHYSICIAN PAYMENT REVIEW COMMISSION, were merged into a single, fifteen-member entity called the MEDICARE PAYMENT ADVISORY COMMISSION (Med-PAC).

Prospective payment system

In 1983, in legislation to shore up the ailing Social Security trust fund (PL 98-21), Congress also put the HOSPITAL INSURANCE (HI) trust fund of MEDICARE on firmer financial footing by creating a new way to pay hospitals. The need was acute. Even though most of the attention was focused on Social Security, whose insolvency was imminent, the Congressional Budget Office had projected that the HI trust fund would run out of money as soon as 1987. Hospital spending was an obvious target; it accounted for two-thirds of the program's costs, and although Congress had since the early 1970s been imposing limits on what hospitals could charge the program, they were still paid essentially what they charged, and they had a built-in incentive to provide more rather than less care.

The prospective payment system (PPS) turned that incentive around. The law created 467 (by 1999 the number was 487) "DIAGNOSIS RELATED GROUPS" of common conditions requiring hospitalization. Payment would be based on the average cost of treating those conditions. If it cost the hospital less than the predetermined payment, it could keep the difference. But if it cost more, the hospital would have to make it up. Not every hospital receives the same payment for the same diagnosis-related group, or DRG; payments are adjusted according to the cost of labor in a particular area, whether the hospital is located in a large city or rural area, whether a hospital serves a "DISPROPORTIONATE SHARE" of low-income patients, and whether it has a teaching program. But the idea was to provide an incentive for hospitals to improve their efficiency.

Although hospitals complained and considerable fine-tuning was required, overall, the PPS system has been considered a major success. (It has been so successful, in fact, that Congress in the 1997 Balanced Budget Act [PL 105-33] ordered the creation of prospective payment systems for outpatient hospital care, HOME HEALTH CARE, and nursing home care.) Medicare's hospital costs, which had been climbing at rates approaching 20 percent annually in the 1970s and early 1980s, quickly slowed. The average length of stay for Medicare patients in the hospital declined from 10 days in 1983 to 7.6 days in 1994. This raised accusations that patients were being discharged too early in some cases (referred to by critics as "sicker and quicker.") Among the protections imposed by Congress to address that complaint is a requirement that patients who feel they are being sent home before they are ready be able to appeal their discharge to a Medicare PEER REVIEW ORGANIZATION (MEDICARE) and stay in the hospital an extra day at no cost to them. More surprisingly, the number of hospital admissions declined sharply as well, although at least some of that decline may have been attributable to a cost-cutting movement throughout the health system of performing more services on an outpatient basis. In the case of Medicare, hospitals had an incentive to shift patients from inpatient to outpatient status, because Medicare reimbursement for outpatient care remained cost-based.

Although many hospitals initially lost money on the PPS system, by the mid-1990s most were able to make money on their Medicare patients. By 1997, inpatient hospital Medicare profit margins averaged 16 percent, leading the Clinton administration to propose a new round of hospital payment cuts in early 1999.

Providers

Any person or entity who delivers medical care is called a provider. The term *providers* generally refers to physicians and hospitals, but it also encompasses mid-level practitioners such as PHYSICIAN ASSISTANTS, NURSE PRACTITIONERS, and physical therapists as well as entities such as nursing homes, HOME HEALTH CARE agencies, and kidney dialysis facilities.

Provider-sponsored organizations (PSOs)

Provider-sponsored organizations are health plans owned and operated by hospitals, doctors, or other health care providers. At the strong urging of hospital and physician groups, who were fighting a losing battle for primacy in running the health care system with insurance companies, Congress in the 1997 Balanced Budget Act (PL 105-33) authorized PSOs to serve MEDICARE beneficiaries under the MEDICARE+CHOICE program. In that legislation, Congress provided PSOs with the ability to circumvent state regulations if states refused to grant the organizations an operating license (physician and hospital groups argued that they were discriminated against because insurance regulators in many states were biased in favor of insurance companies). Insurers argued that if doctors and hospitals wanted to run insurance companies, they should have to meet the same requirements as any other insurer. Health care providers countered that they did not need the same level of financial reserves as insurers, because if they ran into financial difficulties, they could provide care for free, whereas insurers would still have to pay providers. Lawmakers who backed the PSO concept said they hoped PSOs would form in areas of the country where Medicare MANAGED CARE payments were too low to attract managed care organizations from outside the area. The hope was that with the doctors and hospitals

already in place, start-up managed care costs would be lower. PSOs got off to a slow start, however, as with the rest of the Medicare+Choice program. By the end of 1998, only one PSO, Clear Choice Health Plans of Bend, Oregon, had been approved by the HEALTH CARE FINANCING ADMINISTRATION to offer coverage through Medicare+Choice.

Public health

A phrase with a continually shifting definition, *public health* is, in its broadest sense, the effort to improve health and prevent disease in a community or population rather than in individual patients. Originally public health focused on sanitation, particularly on obtaining clean water, proper disposal of human waste, and eradication of rats and other vermin. But as these goals were achieved more or less, and as the modes of transmission of disease became clear, public health began to interact more with the actual practice of medicine (the act of healing individuals), including reporting and quarantines of those with infectious diseases, and later, efforts to immunize populations against preventable ailments. Today, public health efforts look at the roles of nutrition, substance abuse, accident prevention (such as seat belts and bicycle helmets), and pollution, among other things, in determining health status. Public health workers may be medical professionals, but they may also be statisticians, health educators, food and drug inspectors, toxicologists, or environmental scientists. Today, health policy work is also an important part of public health.

Public Health Service

The U.S. Public Health Service (PHS) dates back to 1798, with the creation of the fledgling federal government's first marine hospital, under the Department of the Treasury. The Fifth Congress established the hospital to care for merchant seamen, who were critical to the security of the nation for both commerce and defense purposes. Marine hospitals ultimately spread up and down the East Coast and along other shipping routes, caring for American sailors and British prisoners in the War of 1812 and for combatants on both sides in the Civil War. (The PHS hospitals would later be turned over to the Veterans' Administration.)

The Public Health Service was reorganized in 1870, under the first SURGEON GENERAL OF THE UNITED STATES, John Maynard Woodworth, who reshaped it more along military lines, complete with uniforms and tenure and promotional opportunities based on merit. Congress officially established the Commissioned Corps of the Public Health Service in 1889 (see PUBLIC HEALTH SERVICE, COMMISSIONED CORPS).

In 1912, Congress formally founded the Public Health Service, with a mandate to study "the diseases of man and conditions affecting the propagation and spread thereof." The PHS spent much of the early part of the century combating diseases such as malaria, smallpox, and yellow fever, improving sanitation and other environmental causes of disease, caring for veterans, and manufacturing and distributing vaccines.

In 1939 the service was transferred from the Treasury Department to the Federal Security Agency, later to become the Department of Health, Education, and Welfare, which in turn would become the present day's HEALTH AND HUMAN SERVICES DEPARTMENT (HHS). In 1944 Congress passed the Public Health Service Act (PL 78-410), which codified the agency's authority.

By 1998, 200 years after it began, the PHS included eight health research and delivery agencies, with a combined budget of $29.1 billion for fiscal 1999. The PHS is nominally headed by the U.S. surgeon general; however, the surgeon general's line authority was eliminated in 1966, with most of the PHS put under the direction of the HHS assistant secretary for health. In 1995, the position of assistant secretary for health was downgraded as well, giving the heads of the PHS agencies a direct conduit to the HHS secretary. Ironically, Dr. Philip Lee, who served as the first ASH, as the position is known, under President Lyndon Johnson, also served as the last ASH before the position was reconfigured in 1995.

PHS agencies include:

U.S. Public Health Service, 1999

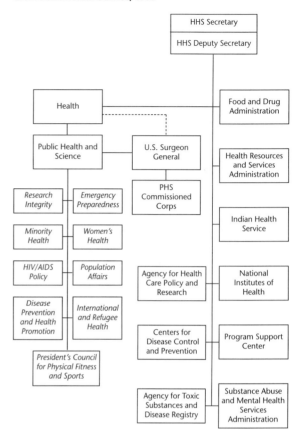

Source: U.S. Public Health Service.

• The NATIONAL INSTITUTES OF HEALTH (NIH), the nation's premier biomedical research establishment. The NIH consists of twenty-four separate institutes, centers, and divisions. With a fiscal 1999 budget of $15.7 billion, NIH funds research both at its campus in Bethesda, Maryland, and around the nation.

• The FOOD AND DRUG ADMINISTRATION (FDA), which regulates a quarter of all products sold in the United States. Its functions include determining the safety and efficacy of prescription drugs, medical devices, and biologic products. The FDA's fiscal 1999 budget was $1.1 billion.

• The CENTERS FOR DISEASE CONTROL AND PREVENTION (CDC), based in Atlanta, Georgia, which surveys and monitors outbreaks of communicable diseases, funds research into prevention strategies, and runs the nation's childhood immunization program. CDC's fiscal 1999 budget was $2.7 billion.

• The AGENCY FOR TOXIC SUBSTANCES AND DISEASE REGISTRY. With a fiscal 1999 budget of $74 million, the agency conducts public health assessments, health studies, surveillance activities, and health education training in communities around waste sites designated as Superfund sites by the U.S. Environmental Protection Agency. The newest of the Public Health Service agencies, the agency was established in 1980, and is based in Atlanta, Georgia.

• The INDIAN HEALTH SERVICE (IHS). Established in 1924, the IHS provides comprehensive health services for an estimated 1.4 million members of 550 recognized tribes of American Indians and Alaska natives through a network of 37 hospitals, 60 health centers, 3 school health centers, and 46 health stations. The IHS received an appropriation of $2.6 billion in fiscal 1999.

• The HEALTH RESOURCES AND SERVICES ADMINISTRATION (HRSA). Established in 1982, HRSA funds health care for medically underserved populations through its network of community and migrant health centers, administers the Ryan White Comprehensive AIDS Resource and Emergency (CARE) program, the MATERNAL AND CHILD HEALTH SERVICES BLOCK GRANT program, and the national ORGAN TRANSPLANT system. HRSA also provides funds and assistance to help train the next generation of health professionals, including operating the NATIONAL HEALTH SERVICE CORPS. HRSA's fiscal 1999 appropriation was $4.3 billion.

• The SUBSTANCE ABUSE AND MENTAL HEALTH SERVICES ADMINISTRATION (SAMHSA). Created in 1992, SAMHSA is the successor agency to the Alcohol, Drug Abuse, and Mental Health Administration (ADAMHA). SAMHSA provides funds for prevention and treatment services for those with substance abuse or mental health problems. The agency also funds research and demonstration projects on prevention and treatment and, with a budget of $2.5 billion in fiscal 1999, monitors the INCIDENCE and PREVALENCE of substance abuse and mental health problems.

• The AGENCY FOR HEALTH CARE POLICY AND RESEARCH (AHCPR). Established in 1989, the AHCPR studies cost, quality, and effectiveness issues associated with the nation's health care system. The AHCPR is the federal government's home for "health services research," which examines how the health care system functions. The AHCPR received a fiscal 1999 appropriation of $171 million.

The assistant secretary for health, as the position was reconfigured by the Clinton administration's "reinventing government" initiative in 1995, is the senior adviser to the HHS secretary on public health and science issues and oversees the Office of Public Health and Science (OPHS). Included in the OPHS are the surgeon general's office (in 1999 Dr. David Satcher, for only the second time in history, served simultaneously in both posts) and a series of smaller offices. Those include the Office of HIV/AIDS Policy, the Office on Minority Health, the OFFICE OF RESEARCH ON WOMEN'S HEALTH, the Office of Disease Prevention and Health Promotion, the Office of Emergency Preparedness, and the Office of International and Refugee Health.

Public Health Service, Commissioned Corps

The Commissioned Corps of the U.S. Public Health Service is headed by the surgeon general and comprises some 6,100 uniformed health care professionals who serve in the eight agencies of the PUBLIC HEALTH SERVICE in all fifty states and around the world. The corps is one of seven uniformed services of the United States (along with the army, navy, marines, air force, coast guard, and Commissioned Corps of the National Oceanic and Atmospheric Administration). As such, in times of national emergencies the corps can be designated as a military service. The corps's mission, according to the HEALTH AND HUMAN SERVICES DEPARTMENT, is "to provide highly-trained and mobile health professionals who carry out programs to promote the health of the Nation, understand and prevent disease and injury, assure safe and effective drugs and medical devices, and deliver health service [sic] to federal beneficiaries, and furnish health expertise in time of war or other national or international emergencies."

The Commissioned Corps, as it is known, was founded by the nation's first surgeon general, John Maynard Woodworth, who was appointed to the post in 1871. Most members of the Commissioned Corps work in the INDIAN HEALTH SERVICE, but they also help staff the NATIONAL INSTITUTES OF HEALTH, the CENTERS FOR DISEASE CONTROL AND PREVENTION (CDC) and the FOOD AND DRUG ADMINISTRATION and serve outside the Department of Health and Human Services in providing health services to the coast guard, the Bureau of Prisons, the Environmental Protection Agency, and the Immigration and Naturalization Service. Members of the Commissioned Corps include not only physicians and nurses but also scientists, dentists, engineers, pharmacists, veterinarians, dietitians, therapists, and health services officers.

Q

Qualified Medicare beneficiary

A qualified Medicare beneficiary (QMB) is a MEDI-CARE beneficiary with income and assets too high to qualify for full coverage under the MEDICAID program but still under 100 percent of the federal poverty line ($8,240 for an individual and $11,060 for a couple in 1999). QMBs (pronounced "quimbees") are eligible to have Medicaid pay all of their Medicare cost-sharing requirements, including monthly PREMIUMS for Part B coverage ($45.50 in 1999), and all required DE-DUCTIBLES and copayments. Although the program has been in existence for a decade, only about three-fourths of those eligible are currently enrolled. (See also DUAL ELIGIBLES.)

Advocates for those with low incomes fear that some QMBs could be adversely affected by a change to the program included in the 1997 Balanced Budget Act (PL 105-33). A provision of that law permits states to pay health care PROVIDERS at Medicaid rates rather than the usually higher Medicare limits. Although providers may not pass any additional cost along to patients, advocates are worried that some providers may stop serving patients in the QMB program, much as many providers currently decline to see Medicaid patients.

Quality improvement organizations

See PEER REVIEW ORGANIZATIONS

R

Rationing

A loaded word in health policy parlance, rationing is, in fact, merely the way health care resources are distributed within a population. The United States currently rations health care by default—those with the most money or best insurance coverage get the most (and usually, but not always, the best) care. In other countries, care is rationed in other ways, frequently through "queues," or waiting lists, for expensive surgery or high-tech treatments, or by limiting the spread of technology. For example, some countries limit the number of magnetic resonance imaging (MRI) machines or positron emission tomography (PET) scanners that are available to the population. Other countries impose age limits for certain procedures, refusing, for example, to transplant kidneys into those over sixty-five years of age. When Oregon proposed its novel rationing program for MEDICAID recipients, critics charged that it was antithetical to American values (see OREGON HEALTH CARE PLAN). Proponents of the program, however, argued that Medicaid was already rationed—those who met eligibility standards got "everything," whereas those who were poor, but not poor enough, or who didn't fall into one of Medicaid's eligibility categories, got nothing. Better to give more people some care than some people no care, they argued (and ultimately prevailed, although no state since has had the stomach to emulate Oregon's example). Most health policy analysts predict that when the huge baby boom population reaches its high health cost years beginning around the year 2010, the United States will have no choice but to implement some sort of overt rationing system.

Referral

Originally an informal method by which patients in need of specialized care were sent to a more advanced practitioner by their personal physician, today *referral* indicates a technique by which managed care plans seek to control the use of medical services by their members. Many plans require that to obtain any care except that provided by a patient's primary care physician, the patient must obtain a written referral from that physician (who is sometimes called a GATEKEEPER). Referrals frequently limit visits to specialists to one or two, after which, if more care is needed, another referral must be obtained. Referrals are also required for laboratory tests, physical therapy or other ancillary medical services, and for admission to a hospital or other treatment facility. Many patients and physicians, however, find referrals needlessly bureaucratic and even intrusive on a patient's preexisting relationship with another physician. As of mid-1998, thirty-one states, for example, had laws requiring that women be able to "directly access" their obstetricians/gynecologists without a referral from their primary care physician, regardless of that plan's rules.

Report cards

Report cards is jargon for tools that can be used by health care consumers, providers, and payers to compare the performance of health plans. Report cards, which remained relatively primitive tools in 1998, purport to measure everything from health care quality and utilization, to cost control, consumer satisfaction, administrative efficiencies, and financial stability.

Residency review committees

Residency review committees (RRCs) are composed of groups of physicians who set standards for training and evaluate medical training programs in each of twenty-six recognized medical specialties. The RRCs report to the ACCREDITATION COUNCIL ON GRADUATE MEDICAL EDUCATION (ACGME), a nonprofit group charged with the responsibility for overseeing the quality of physician training in the nation's estimated 1,000 medical teaching facilities.

Resource-based relative value scale

The resource-based relative value scale (RBRVS) measures the time, training, and skill required to perform a given medical service. The RBRVS, devised for MEDICARE by researchers from Harvard University in 1986, is the basis for the program's physician fee schedule. It has three main factors: physician work (time, skill, and intensity involved in the service), practice expenses, and malpractice costs. The relative values are then adjusted for geographic variations and converted into payment by multiplying the resulting figure by a "conversion factor." Thus, if the relative value for a particular service is $.75 and the conversion factor is $50, the payment for that service would be $37.50. The RBRVS was devised as a way to redress Medicare's tendency to overpay for surgery and other medical procedures and to underpay for so-called cognitive services such as counseling and performing a physical examination. In general, Medicare's physician fee schedule has increased incomes for primary care physicians like internists and decreased them for "proceduralists," such as surgeons.

Respite care

Respite care is a service that provides a paid caregiver to relieve a family member providing support or other care to a family member. Respite care, which is most frequently used for those caring for individuals with Alzheimer's disease, may be provided in the ailing person's home or in an outside facility (including a hospital, nursing home, or adult day care center). MEDICAID allows respite care as an optional service; MEDICARE covers it only as part of its HOSPICE benefit for the terminally ill. The MEDICARE CATASTROPHIC COVERAGE ACT of 1988 (PL 100-360) included the first-ever respite care benefit for Medicare generally, authorizing up to eighty hours per year for unpaid family members or friends who lived with and cared for a "chronically dependent" Medicare beneficiary. But that benefit was repealed before it ever took effect, along with the other new benefits in the law, in 1989.

Retiree health insurance

Many, particularly large, firms offer this health coverage for free or for a fee to workers who are retired from the company. Nearly one-third of MEDICARE beneficiaries—about twelve million individuals in 1999—had some sort of health insurance provided through a former job.

Retiree coverage, however, once widespread, declined throughout the 1990s. Between 1994 and 1998, according to one study of companies with at least five hundred workers, the percentage of employers offering retiree health benefits dropped from 40 percent to 30 percent. (Large employers are more likely than small firms to offer retiree coverage.) A separate study found that many employers who are not actually dropping coverage are cutting back in other ways. In 1991, for example, few or no large employers imposed caps on the amount of benefits provided through retiree health plans; by 1996 39 percent of firms with more than one thousand employees had imposed such caps. Similarly, the percentage of firms requiring retirees to pay PREMIUMS for their coverage increased from 72 percent in 1991 to 88 percent in 1996. Other companies instituted other cost-saving techniques, such as tightening eligibility by requiring workers to be employed for more years in order to qualify for coverage, or increasing cost-sharing requirements such as copayments and DEDUCTIBLES.

Most analysts say the trend toward less generous retiree benefits comes mostly from increasing health care costs in general. But another important factor was the 1992 imposition of a new rule by the Financial Accounting Standards Board requiring companies to show on their current books the estimated future costs of retiree health insurance. The rule is known as FAS 106.

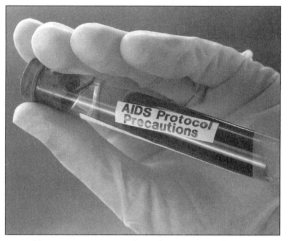

Passed by Congress in 1998, the Ricky Ray Hemophilia Relief Fund Act authorized compensation for the more than seven thousand hemophiliacs who contracted HIV from contaminated clotting factor in the mid-1980s, before blood tests for AIDS were in wide use. Source: National Institute of Allergy and Infectious Diseases

Ribicoff children

So-called for Sen. Abraham Ribicoff, R-Conn., who sponsored the legislation to authorize coverage, this is an optional category of children that states may cover under MEDICAID. Originally, Ribicoff children were any children under age twenty-one who would have been eligible for benefits under the Aid to Families with Dependent Children (AFDC) program if they met the definition of a dependent child. The program permitted coverage of children in low-income families not living at home (such as those in intermediate care facilities for the mentally retarded, those in foster care, or those in psychiatric institutions). The program has largely been superseded by mandated coverage of children in families with incomes under 100 percent of the poverty level born after September 30, 1983. However, until the year 2002, when all children through age nineteen in such families will be covered, the Ribicoff category remains an important pathway to Medicaid coverage for older children.

Ricky Ray Hemophilia Relief Fund Act

This legislation was passed by Congress in 1998 to authorize "compassionate" tax-free payments of up to $100,000 for hemophiliacs and their families who contracted HIV from contaminated "clotting factor" before blood tests for AIDS were in wide use. The measure (PL 105-369) was the culmination of five years of lobbying by the hemophilia community, an estimated half of whose members became HIV positive from using the contaminated clotting factor. Unlike the blood used in

regular blood transfusions, the clotting factor was derived from thousands of donors, which thus substantially increased the recipients' risk of contracting HIV. Ricky Ray was a Florida hemophiliac and the oldest of three brothers, all of whom contracted AIDS through contaminated clotting factor. Ray and his family were shunned by their community in the mid-1980s, before AIDS and its modes of transmission were well understood. He died in 1992 at age fifteen. In 1997, manufacturers of the clotting factor reached a legal settlement with some 7,200 hemophiliacs with HIV and survivors of those who already died to pay them $100,000 each. But because HIV positive hemophiliacs already spend $100,000 a year on clotting factor alone, and another $10,000 to $50,000 on AIDS-related treatment, Congress decided to match the settlement monies. The measure almost did not become law in 1998—indeed, its passage in the Senate was one of the last legislative acts of the 105th Congress—because some senators wanted to extend coverage beyond the hemophilia community to all of those who contracted HIV from tainted blood transfusions. That, however, would have more than doubled the bill's cost.

Risk adjustment

Risk adjustment is a mechanism for spreading the cost of very high users of medical care among the rest of an insured population. The existence of a well-working risk adjuster would eliminate the incentive for insurers to seek to cover those who are least likely to need care and to shun those likely to get sick. The distribution of health care costs among the population makes it obvious why insurance companies would like to cover the healthy: the sickest 1 percent of the population incurs 30 percent of all health care spending in a year; and the sickest 10 percent of the population accounts for 72 percent of health spending. Meanwhile the healthiest 50 percent of the population only incurs 3 percent of annual health care costs. There are two basic types of risk adjustment—prospective and retrospective. Prospective risk adjustment looks at likely risk factors (age, gender, medical history) and sets payments in advance based on anticipated costs that are distributed among insurers. Retrospective risk adjustment looks at the actual claims experience of individuals, and redistributes payments based on patients who cost more than expected, who suffer from certain conditions, or whose costs exceed a certain threshold.

In the 1997 Balanced Budget Act (PL 105-33), Congress ordered the HEALTH CARE FINANCING ADMINISTRATION (HCFA) to develop a risk adjustment mechanism for the MEDICARE managed care program by the year 2000. HCFA announced its proposed methodology on January 15, 1999. It would base risk-adjusted payments on whether or not beneficiaries had been hospitalized for certain conditions in the previous year (affecting payments for potentially up to 12.7 percent of beneficiaries) that could indicate those patients will have higher-than-average health costs in the future. Under HCFA's proposed scenario, certain beneficiaries in managed care could be eligible for extra payments ranging from $1,900 per year to more than $26,000. However, those extra payments would be funded by cutting reimbursement for those without a qualifying hospital stay.

Risk adjusters have proven simpler to theorize than to actually develop and implement, however. They generally require more, and more detailed, data than most plans have available.

Roe v. Wade

Roe v. Wade is the landmark case that legalized ABORTION nationwide. The ruling, written by Justice Harry A. Blackmun and issued on January 22, 1973, declared that the guarantee of liberty in the Fourteenth Amendment to the Constitution extends a right to privacy "broad enough to encompass a woman's decision whether or not to terminate her pregnancy."

But *Roe* also recognized that states have a legitimate interest in protecting both the woman's health and the potential life represented by the fetus. Said the decision: "[A]ppellant and some [friends of the court] argue that the woman's right is absolute and that she is entitled to terminate her pregnancy at whatever time, in whatever way, and for whatever reason she chooses. With this we do not agree. . . . The court's decisions recognizing a right of privacy also acknowledge that some state regulation in areas protected by that right is appropriate. . . . We, therefore, conclude that the right of personal privacy includes the abortion decisions but that this right is not unqualified and must be considered against important state interests in regulation."

The heart of the decision is the so-called trimester framework—dividing the nine-month pregnancy into three equal parts—which Blackmun described as follows: "For the stage prior to approximately the end of the first trimester the abortion decision and its effectuation must be left to the medical judgment of the pregnant woman's attending physician. For the stage subsequent to approximately the end of the first trimester the State, in promoting its interest in the health of the mother, may, if it chooses, regulate the abortion procedure in ways that are reasonably related to maternal health. For the stage subsequent to viability, the State in promoting its interest in the potentiality of human life, may, if it chooses, regulate, and even proscribe, abortion except where it is necessary, in appropriate medical judgment, for the preservation of the life or health of the mother."

In the companion case *Doe v. Bolton,* handed down the same day as *Roe,* the Court made clear that it took a liberal view of what "health" meant: "[T]he medical judgment may be exercised in light of all factors—physical, emotional, psychological, familial, and the woman's age—relevant to the well-being of the patient. All these factors relate to health."

A literal reading of *Roe* would seem to allow states considerable leeway to regulate abortion. But under *Roe*'s original holding, a woman had a "fundamental right" to terminate a pregnancy before fetal viability, and any state efforts to regulate that choice had to survive "strict scrutiny" and demonstrate a "compelling state interest." Under that rubric, the Court in subsequent cases struck down a wide array of abortion restrictions, including twenty-four-hour waiting periods, requirements that all abortions be performed in hospitals, and so-called informed consent laws requiring women seeking abortions to be given information about fetal development and abortion alternatives.

Until the 1989 case *Webster v. Reproductive Health Services of Missouri,* the only major restrictions allowed by the Court were PARENTAL NOTIFICATION AND CONSENT laws, as long as minors could seek permission from a judge if they feared involving their parents (*Bellotti v. Baird,* 1979; *Hodgson v. Minnesota,* 1990, among others), and state and federal laws barring public funding for abortions not needed to save the woman's life (*Harris v. McRae,* 1980, upholding the so-called HYDE AMENDMENT barring federal funding for abortions except in life-threatening situations).

Then, in 1992 the Court discarded the trimester framework altogether in PLANNED PARENTHOOD OF SOUTHEASTERN PENNSYLVANIA V. CASEY. In its place, it substituted a rule under which only state regulations that impose "an undue burden" on a woman's ability to obtain an abortion would be found unconstitutional.

RU486

Formally known as mifepristone, RU486 is a pill that can induce early ABORTION without surgery. Since it was first approved in France in 1988, abortion-rights and antiabortion groups have fought a nearly nonstop battle over whether the drug should be available in the United States. Abortion-rights supporters see the "abortion pill" as a salvation, allowing women to terminate unwanted pregnancies in the privacy of their own home and thus moving the procedure away from abortion clinics, which have become targets of sometimes violent protesters. They also say availability of such "medical abortion" will increase the likelihood that more doctors will provide abortion services, reversing a decline in access. And unlike surgical abortions, which cannot generally be done until a pregnancy is in its seventh week, RU486 works only in the earliest stages of pregnancy. Indeed, at forty-nine days, the outer limit for using the drug most effectively, the embryo is roughly the size of an aspirin. Abortion opponents fear RU486 for much the same reasons proponents want it, including the fact that the highest public support for abortion is at the earliest stages of pregnancy.

The drug is what is known as an antiprogestin. By blocking the action of the hormone progesterone, which prepares the lining of the uterus for pregnancy, RU486 interrupts pregnancy in its early stages (up to seven weeks after a missed menstrual period). In order to work best, RU486 must be combined with a prostaglandin, typically misoprostol, an ulcer medicine that causes uterine contractions. By itself, RU486 works 65 to 80 percent of the time to end a pregnancy; combined with a dose of prostaglandin, the effectiveness jumps to 95 percent. Women who take the drugs and do not abort must undergo the typical surgical procedure.

Medical abortion is not without its difficulties. First, it requires three separate visits to a health professional. The first visit includes an examination, counseling, determination of gestational age; if everything checks out, the woman takes three 200 mg tablets of RU486 and remains under observation for a half-hour. Two days later, the woman returns to take two 200 mcg tablets of miso-

Due largely to the efforts of antiabortion groups, the controversial abortion pill RU486 is not widely available in the United States. Some supporters of the pill, including Lawrence Lader, president of Abortion Rights Mobilization, have pressed the FDA to approve the drug for American distribution. Source: Mark Cardwell, Reuters

prostol to induce contractions and remains at the clinic for up to four hours. About half of the women have their abortions at the clinic during the second visit; 75 percent abort within twenty-four hours after taking the prostaglandin. The combination of drugs can also cause some significant side effects, including sometimes severe cramping and bleeding, as well as nausea, headache, weakness, and fatigue.

Overall, however, the procedure is considered very safe—far safer than carrying a pregnancy to term. Since 1981, women in twenty countries have used RU486 combined with various prostaglandins to induce early abortions. In Europe alone, half a million women have used the procedure. In 1998 the *New England Journal of Medicine* published the results of the U.S. clinical trials, in which the drug was found safe and effective, when combined with a prostaglandin, in terminating pregnancies of forty-nine days or less. Of 2,015 volunteers with pregnancies up to forty-nine days, 2 percent experienced complications severe enough to require hospitalization or surgical intervention; 4 percent of those with pregnancies between fifty and sixty-three days experienced serious side effects.

As of 1999, though, RU486 still was not widely available in the United States, mostly a testament to the efforts of antiabortion groups to keep it out. (Another form of medical abortion, using the drug methotrexate in combination with misoprostol, is available and has been studied; methotrexate is already approved by the Food and Drug Administration [FDA] for cancer chemotherapy.)

From 1988 to 1993, Americans could not even bring RU486 into the country; the FDA under Presidents Ronald Reagan and George Bush issued an "import alert" instructing customs agents to confiscate any pills from Americans returning from outside the country. President Bill Clinton lifted the alert on his second full day in office in 1993, along with a raft of other abortion restrictions from the era of Reagan and Bush.

In 1994, the French maker of the drug, Roussel-Uclaf, donated the U.S. rights to the medication to the Population Council, a nonprofit organization based in New York. The Population Council conducted U.S. clinical trials, applied to the FDA for approval, and arranged for a manufacturer for the drug.

In September 1996, the FDA issued a letter calling the

drug "approvable," pending receipt of more information on the drug's manufacturing and labeling. Final approval was delayed, however, when the person the council contracted with to raise money to manufacture and distribute the drug was found to have committed fraud.

In June 1998, abortion opponents in Congress made an attempt to stop RU486 legislatively. During consideration of the Agriculture Appropriations bill (which includes funding for FDA), the House voted 223–202 for an amendment offered by Rep. Tom Coburn, R-Okla., to bar FDA from granting final approval to any drug "for the inducement of abortion," including RU486. "Should we be in the business of spending federal tax dollars to facilitate the death of children?" Coburn asked on the House floor. "We should be seeking alternatives to abortion rather than making abortion easier." The amendment, however, was dropped in a House-Senate conference, presumably clearing the way for final approval by the FDA.

Ryan White Comprehensive AIDS Resource and Emergency (CARE) Act

Passed by Congress in 1990 and signed reluctantly by President George Bush (PL 101-381), the Ryan White Comprehensive AIDS Resource and Emergency (CARE) program has rapidly become the major source of funding for treatment and detection of AIDS and HIV, the AIDS virus. In fiscal 1999, Congress appropriated $1.4 billion for the Ryan White program, named for an Indiana teenager who contracted AIDS from contaminated clotting factor he took for hemophilia and whose struggle attracted national attention early in the epidemic. White died at age nineteen on April 8, 1990, a little more than a month before the Senate passed the measure and four months before it became law. From fiscal 1991 to fiscal 1999, nearly $6.4 billion in grant funds were awarded under the act, which helps finance services to an estimated 400,000 individuals with HIV/AIDS each year.

The program has five major parts. Title I provides emergency relief grants to cities with demonstrably high rates of AIDS and HIV-positive citizens. Grants can be used to provide health care and support services, prescription drugs, transportation, and counseling to low-income and uninsured individuals. When the measure was passed originally in 1990, fifteen cities qualified for the emergency grants; as of 1998, fifty cities were eligible. Title II provides grants to all fifty states, the District of Columbia, and U.S. territories to improve "the quality, accessibility and organization of health care and support for those with AIDS and HIV." Services that can be provided with Title II money are similar to those allowed in Title I. Title III provides grants to states to provide early intervention and comprehensive primary health care services for people living with AIDS as well as for at-risk populations, including women, intravenous drug users, and the homeless. Title III grants fund such activities as education, counseling, testing, and treatment. Title IV provides grants for coordinated HIV services and access to research for children, youth, women, and families. The final section of the act, which in the 1996 five-year reauthorization measure (PL 104-146) combined several programs from the original measure, includes authorized funding for fifteen AIDS education and training centers to educate health professionals in early diagnosis and treatment of HIV-positive individuals; a grant program to reimburse dental schools for the additional, uncompensated costs of providing services to those with AIDS and HIV; and special projects grants that fund innovative programs to deliver care to special populations with HIV disease.

Although the original measure passed with overwhelming support in both the House (where it was approved 408–14) and the Senate (where the vote was 95–4), heated arguments over AIDS policy held it up for months. The arguments focused particularly on issues related to the confidentiality of AIDS testing and whether the federal government should fund NEEDLE EXCHANGE programs to deter the spread of HIV among intravenous drug users by providing them with clean needles. (The final bill barred funding of such needle exchange programs.) Some conservative law-

Named after an Indiana teenager who died of AIDS, the Ryan White Comprehensive AIDS Resource and Emergency (CARE) Act is the major source of funding for treatment and detection of AIDS and HIV. Speaker of the House Newt Gingrich in 1996 addressed organizers of the National AIDS Candlelight March in front of a quilt honoring White and other well-known people who died of AIDS.
Source: Mike Theiler, Reuters

makers, particularly Sen. Jesse Helms, R-N.C., in the Senate, and Rep. William Dannemeyer, R-Calif., in the House, opposed the bills outright, calling them a payoff to the politically active homosexual lobby. Even President Bush expressed disapproval of the measure, noting in an official administration statement that the bill's "narrow, disease-specific approach sets a dangerous precedent, inviting treatment of other diseases through similar ad hoc arrangements." Nonetheless, Bush, signed the measure on August 18, 1990.

Although the issue of treating AIDS was hardly as controversial when the act was up for reauthorization in 1996, the final measure was held up for several months by a controversy over whether testing of all newborn infants for HIV should be mandatory. With evidence having accumulated that treating pregnant women with the drug AZT could reduce the chances of transmission to newborns, some members of the medical community (including the CENTERS FOR DISEASE CONTROL AND PREVENTION and the AMERICAN MEDICAL ASSOCIATION) argued that testing efforts should be aimed at mothers, not at babies. In the end, a compromise was worked out that would make HIV testing for newborns mandatory if states did not accomplish by other means a reduction in perinatal (pregnant mother to child) transmission of the disease. In order to continue receiving Ryan White funds, states would have to show a 50 percent reduction by March 2000 in the rate of new perinatal transmissions, compared with 1993; show that at least 95 percent of mothers who had received prenatal care during their pregnancy had been tested; or implement mandatory testing for newborns whose mothers had not been tested. AIDS organizations opposed the compromise as a waste of resources, noting that of an estimated 4.5 million live births annually, only about 7,000 were to HIV-infected women, resulting in only about 2,000 infected infants.

S

Safety net facilities

Technically, safety net facilities are health care PROVIDERS who are legally required to provide health care services free or at reduced rates to those who cannot otherwise afford them. In practice, however, the safety net is much larger, including a network of some 1,400 public hospitals owned and operated by states, cities, or counties; 700 COMMUNITY AND MIGRANT HEALTH CENTERS supported by the federal and local governments; and other clinics and practitioners that provide health services to those with low incomes, no insurance, or other access problems. Also considered safety net providers are maternal and child health clinics, local PUBLIC HEALTH departments, veterans' hospitals, and INDIAN HEALTH SERVICE facilities.

Although public hospitals provide more than two-thirds of their services to patients on MEDICAID or without insurance altogether, they are also important to those who are better off. Frequently, public hospitals operate an entire region's only burn unit or neonatal intensive care unit or other specialized but money-losing forms of care. Safety net providers have been under stress in recent years. At the same time the number of uninsured has continued to grow, Medicaid patients, who have traditionally been safety net providers' primary source of revenues, are moving into managed care plans, which don't necessarily send them to the safety net providers. Some safety net providers have responded by forming their own MANAGED CARE plans, usually a combination of hospitals and community health centers, which can provide both inpatient and outpatient services.

Safety net providers have also been affected by recent federal budget cutbacks. As part of the 1997 Balanced Budget Act (PL 105-33), Congress reduced MEDICAID payments for hospitals that serve a "disproportionate share" of low-income patients by $13 billion over five years (see DISPROPORTIONATE SHARE HOSPITAL (MEDICARE AND MEDICAID)). That law also reduced reimbursement for many federally supported clinics that serve the uninsured and poor. Safety net providers are also seeing caseloads rise as a result of the effects of the 1996 welfare reform law (the PERSONAL RESPONSIBILITY AND WORK OPPORTUNITY ACT of 1996; PL 104-193), which eliminated Medicaid coverage for many immigrants and which has had the effect of lowering Medicaid caseloads in general.

SAMHSA

See SUBSTANCE ABUSE AND MENTAL HEALTH SERVICES ADMINISTRATION.

Secondary care

Secondary care is care provided by a medical specialist. The intermediate step between PRIMARY CARE (the first point of contact with the medical system for most patients) and TERTIARY CARE (highly specialized care, normally provided in a hospital). See also SPECIALTY CARE.

Secondary Payer (Medicare)

The Medicare Secondary Payer program is a set of provisions for MEDICARE beneficiaries who also have other insurance to determine which insurance policy pays first. In most situations, Medicare is the "primary payer," meaning that it covers care to the extent of its benefits, with other insurance covering some or all of the gaps. In some cases, however, Medicare is the "secondary payer," meaning that other insurance must pay to the extent of its coverage, with Medicare paying uncovered bills, if any. For example, employers of more than twenty workers must offer workers age sixty-five and over (and their spouses age sixty-five and over) the same coverage offered to other workers. If the Medicare-eligible worker accepts the employer's coverage, that coverage becomes the primary payer, and Medicare the secondary payer. Plans offered by large employers (with more than 100 employees) are also primary payers for employees or dependents who receive Medicare on the basis of disability, as long as the employee is considered to be in "current employment status." And employer-sponsored plans of any size are the primary payer for eighteen months for persons who become eligible for Medicare's END-STAGE RENAL DISEASE (ESRD) program. That leaves employers as the primary payers for a maximum of twenty-one months (eighteen months plus the three-month waiting period for ESRD coverage). The Medicare Secondary Payer program also authorized a "data match" program, using Internal Revenue Service and Social Security Administration records to determine if working Medicare beneficiaries may have employer-based coverage that should be a primary payer. The Medicare Secondary Payer program was temporary throughout the 1980s and 1990s, with periodic extensions, producing periodic savings to the Medicare budget baseline. For example, in fiscal 1995, Medicare Secondary Payer provisions saved the program $3 billion. In the 1997 Balanced Budget Act (PL 105-33), Congress made the program permanent.

Self-insurance

Self-insurance is the practice of (usually) large companies using their own funds to pay health benefits to employees. Self-insured firms often hire an insurance company as a "third-party administrator" to process claims and other paperwork, but the company, not the insurer, pays for the cost of medical care for those covered by the plan. Self-insured companies often purchase "stop-loss" coverage to protect themselves against unexpectedly large expenses. Self-insurance can be financially attractive to companies because self-insured plans are exempt from most state insurance laws (including costly benefit mandates) under the federal EMPLOYEE RETIREMENT INCOME SECURITY ACT (ERISA).

Self-referral curbs

Congress twice, first in 1989 and again in 1993, sought to crack down on MEDICARE reimbursement for laboratory tests, X-rays, and other services provided at facilities owned in whole or in part by physicians who made the REFERRALS. The first set of restrictions, made in the fiscal 1990 BUDGET RECONCILIATION bill (PL 101-239), grew out of a report by the inspector general of the HEALTH AND HUMAN SERVICES DEPARTMENT that found that Medicare patients of physicians who owned or invested in clinical laboratories received 34 percent more lab services than the average Medicare patient in 1987, costing the federal government an extra $28 million that year. The reconciliation bill barred Medicare payments to clinical laboratories when the referring physician had an ownership interest or other financial arrangement with the facility. But the measure included several exceptions—not covered by the ban were laboratory services provided directly by the physician or his or her employee or by an employee under the physician's direct supervision; services provided as part of a group practice; services within prepaid health plans; and services provided in any rural area or in Puerto Rico.

Selling of patient referrals was already illegal. In 1977 legislation (PL 95-142) Congress made it a felony to accept kickbacks for services paid for by the federal Medicare or joint state-federal MEDICAID programs. A 1987 law (PL 100-93) instituted civil penalties to make prosecution easier and sought to close some of the loopholes left in the earlier statute. But most of the ventures the 1990 law sought to block were crafted to get around those earlier laws by not basing direct payments on referrals. Many of the ventures were in the form of "limited partnerships" that provided the doctor/owners a percentage of any profits.

Organized medicine, led by the AMERICAN MEDICAL ASSOCIATION, opposed the new restrictions, noting that in many areas, facilities owned by doctors were the only ones available. But even the editor of the prestigious *New England Journal of Medicine* argued in favor of the self-referral curbs, noting in testimony before Congress that such arrangements "inevitably encourage unnecessary duplication and overutilization of facilities and services, and thereby add significantly to the cost of health care."

Rep. Pete Stark, D-Calif., then-chairman of the House Ways and Means Subcommittee on Health and sponsor of the limitations (which have come to be known as the Stark I and Stark II restrictions), was disappointed that the curbs enacted in 1989 applied only to laboratory services. He was rewarded in 1993, when, as part of that year's budget reconciliation bill (PL 103-66), the self-referral curbs were extended to cover not only laboratory services but also physical and occupational therapy services; radiology or other diagnostic services; radiation therapy services; durable medical equipment; parenteral and enteral nutrients, equipment, and supplies; prosthetics, orthotics, and prosthetic devices; HOME HEALTH services; outpatient prescription drugs; and inpatient and outpatient hospital services. The bill revised and added a series of exceptions to the ban, including ones for services provided to rural residents in rural areas, those provided by group practices and those provided by or under the direct supervision of a physician or group of physicians. It also clarified circumstances in which ownership of investment securities constituted a relationship that triggered the referral ban, and it clarified permissible compensation arrangements and definitions of group practices.

As part of the 1997 Balanced Budget Act (PL 105-33), Congress required that the Justice Department issue binding "advisory opinions" to physicians who submit business plans as to whether the plan would violate the self-referral restrictions.

Senate Appropriations Committee

The Senate Appropriations Committee oversees the "discretionary" portion of the federal budget. The committee writes thirteen separate spending bills each year that are required for the government to run. Through the Labor-Health and Human Services-Education appropriation, the committee sets spending levels for most of the HEALTH AND HUMAN SERVICES DEPARTMENT (HHS), with three major exceptions. MEDICARE and MEDICAID, as "entitlement" programs, are funded according to estimates of how much they will cost; legislative changes to affect those costs must be initiated by "authorizing" committees. (Appropriators do have authority over some very limited portions of the Medicare budget, primarily how much to allocate for Medicare contractors, the private insurance companies that process Medicare claims.) Additionally, for historical reasons, the FOOD AND DRUG ADMINISTRATION, although part of HHS, is funded as part of the Agriculture appropriations bill. The appropriations committee also sets spending levels for other health-related programs, including the INDIAN HEALTH SERVICE (funded in the Interior bill), health care for veterans (funded in the Veterans Affairs Department (VA)–Housing and Urban Development Department (HUD)–Independent agencies bill), health care and insurance for the military (through the Defense bill), health care for those incarcerated in federal prisons (through the Commerce-State-Justice bill), and health insurance for federal employees (through the Treasury-Postal Service bill).

Senate Finance Committee

The Senate Finance Committee has the broadest health jurisdiction of any committee in Congress. Whereas the House Ways and Means Committee shares its health jurisdiction with the Commerce Committee,

The Finance Committee is one of the most powerful in the Senate. Here John Chafee, R-R.I. (left) and Charles Grassley, R-Iowa, lead the discussion of a Medicare bill during an evening markup session. Source: Scott J. Ferrell, Congressional Quarterly

Senate Finance has complete and exclusive jurisdiction over all health programs included in the SOCIAL SECURITY ACT. That gives it authority over MEDICARE, MEDICAID, the MATERNAL AND CHILD HEALTH SERVICES BLOCK GRANT, and the new CHILDREN'S HEALTH INSURANCE PROGRAM (CHIP) created in the 1997 Balanced Budget Act (PL 105-33). Of the committees that oversee health programs, the Senate Finance Committee has always been the most closely divided between Republicans and Democrats (traditionally the majority party has had only a two-vote advantage over the minority, meaning that a single defector could produce a tie vote). As a result, the panel tends to act in a more bipartisan manner than other health committees, and, for that reason, among others, its bills tend to be taken seriously by both the Senate and the House.

Senate Health, Education, Labor and Pensions Committee

Formerly the Labor and Human Resources Committee, the panel was renamed the Committee on Health, Education, Labor and Pensions (HELP) at the start of the 106th Congress. The HELP Committee has the second broadest health jurisdiction in that chamber, after the Finance Committee. The Senate HELP panel oversees most of the health programs run by the HEALTH AND HUMAN SERVICES DEPARTMENT other than MEDICARE and MEDICAID (which are under the Finance Committee's purview), including the vast PUBLIC HEALTH SERVICE (which includes the NATIONAL INSTITUTES OF HEALTH and the CENTERS FOR DISEASE CONTROL AND PREVENTION) and the FOOD AND DRUG ADMINISTRATION. The committee also oversees employee-benefit and worker-safety issues by virtue of its labor jurisdiction, and aging and disability issues under its human resources purview. Like the House Education and Workforce Committee, the Senate Labor panel has a reputation for being more liberal than the Senate as a whole. In 1995 and 1996, the committee's chairman, Sen. Nancy Landon Kassebaum, R-Kan., and its ranking Democrat, Edward Kennedy, of Massachusetts, developed a bipartisan measure that would become PL 104-191, the HEALTH INSURANCE PORTABILITY AND ACCOUNTABILITY ACT (HIPAA).

Single payer

Single payer is the term used to refer to a health care system in which all the bills are paid by a single entity, generally the government. Single payer systems, however, are not the same as government-run medical care. Medicare is, in fact, a single payer system, with the federal government responsible for paying for all Medicare-covered services, which are provided by private health care entities. By contrast, the Veterans' Administration (VA) health system is a government-run enterprise: the hospitals are owned by the federal government, and health care professionals are paid a government salary to provide services. Internationally, Canada has a single payer system, in which the government finances care provided by private doctors and hospitals, whereas Great Britain's system (although it has evolved considerably over the years to reflect more private influences) is more in the mold of the VA, with government-owned facilities and doctors on salary.

Single payer advocates in the United States note that it has many advantages over the existing public/private patchwork system. It is fundamentally simple, easy enough for everyone to understand. It would, by definition, provide universal coverage, insuring everyone. A single payer system would also significantly reduce costs associated with administering more than 1,500 private insurance plans; an estimate of one single payer proposal offered during the health reform debate of 1993–1994 said it would have reduced national health spending by 6 percent in the year 2003. Even a significant subset of doctors supported the single payer concept, based on the theory that it would be better to be hassled administratively by a single entity than have to deal with multiple sets of rules imposed by dozens of payers.

But critics complained that adopting a single payer system would be catastrophically disruptive, essentially putting out of business the entire private health insurance industry. It would entail a huge tax increase—and even though most people would pay no more under a single payer system than they paid before in premiums and other out-of-pocket health care costs, taxes remained anathema to many, if not most, Americans. Other opponents worried that government control of the health care system, particularly price controls, could suppress critical innovations in new treatments or therapies, or even lead to overt RATIONING of new or expensive technologies.

During the 1993–1994 debate over health reform in the United States, there was significant—although not majority—support for proposals to convert the nation's private health insurance system to a single payer program. The proposal, sponsored by Rep. Jim McDermott, D-Wash., in the House and Sen. Paul Wellstone, D-Minn., in the Senate, would have imposed a new payroll tax to fund all health care and imposed strict price controls on health care goods and services. The proposal at one point enjoyed the support of nearly 100 House members, as many cosponsors as signed onto President Bill Clinton's HEALTH SECURITY ACT. Support for the plan on the House Education and Labor Committee (traditionally a liberal stronghold) was so strong that the only way the panel could find enough votes to report out a bill favored by the Clinton administration was by also reporting out (without recommendation for passage) the single payer proposal. In the end, neither bill was acted on by the full House.

Small market variation

Research over the last decade has shown conclusively that doctors in different parts of the country practice medicine in very different ways. What has not been determined, however, is whether the patients who receive more care are actually getting better care, or whether those receiving less care are being undertreated. The phrase *geography is destiny*—meaning that the medical care patients receive is determined by where in the country they live—is associated with John Wennberg, a physician and researcher at Dartmouth University in Hanover, New Hampshire, who pioneered research into variations in medical practice. Wennberg's early research demonstrated that the rates of procedures performed in Boston were vastly different from those performed in Providence, Rhode Island, less than 100 miles away. In 1996, Wennberg produced the first *Dartmouth Atlas of Health Care*, which used data from Medicare's FEE-FOR-SERVICE program to document different practice patterns of physicians and different delivery capacities in 306 separate areas of the United States. For example, on a per person basis, MEDICARE spending is more than twice as high in Miami, Florida, as in Minneapolis, Minnesota. Wennberg's analyses also showed that although, generally, health care utilization is higher in areas with a greater capacity (that is, more hospitalizations in areas with more hospital beds), care also varies depending on how physicians tend to practice. Thus, an area may have a higher-than-average rate of some surgical procedures, but a lower-than-average rate of others.

Social Security Act

This act is the law that governs not only the best-known U.S. retirement program, but also a broad range of other social programs. Few realize that MEDICARE is actually Title XVIII of the Social Security Act, and MEDICAID is Title XIX. Other programs authorized in the Social Security Act include Survivors and Disability Insurance (Title II), Unemployment Insurance (Title III), the MATERNAL AND CHILD HEALTH SERVICES BLOCK GRANT (Title V), the SUPPLEMENTAL SECURI-TY INCOME program (Title XVI), and the Social Services Block Grant (Title XX). The new CHILDREN'S HEALTH INSURANCE PROGRAM (CHIP), authorized in the 1997 Balanced Budget Act (PL 105-33), is Title XXI of the Social Security Act.

Social Security Disability Insurance (SSDI)

SSDI is the program under Social Security that protects workers from loss of income due to disability by providing them with monthly cash payments. Disability insurance represents the "DI" portion of Social Security's core "OASDI" program (the remainder is the "old age and survivor insurance"). Insurance for the DI portion of Social Security is 0.6 percentage points of the 7.65 percent Social Security payroll tax (1.45 percentage points are for MEDICARE; the remaining 5.6 is for old age and survivors' insurance). Congress created SSDI in 1956 to aid workers who retire after age fifty but before

Medicare is just one of the many entitlement programs authorized by the Social Security Act. Ensuring that Social Security and Medicare are financially strong in the next century was the focus of a 1999 economic panel hosted by President Bill Clinton (right) and Vice President Al Gore.
Source: Mark Wilson, Reuters

age sixty-five because of disability; coverage of younger workers was added later.

In order to qualify for SSDI benefits, an individual must have worked the requisite number of quarters in Social Security-covered employment (generally twenty quarters, unless the person is blind or under age thirty-one) and must have a severe impairment rendering him or her unable to perform his or her previous job or any other "substantial gainful activity" as a result of a medically determinable physical or mental impairment that can be expected to result in death or which has lasted or can be expected to last for at least twelve continuous months. SSDI recipients who are certified as "permanently and totally disabled," after a twenty-nine-month period (five months before cash benefits begin and twenty-four months of receiving benefits) are eligible for Medicare coverage.

As of December 1996, an estimated 6 million disabled workers and families, representing 14 percent of all Social Security beneficiaries, were receiving SSDI benefits.

Special Supplemental Food Program for Women, Infants, and Children

This is the former name of the Special Supplemental Nutrition Program for Women, Infants, and Children, or WIC. The program's name was changed in 1994 to reflect its emphasis on nutrition.

Specialty care

Specialty care is that provided by a medical "specialist," generally a medical doctor who has undergone additional training and passed an examination given in one of twenty-six disciplines regulated by the American Board of Medical Specialties. Surgeons, psychiatrists, obstetrician/gynecologists, and cardiologists are all specialists. In many MANAGED CARE PLANS, patients may not obtain care from a specialist without a written REFERRAL from their primary care physician.

Specified Low-Income Medicare Beneficiaries (SLMB)

SLMBs (pronounced "slim-bees") are MEDICARE beneficiaries with incomes between 100 and 120 percent of the federal poverty line. Such incomes are too high to qualify SLMBs for full MEDICAID coverage or for Medicaid coverage of all their Medicare cost-sharing requirements. SLMBs do qualify, however, for a program enacted in 1990 that requires state Medicaid programs to pay their Medicare Part B premium ($45.50 in 1999). The SLMB program is significantly underused; only about 16 percent of those eligible are currently enrolled. (See also DUAL ELIGIBLES.)

Spend-down

Spend-down is the name for the process by which an individual qualifies for MEDICAID coverage by virtue of exhausting his or her income and assets. States have considerable flexibility to determine the level at which a person has "spent down" to Medicaid eligibility, but generally, federal law requires states who operate optional MEDICALLY NEEDY programs to take into account the cost of health insurance premiums and other required cost-sharing, as well as other medical expenses the person has, in determining if the remaining financial situation would qualify the individual for Medicaid coverage.

Spousal impoverishment

Spousal impoverishment refers to a situation under MEDICAID in which a spouse living in the community is impoverished by the program's requirements for payments to augment Medicaid coverage of a spouse in a nursing home. Until passage of the 1988 MEDICARE CATASTROPHIC COVERAGE ACT (PL 100-360), Medicaid required not only that an individual "spend down" virtually all of his or her income or assets before qualifying for Medicaid coverage of a nursing home stay but also required that virtually all of the institutionalized individual's income go toward the cost of the care. After a person had been institutionalized for more than one month, spouses were no longer considered to be living together, and only the income of the institutionalized spouse was considered for determining Medicaid eligibility. If the wife was in an institution and the husband remained at home, the husband could keep any income in his own name. The problem arose most often, however, when it was the husband in the nursing home and the wife at home. If the wife had no income in her name, as was frequently the case, she had to subsist on a welfare-level maintenance allowance from the husband's income while the rest went toward the cost of his nursing home care, giving rise to the term *spousal impoverishment.*

Under provisions of the Medicare Catastrophic Coverage law that were *not* repealed with the rest of the measure in 1989, in any month in which a married person was in a nursing home, no income of the at-home spouse was to be considered available to the institutionalized spouse, and income paid solely to one spouse was to belong to that spouse alone. Income paid in both names was to be considered available in equal portions to both spouses. At the beginning of a continuous period of institutionalization, a couple's total assets would be counted and split in two, with half considered available to each spouse, exempting the couple's house, household goods, and personal effects. If, after division of the assets, the at-home spouse was left with less than $12,000 (indexed to general inflation beginning in 1989), the institutionalized spouse could transfer an amount sufficient to allow the at-home spouse to hold $12,000 worth of assets in his or her own name. In 1997 the minimum asset amount was $15,804. However, amounts greater than $60,000 (also indexed to inflation) would be attributed to the institutionalized spouse and thus become available to pay the nursing home bill. In 1997 the maximum asset limit was $79,020. States could, at their option, raise the $12,000 minimum to any level below the $60,000 maximum.

Beginning on September 30, 1989, states also had to permit the at-home spouse to keep a "maintenance needs allowance" from the other spouse's income sufficient to bring total income to at least 122 percent of the monthly federal poverty threshold for a two-person household, rising to 150 percent by 1992. The maintenance needs allowance could not exceed $1,500 per month, expect in cases in which a higher level was determined by administrative degree or court order. In 1997 the cap on the maintenance allowance was $1,975.50.

Stark and Stark II restrictions

See SELF-REFERRAL CURBS.

State Children's Health Insurance Program

State Children's Health Insurance Program (S-CHIP) is the formal name of the program included in the 1997 Balanced Budget Act (PL 105-33) that provided $48 billion over ten years to states to help provide coverage for an estimated 4 million uninsured children. The program is referred to by the Clinton administration as just the CHILDREN'S HEALTH INSURANCE PROGRAM (CHIP).

Substance Abuse and Mental Health Services Administration

Created in 1992, the Substance Abuse and Mental Health Services Administration (SAMHSA) is the successor agency to the Alcohol, Drug Abuse, and Mental Health Administration (ADAMHA). SAMHSA provides funds to help with the costs of treatment for those with substance abuse problems or mental illness, and it funds research into the causes and prevention of these ills. The agency, with a budget of $2.5 billion in fiscal 1999, also monitors the INCIDENCE and PREVALENCE of substance abuse and mental health treatment. SAMHSA has three main branches, the Center for Mental Health Services, which helps disseminate information on treatments for mental illness, the Center for Substance Abuse Prevention, which spearheads federal efforts to prevent alcohol and substance abuse; and the Center for Substance Abuse Treatment, which studies ways to improve treatment services and make them more available.

Substitution

See CROWD-OUT.

Suicide, assisted

Defined generally, assisted suicide is the practice of helping someone, usually someone with a terminal illness, end his or her own life. From the perspective of health professionals, the term means taking "affirmative steps" to end someone's life rather than merely withholding treatment or nourishment. But the difference between assisted suicide and murder or euthanasia is a fine line, as Dr. Jack Kevorkian, a Michigan pathologist who said he helped more than 130 people kill themselves between 1990 and 1998, has demonstrated.

Kevorkian frequently provided a carbon monoxide machine to allow patients with terminal illnesses to end their lives. Between 1994 and 1996 Kevorkian, whose license to practice medicine was revoked by Michigan and California authorities, was tried and acquitted three times on assisted suicide charges. A fourth trial ended in a mistrial. But in 1998 Kevorkian was arrested for first-degree murder after he appeared in a videotape broadcast on the newsmagazine *60 Minutes.* The videotape showed him delivering what he said was a fatal injection of potassium chloride to fifty-two-year-old Thomas Youk, a Michigan man suffering from Lou Gehrig's disease, a uniformly fatal muscle malady. A Michigan jury convicted Kevorkian of second-degree murder in March 1999.

Kevorkian said he wanted to force Americans to debate the issue of assisted suicide and *euthanasia* (the affirmative "mercy" killing of a suffering individual).

But even without him, the debate over "end-of-life" issues was already well underway.

In anticipation of two forthcoming Supreme Court rulings, Congress in early 1997 moved to outlaw federal funding for assisted suicide. The Assisted Suicide Funding Restriction Act of 1997 (PL 105-12), signed by President Bill Clinton April 30, barred the use of federal funds "to provide any health care item or services furnished for the purpose of causing, or for the purpose of assisting in causing, the death of any individual, such as by assisted suicide, euthanasia, or mercy killing." The measure, however, specifically exempted from the ban the withdrawing of medical care, withholding of food or water, and providing of pain relief "even if such use may increase the risk of death."

The Supreme Court, however, in the two cases testing the issues, did not find any constitutional right to assisted suicide in the decisions it issued in June 1997. In *Vacco v. Quill* and *Washington v. Glucksberg* the Court upheld assisted suicide bans in New York and Washington State, respectively. But at the same time, the Court also did not find any reason that states could not permit assisted suicide if they so chose.

So far, Oregon is the only state to test that side of the assisted suicide equation. In 1994, voters used the initiative process to approve the "Death with Dignity Act," which permitted state residents who were determined to be mentally competent and to have less than six months to live to request prescriptions for lethal doses of drugs. After a protracted court fight that culminated in the Supreme Court's rejecting a challenge to the law on October 14, 1997, voters in November 1997 reaffirmed their support for the measure by a 60–40 margin, and it took effect later that month. In the measure's first year of operation, ten state residents used the law to obtain lethal doses of barbiturates to kill themselves. Eight actually committed suicide; the other two died of their ailments.

Meanwhile, some lawmakers in Washington tried to overturn the Oregon law. Before the measure took effect in 1997, House and Senate Judiciary Committee Chairmen Henry Hyde, R-Ill., and Orrin Hatch, R-Utah, wrote to the federal Drug Enforcement Administration asking if Oregon physicians could legally provide drugs for assisting death that were included on the federal government's list of "controlled substances." So as not to interfere with the Oregon vote, the DEA waited until the day after the election to respond to the letter. Its determination was that physicians could not fulfill the requirements of the Oregon law without running afoul of the federal Controlled Substances Act. That law permits physicians to prescribe drugs only for "legitimate medical purposes," DEA administrator Thomas Constantine wrote, and assisted suicide or euthanasia was not a legitimate medical purpose.

In June 1998, however, Attorney General Janet Reno overruled the DEA's interpretation. "The state of Oregon has reached the considered judgment that physician-assisted suicide should be authorized under narrow conditions and in compliance with certain detailed procedures," Acting Assistant Attorney General L. Anthony Sutin wrote in a letter to Oregon Democratic senator Ron Wyden advising him of Reno's decision. "Under these circumstances, we have concluded that the [Controlled Substances Act] does not authorize DEA to prosecute, or to revoke the DEA registration of, a physician who has assisted in a suicide in compliance with Oregon law."

In response to Reno's overturning of the DEA, anti-assisted suicide legislators immediately set out to overturn Reno. In June 1998 they introduced the "Lethal Drug Abuse Prevention Act," which would have barred physicians from prescribing drugs on the federal list of controlled substances "with the purpose of causing, or assisting in causing, the suicide or euthanasia of any individual." In the Senate the measure was sponsored by Assistant Majority Leader Don Nickles, R-Okla., and in the House by Judiciary chairman Hyde.

By September the bill had been approved by both the House and Senate Judiciary Committees and was set for floor action in both chambers. But neither house ended up voting on the measure. That was because a coalition of health professional and patient groups, many of which opposed assisted suicide, launched an intense—and ultimately successful—lobbying campaign to defeat the measure.

They argued that giving the DEA the affirmative authority to police cases of suspected assisted suicide or euthanasia would make it less likely that doctors would use appropriate levels of medication to control intractable pain for terminal patients, thereby taking an already bad problem and making it worse. "We're concerned that using the federal government, the DEA, as a watchdog over physicians will have a very chilling effect on physicians treating patients at the end of life with heavy doses of pain medication," said Thomas Reardon, president-elect of the AMERICAN MEDICAL ASSOCIATION (AMA). "So we're concerned that this will really negatively impact the quality of care for many terminally ill patients." (The AMA was on record as opposing assisted suicide, noting that "physician assisted suicide is against the Code of Medical Ethics and incompatible with the physician's role as healer and caregiver.")

Supplemental Security Income (SSI)

SSI is a federal entitlement program that provides cash assistance to low-income aged, blind, and disabled individuals. Although it is run by the Social Security Administration, SSI is not the same as the SOCIAL SECURITY DISABILITY INSURANCE program (SSDI). The latter is not a means-tested program for those with low incomes and requires qualifying individuals to be fully vested in the Social Security system. Rather, SSI, created in 1972 by PL 92-603 and begun in 1974, was intended to replace a series of state programs as well as the original program of Aid to the Old-Aged and Blind established under the original Social Security program as passed in 1935 and the Aid to the Permanently and Totally Disabled program enacted in 1950. As envisioned at its creation, SSI was intended to "provide a positive assurance that the nation's aged, blind, and disabled people would no longer have to subsist on below poverty-level incomes" by providing a uniform, national income support level. SSI payments are to supplement Social Security income supports, particularly for those individuals who are not fully qualified for Social Security or are qualified only for minimal payments.

In June 1998, SSI provided about $2.3 billion in payments to some 6.6 million beneficiaries. The vast majority of SSI beneficiaries are disabled (about 5 million); 1 million are children, about 1.4 million are elderly, and some 85,000 are blind. About 45 percent of SSI beneficiaries receive supplements from states in addition to the federal payments. In 1999 the maximum SSI monthly payment was $500 for individuals and $751 for couples.

SSI, unlike other Social Security programs, is funded from general revenues rather than from dedicated Social Security payroll taxes. SSI eligibility also confers automatic eligibility for MEDICAID. Most elderly individuals in nursing homes obtain Medicaid coverage for the costs of their care by qualifying for SSI after "spending down." The 1996 welfare reform bill, PERSONAL RESPONSIBILITY AND WORK OPPORTUNITY RECONCILIATION ACT of 1996 (PL 104-193), made significant changes to the SSI program and its relationship to Medicaid. For example, it made it significantly more difficult for mentally disabled children to qualify for SSI (enrollment had been skyrocketing since a 1990 Supreme Court decision, *Sullivan v. Zebley,* leading to charges that children with minor behavioral problems were being added to the SSI and Medicaid rolls). The law also barred legal aliens who entered the United States on or after the date of enactment (August 22, 1996) from receiving any "federal means-tested public benefit," including SSI and Medicaid, for five years from their date of entry; this affected an estimated 500,000 immigrants. Congress, however, restored the eligibility of some two-thirds of those legal aliens for SSI and Medicaid as part of the 1997 Balanced Budget Act (PL 105-33). Made reeligible for benefits were legal immigrants who were receiving SSI as of August 22, 1996, based on a disability; those receiving SSI on that date because they were elderly but who could requalify based on a disability; and those who were in the United States as of August 22, 1996, and subsequently became disabled. Disabled legal immigrants who entered the country after August 22, 1996, but before June 1, 1997, would also be eligible for benefits. Remaining legal immigrants who entered the United States after August 22, 1996, would still be ineligible for SSI or Medicaid for five years, and in any case until they became citizens.

Supplementary Medical Insurance (SMI)

Also known as MEDICARE Part B, SMI is an optional program that covers a set percentage of the cost of physician and other outpatient care. SMI, which cost $68.6 billion in 1996, is funded partially by PREMIUMS paid by the program's beneficiaries ($45.50 per month in 1999), with the rest coming from "general revenues," which includes income taxes and other fees paid to the U.S. Treasury. Originally, Part B premiums were to cover half of the program's costs, but when Part B spending began to rise rapidly shortly after the program was launched, Congress stepped in to make sure premiums would remain affordable. In the 1997 Balanced Budget Act (PL 105-33), Congress permanently fixed the Part B premium at the amount estimated to cover 25 percent of program costs. Part B, which is available to anyone over age sixty-five as well as to those under sixty-five who are eligible for Part A coverage, covers physician fees and other outpatient costs, such as laboratory tests, durable medical equipment and supplies, and ambulance services. Although its overall spending per year is less than Part A, Part B is more heavily used. In 1996, 84 percent of the program's 36 million beneficiaries used services covered by Part B. As of 1999, Part B did not cover the cost of prescription drugs, although President Bill Clinton and some in Congress were agitating to add such coverage.

Surgeon general of the United States

The surgeon general is the chief spokesman for PUBLIC HEALTH in the federal government. Indeed, one of the principal duties of the surgeon general is to "protect and advance the health of the nation through educating the public; advocating for effective disease prevention and health promotion programs and activities, and providing a highly recognized symbol of national commit-

Surgeons General of the U.S. Public Health Service

Name	Years served
John M. Woodworth	1871–1879
John B. Hamilton	1879–1891
Walter Wyman	1891–1911
Rupert Blue	1912–1920
Hugh S. Cumming	1920–1936
Thomas Parran	1936–1948
Leonard A. Scheele	1948–1956
Leroy E. Burney	1956–1961
Luther L. Terry	1961–1965
William H. Stewart	1965–1969
Jesse L. Steinfeld	1969–1973
S. Paul Ehrlich (acting)	1973–1977*
Julius B. Richmond	1977–1981
C. Everett Koop	1981–1989
Antonia C. Novello	1990–1993
M. Joycelyn Elders	1993–1994
David Satcher	1998–

*Never confirmed.

ment to protecting and improving the public's health."

The position of surgeon general has changed significantly over the years, waxing and waning in importance and prominence. The first surgeon general, John Maynard Woodworth, was appointed in 1871 to run a newly reorganized Marine Hospital Service as a national hospital system under the direction of a chief medical officer known as the supervising surgeon. Woodworth went on to found the Commissioned Corps of the Public Health Service to run the hospital system and be ready to move about the country as needed to address health needs or emergencies (see PUBLIC HEALTH SERVICE, COMMISSIONED CORPS). The surgeon general remains the titular head of the Commissioned Corps, one of seven uniformed services in the United States, and holds a rank equivalent to a four-star admiral.

Until 1966, the surgeon general remained the head of the PUBLIC HEALTH SERVICE, with full program, administrative, and financial management authority. But in 1966, that line authority was transferred to the new

As surgeon general from 1981 to 1989, C. Everett Koop (left) spoke out frequently on tobacco issues. Even after leaving public office, he continued to provide advice on tobacco policy to government officials, serving with former FDA commissioner David Kessler as cochair of the Advisory Committee on Tobacco Policy and Public Health. *Source: Rick Wilking, Reuters*

post of assistant secretary for health (ASH). The surgeon general was made a principal deputy to the ASH with responsibility for "advising and assisting on professional medical matters."

The position was the subject of controversy from 1973 to 1977, when many lawmakers wanted it abolished. From 1977 to 1981, the surgeon general and assistant secretary for health positions were held by the same person, Julius Richmond (a situation repeated with the confirmation of the former director of the CENTERS FOR DISEASE CONTROL AND PREVENTION David Satcher in 1998). In 1981 the surgeon general's office was reestablished as a separate entity.

But surgeons general in the modern era have been best known as the "nation's family doctor." In 1964, Surgeon General Luther Terry first informed the nation of the link between smoking and lung cancer. Surgeon General C. Everett Koop, an antiabortion activist and darling of the conservatives who was appointed by President Ronald Reagan in 1981, ultimately won the admiration of more liberal lawmakers who had opposed his appointment. Not only did Koop continue in the tradition of surgeons general by speaking out on tobacco issues—one of his reports detailed the scientific basis for

declaring nicotine addictive—he also angered some of his conservative backers with his blunt and open handling of sexual issues associated with the emerging AIDS epidemic. President Bill Clinton's first surgeon general, Joycelyn Elders (his former health secretary from Arkansas), ultimately proved so controversial—in effect calling for children to be taught masturbation—that Clinton fired her.

The surgeon general's post remained vacant from Elders's departure in 1994 until Satcher's confirmation in 1998, as Congress and President Clinton sparred over whether the post should be filled and whether that person's position on abortion should be a litmus test. Clinton's first nominee to fill the post following Elders's departure, Tennessee obstetrician/gynecologist Henry Foster, withdrew from consideration in 1995 after the Senate failed to break a filibuster over his nomination. Antiabortion forces objected to Foster because he had performed abortions early in his career. Abortion opponents also held up Satcher's nomination because he supported President Clinton's veto of legislation to ban so-called PARTIAL-BIRTH ABORTION. Satcher was sworn in as surgeon general on February 13, 1998.

T

Taft-Hartley plans

This is the name by which "multiemployer" health and welfare plans are known. These are health, pension, or welfare plans to which more than one employer is required to contribute and which are maintained pursuant to one or more collective bargaining agreements between one or more labor unions and more than one employer. Multiemployer plans must be cosponsored by a labor union and must comply with the structural requirements of the 1947 Taft-Hartley Act. Among those requirements are that the plan must be governed equally by labor and management trustees and that the plan must be established and maintained legally separate from either the union or the employers.

Taft-Hartley plans are most common in highly unionized industries in which workers typically change employers often—since they do not have to change health plans if their new employer participates. Among the industries with Taft-Hartley plans are building and construction, entertainment, and mining. "The intermittent and mobile employment patterns of most of these industries would prevent the workers from obtaining health benefit coverage absent a central pooled trust fund through which portable coverage is provided to workers as they move from employer to employer," testified James S. Ray on behalf of the National Coordinating Committee for Multiemployer Plans before a House subcommittee in May 1999. "Moreover, most employers in these industries are small and would not maintain their own employee health plans, particularly for transient workers," Ray said.

Technology assessment

Research that determines if and how well a particular therapy works, technology assessment is taking on a new emphasis in the age of cost-conscious medicine. According to the INSTITUTE OF MEDICINE of the National Academy of Sciences, technology assessment can evaluate medical techniques, drugs, equipment, or procedures, according to their safety, effectiveness, feasibility, cost, and cost-effectiveness. Technology assessment also looks at the social, economic, and ethical consequences, both intended and unintended, of the subject. Technology assessment is a critical element of EVIDENCE BASED MEDICINE, in which practitioners are encouraged to use the most effective therapies. But technology assessment can raise thorny issues. For example, although a new surgical technique might be more effective and cheaper than another technique, it may be so safe that it could be used in situations where surgery might not have been previously judged a good risk. Overall, that could end up costing society as a whole more, and it could risk the life or health of some patients who might otherwise have not undergone the procedure at all.

TennCare

One of two major statewide efforts to expand MEDICAID to cover all the poor, not just those "categorically eligible" for the program, TennCare was formally launched in Tennessee in 1994, during the national debate over health care reform. Unlike in Oregon, which sought to expand coverage by offering fewer benefits to more people, TennCare sought to expand coverage by moving its entire Medicaid population to managed care (see OREGON HEALTH PLAN). The state had hoped to use the savings from managed care to cover not only the Medicaid-eligible population but also the uninsured and the "uninsurable," those who were turned down for coverage by private insurers because of their health status.

In 1995, TennCare reached 90 percent of its target enrollment and closed down enrollment for the uninsured. Still eligible were those who would have been eligible for Medicaid under federal guidelines, as well as those who could show they could not obtain other insurance. In 1997, Tennessee opened the program to all children under age nineteen with no other access to insurance, regardless of family income. In 1998, using funds from the CHILDREN'S HEALTH INSURANCE PROGRAM (CHIP) included in the 1997 Balanced Budget Act (PL 105-33), Tennessee expanded TennCare again to cover all children in families with incomes under 200 percent of poverty, although on a modified open enrollment basis.

In 1998, TennCare contracted with twelve HEALTH MAINTENANCE ORGANIZATIONS (HMOS), spread over twelve regions of the state, each of which received a set fee from the state. The HMOs are responsible for providing all "medically necessary" services (including inpatient and outpatient hospital care, physician services, prescription drugs, laboratory and X-ray services, medical supplies, HOME HEALTH CARE, HOSPICE care, and ambulance transportation). TennCare organizations are not required to cover LONG-TERM-CARE services covered by Medicaid; that responsibility remained with the state, as under the previous Medicaid program.

Implementation of TennCare did not go smoothly. The HMOs were responsible for contracting with individual health care PROVIDERS, many of whom resisted the low payment rates offered them. That, in turn, made access difficult for many patients. Despite the low payments they paid to providers, however, many of the managed care plans lost money nonetheless. One problem was the state's closure of the program to the uninsured while leaving it open to the uninsurable, who are more expensive to serve. TennCare's failure to cover all of the state's uninsured population has also caused problems. In 1997, according to the Census Bureau, 13.6 percent of Tennessee's population under sixty-five remained uninsured; twenty-two states had lower rates that year. With so many remaining uninsured, hospitals, particularly public hospitals and those that serve a large proportion of low-income and uninsured patients, complained that they were losing money on TennCare, which promised lower payments, but for more patients. Instead, the hospitals say, they still have large numbers of uninsured patients, and lower payments for those who are covered.

Tertiary care

The most advanced form of health care, tertiary care is available primarily at large academic medical centers that do the most cutting-edge research. Tertiary care hospitals perform the most technical and advanced procedures, whereas community hospitals provide more routine services.

Title X Family Planning Program

Title X of the Public Health Service Act is the nation's principal family planning program. Although Title X (known as Title Ten) funds may not be used to pay for abortions—the program's enactment in 1970 predated the 1973 Supreme Court's landmark ruling legalizing the procedure nationwide—Title X remains mired in the ABORTION debate and is one of the federal government's most contentious programs. Although it has been kept running by stop-gap funding, the program has not been formally reauthorized since 1984, largely because of unresolved fights over whether clinics funded by Title X should be allowed to refer patients for abortions and whether minors should be able to receive services without the knowledge of their parents. (See PARENTAL NOTIFICATION; GAG RULE.)

In 1994, the last year for which statistics are available,

an estimated 4.2 million women received services from 4,200 clinics funded by Title X. Each year publicly funded family planning services prevent an estimated 1.3 million pregnancies and perform more than 600,000 abortions. Title X clients are predominantly young (30 percent are teenagers) and poor (more than half have incomes below the federal poverty line).

Although Title X has been kept alive without formal authorization for a decade-and-a-half through the annual appropriations process, its funding has suffered. In constant dollars, funding declined by more than 65 percent between 1980 and 1994. For fiscal 1999 the program received an appropriation of $215 million; had funding merely kept up with inflation it would have received more than twice that amount.

The first broad attacks on the program came in 1981, when the Reagan administration proposed to make it part of a major health program block grant, thus making services optional for states. In exchange for keeping the program intact, Democrats agreed to a 25 percent funding cut, as well as creation of the companion ADO-LESCENT FAMILY LIFE PROGRAM, to provide services to pregnant teenagers and to discourage sexual activity among teenagers. That program, unlike Title X, required PARENTAL CONSENT for most services and barred abortion counseling or referrals.

In 1983 the Reagan administration proposed a requirement that parents be notified when minors seek family planning services. The regulations, dubbed the "squeal rule" by critics, were ultimately struck down by federal courts as contrary to congressional intent for the law. In 1984 abortion opponents would unsuccessfully attempt to force votes on the regulations as part of the Title X reauthorization. The bill reauthorizing Title X and the Adolescent Family Life Program for one year would be the last time either program made it through the reauthorization process; both programs have been kept alive only by appropriators' ignoring rules barring funding for unauthorized activities.

In 1985, backers of Title X in the House of Representatives tried to prevent parental notification amendments by trying to pass a reauthorization bill on the "suspension" calendar, which bars amendments but requires a two-thirds vote. But opponents cried foul, and the 214–197 vote was not enough to pass the bill. In 1987 the issue was further complicated by publication of controversial rules that would bar Title X clinics from making abortion referrals and required grantees who performed abortions with nonfederal funds to physically separate the activities.

In 1989 it finally appeared that the program might get reauthorized when the Senate Labor and Human Resources Committee unanimously approved a three-year reauthorization, allowing funding for the state of Utah, which has a state law requiring parental involvement for contraceptive services, through another section of the Public Health Service Act, leaving Title X's confidentiality requirement intact. But the bill was pulled from the floor in 1990 after a parental notification amendment was added.

The House passed a five-year reauthorization in 1992, which also would have overturned the counseling ban, upheld by the Supreme Court a year earlier in the case *Rust v. Sullivan.* That measure, merged with a Senate bill passed in 1991 that would have overturned the ban but not reauthorized the program, was sent to President George Bush, who vetoed it on September 25. "I have repeatedly informed the Congress that I would disapprove any legislation that would transform this program into a vehicle for the promotion of abortion," said the president in his veto statement. "Unfortunately, the Congress has seen fit to entangle this family planning program in the politics of abortion." The Senate voted 73–26 to override Bush's veto, but the House fell ten votes short on October 2 with a vote of 266–148.

In 1993 the House again passed a Title X reauthorization, which again would have codified the abortion counseling guidelines in effect from 1981 to 1988. Surprisingly, the House turned back an effort to impose a restrictive parental notification requirement for family planning clinics affiliated with abortion providers. The Senate, however, never took up the House bill.

The new Republican-led Congress in 1995 tried to kill the Title X program outright. But even the firmly antiabortion House was not ready to pull the plug on family planning. An amendment to eliminate the program's $193 million in funding offered by House Appropriations Chairman Bob Livingston, R-La., was defeated by a vote of 207–221. That included fifty-three Republicans, most of them moderates.

In 1996, Livingston tried another tack—to reduce the income level of clients Title X clinics could serve. Under existing law, people with incomes up to 250 percent of poverty were eligible for reduced-price care; Livingston proposed to reduce that to 150 percent. But Livingston's own committee voted down his proposal, adopting instead a substitute offered by the Labor–Health and Human Services (HHS) subcommittee chairman John Porter, R-Ill., restating existing law. During floor debate, the House also rejected an amendment offered by Rep. Ernest Istook, R-Okla., to require parental consent before minors could receive contraceptives from clinics funded by Title X, or else wait five business days and notify the minor's custodial parent or legal guardian. Instead, the House adopted a substitute amendment that retained existing law requiring clinics to encourage family involvement.

In 1997, Istook's amendment met the same fate as in 1996. The House did, however, vote to cut $9 million and shift it to other programs. That cut was later restored. In 1998 the parental notification amendment would pass, although it would be dropped in conference.

TRICARE

Formerly CHAMPUS, TRICARE is the program for providing health care services to military dependents and retirees outside of facilities operated directly by the Department of Defense (DoD). Under federal law, active-duty personnel and their dependents are entitled to receive services from DoD-run medical facilities; retirees and their dependents may receive care there under certain circumstances. For all except active-duty personnel, however, care is provided by military medical facilities only on a space-available basis. That led Congress in 1966 to expand a 1956 law providing care for military dependents. The new Civilian Health and Medical Program of the Uniformed Services (CHAMPUS)

provided for care delivered by private or public providers under contract to the DoD. TRICARE, which has been gradually replacing CHAMPUS since the early 1990s, pays for care that is not available from the military, or for those who live too far from military medical care. Some 5.5 million Americans are eligible for TRICARE, which offers three options; TRICARE Prime, a HEALTH MAINTENANCE ORGANIZATION (HMO)–type plan; TRICARE Extra, a PREFERRED PROVIDER ORGANIZATION (PPO)–type plan; or TRICARE Standard, a traditional fee-for-service-type plan. As with most private insurance, out-of-pocket cost-sharing requirements are lowest in the HMO and highest in the FEE-FOR-SERVICE plan.

Tuskeegee experiments

The exposure of a notorious study of syphilis undertaken by the U.S. PUBLIC HEALTH SERVICE at the Tuskeegee Institute helped revolutionize rules regarding the use of human subjects in scientific research. The study had its origins in 1928, when a private foundation joined with U.S. public health workers in an effort to improve the health of African Americans in the South; earlier studies had shown a high prevalence of syphilis among black men. But funding for the project ran out before treatment programs could be fully implemented, and instead, the Public Health Service decided to study the effects of untreated syphilis.

Federal researchers enlisted the aid of the Tuskeegee Institute, founded by Booker T. Washington, which was highly regarded in the African-American community. Study participants were offered free physicals and other medical care, but those with syphilis were not told they had the disease. Later, researchers prevented the men with syphilis from being treated by draft boards during World War II, and the men were kept out of treatments using penicillin when it was first found to be effective in curing the disease. The men were kept in the dark about their condition until the study was made public in 1972 by the Associated Press.

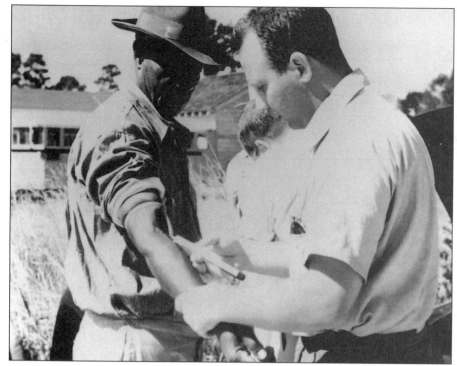

A government study originally intended to improve the health of African Americans in the South, the Tuskeegee experiments prevented men with syphilis from receiving penicillin that would have cured the disease. Here, a government doctor draws blood from a participant in the experiments. Source: Center for Disease Control

News of the study triggered 1973 hearings by the Senate Committee on Labor and Public Health, and led to a major rewrite of federal regulations on research protocols using human subjects. In December 1974 the federal government paid $10 million in an out-of-court settlement to the research subjects and their families.

But although the study ended some three decades ago, its effects have still not disappeared. A significant portion of the African-American community remains suspicious of government health officials, which has made public health efforts to control the spread of AIDS and HIV problematic.

U

Uncompensated care

Uncompensated care refers to medical care provided free, although not necessarily intentionally so. The term is often defined to include both charity care and "bad debt," care for which bills are rendered but not paid. In the past, health care providers often made up the cost of their uncompensated care by passing it along to other payers (see COST SHIFTING). But managed care, with its strict payment limits, has strained the ability of some hospitals to shift costs to other payers, leaving analysts to worry that care will be more difficult for the uninsured to obtain.

Underinsured

Different from having no insurance, being at risk for financial catastrophe despite coverage is known as being underinsured. Policy analysts define *underinsurance* as being at risk of having to spend more than 10 percent of income on a major medical event. Between 1977 and 1987, the number of underinsured Americans under age sixty-five grew by half, to an estimated 29 million individuals, according to a study published in 1995 in the *Journal of the American Medical Association.* A 1998 study by Consumers Union found that an estimated 11 million families, one of every eight, spent more than 10 percent of their income on health care (premiums not paid by employers plus required out-of-pocket costs) in 1996. Eighty percent of those families had insurance for all family members.

Underwriting

Underwriting is the process by which an insurer investigates an individual's medical history and health status to determine whether or not it will issue insurance and at what cost. The underwriting process may result in insurers' placing temporary or permanent limitations on a PREEXISTING CONDITION.

Uninsured

Estimates vary, but analysts agreed that in 1997 more than 40 million Americans lacked health insurance—up 10 million from a decade earlier. That represented about 17 percent of the nation's nonelderly population (virtually everyone over sixty-five has access to coverage through MEDICARE). Finding a way to provide coverage to the uninsured was a major goal of the failed 1993–1994 effort to reshape the nation's health care system (as was slowing the spiraling costs of health care), but the subject has been discussed infrequently since then, as other issues have topped the nation's health care agenda.

Contrary to popular perception, most of the uninsured are not poor, nor are they unemployed. That's because many of the very poorest Americans, along with those who cannot work because of disability, are covered by MEDICAID (or, in the case of some disabled, Medicare). Rather, in 1995, 46 percent of the uninsured had incomes higher than twice the poverty level, 32 percent had incomes higher than poverty but below 200 percent of that threshold, and 22 percent were poor (largely able-bodied, single adults who do not fit one of Medicaid's eligibility "categories"). Slightly more men

Nonelderly Americans with Selected Sources of Health Insurance Coverage, 1987–1997

	1987	1988	1989	1990	1991	1992	1993	1994	1995	1996	1997[a]
						(millions)					
Total population	214.4	216.6	218.5	220.6	222.9	225.5	228.0	229.9	231.9	234.0	236.2
Total private	162.8	162.9	164.3	162.1	161.3	160.5	161.5	162.8	163.9	165.8	167.5
Employment-based coverage	148.5	149.4	149.8	147.7	147.7	145.9	144.9	146.3	147.9	149.8	151.7
own name	72.5	73.5	74.0	73.1	73.1	71.7	74.9	75.2	75.9	76.9	77.4
dependent coverage	75.9	75.9	75.8	74.7	74.6	74.3	69.9	71.1	72.1	72.9	74.3
Other private coverage	14.3	13.5	14.5	14.3	13.6	14.6	16.6	16.4	16.0	16.0	15.8
Total public	28.5	28.8	28.7	31.9	34.4	36.0	38.1	38.9	38.4	37.4	34.9
Medicare	3.1	3.2	3.2	3.4	3.5	3.9	3.7	3.7	4.1	4.6	4.7
Medicaid	18.4	18.9	19.2	22.4	24.8	26.5	29.0	28.7	29.0	28.2	26.0
CHAMPUS/CHAMPVA[b]	8.5	8.2	7.9	7.9	7.9	7.5	7.4	8.7	7.4	6.8	6.6
No health insurance	31.8	33.6	34.3	35.6	36.3	38.3	39.3	39.4	40.3	41.4	43.1
						(percentage)					
Total population	100.0%	100.0%	100.0%	100.0%	100.0%	100.0%	100.0%	100.0%	100.0%	100.0%	100.0%
Total private	75.9	75.2	75.2	73.5	72.4	71.2	70.8	70.8	70.7	70.9	70.9
Employment-based coverage	69.2	69.0	68.6	67.0	66.3	64.7	63.5	63.6	63.8	64.0	64.2
own name	33.8	33.9	33.9	33.1	32.8	31.8	32.9	32.7	32.7	32.9	32.8
dependent coverage	35.4	35.0	34.7	33.8	33.5	32.9	30.7	30.9	31.1	31.2	31.5
Other private coverage	6.7	6.3	6.6	6.5	6.1	6.5	7.3	7.1	6.9	6.8	6.7
Total public	13.3	13.3	13.2	14.5	15.5	16.0	16.7	16.9	16.6	16.0	14.8
Medicare	1.4	1.5	1.5	1.6	1.6	1.7	1.6	1.6	1.8	2.0	2.0
Medicaid	8.6	8.7	8.8	10.2	11.1	11.8	12.7	12.5	12.5	12.1	11.0
CHAMPUS/CHAMPVA[b]	4.0	3.8	3.6	3.6	3.5	3.3	3.3	3.8	3.2	2.9	2.8
No health insurance	14.8	15.5	15.7	16.1	16.3	17.0	17.3	17.1	17.4	17.7	18.3

Source: Employee Benefit Research Institute (www.ebri.org) estimates of the March 1988–1998 Current Population Survey.

Notes: Details may not add to totals because individuals may receive coverage from more than one source.

a. Medicaid and uninsured data are not completely consistent with data from previous years. Starting with the March 1998 Current Population Survey (CPS), the Bureau of the Census modified its definition of the population with Medicaid and the population without health insurance coverage. Previously, individuals covered solely by the Indian Health Service were counted in the Medicaid population. Beginning with data from the March 1998 CPS, individuals covered solely by the Indian Health Service are counted as uninsured. This change decreased the Medicaid population and increased the uninsured population by 300,000, or 0.2 percent.

b. CHAMPUS: Civilian Health and Medical Program of the Uniformed Services; CHAMPVA: Civilian Health and Medical Program of the Department of Veterans Affairs.

than women were uninsured (55 percent, compared with 45 percent), and a plurality (43 percent) were between eighteen and thirty-four years old. A total of 38 percent were age thirty-five to sixty-four, and 19 percent were under age eighteen.

Eighty percent of those without insurance are workers, or live in a family with someone who works full-time all year. Only 10 percent of the uninsured live in a family with no one who works. But many of those workers are in jobs in the service sector that pay low wages—72 percent of uninsured workers earned less than $20,000 in 1995. And nearly half (48 percent) worked for firms with fewer than twenty-five workers. Smaller firms are less likely to offer insurance, or, if they do, more often require workers to pay the full premiums. Nearly two-thirds of the uninsured said they did not have coverage because they could not afford it; only 8 percent said it was because they thought they did not need or want insurance.

Most of the uninsured stay that way for a lengthy period. In 1997, only 15 percent of those who reported having been uninsured at any time in the previous two years were without coverage for three months or less. At the same time, 44 percent were uninsured for two years or more, and 20 percent, from twelve to twenty-three months.

Although every American theoretically has access to needed health care through public facilities, having insurance does make a difference in health status. In 1997, uninsured adults were four times as likely as those with coverage to report not getting needed medical care—30 percent, compared with 7 percent with private coverage. Fifty-five percent of the uninsured in one survey said they delayed getting care because they could not afford it, compared with 6 percent with private coverage. One in five uninsured children had no family doctor or other "usual source of care" in 1996, compared with only 6 percent of those with private coverage; 33 percent of uninsured children did not see a doctor for a year or more in 1993–1994, twice the percentage of those with coverage. And both adults and children were less likely to receive preventive care; uninsured women with breast cancer were more likely to have the disease diagnosed in the later stages, when it is less treatable.

Medicaid expansions between 1984 and 1990 helped mask the rise of the uninsured; during that time Congress extended eligibility to a half-million pregnant women, 4 million to 5 million children, and more than 4 million elderly and disabled individuals. Between 1988 and 1993, however, private coverage declined, and in 1996 about 64 percent of nonelderly Americans had employer-provided coverage, down from 69.2 percent in 1987. The trend has not so much been for employers to drop coverage altogether as it has for them to raise costs for workers who participate, putting coverage out of reach for low-income workers. From 1988 to 1996, although premiums increased on average by roughly 7.5 percent per year, employee contributions rose by 18.3 percent for individuals. For families, premiums rose by 9.8 percent per year; employee contributions rose by 11.9 percent.

Lawmakers have not completely ignored the plight of the uninsured. In 1996, Congress addressed the issue

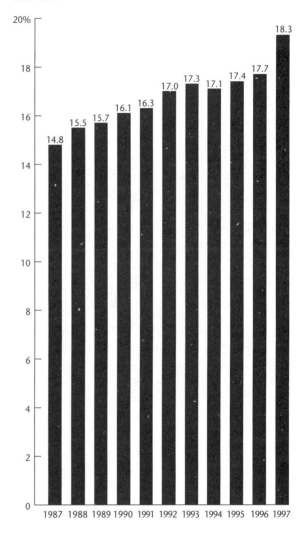

Percentage of Nonelderly Americans Without Health Insurance, 1987–1997

Source: Employee Benefit Research Institute (www.ebri.org) estimates of the March 1988–1998 Curent Population Survey.

in a very modest way in the HEALTH INSURANCE PORTABILITY AND ACCOUNTABILITY ACT (HIPAA), PL 104-191, which was aimed primarily at helping those who already had insurance keep it. The measure's "portability" provisions made it more difficult for insurers to cancel or deny coverage to those with "preexisting" health conditions, and required insurers to sell individual policies to those previously covered as part of a group who had not had a break in coverage.

As part of the 1997 Balanced Budget Act (PL 105-33), Congress addressed the issue of the uninsured more directly, approving a new CHILDREN'S HEALTH INSURANCE PROGRAM (CHIP) that was estimated to cover up to half of the 10 million Americans under age eighteen who lacked coverage.

President Bill Clinton continued to try to expand coverage incrementally, proposing first a plan to help the temporarily unemployed pay for extended coverage under COBRA CONTINUATION and later a scheme to allow those under age sixty-five to "buy in" to Medicare coverage. Neither proposal, however, was given much attention in Congress in 1997 or 1998.

Unions, doctor

By the mid-1990s, with antipathy growing towards managed care, an increasing number of doctors sought to strengthen their bargaining power by joining unions. By 1999, an estimated thirty-eight thousand physicians belonged to a union. And over the objections of its board, the AMERICAN MEDICAL ASSOCIATION'S House of Delegates shocked the nation in June 1999 by voting to form a bargaining unit for doctors.

But most doctors were unable to join unions even if they wanted to. That is because federal antitrust laws blocked any joint action by doctors who were not salaried employees. As of 1999, that restriction left only an estimated 15 percent of the nation's six hundred thousand practicing physicians eligible to participate in the bargaining unit the AMA voted to form.

Some doctors in private practice did try to argue that managed care plans that dictated not only the terms of contracts, but also the way doctors practiced medicine, in effect made those doctors "de facto" employees, entitled to collective bargaining rights under federal law. But in May 1999, the National Labor Relations Board ruled that even if plans do control some elements of doctors' practices, that control is not enough to establish an employer-employee relationship.

The American Medical Association (AMA) announced in June 1999 that it would form a doctors' union. Opposed by antitrust law barring joint action by unsalaried physicians, the AMA, led by Dr. Thomas R. Reardon, sought an exemption to the law from Capitol Hill, via the "Quality Health Care Coalition Act of 1999." Source: Scott J. Ferrell, Congressional Quarterly

The AMA turned to Capitol Hill to support antitrust relief in the form of legislation introduced in the 106th Congress by Rep. Tom Campbell, R-Calif. The "Quality Health Care Coalition Act of 1999" would "correct the dangerous imbalance in the health care marketplace by returning professional medical decision making to physicians," testified AMA Executive Vice President E. Ratcliffe Anderson Jr., M.D., before the House Judiciary Committee in June 1999. "In many markets physicians have virtually no bargaining power with dominant health plans that refuse to negotiate any terms of their contracts—including terms with important patient care implications. As a result, plans present physicians with nonnegotiable contract terms that no businessperson with any bargaining power would agree to. Consequently, the power of health plans alone to determine the kind of health care that patients receive is virtually unchecked."

The bill would create a limited antitrust exemption for physicians, dentists, pharmacists, and other health care professionals who are not otherwise employees. It would allow them to negotiate collectively over fees and to refuse to deal with a plan that did not meet their demands.

The Clinton administration opposed the bill. "This bill would allow nonemployee, health care professionals collectively to raise their fees to health insurers without fear of antitrust liability and without regard to competitive market forces fostered by the antitrust laws," Assistant Attorney General for Antitrust Joel Klein told the same Judiciary Committee hearing. Klein added that the cost would likely be passed on to consumers. "There is no justification to accord special status to health care professionals under the antitrust laws, differentiating them from other professionals and independent contractors such as architects, engineers, or lawyers."

United Nations Population Fund

U.S. funding for the United Nations Population Fund, formally the United Nations Fund for Population Activities (UNFPA), a UN agency it helped found in 1969, has been a bone of contention almost ever since. ABORTION opponents have since the mid-1980s sought to end U.S. contributions because of the UNFPA's continuing support of activities in China, whose government has practiced coercive sterilization and abortion policies in support of its "one child per family" population control efforts.

According to the organization, the UNFPA provides assistance to developing countries "to improve reproductive health and family planning services on the basis of individual choice, and to formulate population policies in support of efforts towards sustainable development." Among UNFPA's mandates, as imposed by the UN Economic and Social Council, is "to assist developing countries, at their request, in dealing with their population problems in the forms and means best suited to the individual countries' needs." In 1996 the agency provided support to 169 countries; UNFPA directly managed a quarter of the world's population assistance.

Overcoming population problems in developing countries, including India, is the primary responsibility of the UN Population Fund. According to the World Bank, India will not reach its goal of zero population growth until the end of the twenty-first century, when its population is expected to be 1.88 billion, double the current figure.
Source: Sunil Malhotra, Reuters

The organization does not provide any support for abortion or abortion-related activities. Rather, it says "UNFPA seeks to prevent abortion by increasing access to family planning services, and to reduce maternal deaths through better management of complications of unsafe abortions."

In 1986, Congress "defunded" UNFPA, by barring aid to any group that "participates in the management of a program of coercive abortion or involuntary sterilization." That ban lasted until 1993, when, under President Bill Clinton, Congress appropriated $50 million for the agency, which insisted its activities in China were intended to eliminate involuntary population control policies and that it only operated in areas where quotas had been removed. But when Republicans took over Congress in 1995, the issue of UNFPA funding was back on the table. In 1998, funding, which was only $20 million the previous year, was again cut entirely.

United Network for Organ Sharing

The United Network for Organ Sharing (UNOS) is a private, nonprofit organization that operates the nation's organ distribution system, under contract to the HEALTH AND HUMAN SERVICES DEPARTMENT (HHS). In 1998, UNOS and HHS got into a heated dispute over proposed new HHS rules that would have required that organs be distributed nationally, rather than regionally. Under the previous system, organs for transplant were first offered locally, since transportation time cut down on their viability. But advances in medicine made it more feasible to fly organs even across the country without increasing the chances of an unsuccessful transplant. Thus, HHS proposed that organs be distributed to the patient with the most serious need and with the best chance of benefiting from the organ, regardless of where that patient was located. UNOS charged that such a plan could put smaller transplant centers out of business, because most of the organs would end up going to the largest transplant centers with the most patients. In the end, Congress delayed the rules by a year, until 1999, in an effort to let UNOS and HHS work out their disagreements.

Universal coverage

Universal coverage is a term referring to a health system that guarantees insurance to all citizens. Universal coverage can be provided by a state government, but it is generally a national responsibility. There are various ways to guarantee universal coverage. One, obviously, is a government-run system, such as those in Canada or Great Britain, where the government pays directly for health care services provided to its citizens, either by private doctors and hospitals (as in Canada) or by those on government salary (as in Britain). But combination systems can also provide coverage for all. During the 1993–1994 health reform debate, President Bill Clinton wanted to guarantee universal coverage by requiring employers to provide insurance to their workers, with the government providing subsidies for everyone else. A large subset of Democrats wanted a SINGLE PAYER system similar to Canada's, in which the government would pay private health care providers (the way MEDICARE works). Some Republicans wanted to guarantee universal coverage through a third mechanism, an "individual mandate," that would require every person to purchase insurance coverage (just as drivers are required to carry car insurance), with subsidies for those with low incomes. Universal coverage is not the same as "universal access," which simply requires that insurance companies sell coverage to all comers, regardless of their health status. As of 1998, the United States did not have universal access, either, although the 1996 HEALTH INSURANCE PORTABILITY AND ACCOUNTABILITY ACT (PL 104-191) did eliminate some restrictions on individuals' ability to get and keep coverage.

U.S. Department of Health and Human Services (HHS)

See HEALTH AND HUMAN SERVICES DEPARTMENT.

U.S. Public Health Service

See PUBLIC HEALTH SERVICE.

Utilization review

Utilization review (UR) refers to an insurance company practice that decides if care recommended or provided to a patient is appropriate and of high quality. "Retrospective" utilization review, reviews patient records after the fact to determine whether the care provided was the best and most cost-effective. "Prospective" utilization review occurs after care is prescribed, but before it is delivered. Critics of UR note that it may be undertaken by health professionals who are not doctors (typically, first-line reviewers are nurses), and that health plans may deny coverage for purely economic reasons—that is, because it is too expensive. Defenders of the practice, however, note that it can help standardize and raise the quality of care for all patients.

V

Veterans health care

Among the groups that are guaranteed health care by federal law are the nation's veterans. But whereas MEDICARE and MEDICAID pay for care provided by private health care entities or those run by state or local governments, the federal government itself runs the Veterans' Administration (VA) health care program, which in fiscal 1999 provided care to an estimated 3.6 million veterans and their dependents at 172 medical centers (at least one in each of the lower forty-eight states), 551 outpatient, community, and outreach clinics, 131 nursing home units, 40 transitional "domiciliaries," where patients are provided nonskilled nursing care, and 73 home care programs. In fiscal 1999 the Veterans Administration received an appropriation of $17.3 billion.

Not every veteran is eligible for health care services provided by the VA. Originally, only those with service-related ailments or who could not otherwise afford care were guaranteed care in VA facilities. In 1996, Congress overhauled eligibility rules in legislation (PL 104-262) designed to de-emphasize inpatient care and move more patients into less expensive outpatient clinics. Previously, the system guaranteed outpatient care only to severely disabled veterans with injuries connected to their military services and a few other categories of veterans. Other groups eligible for VA care, such as less disabled or low-income veterans, often had to have been in a VA hospital already or meet other complex legal requirements to receive outpatient treatment.

The 1996 legislation eliminated statutory restrictions governing which categories of veterans were eligible for the full range of VA health care, which included treatment in outpatient clinics, home care, and other servic-

Until 1996, only veterans unable to afford health care or those with service-related ailments, such as Panama veteran Patrick McElrath (right, pictured in 1991 with Colin Powell, chairman of the Joint Chiefs of Staff), were eligible for government-funded health care. Legislation passed in 1996 loosened eligibility requirements. Source: Win McNamee, Reuters

es as well as hospitalization. It gave the VA authority to treat all veterans as it saw fit as long as it stayed within its budget (which the bill also capped). The bill required the VA to set up a priority system to decide which categories of veterans would receive care and in what order.

VA clinicians also conduct medical research. In addition to pioneering treatments for such battle-related conditions as post-traumatic stress disorder, exposure to Agent Orange (a defoliant later found to cause health problems), and artificial limbs, VA researchers helped develop such medical advances as cardiac pacemakers and CT scanners. The first kidney transplant in the United States was performed in a VA medical facility.

Voluntary health agencies

Voluntary health agencies (VHAs) are private, non-profit groups that work "to improve health by providing patient and family services, community services, public and professional education, medical research support and health related advocacy," according to the National Health Council, the umbrella organization for 132 health-related groups, 41 of them VHAs. Major VHAs include the American Red Cross, American Cancer Society, the March of Dimes Birth Defects Foundation, and the National Easter Seal Society.

W

Webster v. Reproductive Health Services

Webster v. Reproductive Health Services was a pivotal abortion case decided by the U.S. Supreme Court on July 3, 1989. The Court upheld a series of restrictions on the procedure, including banning the use of public employees or facilities for abortion and requiring physicians to perform tests to determine viability on fetuses of more than twenty weeks gestation. In upholding the restrictions on a 5–4 vote, the court signaled—but did not expressly say—that it no longer considered abortion a fundamental right. Thus, both sides agreed, it essentially invited states to pass their own laws limiting abortion.

The *Webster* decision, handed down on the final day of the term, produced seven separate opinions, with no single opinion joined by more than three justices. But the plurality opinion, written by Chief Justice William Rehnquist, pointedly declined to overturn ROE V. WADE, although it noted that "we would modify and narrow *Roe* and succeeding cases."

In some ways the *Webster* decision had the opposite effect than the justices intended. Rather than spurring states to pass new abortion restrictions, the threat to *Roe* and the real possibility that the right to abortion could be eliminated with the vote of one more justice mobilized abortion-rights forces. In the subsequent months, both the House of Representatives and the Senate voted to roll back various restrictions imposed over the previous decade, including the ban on federal funding of abortion in cases of rape or incest, and barring the District of Columbia from using its own tax dollars to pay for abortions. Four vetoes from President George Bush, however, prevented any of the restrictions from actually being eliminated. The Court clarified the *Webster* deci-

Four years after the Supreme Court's decision in Webster v. Reproductive Health Services *(1989), which upheld several abortion restrictions, antiabortion activists rallied to protect the restrictions threatened by the Freedom of Choice Act (above). Spurred by* Webster *to redouble their efforts, abortion rights activists pressed Congress for legislative relief and held dramatic public demonstrations (next page).*

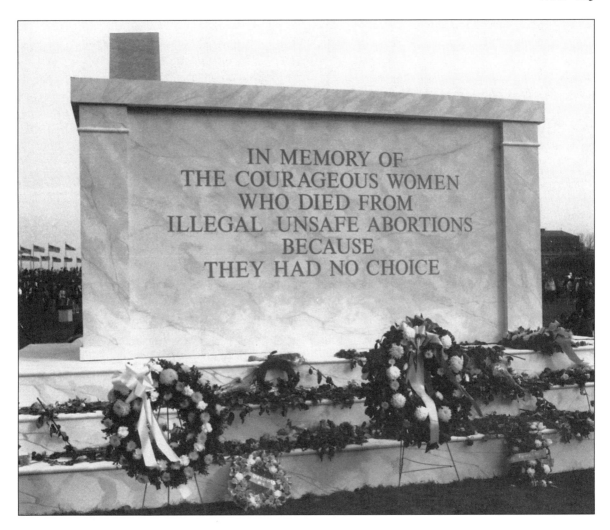

sion three years later, in *PLANNED PARENTHOOD OF SOUTHEASTERN PENNSYLVANIA V. CASEY.*

WIC

Technically the Special Supplemental Nutrition Program for Women, Infants, and Children, WIC provides food, nutritional counseling, and access to health services for an estimated 7.4 million Americans monthly, about 60 percent of those who are eligible. Permanently authorized in 1974, WIC is available to pregnant or postpartum women, infants, and children up to age five in families with incomes up to 185 percent of the federal poverty level and who are determined by a health professional to be at "nutritional risk." Risk factors can include medical conditions (such as anemia, underweight, or a history of complications with pregnancy) or failure to consume an adequate diet. WIC, which is administered by the U.S. Agriculture Department's Food and Nutrition Service, received a $3.9 billion appropriation in fiscal 1998. Of the total WIC population in that year, 3.8 million were children, 1.9 million were infants, and 1.7 million were pregnant or postpartum women.

WIC participants receive food "vouchers" they can

use to purchase foods high in protein, calcium, iron, and vitamins A and C, such as milk, cheese, iron-fortified cereals, fruit or vegetable juice, and peanut butter. Although WIC mothers are encouraged to breast-feed their babies, those who do not can receive formula from WIC programs that states obtain through special discount agreements with manufacturers. The WIC Farmer's Market Nutrition Program, established in 1992, gives WIC participants additional vouchers they can use to purchase fresh produce at participating farmers' markets. Twelve million dollars of WIC's total appropriation is set aside for the farmers' market program.

Women's Health, Office of Research on

Established in statute in the 1993 National Institutes of Health (NIH) Revitalization Act (PL 103-43), the office, located within the office of the director of the NIH, is charged with ensuring that issues relating to women's health are adequately identified and addressed in research activities. The office is also charged with recruiting women to participate in clinical trials. The 1993 bill required that women and members of minority groups be included as subjects in research projects in most cases. Women and minorities could be excluded only if there were scientific reasons to assume that the variables being studied did not affect women or minorities differently from men.

The 1993 requirements grew out of a 1990 study by the General Accounting Office that found that the NIH had not been enforcing its own 1986 policy requiring inclusion of women in research trials. In many cases, researchers worried that women could become pregnant and endanger themselves and their babies, or, more commonly, they worried that women's different chemical make-up would confound the study results. As a result of the near-systematic exclusion, however, many landmark studies told nothing about the effect of certain treatments on women.

Z

Zidovudine

The formal name of the drug AZT, zidovudine was the first effective medication to fight the virus that causes AIDS. Zidovudine, which was originally developed by federal researchers, has been shown to delay the onset of AIDS when taken before patients become symptomatic. The drug has been particularly effective when taken by pregnant women, having been shown to prevent mother-to-infant transmission of the AIDS virus.

Reference Material

Health Care Policy Acronyms

AAPCC adjusted average per capita cost.

ACGME Accreditation Council on Graduate Medical Education.

ACOG American College of Obstetricians and Gynecologists.

ACR adjusted community rate.

ADA Americans with Disabilities Act.

ADAMHA Alcohol, Drug Abuse and Mental Health Administration, U.S. (since reorganized).

ADL activity of daily living.

AFDC Aid to Families with Dependent Children, a welfare program replaced in 1996 by the Temporary Aid for Needy Families program.

AFLA Adolescent Family Life Act.

AHC academic health center (*same as* academic medical center).

AHCPR Agency for Health Care Policy and Research.

AIDS Acquired Immune Deficiency Syndrome; *also* Acquired Immunodeficiency Syndrome.

AMA American Medical Association.

AMC academic medical center (*same as* academic health center).

ATSDR Agency for Toxic Substances and Disease Registry, U.S.

CalPERS California Public Employee Retirement System.

CBO Congressional Budget Office.

CDC Centers for Disease Control and Prevention, U.S.

CHAMPUS Civilian Health and Medical Program of the Uniformed Services.

CHDR Center for Health Dispute Resolution (Medicare).

CHIP Children's Health Insurance Program.

CLIA Clinical Laboratory Improvement Act.

COBRA Consolidated Omnibus Budget Reconciliation Act (PL 99-272), the fiscal 1986 budget reconciliation bill.

COGME Council on Graduate Medical Education.

CPT Current Procedural Terminology, a coding mechanism for health care services.

CRNA certified registered nurse anesthetist.

DEA Drug Enforcement Administration.

DEFRA Deficit Reduction Act (PL 98-369), the fiscal 1984 budget reconciliation bill.

DME durable medical equipment; *also* direct medical education (payments, Medicare).

DNR "do not resuscitate," an order for terminal patients in hospitals or nursing homes.

DSH disproportionate share payments.

EMTALA Emergency Medical Treatment and Active Labor Act.

EPSDT Early and Periodic Screening, Diagnostic and Treatment program (Medicaid).

ERISA Employee Retirement Income Security Act.

ESRD End-Stage Renal Disease program (Medicare).

FACE Act Freedom of Access to Clinic Entrances Act.

FDA Food and Drug Administration, U.S.

FEHBP Federal Employee Health Benefits Program.

FMAP Federal Medical Assistance Percentage (Medicaid).

FMG foreign medical graduate (*same as* international medical graduate).

FQHC federally qualified health center.

GME graduate medical education.

HCFA Health Care Financing Administration, U.S.

HEDIS Health Plan Employer Data and Information Set.

HEW Health, Education and Welfare Department, U.S.; former name of Department of Health and Human Services.

HI Hospital Insurance program (Medicare).

HIPAA Health Insurance Portability and Accountability Act of 1996.

HMO health maintenance organization (managed care).

HIV Human Immunodeficiency Virus.

HPSA health professional shortage area.

HRSA Health Resources and Services Administration, U.S.

IADL instrumental activity of daily living.

ICF-MR intermediate care facility for the mentally retarded (Medicaid).

IME indirect medical education (payments, Medicare).

IMG international medical graduate (*same as* foreign medical graduate).

IoM Institute of Medicine of the National Academy of Sciences.

JCAHO Joint Commission on the Accreditation of Healthcare Organizations.

MedPAC Medicare Payment Advisory Commission.

MSA medical savings account.

MVPS Medicare Volume Performance Standard.

NAIC National Association of Insurance Commissioners.

NARAL National Abortion and Reproductive Rights Action League.

NCCAM National Center for Complementary and Alternative Medicine.

NCQA National Committee for Quality Assurance.

NFIB National Federation of Independent Business.

NIH National Institutes of Health, U.S.

NLEA Nutrition Labeling and Education Act (PL 101-535).

NRLC National Right to Life Committee.

OBRA Omnibus Budget Reconciliation Act; formal name of five separate budget reconciliation bills: fiscal 1987 (PL 99-509), fiscal 1988–1989 (PL 100-203), fiscal 1990 (PL 101-239), fiscal 1991 (PL 101-508), and fiscal 1994 (PL 103-66).

PA physician assistant.

PACE Program of All-inclusive Care for the Elderly.

PDUFA Prescription Drug User Fee Act (PL 102-571).

PHS Public Health Service; *also known as* USPHS.

PPO preferred provider organization (managed care).

POS point of service plan (managed care).

PPRC Physician Payment Review Commission; with Prospective Payment Assessment Commission (ProPAC), folded into Medicare Payment Advisory Commission (MedPAC) in 1997.

ProPAC Prospective Payment Assessment Commission; with Physician Payment Review Commission (PPRC), folded into Medicare Payment Advisory Commission (MedPAC) in 1997.

PSO provider-sponsored organization.

PSRO professional standards review organization (Medicare).

QMB qualified Medicare beneficiary.

RBRVS resource-based relative value scale (Medicare).

RN registered nurse.

RRC residency review committee.

SAMHSA Substance Abuse and Mental Health Services Administration, U.S.

SLMB Specified Low-Income Medicare Beneficiary.

SMI Supplementary Medical Insurance (Medicare).

SSDI Social Security Disability Income program.

SSI Supplemental Security Income program.

S-CHIP State Children's Health Insurance Program.

TANF Temporary Aid for Needy Families program, the welfare program replacement for Aid to Families with Dependent Children.

TEFRA Tax Equity and Fiscal Responsibility Act (PL 97-248), the fiscal 1983 budget reconciliation bill.

UNFPA Technically, United Nations Fund for Population Activities; known mostly as the UN Population Fund.

UNOS United Network for Organ Sharing.

Congressional Committees Responsible for Health Care Policy

House Committees

Appropriations Committee

Address: H-218 Capitol Bldg., Washington, D.C. 20510
Phone: (202) 225-2771

REPUBLICANS (34)
C.W. Bill Young, Fla., chairman
Ralph Regula, Ohio
Jerry Lewis, Calif.
John Edward Porter, Ill.
Harold Rogers, Ky.
Joe Skeen, N.M.
Frank R. Wolf, Va.
Tom DeLay, Texas
Jim Kolbe, Ariz.
Ron Packard, Calif.
Sonny Callahan, Ala.
James T. Walsh, N.Y.
Charles H. Taylor, N.C.
David L. Hobson, Ohio
Ernest Istook, Okla.
Henry Bonilla, Texas
Joe Knollenberg, Mich.
Dan Miller, Fla.
Jay Dickey, Ark.
Jack Kingston, Ga.
Rodney Frelinghuysen, N.J.
Roger Wicker, Miss.
George Nethercutt, Wash.
Randy Cunningham, Calif.
Todd Tiahrt, Kan.
Zach Wamp, Tenn.
Tom Latham, Iowa
Anne M. Northup, Ky.
Robert B. Aderholt, Ala.
Jo Ann Emerson, Mo.
John E. Sununu, N.H.
Kay Granger, Texas
John E. Peterson, Pa.
Roy Blunt, Mo.

DEMOCRATS (27)
David R. Obey, Wis., ranking member
John P. Murtha, Pa.
Norm Dicks, Wash.
Martin Olav Sabo, Minn.
Julian C. Dixon, Calif.
Steny H. Hoyer, Md.
Alan B. Mollohan, W.Va.
Marcy Kaptur, Ohio
Nancy Pelosi, Calif.
Peter J. Visclosky, Ind.
Nita M. Lowey, N.Y.
Jose E. Serrano, N.Y.
Rosa DeLauro, Conn.
James P. Moran, Va.
John W. Olver, Mass.
Ed Pastor, Ariz.
Carrie P. Meek, Fla.
David E. Price, N.C.
Chet Edwards, Texas
Robert E. Cramer, Ala.
Maurice D. Hinchey, N.Y.
Lucille Roybal-Allard, Calif.
Sam Farr, Calif.
Jesse L. Jackson Jr., Ill.
Carolyn Cheeks Kilpatrick, Mich.
Allen Boyd, Fla.
Michael P. Forbes, N.Y.

Subcommittee on Labor, Health and Human Services and Education

REPUBLICANS (9)
John Edward Porter, Ill., chairman
C.W. Bill Young, Fla.
Henry Bonilla, Texas
Ernest Istook, Okla.
Dan Miller, Fla.
Jay Dickey, Ark.
Roger Wicker, Miss.
Anne M. Northup, Ky.
Randy Cunningham, Calif.

DEMOCRATS (6)
David R. Obey, Wis., ranking member
Steny H. Hoyer, Md.
Nancy Pelosi, Calif.
Nita M. Lowey, N.Y.
Rosa DeLauro, Conn.
Jesse L. Jackson Jr., Ill.

Commerce Committee

Address: 2125 Rayburn Bldg., Washington, D.C. 20515
Phone: (202) 225-2927

REPUBLICANS (29)
Tom Bliley, Va., chairman
W.J. Tauzin, La.
Michael G. Oxley, Ohio
Michael Bilirakis, Fla.
Joe L. Barton, Texas
Fred Upton, Mich.
Cliff Stearns, Fla.
Paul E. Gillmor, Ohio
James C. Greenwood, Pa.
Christopher Cox, Calif.
Nathan Deal, Ga.
Steve Largent, Okla.
Richard M. Burr, N.C.
Brian P. Bilbray, Calif.
Edward Whitfield, Ky.
Greg Ganske, Iowa
Charlie Norwood, Ga.
Tom Coburn, Okla.
Rick A. Lazio, N.Y.
Barbara Cubin, Wyo.
James E. Rogan, Calif.
John M. Shimkus, Ill.
Heather A. Wilson, N.M.
John Shadegg, Ariz.
Charles W. Pickering Jr., Miss.
Vito J. Fossella, N.Y.
Roy Blunt, Mo.
Ed Bryant, Tenn.
Robert L. Ehrlich Jr., Md.

DEMOCRATS (24)
John D. Dingell, Mich., ranking member
Henry A. Waxman, Calif.
Edward J. Markey, Mass.
Ralph M. Hall, Texas
Rick Boucher, Va.
Edolphus Towns, N.Y.
Frank Pallone Jr., N.J.
Sherrod Brown, Ohio
Bart Gordon, Tenn.
Peter Deutsch, Fla.
Bobby L. Rush, Ill.
Anna G. Eshoo, Calif.
Ron Klink, Pa.
Bart Stupak, Mich.
Eliot L. Engel, N.Y.
Tom Sawyer, Ohio
Albert R. Wynn, Md.
Gene Green, Texas
Karen McCarthy, Mo.
Ted Strickland, Ohio
Diana DeGette, Colo.
Thomas M. Barrett, Wis.
Bill Luther, Minn.
Lois Capps, Calif.

Subcommittee on Health and Environment

REPUBLICANS (16)
Michael Bilirakis, Fla., chairman
Fred Upton, Mich.
Cliff Stearns, Fla.
James C. Greenwood, Pa.
Nathan Deal, Ga.
Richard M. Burr, N.C.
Brian P. Bilbray, Calif.
Edward Whitfield, Ky.
Greg Ganske, Iowa
Charlie Norwood, Ga.
Tom Coburn, Okla.
Rick A. Lazio, N.Y.
Barbara Cubin, Wyo.
John Shadegg, Ariz.
Charles W. Pickering Jr., Miss.
Ed Bryant, Tenn.

DEMOCRATS (13)
Sherrod Brown, Ohio, ranking member
Henry A. Waxman, Calif.
Frank Pallone Jr., N.J.
Peter Deutsch, Fla.
Bart Stupak, Mich.
Ted Strickland, Ohio
Diana DeGette, Colo.
Thomas M. Barrett, Wis.
Gene Green, Texas
Lois Capps, Calif.
Ralph M. Hall, Texas
Edolphus Towns, N.Y.
Anna G. Eshoo, Calif.

Education and Workforce Committee

Address: 2181 Rayburn Bldg., Washington, D.C. 20515
Phone: (202) 225-4527

REPUBLICANS (27)
Bill Goodling, Pa., chairman
Tom Petri, Wis.
Marge Roukema, N.J.
Cass Ballenger, N.C.
Bill Barrett, Neb.
John A. Boehner, Ohio
Peter Hoekstra, Mich.
Howard P. McKeon, Calif.
Michael N. Castle, Del.
Sam Johnson, Texas
James M. Talent, Mo.
James C. Greenwood, Pa.
Lindsey Graham, S.C.
Mark Souder, Ind.
David M. McIntosh, Ind.
Charlie Norwood, Ga.
Ron Paul, Texas
Bob Schaffer, Colo.
Fred Upton, Mich.
Nathan Deal, Ga.
Van Hilleary, Tenn.
Vernon J. Ehlers, Mich.
Matt Salmon, Ariz.
Tom Tancredo, Colo.
Ernie Fletcher, Ky.
Jim DeMint, S.C.
Johnny Isakson, Ga.

DEMOCRATS (22)
William L. Clay, Mo., ranking member
George Miller, Calif.
Dale E. Kildee, Mich.
Matthew G. Martinez, Calif.
Major R. Owens, N.Y.
Donald M. Payne, N.J.
Patsy T. Mink, Hawaii
Robert E. Andrews, N.J.
Tim Roemer, Ind.
Robert C. Scott, Va.
Lynn Woolsey, Calif.
Carlos Romero-Barcelo, P.R.
Chaka Fattah, Pa.
Ruben Hinojosa, Texas
Carolyn McCarthy, N.Y.
John F. Tierney, Mass.
Ron Kind, Wis.
Loretta Sanchez, Calif.
Harold E. Ford Jr., Tenn.
Dennis J. Kucinich, Ohio
David Wu, Ore.
Rush D. Holt, N.J.

Subcommittee on Employer-Employee Relations

REPUBLICANS (11)
John A. Boehner, Ohio, chairman
James M. Talent, Mo.
Tom Petri, Wis.
Marge Roukema, N.J.
Cass Ballenger, N.C.
Bill Goodling, Pa.
Howard P. McKeon, Calif.
Peter Hoekstra, Mich.
Matt Salmon, Ariz.
Ernie Fletcher, Ky., vice chairman
Jim DeMint, S.C.

DEMOCRATS *(8)*
Robert E. Andrews, N.J., ranking member
Dale E. Kildee, Mich.
Donald M. Payne, N.J.
Carlos Romero-Barcelo, P.R.
Carolyn McCarthy, N.Y.
John F. Tierney, Mass.
David Wu, Ore.
Rush D. Holt, N.J.

Ways and Means Committee

Address: 1102 Longworth Bldg., Washington, D.C. 20515
Phone: (202) 225-3625

REPUBLICANS (23)
Bill Archer, Texas, chairman
Philip M. Crane, Ill.
Bill Thomas, Calif.
E. Clay Shaw Jr., Fla.
Nancy L. Johnson, Conn.
Amo Houghton, N.Y.
Wally Herger, Calif.
Jim McCrery, La.
Dave Camp, Mich.
Jim Ramstad, Minn.
Jim Nussle, Iowa
Sam Johnson, Texas
Jennifer Dunn, Wash.
Mac Collins, Ga.
Rob Portman, Ohio
Phil English, Pa.
Wes Watkins, Okla.
J.D. Hayworth, Ariz.
Jerry Weller, Ill.
Kenny Hulshof, Mo.
Scott McInnis, Colo.
Ron Lewis, Ky.
Mark Foley, Fla.

DEMOCRATS (16)
Charles B. Rangel, N.Y., ranking member
Pete Stark, Calif.
Robert T. Matsui, Calif.
William J. Coyne, Pa.
Sander M. Levin, Mich.
Benjamin L. Cardin, Md.
Jim McDermott, Wash.
Jerry Kleczka, Wis.
John Lewis, Ga.
Richard E. Neal, Mass.
Michael R. McNulty, N.Y.
William J. Jefferson, La.
John Tanner, Tenn.
Xavier Becerra, Calif.
Karen L. Thurman, Fla.
Lloyd Doggett, Texas

Subcommittee on Health

REPUBLICANS (8)
Bill Thomas, Calif., chairman
Nancy L. Johnson, Conn.
Jim McCrery, La.

DEMOCRATS (5)
Pete Stark, Calif., ranking member
Jerry Kleczka, Wis.
John Lewis, Ga.

(Continued)

(Continued)

REPUBLICANS	DEMOCRATS
Philip M. Crane, Ill.	*Jim McDermott, Wash.*
Sam Johnson, Texas	*Karen L. Thurman, Fla.*
Dave Camp, Mich.	
Jim Ramstad, Minn.	
Phil English, Pa.	

Senate Committees

Appropriations Committee

Address: S-128 Capitol, Washington, D.C. 20510
Phone: (202) 224-3471

REPUBLICANS (15)	DEMOCRATS (13)
Ted Stevens, Alaska, chairman	*Robert C. Byrd, W.Va., ranking member*
Thad Cochran, Miss.	*Daniel K. Inouye, Hawaii*
Arlen Specter, Pa.	*Ernest F. Hollings, S.C.*
Pete V. Domenici, N.M.	*Patrick J. Leahy, Vt.*
Christopher S. Bond, Mo.	*Frank R. Lautenberg, N.J.*
Slade Gorton, Wash.	*Tom Harkin, Iowa*
Mitch McConnell, Ky.	*Barbara A. Mikulski, Md.*
Conrad Burns, Mont.	*Harry Reid, Nev.*
Richard C. Shelby, Ala.	*Herb Kohl, Wis.*
Judd Gregg, N.H.	*Patty Murray, Wash.*
Robert F. Bennett, Utah	*Byron L. Dorgan, N.D.*
Ben Nighthorse Campbell, Colo.	*Dianne Feinstein, Calif.*
Larry E. Craig, Idaho	*Richard J. Durbin, Ill.*
Kay Bailey Hutchison, Texas	
Jon Kyl, Ariz.	

Subcommittee on Labor, Health and Human Services and Education

REPUBLICANS (8)	DEMOCRATS (7)
Arlen Specter, Pa., chairman	*Tom Harkin, Iowa, ranking member*
Thad Cochran, Miss.	*Ernest F. Hollings, S.C.*
Slade Gorton, Wash.	*Daniel K. Inouye, Hawaii*
Judd Gregg, N.H.	*Harry Reid, Nev.*
Larry E. Craig, Idaho	*Herb Kohl, Wis.*
Kay Bailey Hutchison, Texas	*Patty Murray, Wash.*
Ted Stevens, Alaska	*Dianne Feinstein, Calif.*
Jon Kyl, Ariz.	

Finance Committee

Address: SD-219 Dirksen Bldg., Washington, D.C. 20510
Phone: (202) 224-4515

REPUBLICANS (11)
William V. Roth Jr., Del., chairman
John H. Chafee, R.I.
Charles E. Grassley, Iowa
Orrin G. Hatch, Utah
Frank H. Murkowski, Alaska
Don Nickles, Okla.
Phil Gramm, Texas
Trent Lott, Miss.
James M. Jeffords, Vt.
Connie Mack, Fla.
Fred Thompson, Tenn.

DEMOCRATS (9)
Daniel Patrick Moynihan, N.Y.,
   ranking member
Max Baucus, Mont.
John D. Rockefeller IV, W.Va.
John B. Breaux, La.
Kent Conrad, N.D.
Bob Graham, Fla.
Richard H. Bryan, Nev.
Bob Kerrey, Neb.
Charles S. Robb, Va.

Subcommittee on Health Care

REPUBLICANS (8)
John H. Chafee, R.I., chairman
William V. Roth Jr., Del.
James M. Jeffords, Vt.
Charles E. Grassley, Iowa
Phil Gramm, Texas
Don Nickles, Okla.
Orrin G. Hatch, Utah
Fred Thompson, Tenn.

DEMOCRATS (7)
John D. Rockefeller IV, W.Va.,
   ranking member
Max Baucus, Mont.
John B. Breaux, La.
Kent Conrad, N.D.
Bob Graham, Fla.
Richard H. Bryan, Nev.
Bob Kerrey, Neb.

Health, Education, Labor and Pensions Committee

Addess: SD-428 Dirksen Bldg., Washington, D.C. 20510
Phone: (202) 224-5375

REPUBLICANS (10)
James M. Jeffords, Vt., chairman
Judd Gregg, N.H.
Bill Frist, Tenn.
Mike DeWine, Ohio
Michael B. Enzi, Wyo.
Tim Hutchinson, Ark.
Susan Collins, Maine
Sam Brownback, Kan.
Chuck Hagel, Neb.
Jeff Sessions, Ala.

DEMOCRATS (8)
Edward M. Kennedy, Mass.,
   ranking member
Christopher J. Dodd, Conn.
Tom Harkin, Iowa
Barbara A. Mikulski, Md.
Jeff Bingaman, N.M.
Paul Wellstone, Minn.
Patty Murray, Wash.
Jack Reed, R.I.

Subcommittee on Public Health

REPUBLICANS (6)
Bill Frist, Tenn., chairman
Judd Gregg, N.H.
Michael B. Enzi, Wyo.
Susan Collins, Maine
Sam Brownback, Kan.
Jeff Sessions, Ala.

DEMOCRATS (5)
Edward M. Kennedy, Mass.,
  ranking member
Jack Reed, R.I.
Tom Harkin, Iowa
Barbara A. Mikulski, Md.
Jeff Bingaman, N.M.

Special Committee on Aging

Address: SD-G31 Dirksen Bldg., Washington, D.C. 20510
Phone: (202) 224-5364

REPUBLICANS (11)
Charles E. Grassley, Iowa, chairman
James M. Jeffords, Vt.
Larry E. Craig, Idaho
Conrad Burns, Mont.
Richard C. Shelby, Ala.
Rick Santorum, Pa.
Chuck Hagel, Neb.
Susan Collins, Maine
Michael B. Enzi, Wyo.
Jim Bunning, Ky.
Tim Hutchinson, Ark.

DEMOCRATS (9)
John B. Breaux, La., ranking member
Harry Reid, Nev.
Herb Kohl, Wis.
Russell D. Feingold, Wis.
Ron Wyden, Ore.
Jack Reed, R.I.
Richard H. Bryan, Nev.
Evan Bayh, Ind.
Blanche Lincoln, Ark.

Sources of Further Information

The following organizations can provide extensive information on the topics covered in this book. All maintain highly useful websites. This is not intended to be an exhaustive list of health policy sources; rather, it provides a starting point for those wishing to delve more deeply into the subject.

For organizations that maintain a Washington, D.C., office in addition to a main headquarters in another city, the address of the Washington office is provided, because that is generally the office that provides policy information.

Government

Department of Health and Human Services
Hubert H. Humphrey Building
200 Independence Ave. S.W.
Washington, D.C. 20201
Main Public Affairs: 202/690-7850
Internet: www.hhs.gov

HHS oversees federal health agencies and programs, including the National Institutes of Health, Centers for Disease Control and Prevention, and Medicare and Medicaid.

Health Care Financing Administration
Hubert H. Humphrey Building
200 Independence Ave. S.W.
Washington, D.C. 20201
202/690-6145
Internet: www.hcfa.gov

HCFA oversees the operations of Medicare, Medicaid, and the Children's Health Insurance Program (CHIP).

THOMAS—Legislative Information on the Internet
Internet: http://thomas.loc.gov/

Maintained by the Library of Congress, THOMAS is the official site for online information related to Congress. The site also includes links to House and Senate committees and individual member offices.

Foundations and Think Tanks

Alliance for Health Reform
1900 L St. N.W.
Suite 512
Washington, D.C. 20036
202/466-5626
Internet: www.allhealth.organization

The Alliance is a nonpartisan group that produces publications and holds briefings on a variety of health policy issues currently before Congress and the nation.

American Enterprise Institute for Public Policy Research
1150 17th St. N.W.
Suite 1100
Washington, D.C. 20036
202/862-5800
Internet: www.aei.org

AEI is one of the few major think tanks in Washington that is home to both liberal and conservative scholars.

The Brookings Institution
1775 Massachusetts Ave. N.W.
Washington, D.C. 20036
202/797-6000
Internet: www.brookings.org

Brookings is Washington's leading liberal think tank.

The Cato Institute

1000 Massachusetts Ave. N.W.
Washington, D.C. 20001
202/842-0200
Internet: www.cato.org

The Cato Institute is a think tank representing the libertarian point of view.

Center on Budget and Policy Priorities

777 N. Capitol St. N.E.
Suite 705
Washington, D.C. 20002
202/408-1080
Internet: www.cbpp.org

The liberal-leaning CBPP conducts research on health, welfare, and tax issues.

Center for Studying Health System Change

600 Maryland Ave. S.W.
Washington, D.C. 20024
202/484-3475
Internet: www.hschange.com

Funded by the Robert Wood Johnson Foundation (see below) the Center conducts research on the changes in financing, insurance, and delivery of health care.

The Commonwealth Fund

One East 75th St.
New York, N.Y. 10021-2692
212/606-3800
Internet: www.cmwf.organization

The Commonwealth Fund makes grants related to health policy, with a special emphasis on women's health.

Employee Benefit Research Institute

2121 K St. N.W.
Washington, D.C. 20037
202/659-0670
Internet: www.ebri.org

Funded by employers, unions, and employee benefits firms, EBRI is known for producing reliable information on health insurance and pensions topics.

The Heritage Foundation

214 Massachusetts Ave. N.E.
Washington, D.C. 20002
202/546-4400
Internet: www.heritage.org

The Heritage Foundation is Washington's leading conservative think tank.

The Henry J. Kaiser Family Foundation

2400 Sand Hill Rd.
Menlo Park, Calif. 94025
650/854-9400
Internet: www.kff.org

Not associated with the managed care company Kaiser Permanente, the Kaiser Family Foundation is a philanthropy that makes grants on health policy, AIDS, and reproductive health issues.

National Center for Policy Analysis

Metropolitan Square
655 15th St. N.W.
Suite 375
Washington, D.C. 20005
202/628-6671
Internet: www.ncpa.org

NCPA is a conservative think tank based in Dallas, Texas.

National Committee for Quality Assurance

200 L St. N.W.
Suite 500
Washington, D.C. 20036
202/955-3500
Internet: www.ncqa.org

NCQA develops standards for and accredits managed care organizations.

The Robert Wood Johnson Foundation

College Road
P.O. Box 2316
Princeton, N.J. 08543-2316
Internet: www.rwjf.org

The largest of the health policy philanthropies, RWJF funds a wide variety of projects related to health and health care.

The Urban Institute
2100 M St. N.W.
Washington, D.C. 20037
202/261-5700
Internet:www.urban.org

Originally founded as a think tank to research problems of cities, today the Urban Institute is a major source of research on health and welfare issues.

Interest Groups

AARP
601 E St. N.W.
Washington, D.C. 20049
202/434-2277
Internet: www.aarp.org

AARP represents the interests of people over age fifty, with a particular emphasis on Medicare and Social Security.

American Association of Health Plans
1129 20th St. N.W.
Suite 600
Washington, D.C. 20036
202/778-3200
Internet: www.aahp.org

AAHP represents the managed care industry in Washington, D.C.

American Health Care Association
1201 L St. N.W.
Washington, D.C. 20005-4014
202/842-4444
Internet: www.ahca.org

Despite its name, the AHCA actually represents only the long-term care community: nursing homes, assisted living facilities, and "subacute" care providers.

American Hospital Association
Liberty Place, Suite 700
325 7th St. N.W.
Washington, D.C. 20004-2802
202/638-1100
Internet: www.aha.org

The AHA represents the nation's estimated five thousand community hospitals and health networks.

American Medical Association
1101 Vermont Ave. N.W.
Washington, D.C. 20005
202/789-7400
Internet: www.ama-assn.org

The AMA represents the nation's physicians.

American Nurses Association
600 Maryland Ave. S.W.
Washington, D.C. 20024
202/651-7027
Internet: www.nursingworld.org

The ANA represents the nation's nurses.

Blue Cross and Blue Shield Association
1310 G St. N.W.
Washington, D.C. 20005
202/626-4780
Internet: www.bluecares.com

The BCBSA is the federation of the nation's independent Blue Cross and Blue Shield plans.

Familes USA
1334 G St. N.W.
Washington, D.C. 20005
Phone: 202/628-3030
Internet: www.famliesusa.org

Families USA is a consumer advocacy group for affordable health and long-term care.

Health Insurance Association of America
555 13th St. N.W.
Suite 600 East
Washington, D.C. 20004
202/824-1600
Internet: www.hiaa.org

The HIAA represents the health insurance industry in Washington, D.C.

Medicare Rights Center
1460 Broadway
New York, N.Y. 10036
212/869-3850
Internet: www.Medicarerights.org

The MRC is a national not-for-profit organization that helps consumers navigate Medicare's complex rules and procedures through counseling, public education, and advocacy.

National Abortion and Reproductive Rights Action League

1156 15th St. N.W.
Suite 700
Washington, D.C. 20005
202/973-3000
Internet: www.naral.org

NARAL is an advocacy organization for reproductive and abortion rights.

National Right to Life Committee

419 7th St. N.W.
Suite 500
Washington, D.C. 20004
202/626-8800
Internet: www.nrlc.org

NRLC is Washington's leading antiabortion organization. The group also works against euthanasia and health care rationing.

Pharmaceutical Research and Manufacturers' Association

1100 15th St. N.W.
Washington, D.C. 20005
202/835-3400
Internet: www.phrma.org

PhRMA represents makers of "brand name" prescription drugs.

Physicians for a National Health Program

332 South Michigan Ave.
Suite 500
Chicago, Ill. 60604
312/554-0382
Internet: www.pnhp.org

PNHP represents doctors who support creation of a national "single-payer" health system.

Index

Note: Page references in italics indicate photographs or illustrations.

Physician Payment Review Commission
(PPRC), 24, 130, 162, 171
Physicians
on Clinical Laboratory Improvement
Act, 34
group-model HMOs and, 81
health care spending on, 76
Medicaid and, 111
participating (Medicare), 156
private contracting and, 170
Planned Parenthood Federation of Amer-
ica (PPFA), 163–164
*Planned Parenthood of Central Missouri v.
Danforth* (1976), 5
*Planned Parenthood of Kansas City, Mo. v.
Ashcroft* (1983), 6
*Planned Parenthood of Southeastern Pa. v.
Casey* (1992), 7, 58, 164, 181, 213
Play or pay system, 161, 165
Point-of-service (POS) plans, 20, 107–108,
127, 158, 165
Population Council, 182
Portability, 165
See also Health Insurance Portability
and Accountability Act of 1986
(HIPAA) (PL 104-191)
Porter, John, 201
Poverty statistics, 165–166
Powell, Colin, *210*
Powers of attorney. *See* Durable powers
of attorney for healthcare
Practice guidelines, clinical, 34
Practice plans, academic health center, 9,
67
Preexisting conditions, 36, 77, 131, 166,
205–206
Preferred provider networks, 15, 166
Preferred provider organizations (PPOs),
166–167
Blue Cross/Blue Shield Association
(BCBSA), 20
contraceptive coverage by, 38
managed care and, 105, 108
Medicare+Choice and, 127
NCQA and, 139
TRICARE Extra as, 201
Premium caps, 84
Premiums, 167
Premium support program, Medicare,
137, 138, 167
Prenatal care, 111, 158
Prescription drugs
facilities fees, 168
generic, 62–63, 114–115
Medicaid and, 111
Medicare and, 138
Medicare Catastrophic Coverage Act
and, 129
Patients' Bill of Rights and, 158
pharmacy benefit managers and, 162
spending on, 76

Prescription Drug User Fee Act (PDUFA)
(PL 102-571) (1992), 57, 89, 167–168
President's Commission for the Study of
Ethical Problems in Medicine and
Biomedical and Behavioral Research,
54
Prevalence, 168
of substance abuse and mental illness,
192
Preventive care, 107, 123
Preventive Health Services Block Grant,
CDC and, 29
Price Waterhouse LLP study on lifetime
limits, 101
Primary care, 168, 185
clinical nurse specialists and, 34
community health centers and, 36
federally qualified health centers and,
53
HRSA and, 83
Medicare and, 125
primary care case management
(PCCM), 113–114
Primary care physicians (PCPs), 168–169
as gatekeepers, 62, 107
graduate education for, 66
nurse practitioners and, 145
PPOs and, 167
for women, Patients' Bill of Rights and,
158
Privacy, medical records, 79
See also Confidentiality, medical
records
Private contracting (Medicare), 169–170
Private fee-for-service (Medicare), 170
Private right of action, medical records
confidentiality and, 118
Professional Standards Review Organiza-
tions (PSROs), 124
Program of All-inclusive Care for the
Elderly (PACE), 170
Program on Long-Term Care, Research
Triangle Park Institute, N.C., 146
Prospective Payment Assessment Com-
mission (ProPAC), 130, 162, 171
Prospective payment system (PPS), 87,
124, 171
Prospective utilization review, 209
Providers, health care, 172
health services research and, 86
qualified Medicare beneficiaries and,
176
safety net facilities of, 185
TennCare and, 199
unique identifiers for, 74
Provider-sponsored organizations
(PSOs), 172
Medicare+Choice and, 127
Prudent layperson, 127
Pryor, David, 114–115
Public accommodation, 18

Public Citizen Health Research Group,
116, 157
Public health, 172
safety net facilities and, 185
surgeon general of the United States
and, 195
Public Health Service, U.S. (PHS), 69–70,
172–174
agencies of, 173–174
Commissioned Corps, 139, 174–175, 196
health jurisdiction in Congress of, 81
health professional shortage areas and,
82–83
House Commerce Committee and, 89
Senate HELP Committee and, 188
surgeon general of the United States
and, 196
Tuskeegee experiments and, 201–202
Public Health Service Act (PL 78-410)
(1944), 173
adolescent family life program (Title
XX), 10–11
federal family planning program (Title
X), 61, 83, 152–153, 199–201
Public Housing, Health Care for Residents of, 83
Public Service Agencies, 12
Punitive damages, medical malpractice,
116
Purchasing cooperatives, health care,
84–85, 108
Pure Food and Drug Act of 1906, 53, 56

Q
Qualified Individuals-1 (QI-1) program,
45
Qualified Individuals-2 (QI-2) program,
45
Qualified Medicare beneficiaries
(QMBs), 45, 176
Quality Health Care Coalition Act of
1999, 206
Quality Improvement Organizations
(QIOs), 160
Qui tam actions, 52

R
Railroad Retirement benefits, Medicare
Part A and, 122
RAND Corporation, 116
Ransdell Act of 1930, 140
Rationing, health care, 142, 147–148, 170,
177
Ray, James S., 198
Ray, Ricky. *See* Ricky Ray Hemophilia Re-
lief Fund Act (PL 105-369) (1998)
Reagan, Ronald
gag rule and, 7
Medicare Catastrophic Coverage Act
and, 128, 129
prescription drug user fees and, 167